Literary Slumming

Literary Slumming

Slang and Class in Nineteenth-Century France

Eliza Jane Smith

LEXINGTON BOOKS
Lanham • Boulder • New York • London

Published by Lexington Books
An imprint of The Rowman & Littlefield Publishing Group, Inc.
4501 Forbes Boulevard, Suite 200, Lanham, Maryland 20706
www.rowman.com

6 Tinworth Street, London SE11 5AL, United Kingdom

Copyright © 2021 by The Rowman and Littlefield Publishing Group, Inc.

All rights reserved. No part of this book may be reproduced in any form or by any electronic or mechanical means, including information storage and retrieval systems, without written permission from the publisher, except by a reviewer who may quote passages in a review.

British Library Cataloguing in Publication Information Available

Library of Congress Cataloging-in-Publication Data

Names: Smith, Eliza Jane, author.
Title: Literary slumming : slang and class in nineteenth-century France / Eliza Jane Smith.
Description: Lanham : Lexington Books, [2021] | Includes bibliographical references and index. | Summary: "Literary Slumming: Slang and Class in Nineteenth-Century France reveals how the use of slang in French literature and culture led to the emergence of a sociolinguistic phenomenon that prioritized criminal life and culture in a way that expanded class boundaries and increased visibility for minorities within the public sphere"— Provided by publisher.
Identifiers: LCCN 2021018580 (print) | LCCN 2021018581 (ebook) | ISBN 9781793621146 (cloth) | ISBN 9781793621153 (epub) ISBN 9781793621160 (pbk)
Subjects: LCSH: French literature—19th century—History and criticism. | Cant in literature. | Criminals in literature. | Working class in literature. | Literature and society—France. | French language—Slang. | LCGFT: Literary criticism.
Classification: LCC PQ283 .S65 2021 (print) | LCC PQ283 (ebook) | DDC 840.9/3526927—dc23
LC record available at https://lccn.loc.gov/2021018580
LC ebook record available at https://lccn.loc.gov/2021018581

For Mom, Dad, Buddy, & Jake.
Forever thicker than thieves.

Contents

List of Figures	ix
Acknowledgments	xi
Prologue: Slang as Premodern Anti-Language	xiii
Introduction: Literary Slumming in Nineteenth-Century France	1
1 Slang as Criminal Code	29
2 Slang as Embodied Language	59
3 Slang as Language Politics	93
4 Slang as the Language of Misery	131
5 Slang as the Language of Parisians	165
6 Slang as the Language of Whores	197
Epilogue: Literary Slumming across Cultures	251
Bibliography	261
Index	271
About the Author	281

List of Figures

Figure 2.1	"Tortillard."	64
Figure 2.2	"Le Maître d'école."	65
Figure 2.3	"Bras-Rouge."	66
Figure 2.4	"Saint Jerome in a Woman's Dress."	75
Figure 2.5	"Thomas Seyton et la comtesse Sarah."	76
Figure 6.1	"—J'ai cancanné que j'en ai pus de jambes, j'ai mal au cou d'avoir crié . . . et bu que le palais m'en ratisse . . . Tu n'es donc pas un homme?"	198
Figure 6.2	"La Chouette."	208
Figure 6.3	"Fleur-de-Marie."	210
Figure 6.4	Detail from "The Annunciation" by Fra Angelico.	211
Figure 6.5	Esther and the baron de Nucingen.	212
Figure 6.6	Asie.	213
Figure 6.7	Actress Marlene Dietrich in *Blonde Venus* (1932). Directed by Josef von Sternberg.	220
Figure 6.8	Actress Greta Garbo in *The Temptress* (1926). Directed by Fred Niblo.	224
Figure 6.9	"Germinie Lacerteux se montrant dans sa robe de demoiselle d'honneur à Mademoiselle de Varandeuil."	229
Figure 6.10	"Germinie Lacerteux chez Gautruche."	230
Figure 6.11	"Attaque hystéro-épileptique: arc de cercle."	233
Figure 6.12	Photographie d'Augustine *Iconographie photographique de la Salpêtrière* by Bourneville and Régnard.	234
Figure 6.13	"Nana, en Vénus, chantant."	236

Acknowledgments

I would like to thank Holly Buchanan who graciously aided me throughout the publication process of this book. I am indebted to the University of California, Santa Barbara, and the Borchard Foundation for their charitable funding which allowed me to conduct research in Paris, France, from 2014 to 2016. I owe a special thanks to the late Dominique Kalifa, who generously invited me to Paris I, Panthéon-Sorbonne as a *chercheur invité* and offered invaluable mentorship.

Over the years, I have been incredibly fortunate to work with several fabulous women scholars: Cynthia Brown, Mary Bucholtz, Dominique Jullien, Catherine Nesci, Dora Polachek, and Jean Marie Schultz. This book would not have materialized without their relentless dedication to my intellectual and professional growth, and for that I am most grateful.

I would like to extend my sincere appreciation to the following family members and friends for their unconditional support: Jessica Andrianos, Aria Dal Molin, Sylvain Dufraisse, Osiris Gómez, Marilynn Johnson, Sumire Ogata, Chris Murray, and Melissa Trujillo. Heartfelt acknowledgment is due to Jessica Hope Jordan, who spent many hours reading this manuscript and offered her most dazzling insights.

Most importantly, thank you to my family: Bonnie Visker Smith, Bruce Smith, Buddy Smith, and Jake Smith. This book on slang (and other wild expressions of criminal debauchery) is for you.

Prologue
Slang as Premodern Anti-Language

The advent of slang as a coded anti-language dates back to the Middle Ages. The character of the criminal who speaks slang coincides with the appearance of jargon (*gergon*) in fifteenth-century French Mystery plays, such as *Viel Testament, Passion Jesucrist, Actes des Apostres,* and *Vie de St. Christophe.* In his multivolume *History of the French Language* (*Histoire de la langue française*), linguist Ferdinand Brunot explains that French dialects and slang in medieval mystery plays appeared mainly in order to convey their social status.[1] The term "jargon" referred to the coded criminal language of the Coquillars (*les Coquillards*), an organization of about one thousand thieves who received their name from the shell (*coquille*) they attached to their collars, like the pilgrims of Saint-Jacques-de Compostelle.[2] These criminals disguised themselves as ruined pilgrims to trick compassionate Christians into giving them money.[3] Following the Mystery plays, French poet François Villon wrote Ballads I through XI in the language of the Coquillars.[4] The slang of the Coquillars was marked by a replacement of the first consonant of a word with the letter "L" and dropping the final consonant of the ending. For example, *pardessus* became *lardeuss*, *en douce* became *en loucedé*, and *borgne* became *lorgnebé*. Written without any definitions or explanations, Villon's use of jargon, coupled with his lack of linguistic guidance, suggests that jargon functions primarily as a language for which an initiation is required. Nevertheless, even though the trial of the Coquillars had already taken place in which official court documents from 1455 noted the jargon of this professional criminal organization, a minority of the population would have been familiar with the ballads' lexicon.[5]

Following Villon's *Ballades en jargon*, Pechon de Ruby penned *The Magnanimous Life of Dealers, Bandits, and Bohemians* (*La Vie genereuse des Mercelots, des Gueux et Bohemiens*, 1596), a picaresque tale of the author as a young man who leaves his father's household and is initiated into the Order of the Wandering Thugs (*les gueux*). As the protagonist Pechon makes his way from wandering merchants to wandering beggars, and then finally among Bohemians, jargon used as a criminal code links together all the social groups: in order for Pechon to join each group, a linguistic initiation must first take place, as the wandering merchants (*les mercelots*) will only induct Pechon after he masters their language.[6]

Following Pechon's *The Magnanimous Life*, until the publication of Eugène-François Vidocq's *Memoirs* in the early nineteenth century, only a few French literary works treating criminal characters and slang appeared. Guillaume Bouchet's *Fifteenth Evening* (*Quinzième serée*), which was published posthumously in the second volume of his oeuvre *Evenings* (*Les Sérées*) entitled *Robbers, Thieves, Highwaymen, & Swindlers* (*Des Larrons, des Voleurs, des Picoureurs, & Mattois*, 1597), takes place during the One-Hundred Years War in France. The text meditates on, in the form of a vigil (*veillée*), incidences of ruse and theft (sometimes justified, and sometimes not), while valorizing the cunning nature of various beggars and thieves.[7] Also including a dictionary on jargon, in 1630, Olivier Chereau's *Jargon or the Language of Reformed Slang* (*Le Jargon ou Langage de l'Argot Reformé*) appears as a detailed work on the criminal organizations of Bohemians and wanderers. In 1722, the terror that Louis-Dominique Cartouche and his gang wrought on the inhabitants of Paris inspired Nicolas Ragot de Granval to write *Vice Punished* (*Vice puni*).[8] The criminal organization "The Chauffeurs of Orgères" (*Les Chauffeurs d'Orgères*), in the late eighteenth century, led to the publication of *The Rat of Châtelet* (*Le rat du Châtelet*, 1790), an anonymous work of nearly thirty pages that uses both slang and the vernacular.

In spite of an early relative lack of French literary representations of criminal types, the relationship between criminality and marginalized social groups, such as the Bohemians and Jews, as well as criminal language, surfaces in a variety of genres beginning in the fifteenth century. These early works, whether poems, dictionaries, or short novels, serve as the foundation for the later literary representations of slang speakers in the nineteenth century. However, earlier texts that included *jargon* and thieving characters could not be diffused to a readership *en masse*, and the authors of these works did not necessarily have the same literary restrictions that came about with the institutionalization of the French Academy in the seventeenth century. Although these works provided an early basis for what would fully develop as the slang-speaking criminal type in the early nineteenth century, they did not circulate to the general public in ways that literary slumming did after 1789. The portrayal of slang as a criminal code is pervasive in the early nineteenth century; however, it is characterized by a difference in literary standards, readership, and authorial intentions, which were mainly economically driven.

Mass distribution via the press to a socially varied audience allowed for the establishment of slang's first indexical order within the collective imaginary and the dips into forbidden criminal realms permitted consensual identity-play as well as the development of a complicity between the writer and his readers. From this perspective, the coded jargon of gypsies, wandering beggars, or other mobile social groups in premodern texts do not align in terms of authorial intention, the social circumstances surrounding literary conventions, and the technology that allowed for mass consumption of these works in the nineteenth century and that is revealed in the following chapters.

NOTES

1. Brunot, *Histoire de la langue française*, 553–565.
2. Daniel Heller-Roazen translates *Coquillards* as "People of the Shell" or "Shellsters" (20).
3. Cellard, *Anthologie*, 33.
4. Cérésa, *Les Princes de l'argot*, 15–16.
5. Villon himself associated with the Coquillars, and often cites them by name in the opening lines of his ballads. For example, Ballad II begins: *Coquillars enaruans a ruel* [. . .].
6. Unlike the jargon in Villon's ballads that lacks definitions, Pechon includes a glossary for the jargon of petty merchants (*bleschien*).
7. The *veillée* was a storytelling practice that was common in villages. As Martyn Lyons notes, it was not a ritual that included the reading of texts: "[T]he *veillée* is best seen as a traditional form of peasant sociability centered on work, which retained elements of collective celebration, in which oral transmission had little need of books" (Lyons, *Readers*, 136).
8. Louis-Dominique Cartouche was the head of a notorious gang of thieving highwaymen in Paris during the Régence (1715–1723). In the eighteenth century, Cartouche was a well-known criminal, shrouded in various anecdotes, who suffered a public execution by wheel. He appears in French literary and popular culture from the eighteenth through the twenty-first centuries.

Introduction
Literary Slumming in Nineteenth-Century France

The opening scene of Eugène Sue's epic serial novel *The Mysteries of Paris* (1842–1843) reveals a portrait of the nineteenth-century Parisian underworld, characterized by a lowly tavern called a "joint," which is filled with criminals and run by an "ogre" or "ogress":

> Serving the scum of Paris, inns of this variety are packed with freed convicts, swindlers, thieves, and assassins [. . .]. This opening should alert readers to the sinister scenes that await them. If they proceed, they will find themselves in strange places, foul urban abscesses that teem with criminals as terrifying and revolting as swamp creatures.[1]

With its prospects of villainy, violence, and even death, Sue's dark narrative thus lures his bourgeois readers with the temptations of vicariously exploring an uncharted criminal underworld. To satisfy such bourgeois curiosity, Sue immerses his readers in a world of murderers, thieves, and prostitutes who speak in a "mysterious language, full of morbid imagery and metaphors steeped in blood."[2] The "mysterious" language was slang (*argot*), a form of criminal code that had been built on earlier secret languages, and which pervaded nineteenth-century novels in France. The use of slang in these works allowed for the crafting of criminal characters that were both believable and recognizable for contemporary readers. However, nineteenth-century French literary critics and politicians condemned the use of slang in French literature, calling instead for a return to the rigid prescriptivism of the seventeenth and eighteenth centuries. Nevertheless, the use of bizarre expressions and words with vulgar, immoral connotations soon filled the dialogue in French-serialized novels, as crooked characters began to hold the literary spotlight. Their use of slang and the exploits of their evil dealings soon became easily accessible to the bourgeoisie and upper classes due to the cheaper printing and distribution of literary works in the early nineteenth century.[3] Writers such as Eugène-François Vidocq, Eugène Sue, Honoré de Balzac, Victor Hugo, the brothers Edmond and Jules de Goncourt, and Émile Zola each altered nineteenth-century slang's referential meanings through their individual stylizations of its connotations of the criminal and lower classes. Thus, as a social index, after 1789, slang had begun to subvert an already crumbling social hierarchy, while simultaneously appealing to bourgeois readers who could vicariously explore the secret realms of the lower-class and/or criminal ways-of-life.

Of course, in the nineteenth century, slang was an urban language. In his study of the nineteenth-century Parisian underworld, historian Dominique Kalifa explores the collective construction of the urban birthplace of the slang speaker, or the underworld (*les bas-fonds*). For Kalifa, the relationship between the social and geographical topography of the early nineteenth century reflected a hazy reality, leading one to question whether "these dregs of society and thugs, did they really exist?"[4] While one can, of course, never be certain, it is true that traits such as "misery, vice, and crime" (*la misère, le vice, et le crime*) became associated with certain perceived characteristics of the slang speaker (*l'argotier*) due to realist representations of the criminal underworld that had become a focus of French literary and political discourses.[5] The cultural construction of concepts such as the *bas-fonds* (underworld), a place "born at the crossroads of literature, philanthropy, desire for reform and increased morality, brought about by the elites," further revealed a passion for a social "escape" and "exoticism" where emotions could be sensationalized.[6] According to Kalifa, the imagined representation of a place that was simultaneously real and fictive informs the emergence of additional conceptions of space in the nineteenth century, such as that of the slum. In addition, in the nineteenth century, Kalifa argues that the media granted visibility to social issues, thus creating a "homogenous imaginary of the norm," with investigations transforming crime into a representable entity.[7] Other scholars, such as literary critic Nicolas Gauthier, have argued that the representations of criminal culture in French novels from 1840 to 1860 were actually more heterogenous. While writers of city-mysteries regurgitated similar elements of successful novels, such as Sue's *The Mysteries of Paris* (1842–1843), Gauthier asserts that each author incorporated their own unique stylistic features, rendering the genre more intangible in terms of definition. Furthermore, Gauthier affirms that slang in French novels, specifically city-mysteries, appears incidentally as an accessory of the criminal persona.[8]

However, for the purposes of this book, I will argue that slang serves as the primary feature through which nineteenth-century French writers crafted their criminal characters, building on literary portraits from previous centuries as well. Although I agree that each of these works contains their own distinct originality, I am more interested in the creation of an imagined, collective view of the criminal and his language, similar to the one that Kalifa describes in relation to the underworld, and the ways in which representations of this figure in French literature and its diffusion via the press informed the social construction of the slang speaker. I will demonstrate that not only did French society, notably within the literary realm, impact the evolution of this slang speech, but the prevalence of slang in literary works also affected society. Both the realities and myths surrounding the behaviors, speech, and ways-of-life of the dangerous classes initially reveals a social agreement on what constituted the criminal persona in nineteenth-century France, a persona that undergoes a linguistic transformation across this time period.

Whether the slang documented in nineteenth-century French memoirs, novels, and dictionaries was authentic really did not matter, as it instead served a larger literary purpose of fulfilling an upper-class fascination with society's untouchables through the mass consumption of literary works that dealt with crime, sexual deviancy, and immorality. This fascination with lower-class and criminal life was not limited to France, of course, as such narratives were also a part of nineteenth-century American realist literature stemming from both the larger literary movement of Realism and the determinist Social Darwinist philosophy extant at the time.

At this discursive crossroads in nineteenth-century France, the fascination with, as well as a fear of, the criminal and working classes, which were often viewed as interchangeable within the collective imaginary, began to pervade artistic, literary, and political domains. Predominately bourgeois, such domains maintained hegemonic control over the presentation and stylization of criminal subcultures. As a matter of fact, cultural portrayals of the slang speaker could not exist outside of a dominant discourse that expressed middle-class ideologies. Thus, an evolution of a more realistic portrayal of the criminal type in nineteenth-century French literature that was designed for middle-class readership created new linguistic possibilities, as well as artistic and social ones, through modes of cultural subversion. Therefore, this book reveals how the French bourgeoisie, while excluded from originating slang, nevertheless shifted the social indexes of lower-class slang in ways that generated a new creative literary space for the lower and criminal classes and other minorities.

Nonetheless, a dearth of lower-class writers in the nineteenth century meant that these representations of slang speakers, of course, emanated from an upper-class imaginary.[9] In view of the privileged backgrounds of many of the writers, the ways in which both novelists and lexicographers acquired knowledge of the criminal code of slang were varied. In some cases, former criminals, such as Vidocq, underwent both a moral and social reform that led them to publish their insider knowledge as memoir. In other instances, writers, such as Sue, Balzac, and Hugo, primarily relied on Vidocq's experience as a resource. In contrast, Hugo invented slang words that he passed off as criminal lexicon, which became a pivotal feature of his novels. Lexicographers, such as Alfred Delvau, held a firsthand knowledge of slang due to their ostensible experience spent among the criminal classes. For other writers, such as the Goncourt brothers and Zola, a reliance on medical texts and their firsthand encounters with prostitutes provided the basis for their portrayals of working-class women who spoke slang.

Although French literary scholars and historians have addressed the aesthetic, cultural, and political impacts of representations of the criminal underworld from the sixteenth to the twentieth century, these studies, while extremely significant, have yet to analyze slang as the basis of the criminal character and its sociolinguistic effects in French realist works on artistic and social parameters in the nineteenth century, especially for the lower classes and women.[10] In fact, very little scholarship in recent years focuses specifically on slang in nineteenth-century French literature. In her book *Political Stylistics*, literary critic, Pascale Gaitet explores the invasion of both popular language and slang in narratives as indirect free speech that occurred during the fin-de-siècle into the early twentieth century. Through Gaitet's analysis of Émile Zola's *The Drinking Den* (*L'Assommoir*, 1876), Louis-Ferdinand Céline's *Journey to the End of the Night* (*Voyage au bout de la nuit*, 1932), and Raymond Queneau's *Zazie in the Metro* (*Zazie dans le métro*, 1959), she reveals the ways in which these French writers defied previous literary standards, while nevertheless creating canonical works of literature through linguistic portrayals of the worker. However, I will add that the positive reception these works received was made possible due to the century-long process of literary, linguistic, and technological innovation that took place in the nineteenth century. The mass distribution of slang language in French literature was made possible by increased affordability of printing and the rise of the publishing industry, which, in turn, set in motion a breakdown of previous literary standards that had been established in the seventeenth century. Despite the ubiquity of slang language in nineteenth-century French literature and its effects on literature, as well as film in the twentieth century, an extensive study of its sociolinguistic evolution and impact has yet to be undertaken by scholars.

My analysis builds on the previous critical conversation on slang in French literature by contributing a comprehensive sociolinguistic study of criminal characters and their language, which I argue is the basis of their identity, through an interdisciplinary approach that additionally takes on the embodied aspect of criminal codes as expressed through appearance, dance, gesture, and sexuality. Because the body, in ways similar to speech, is capable of its own language expression, it can also be read as expressing a kind of slang, especially the criminal body. These embodied characteristics of slang in the working and criminal classes, as well as their use of their slang speech, in French literature provide the basis of slang's indexes and indexical orders, which contribute to more "realistic" portrayals of slang speakers during the nineteenth century, thus allowing for more complex portrayals of social identities. More importantly, this study on highly subversive, slang-speaking characters in French literature reveals a wide-sweeping sociolinguistic trend that I call *literary slumming*, taking place within France (and elsewhere), that not only speaks to a collective social progress but further marks a significant shift in the relationship between dominant and oppressed cultures, the effects of which emerge more completely in the twentieth century.

SOCIOLINGUISTIC ANALYSIS

The process of cultural and linguistic appropriation of criminal culture by bourgeois and upper-class writers evolved throughout the nineteenth century. As many writers worked to rebrand the slang speaker for both stylistic and economic purposes, these writers also slowly shaped the characteristics of the slang speaker from different aspects, such as their physical appearance, profession, sex and gender, and morals. While these representations of criminal and working-class culture remained in the hands of the middle and upper classes, these writers did not merely aspire to represent a language, but rather to construct an entire narrative around slang that addressed questions pertaining to the language's past, the identity of its speakers, as well as the linguistic, semiotic, and social shifts of the language from the Middle Ages to the nineteenth century. Therefore, the slang narratives written by these nineteenth-century writers are highly intertextual, while nevertheless establish uniquely individual portrayals of slang that suits each writers' characters.

Of course, the character constructions of slang speakers in the nineteenth century are based primarily in language, in addition to morality, physicality, and even geography. In terms of such constructions, linguistic anthropologist Asif Agha refers to *characterological figures* as "any image of personhood that is performable through a semiotic display or enactment (such as an utterance)."[11] These "characterological figures" become stereotypes, defined by their utterances, gestures, and accent, to such an extent that "*any* animator can inhabit that figure by uttering the form."[12] Similarly, the realist portrayal of the slang speaker in nineteenth-century France was not simply a matter of imitating lower-class speech habits but was instead *the establishment* of specific character traits that indexed to readers a criminal or working-class figure to the extent that such characterological figures emerged in the wider culture.

The sociolinguistic concept of *indexicality*, according to linguistic anthropologist Michael Silverstein, refers to the context-bounded expressions and ways of speaking that reference, or "index," their attached cultural ideologies, such as social milieu, behavior, gender, morality, race, and social interaction. When analyzing the complex construction and presentation of slang throughout the nineteenth century, the non-referential indexes that bourgeois writers included as fundamental to criminal characters thus reveal the social and/or class information of a dominated culture by those who were dominant. For Silverstein, there further exist two kinds of indexicality: (1) *referential* and (2) *non-referential*. For instance, an example of referential indexicality is the use of pronouns. For those versed in basic French pragmatics, the informal subject pronoun, *tu* (you), immediately indexes an informal conversational setting, such as between peers, intimate partners, family or friends, or a person of authority and their social inferior. A similar phenomenon happens with the formal subject pronoun, *vous* (you). Without even knowing the identity of the conversationalists, one can therefore immediately deduce valuable social and class information, which thus renders the pronoun context-bounded: there is a formal conversation occurring, or perhaps someone is addressing a group of persons; however, in any case, *vous* nevertheless implies formality as well as social and/or class distance.

The use of the pronouns, *tu* and *vous*, which pertain to the literal meaning of what is being spoken, non-referential indexes, or social indexes infused within language, do not. In other words, the choice of a certain dialect or sociolect, such as slang, could be considered a non-referential index because it communicates a social context to both conversationalists and listeners alike.[13] Therefore, accents, physical appearance, gestures, and even pronunciation can function as non-referential indexes which indicate the communicative context, for example, the social status of the speaker, the social relationship between speaker and addressee, or gender, race, or age; however, non-referential indexes do not contribute to the referential, or literal, meaning.[14] Additionally, as Barbara Johnstone states, "Indexical forms can both evoke and construct identities."[15] In nineteenth-century France, speaking slang rather than Standard French thus indexed information about the speaker's socioeconomic status, education, profession, and even morality, as well as served as the literary basis for the creation of working-class and criminal character types.

Simultaneously, such indexes are subject to an infinite number of interpretations. Thus, an analysis of the use of slang in French-serialized novels, memoirs, and dictionaries, and the discourse surrounding them reveals variations in interpretation, as well as their linkage to a particular time period and social setting. For linguist Penelope Eckhert, the "variables," such as lexicon, accent, and pronunciation, do not contain a fixed ideological meaning, but rather exist within an *indexical field*, or a "constellation of meanings that are ideologically linked."[16] The non-referential indexes reinforced within French serials, memoirs, novels, public debates, and dictionaries were therefore a part of a more fluid system of ideological interpretation, one that clearly shifts throughout the nineteenth century. From a criminal code to trendy Parisian speech, slang indexed a wide variety of demographics. For instance, slang, as an index of a hip Parisian in the second half of the century, could also index degrees of criminality or immorality because these indexes, although different from one another, nevertheless existed within the same indexical field. However, it was not until the publication of Victor Hugo's novel *Les Misérables* (1862), that an entirely new indexical order emerged, one in which the slang speaker became a victim of social misery and poverty, qualities that now positioned criminals and working-class types as Christ-like figures in need of assistance from the upper classes.

LITERAL AND LITERARY SLUMMING

The literary appropriation of slang by bourgeois and upper-class writers in the nineteenth-century, a space in which the lower, illiterate classes did not yet have authorial access, thus surfaces as a kind of *literary slumming*, a sociolinguistic occurrence where writers from privileged backgrounds slipped into forbidden social realms and appropriated aspects of lower-class culture, and then fashioned it for a bourgeois public in a way that created a collective, cultural image of what it meant to be socially disadvantaged, criminal, immoral, or sexually deviant. An indulgence in literary slumming in the nineteenth century corresponded to a literal slumming that necessitated a geographic location. Whereas the misfit criminal of the premodern era relied on constant mobility, the villains of Vidocq, Sue, and Balzac found a strong footing in the urban environment. The urban setting provided more criminal opportunities, in addition to allowing for the ability to hide easily because of the mass influx of people and the labyrinth-like urban topography of Paris in the pre-Haussmann period. As David Harvey points out, "[t]he rapid and seemingly chaotic growth of Paris in the early nineteenth century rendered city life difficult to decipher, decode, and represent."[17] From this perspective one can view Paris, according to Harvey, as simultaneously "an incomprehensible labyrinth of kaleidoscopic qualities" and a conglomeration of "persistent nodal points" that transform the city space into "something more permanent and solid."[18] Most notably, "[t]he ecology of the city and the personalities of its inhabitants are mirror images of each other," a dynamic that fully emerges between criminals and space.[19] The locations that become indexical of criminality in nineteenth-century French literature includes specific Parisian districts like

La Cité in the center of Paris and peripheral districts north or south of the city-center, in addition to taverns, brothels, soup houses, and prisons.[20]

As Mary Bucholtz explains, the mapping of geographic regions and its slang speakers can communicate social "ideology rather than practice."[21] Within the collective imaginary, specific Parisian districts indexed the thieves, murderers, and prostitutes that haunted the criminal underworld. These geographical spaces contextualized language in a similar way that social status would, albeit through the reinforced demarcation of certain physical spaces in relation to speech practices. As Andrea Goulet notes, with regards to the Parisian underground, "the nineteenth century gave subterranean space a new set of symbolic associations that added class stratifications to the mythology of the labyrinth."[22] In his discussion on George W. M. Reynolds' *The Mysteries of London* (1844) and Sue's *The Mysteries of Paris*, David L. Pike points out that "[b]oth texts depicted an underground city existing metaphorically as well as physically beneath the everyday middle-class metropolis, but Sue defined his space through the language of argot as much as through the quartiers in which it was noted."[23] From a sociolinguistic perspective, then, in early nineteenth-century depictions of criminal slang in French literature, geography is as much of an index of language as language is of geography.

As practice, in the nineteenth century, *literal slumming* was common among the bourgeoisie and the upper classes, as well as quite popular. Disguising oneself and frequenting lower-class districts, whether as a form of charity or entertainment, in fact occurred in both France and England. In his book *Slumming: Sexual and Social Politics in Victorian London*, Seth Koven describes the upper-class eroticization and romanticization of slums in nineteenth-century London. According to Koven, these "tourist sites" functioned as "sites of spectacular brutality and sexual degradation" that attracted an indeterminate number of men and women.[24] Critic Edward Tannenbaum also acknowledges a bourgeois interest in a lifestyle that was completely foreign to them; however, one that nevertheless remained within their geographical grasp: novels, such as *The Mysteries of Paris*, "appeal[ed] to the bourgeois tourist's taste for the exotic."[25] It is important to note that this exoticism, Gauthier asserts, also emerges at the insistence of the author.[26]

In Sue's novel, particular sites function as geographical crossroads where characters from the upper and lower classes encounter one another. For instance, the house at 17 Rue du Temple in Sue's *The Mysteries of Paris* provides a physical location for characters of a variety of social backgrounds to interact with one another. As Stephen Knight points out, the reader thus becomes aware that the house "is not a natural place for aristocrats to be."[27] Nonetheless, the aristocrats' cultural, social, and linguistic dominance allows them to enter such an establishment to take part in the events. At the same time, Knight acknowledges that the house gives Sue the freedom to represent "considerable variations of life and attitudes in the lower-income levels."[28] Sue's novel thus notably presents the slumming of upper-class characters who get to experience crime and poverty firsthand. Furthermore, although the difference between self-denial and self-interest remains ambiguous, slumming under the guise of charity and social reform gives the upper-classes larger access (both literally and literary) to the seedy haunts of society's untouchables. For Sue's aristocratic protagonist, Rodolphe, charity is only another form of aristocratic power, as well as play, as Dominique Jullien has argued.[29] If playing God is the ultimate form of upper-class diversion, then slumming is the ultimate means through which the upper-class characters can exercise their cultural and social power. At the same time, slumming is also a means through which a sense of control over the wild bodies of the lower class and criminals can be established.

While Vidocq's account of slumming was firsthand, Hugo, Sue, and Balzac instead create an air of authenticity via a narrator who serves as an interlocutory guide for his fellow bourgeois readers. In their respective works, each author establishes a sense of authority by flaunting their experiences slumming as well as their insider knowledge of criminal lifestyles. These so-called firsthand accounts contribute to the exoticization of the lower classes that Tannenbaum describes. For example, once Vidocq reforms from his criminal lifestyle, he tells of his time spent in seedy districts of Paris as he sought to crack down on crime:

> In a capital as populous as Paris, the bad areas are ordinarily numerous; it is there that all the corrupted men meet: in order to meet them and watch them, I assiduously frequented the places of ill-repute, presenting myself sometimes under one name or at times under another, and changing very often my disguise like a person who needs to evade the watchful eye of the police. All of the thieves that I habitually saw would have sworn that I was one of theirs.[30]

Vidocq's firsthand description of slumming underscores his three identities: (1) Vidocq the narrator, (2) Vidocq the bourgeois police detective, and (3) Vidocq the criminal protagonist. Vidocq, as narrator and detective, functions on the same social and moral plane as his bourgeois readers; however, Vidocq, the criminal, functions on the same social and moral plane as his fellow thieves that appear in his memoir (and who really existed). While Vidocq's position as a kind of undercover agent allows for the emergence of this double identity, such literary slumming that these nineteenth-century writers engaged in also allowed for the creation of two simultaneous social identities. Notably, this double identity of the writer also granted readers permission to engage in a vicarious cultural voyeurism as they gained access to the depths of the criminal underworld without having to compromise their bourgeois or upper-class moral integrity.

While in the nineteenth century, the term "slumming" had a negative connotation, this practice nevertheless permitted one to experience a different way-of-life as well as a completely new identity. For Koven, such mobility remains at the heart of slumming, which he defines as the "activities undertaken by people of wealth, social standing, or education in urban spaces inhabited by the poor [. . .] figured as some sort of 'descent,' across urban spatial and class, gender and sexual boundaries."[31] Like the physical descent into the city's ghettos, a literary cultural descent also occurred. Writers crossed social, sexual, and spatial frontiers; however, they did so within the confines of a figurative space. The construction of the *literary slum*, in terms of both content and format, thus allowed for multiple acts of bourgeois identity-play, charity, voyeurism, and detective-like social investigations to occur.

The French equivalent *s'encanailler* of the English term slumming first appeared in the *Dictionary of the French Academy* (*Dictionnaire de l'académie française*, 1694) and was defined as "to haunt the dregs of society, to do business with the dregs of society."[32] The definition, which remained unchanged in subsequent editions of the dictionary, reveals the act of slumming as a physical encounter with the lower classes and/or a commercial exchange.[33] Unlike the discourses that shaped acts of slumming in nineteenth-century Britain, which instead focused on acts of charity and/or engagement in sexual acts, the French discourse on slumming contained a distinct economic slant. This notion of exchange not only evoked criminal dealings but also equally applied to the linguistic exchange of slang that took place across class lines: first, an increase in the discourse surrounding slang in the nineteenth century was due in part to writers' desire for financial gain, an act that was viewed by some literary critics and politicians as a kind of criminal dealing in itself. Second, such financial gain was predicated on disclosing the inner workings of criminal society in ways that also increased slang's cultural capital. As these writers emphasized the social value of knowing slang, they also deemed slang as the trendy way of speaking for Parisians.

The pervasiveness of slang in nineteenth-century French literature, reference works, and public debates naturally increased the upper-class reader's "register range," in other words, "the variety of registers with which he or she is acquainted [and that] equips a person with portable emblems of identity."[34] According to Agha, the way in which a person gains access to these registers is through continual "processes of socialization."[35] Writers and lexicographers who cultivated a practice of literary slumming thus provided an opportunity for socialization in which the upper-class reader could interact with this new register of slang. The writers' constructions of slang and its speakers further contributed to slang's enregisterment, or the sociolinguistic concept that refers to the conversion of lexical items into a socially sanctioned linguistic register, which culminated in the publication of French slang dictionaries.[36] As indexes become more collectively synonymous with the demographics they represent, enregisterment is more likely to occur. Thus, the portrayal of slang as a criminal code in serial novels and dictionaries embedded, or enregistered, the language itself as also criminal in the minds of bourgeois readers.

In nineteenth-century France, writers ignored the generic standards imposed under Louis XIV in order to capture more authentically the culture of society's untouchables, while also establishing themselves as writers of note, again, ultimately for profit. The use of slang thus became the basis for the construction of the criminal classes in literature, in addition to other artistic factors, such as body stylization and performance, all of which resulted in the sociolinguistic phenomenon that I term, *literary slumming*, or the practice of upper-class appropriation, imitation, marketing, and revealing of lower-class culture, all on a mass scale. Literary slumming therefore refers not only to what was then considered to be lowbrow content but also to the perceived cheapening of literary production in the form of the serialized novel, the merits of which were hotly contested in public debates during the 1840s. In other words, one can view such serial novels as the symbolic slums of the nineteenth-century literary world.

In addition to such cultural appropriation, both writers and readers were able to engage in a form of identity-play from the safety of their home. Through their voyeuristic voyage into the deepest, darkest corners of French society, bourgeois writers and readers were slumming in a manner that only existed purely within their imaginary. By defining and inventing identities for the criminal and working classes, middle- and upper-class writers also simultaneously defined, altered, and questioned their own class identities. By creating a literary space that defied convention in terms of content and style, in addition to a format of newspaper serials, a kaleidoscope of character types from all social strata ultimately served to dilute class identities. This blurring of social lines in the literary realm, as well as the establishment of the writer as a cultural intermediary between society and anti-society, not only solidified an author's credibility but also served as the basis of his own identity-play. Through a validation of more nuanced identities, including of his own, the writer accorded his bourgeois readers permission to explore new social possibilities for themselves, even if this exploration remained confined only to their imagination.

While it can also be argued that literary slumming had already occurred in previous centuries, it is my assertion here instead that the nineteenth century marks a turning point in the representation of slang speakers due to the mass distribution of literary works to the public. Through technological advances in the printing press, French readers acquired access to these characterological figures on an unprecedented scale as newspapers were distributed widely and as subscription costs were halved. Consequently, slang underwent processes of enregisterment and iconization,[37] effectively becoming synonymous with the figure of the criminal in the minds of the collective imaginary. Although early modern French writers also created criminal characters, such as Pechon de Ruby and Guillaume Bouchet, as, of course, did Shakespeare and others, only a minority of privileged readers (or theater-goers) previously had access to these works. In contrast, the literary slumming of the nineteenth century involved a mass community of readers.

As the demand for literary criminal characters grew in nineteenth-century France, one witnesses a shift from parody in the depiction of these characters to a more realistic representation of lower-class language, mannerisms, and morals. As the literary movement of realism took hold, writers begin to showcase both their knowledge and their firsthand experience of criminal and working-class types. Such testimony to an otherwise inaccessible world thus redefined the role of the writer as a cultural intermediary, as well as revealed both the literary and economic values of acquiring languages and information that had previously held little to no cultural capital.

These writers' insider knowledge of lower-class and criminal life suggests their invasion of a territory that was simultaneously both physical and cultural, thus resulting in an (re)appropriation of both the literal and symbolic slums. As aforementioned, upper-class writers appropriated and managed representations of slang speakers, while exploiting them for economic reasons. In spite of these motivations, in the first half of the nineteenth century, the writers' portrayals of slang speakers included claims of their insider knowledge through firsthand experiences, whereas in the second half of the nineteenth-century writers instead incorporated slang into the narrative voice through the use of free indirect speech.[38] This turn marks an increasing fluidity in terms of literary and linguistic transgressions: by the late nineteenth century, slang had now become more than mere dialogue between criminal characters, thus pervading the text more freely.

SLANG AS CRIMINAL CODE

In terms of an exact definition of slang, an ambiguity still exists. In comparison to jargon or patois, the main difference is that slang functioned as a secret criminal code, or what linguist M.A.K. Halliday refers to as an "anti-language," or a language that exists within an "anti-society." For Halliday, such an "anti-society" exists within every modern society and functions as "a society that is set up within another society as a conscious alternative to it," or as a form of resistance that reflects a counter-social construction, including that of identity.³⁹ Although Halliday explains that it is not clear how anti-societies form, they are nevertheless both generated and maintained by anti-languages:

> There is continuity between language and anti-language, just as there is continuity between society and anti-society. But there is also tension between them, reflecting the fact that they are variants of one and the same underlying semiotic. They may express different social structures; but they are part and parcel of the same social system.⁴⁰

These two realities must exist simultaneously in tension with each other to exist at all, as the anti-language reconstructs a new reality from one that is already in existence; this is its sole purpose.⁴¹ As Halliday notes, anti-languages are often secretive; however, their classified nature is not why they form.⁴² For instance, one possible form of an anti-language is a re-lexicalization of the language proper in which words already in use are reappropriated, however, with a different meaning.⁴³ This re-lexicalization occurs frequently in early nineteenth-century French literary representations of criminal slang, as shape-shifting criminal types infuse French words with new social meaning. Terms such as *baker* (the devil), *sick* (in prison), *wild boar* (confessor), and *aunt* (a man who has sex with other men) exist in Standard French, and in this context, contain neutral meanings.⁴⁴ However, in the context of an anti-society, the speakers of these words pervert their meaning, using them to communicate their criminal plans, in ways similar to how a believable disguise serves a criminal agenda.

The main issue for defining slang as an anti-language, however, is that the connotation of the term itself, slang, does not remain static, rather it evolves across the nineteenth century; therefore, the definition of slang depends more on the perception of each writer. As Daniel Heller-Roazen points out, typically "[s]lang refers to words and phrases that, within a single tongue, belong to particular segments of society [. . .]. Such expressions tend to live short lives, their fates being tied to fashion."⁴⁵ In contrast, he defines "jargon" as "the terms and formulae employed by people who share a certain practice, activity, or knowledge" and notes further that "cant" is the term for the English slang of criminals who seek to conceal their evil-doings by speaking in code.⁴⁶ For centuries, the French term for slang, *argot*, housed the same definition as that for its English equivalent, cant. Originally, *argot* referred to a network of thieves and beggars (*Argot* with a capital A) before connoting a secret language that criminals used to communicate with one another.

The first known document revealing the jargon (*gergon*) of beggars and thieves is a dossier from 1455 concerning the trial of the *Coquillars* (*les Coquillards*), a group of nearly a thousand thieves and beggars who communicated in a language called *blesquin*, a sort of precursor to slang, which originated from the *blesches*, or thief apprentices.[47] This criminal organization received their name from the shell (*coquille*) that they attached to their collars, like the pilgrims of Saint-Jacques-de Compostelle, in order to pretend to be ruined pilgrims, while tricking compassionate Christians into giving them money.[48] Jacques Cellard defines them as the following:

> The Shell is not a gang in the modern sense [. . .]. One must represent it as a professional network of shrewd gangsters who were well organized, dispersed, and diversified, and whose confidants, i.e. those specialists of all delinquent domains, 'exchange' (and undoubtedly sell) information and services.[49]

During their trial, some of the *Coquillars* were hanged, while others were banished.

Literary critic Claudine Nédélec has analyzed the initial introduction of slang into French literature in four pivotal texts published between 1596 and 1630.[50] According to Nédélec, these texts were part autobiography and part fiction, encapsulate a "spectacle of misery," and function as the début of a "burlesque" aesthetic. Unlike François Villon's slang ballads, I–XI, that remained un-decoded for the reader, the writers of the texts analyzed by Nédélec treated slang as a cryptic entity that could only be deciphered by an initiated member (or former member) of an extensive criminal order. By incorporating glossaries, footnotes, italics, parentheses, and other translations, early slang writers played the role of guide, while taking painstaking measures to initiate their reader into the world of beggars and thieves. At the same time, the portrayal of the earlier slang speaker became a hybrid figure of beggar and criminal who belonged to a well-organized criminal hierarchy. Despite its initiation on the part of the writer, the representation of this figure nevertheless still existed mainly in the realm of the farcical.

In 1680, Pierre Richelet defined the French term *jargon* for the first time as "a kind of particular language made to please. A kind of crude language that cannot be called a true language."[51] While his definition does not mention criminals explicitly, it does downplay slang's validity as an actual language. Instead, Richelet reduces it to a kind of language play that is vulgar at heart. However, he does define *narquois*, which is another synonym for criminal slang, as "the slang of thugs" (*le jargon des gueux*).[52] In the eighteenth century, works that contained slang would slowly cease, as censorship from regulatory institutions such as the French Academy and the Catholic Church began to tighten around writers deemed subversive to the Royal court.[53] Following the Revolution of 1789, the Royal court's censorship fell into the hands of the State. In 1835, the *Dictionary of the French Academy* defined "*Argot*" as the "language of thugs and thieves, which is only comprehensible amongst them."[54] Officially, slang had become the coded language of criminals, while its appearance in literary works was still considered radical.

THE NINETEENTH-CENTURY SOCIOLINGUISTIC EVOLUTION OF FRENCH SLANG

By the time Vidocq published *Thieves* (*Les voleurs*) in 1837, a linguistic crossroads had appeared between the ancient slang of thugs (*les gueux*) and the nineteenth-century slang speaker (*l'argotier*) whose language "cedes the place more and more to that of the vulgar classes or of specialized professions."[55] As Kalifa remarks, the portrayal of criminal types that had begun in the Middle Ages in the form of wandering vagabonds and Bohemians had reinserted itself into a clearer social dimension in the nineteenth century.[56] In *Memoirs*, Vidocq states that slang does not include a different lexicon, but rather it is simply the imposition of new meanings onto French words.[57] This is the precise definition of re-lexicalization that Halliday mentions with regards to anti-languages. For Vidocq, then, criminal slang is merely the re-appropriation of Standard French words.

In contrast, in Sue's *The Mysteries of Paris*, the first sentence immediately establishes slang as a criminal code. Reading as a dictionary entry, the opening of the novel informs the reader of the language that will be presented within: "In the slang of murderers and thieves, a 'joint' is the lowest sort of drinking establishment."[58] Per this entry, such slang can only refer to the speech practices of the most vile social specimens, and thus Sue's consistent association of this dangerous language with the criminal classes and the Parisian underworld gives readers a clear definition of slang without an explicit explanation. In the first chapter, he promises an honest representation of criminal behaviors, moral codes, women, and language.[59] Here, Sue further establishes a relationship between morals and language, while still hinting at the literariness that is inherent to slang in terms of the realism its images conjure. Through the alignment of slang with a certain social type and location, French writers Vidocq, Balzac, and Sue are able to both contextualize and define for their readers each author's precise definition of slang.

Like Vidocq, Balzac's work also provides an image of the criminal hierarchy with mention of their practices and coded words.[60] He additionally occasionally breaks down the etymology of slang to give his readers a more philological explanation of its evolution. For example, in a conversation between criminal mastermind, Vautrin and his aunt, Jacqueline Collin (a.k.a. Asia), the narrator interrupts their dialogue to comment on the nature of slang endings that corrupted Standard French words.[61] In spite of an emphasis on etymology and slang's poetic value, Balzac continues to demarcate slang as a language of criminals by acknowledging the presence of other types of jargon that exist within society.[62] For Balzac, the different jargon that circulates in society differs from slang in that it functions as a stylistic choice, whereas criminal speech has nothing to do with style, but rather with the moral deterioration that begets social deterioration. Since all slang is not created equal, the true place of criminal slang in nineteenth-century literary works is that of character construction. In spite of this differentiation, in *Splendors*, Balzac gives his readers a glimpse into the metaphoric qualities of criminal slang in his "Philosophical, Linguistic and Literary Essay on Slang, Prostitutes and Thieves" (*Essai philosophique, linguistique et littéraire sur l'argot, les filles et les voleurs*).[63] Balzac's explicit acknowledgment of the poetic value of this anti-language would later become fully developed in Victor Hugo's *Les Misérables*.

While slang initially referred to a criminal code, throughout the nineteenth century it eventually began to refer to the Parisian vernacular that was used among the working classes. However, both of these connotations of slang surfaced in nineteenth-century dictionaries. As Jean René Klein points out, slang dictionaries of the nineteenth century fell into one of two categories: (1) collections of the vernacular (*la langue populaire*) or (2) collections of criminal jargon.[64] For writers in the first half of the nineteenth century, such as Vidocq, Balzac, Sue, and even Hugo (with regards to his earlier works such as *The Last Day of a Condemned Man*, 1829), slang connoted stronger criminal ties, whereas for writers of the second half of the century, such as Zola, the Goncourt brothers, and in Hugo's later works, slang referred more broadly to the Parisian working classes, while still implying various degrees of criminality and moral degeneration.

This late-century shift with its emphasis on the Parisian working classes became apparent in dictionary titles as well. Reference works, such as Lorédan Larchey's *The Eccentricities of the French Language* (*Les Excentricités de la langue française*, 1859); Alfred Delvau's *Dictionary of Green Tongue: Comparative Parisian Slang* (*Dictionnaire de la langue verte: argots parisiens comparés*, 1866); and Lucien Rigaud's *Dictionary of Parisian Jargon: Ancient and Modern Slang* (*Dictionnaire du jargon parisien: l'argot ancien et l'argot moderne*, 1878) portrayed slang as an urban phenomenon, a linguistic anomaly originating in the City of Light. Curiously, slang then became less of a criminal code in the eyes of outside observers who felt excluded from it, and who therefore sought both to contain and appropriate it, and instead transformed into a part of daily reality for the Parisian public.

In spite of this marketing of slang and the mass extent to which literary slumming took place, the manipulation of the identity of the slang speaker and the connotations of the language, whether positive or negative by societal standards, not only changed the social discourse vis-à-vis slang but also expanded the creative possibilities within literature, while simultaneously enlarging the realm of possibility regarding the social and class identities of both writer and reader. A dip into the realm of criminality, working-class misery, and sexual deviance constitutes the writer's literary slumming as he seeks to define a world that socially does not belong to him. The basis of this literary slumming, which provides the indulgent bourgeois reader insight into unchartered social territories, is slang. Within the context of this literary antisociety, the writer satisfies a need to play with his own identity, in addition to allowing his reader to experience a different reality without risking firsthand moral contamination. As long as the writer establishes a position of moral superiority that aligns himself with bourgeois values, he is able to transgress (at least partially) linguistic, literary, and social boundaries.

This book provides an in-depth exploration of the sociolinguistic evolution of slang in French literature and dictionaries throughout the nineteenth century to reveal the presence of literary slumming and its artistic and social impact in France. In chapter 1, "Slang as Criminal Code," I examine the use of slang as the principal signifier for criminal identity in three early nineteenth-century works: Eugène François Vidocq's *Memoirs* (1828), Eugène Sue's *The Mysteries of Paris* (1842–43), and Honoré de Balzac's *Splendors and Miseries of Courtesans* (1838–1847). These texts were the first successful works that directly treated criminal life and slang in France, reaching the masses at an unprecedented level.[65] Vidocq, a former criminal who eventually became the chief of the "Security Brigade" (*la brigade de sûreté*) in Paris, and then founder of his own police agency, exercised a powerful influence on contemporary writers such as Balzac, Sue, and Hugo who, belonging to higher social circles, did not have direct access to the urban underworld, and therefore relied on the authenticity of such works. The early nineteenth-century portrayal of French slang as the coded language of criminals parallels earlier works from the Middle Ages and the premodern period. Due to the reinforcement of this image, the language itself, whether fact or fiction, became infused with a mixture of information concerning the slang speaker's class status, such as criminal and/or working class, profession (thief, murderer, and prostitute), as well as morality (nonexistent), thanks to its extensive literary portrayal as such.

In the early nineteenth century, a public battle soon ensued over the use of slang in French literature, while the literary works of Vidocq, Sue, and Balzac demonstrated the power of language to single-handedly establish the basis of a social identity. In fact, these writers reinforced the association between slang and criminality to such an extent that it established the first indexical order. Indexical orders represent such a high degree of indexicality that a collective agreement on the social appropriateness of certain indexes within a culture has occurred. To speak slang in the early nineteenth century equaled a criminal status for readers. Even the conflation of dialects or foreign languages with slang within these literary works resulted in a kind of "linguistic scapegoating," in which the criminal index became attached to these languages as well.

In addition to language serving as the basis of criminal identity, the monopolization of a literary space by middle-class writers revealed the dual identity of the writer who established himself as an upstanding, trustworthy guide for his readers. The writer's initiation into the criminal realm meant that he indeed knew of the ins-and-outs of this forbidden anti-society and thus could easily pass between the underworld and the overworld. At the same time, Vidocq, Sue, and Balzac all needed to prove themselves on the right side of the law, despite their descent into the dregs of society. The writers' authenticity was thus twofold: first, they had to be authentically versed in criminal life, and second, they had to be authentically bourgeois, which was an index of their incorruptible morality. Ultimately, this identity-play of the writer granted his readers the same freedom to indulge in lowbrow content matter without risking their personal integrity. At the same time, these early works propelled the representation of the lower classes to the literary forefront, introducing additional non-referential indexes of the criminal type that functioned in conjunction with language as part of the first indexical order.

In chapter 2, "Slang as Embodied Language," varieties of bodily performance and stylization, mainly disguise and cross-dressing, became inherent features of the criminal, which, as this study argues, resulted in a kind of *embodied sociolinguistics*, and, as is argued further, which ultimately became the corporal equivalent of spoken slang that played an important role in the eventual iconization of criminal identity. In many ways, the cultural discourse on slang speakers and their language also functioned as discourse on their bodies as attempts at defining, containing, and eliminating slang coexisted alongside attempts at defining, containing, and eliminating their bodies. Chapter 2 demonstrates that the representation of criminal characters in French literature display an embodied slang that indexes similar social information as spoken slang. The work of nineteenth-century authors Vidocq, Sue, and Balzac presents multiple criminal identities through the stylization of characters' appearances as well as their gender, language, voice, and bodily movements. In these representations, the criminal's propensity for suggestive dance and improvised song in the public domain, especially in indexically linked regions of the cityscape, unsavory haunts, and prisons, contributed to an embodied slang that reinforced the relationship between performance and crime, thus marking dance and song as indexes of immorality, as well as potential identity markers of criminals. The shape-shifting tendencies of murderers and thieves as revealed in Vidocq, Sue, and Balzac's respective works therefore establishes both the body and spoken language as key tools for bourgeois and upper-class readers to be able to identify and avoid criminals.

For French novelists, in the nineteenth century, the emergence of a media regime (*régime médiatique*) and innovations within the printing press industry meant more money for more words, regardless of quality. Chapter 3, "Slang as Language Politics," explores the ways in which the newspaper industry in the 1830s and 1840s propelled criminals to the forefront of the literary realm, leading to the iconization of slang within the social imaginary. During this time period, the worlds of journalism and literature began to intersect with the invention of the serialized novel (*le roman feuilleton*), which resulted in a mutual literary slumming: as bourgeois writers appropriated and branded lower-class culture, in turn, minority subcultures invaded bourgeois spaces both on and off the page. This collision of cultures, in addition to the growing public fascination with crime, propelled slang to the forefront of the public mind, creating what Agha terms a "semiotic encounter" between readers.[66] As a metonymy for deviant bodies and an index of criminality, both spoken slang and embodied practices became the basis of the criminal archetype in early nineteenth-century French literature. The formulaic nature of these character portraits that relied heavily on linguistic practices and embodiment further effectively rendered the press as the medium through which the iconization of this anti-language could occur due to the mass distribution of lowbrow novels and the resulting democratization of literature for readers.

The need to identify, categorize, and reveal the various social actors of July Monarchy France manifested itself in the literary works of the time through the panoramic representation of social types and their speech practices, to such an extent that marginalized social types became star characters. The pejorative characterizations of slang were not merely an attempt at controlling a dangerous language, but rather at controlling the dangerous bodies from which this language originated and that housed the potential to undermine bourgeois values. An analysis of language politics dating back to the sixteenth century, as well as the ways in which the attempt to standardize French through the elimination of spoken regional dialects and of certain words, expressions, and topics from written texts, reveals the scandalous nature of writing criminal culture, which culminated in the argument among critics known as the "dispute of the serialized novel" (*la querelle du roman-feuilleton*, 1836–1848).

Early critics involved in the dispute, such as Sainte-Beuve, Louis Desnoyers, and Alfred Nettement, either attacked or defended the moral nature of the serialized genre before addressing the dangerous properties of slang. The critique against the serialized novel was, in part, due to its fabrication, the mass production of which created suspicion concerning motives that were more economically, rather than artistically, based. The collaboration between newspapers, authors, and editors led to a kind of cookie-cutter literature, in which certain aspects of the *feuilleton* narrative and structure appeared over and over, establishing these elements as the tried-and-true formulae of serialized literature. These public debates introduced important issues on the politics of spoken versus written languages, as well as the link between language and political dominance, a main concern shared by critics who were against the shift toward a democratization of literature. Finally, the literary slumming that bourgeois and upper-class writers engaged in during this time revealed a primarily monetary interest. Even for writers like Sue, who later became social activists on behalf of the working classes, the initial driving force of their work was money and the establishment of literary legacy. However, this economic motivation resulted in seedier literary content, including language, which ultimately led to the iconization of slang in the early nineteenth century through newspapers.

In the latter half of the nineteenth century, a shift in slang's social connotation from that of criminals to the working classes took place. Chapter 4, "Slang as the Language of Misery," explores the indexical shift of the language through an analysis of Victor Hugo's portrayal of the common people (*le peuple*) through his use of slang in *Les Misérables* (1862). This text serves as a sociolinguistic crossroads by representing the emergence of slang's new social association that of the misery-stricken working classes. Although the anti-language contained in Hugo's novel continues to index remnants of criminality, and an overall negative portrayal of slang persists, at the same time, the glorification of the working-class slang speaker comes into view. In *Les Misérables*, immorality no longer functions as the main source of criminal tendencies. Instead, Hugo provides an in-depth investigation into misery (*la misère*) as the source of criminality, thus resulting in a radical rebranding of criminal types as products of poverty and social injustice as well as Christ-like figures worthy of upper-class assistance rather than contempt. *Les Misérables* thus reveals the power of language simultaneously to condemn and romanticize the common people. In spite of Hugo's unfavorable attitude toward this dangerous language, the inclusion of a Christian-inspired narrative now partially informs the representation of the slang speaker, thus forcing readers to ponder issues regarding charity, innocence, and guilt, as well as judgment. Moreover, Hugo's refusal to serialize his work rendered themes associated with society's outcasts more canonical from a literary perspective, or as accessible to a readership possessing finer literary tastes.[67]

Unlike earlier works, such as those discussed in chapters 1 and 2, Hugo's work marks a different indexicality of slang, while still building on the initial indexicalities that existed in his earlier works such as *The Last Day of a Condemned Man* (1829) and *The Hunchback of Notre-Dame* (1831). In these earlier novels, slang functions as a criminal code, thus alluding to the criminal of the premodern era. Although Hugo emphasizes the initial criminal indexes of slang within these works, a strong poetic mechanism nevertheless characterizes his oeuvre. This poetic aspect that partly exists in Balzac's *Splendors and Miseries of Courtesans* becomes fully realized in *Les Misérables*, thus differing aesthetically from those that preceded it. Rather than incorporating slang for its shock value, Hugo exploits this criminal code principally to fulfill a stylistic objective.

In *Les Misérables*, one witnesses a return to the classical hallmarks of French literature: an emphasis on aesthetics, images of classical Greek mythology and Christianity, and the use of poetic devices, such as allegory and metaphor. At the same time, lowbrow elements enter the realm of higher literary arts with representations of immoral figures who straddle ambiguous social lines between criminal and worker, depictions of Parisian prisons and the underground, and slang. In fact, Hugo devotes an entire section to slang that simultaneously describes its gruesome nature, while poetically lauding its rootedness in metaphor. Hugo's version of literary slumming takes place within the context of upper-class aesthetic ideals (antiquity, Christianity, and classical poetry), as the author partakes in a form of literary slumming that would positively appeal to the middle and upper classes. Finally, Hugo's paradoxical presentation of the language marks the emergence of a new indexical order and establishes the second half of the nineteenth century as one of creative possibility in terms of redefining both literary and social norms.

During the same time that writers engaged in literary slumming within fiction, lexicographers began to produce slang dictionaries as a guide for the uninitiated reader. Like the narrators in Vidocq's *Memoirs*, Sue's *Mysteries*, and Balzac's *Splendors*, these lexicographers established a new role for themselves as cultural intermediaries and linguistic *flâneurs*, as they explored the cityscape firsthand, picking up new words. Chapter 5, "Slang as the Language of Parisians," explores both slang's codification and enregisterment in dictionaries and glossaries, as well as the progressive association of slang with the Parisian people, in addition to the extent to which lexicographers engaged in their own form of literary slumming, by analyzing five slang dictionaries: Eugène-François Vidocq's *Thieves: The Physiology of Their Ways and of Their Language* (*Les voleurs: physiologie de leurs mœurs et de leur langage*, 1836); Lorédan Larchey's *The Eccentricities of the French Language* (*Les excentricités de la langue française*, 1859);[68] Alfred Delvau's *Dictionary of Green Tongue: Comparative Parisian Slang* (*Dictionnaire de la langue verte: argots parisiens comparés*, 1866); Lucien Rigaud's *Dictionary of Parisian Jargon: Ancient and Modern Slang* (*Dictionnaire du jargon parisien. L'argot ancien et l'argot moderne*, 1878); and Jules Lermina and Henri Lévêque's *Thematic French-Slang Dictionary* (*Dictionnaire thématique français-argot*, 1897). While not fiction, many of the slang dictionaries and glossaries of the nineteenth century contained much more than a catalog of words and their definitions. In fact, most of them featured an entire philological origin story, in addition to a profile of the slang speaker that included his "performance" of the language. In the nineteenth century, dictionary writers thus exercised great power in terms of determining slang's indexical associations.

As the lexicographers' stories and definitions vary from one source to another, an indexical evolution also takes place, one that mirrors the evolutions occurring in fictional works as well. The publication and the subsequent re-editions of these slang dictionaries in the nineteenth century reveal a major shift in the marketing of slang from a criminal code to a fashionable, urban language that contains greater creative possibility than Standard French. Ultimately, this codification and enregisterment of slang promoted the social evolution of the language, while, at the same time, it reflected a prescriptivism in which the nonstandard underwent standardization through the act of categorizing as well as the increasing publication of reference works on slang.

In terms of the slang dictionaries of the late nineteenth century, such as Delvau's *Dictionary of Green Tongue* (*Dictionnaire de la langue verte*, 1866), these works aided the "legitimizing marginal subcultures and promot[ed] their integration into mainstream society."[69] Literary slumming thus permitted lexicographers to ostensibly contain and control slang, to market their works to a bourgeois public who sought out such reference works, and ultimately, to initiate the process of standardizing the nonstandard. During this process, the role of the lexicographer evolved into a position of meaning-maker through the construction of an origin narrative as well as through personal descents and jaunts into the Parisian streets, neighborhoods, and bars and cafés that established the lexicographer's linguistic authority. Proclamations of these *flâneur-esque* experiences marked these reference works as containing a high degree of authenticity because of the extent to which a lexicographer, especially in the second half of the nineteenth century, professed a willingness to frequent a variety of city districts and demographics, thus ensuring a higher degree of credibility with regard to a dictionary's lexicon. While not literature in the traditional sense, the prefaces and the long definitions within these reference works reveal detailed stories constructed by the lexicographer around slang and its speakers. The so-called fictional nature of these narratives therefore results in a kind of hybrid text that provides a crossroads between the literary and the referential. Literary slumming was therefore not simply an activity that fiction writers alone engaged in but also nonfiction lexicographers who straddled the boundary between truth and fantasy.

Finally, chapter 6, "Slang as the Language of Whores," looks at the relationship between slang, the body, and women's agency in two novels: Edmond and Jules de Goncourt's *Germinie Lacerteux* (1865) and Émile Zola's *Nana* (1880). These works notably represent the woman slang speaker as indexing working-class masculinity through the vulgar use of her language, while exercising a sensual, yet frenetic, embodied language. The paradoxical combination of her linguistic practices with her bodily ones in effect serves to disrupt male sexual fantasies and return subjectivity to an otherwise objectified social type—the prostitute. Chapter 6's analysis of the gender-specific literary slumming of the Goncourt brothers and Zola therefore opens up a discussion on gendered speech in nineteenth-century France with regards to what constituted "women's speech."

Unlike Fleur-de-Marie in Sue's *Mysteries* and Esther in Balzac's *Splendors*, the masculinized image of the woman slang speaker in the second half of the nineteenth century is less subdued in terms of both her profession as prostitute and speech practices. Earlier literary portrayals of prostitutes offered the possibility of moral reformation; however, for characters such as Germinie and Nana, these women remain prisoner to their bodily, moral, and linguistic decay, and thus have no chance at moral redemption. Although they index sexual deviancy through their speech practices, women slang speakers in the second half of the century also possessed a violently chaotic body that explicitly transgressed gender, linguistic, and social norms, and thus constituted an embodied form of slang that fundamentally altered the public image of the woman slang speaker.

Even though early portrayals of masculine criminal bodies also possessed a certain mobility and erratic movement that functioned in conjunction with slang to define them as explicitly "criminal," the prostitute's mobile body united sexuality and performance, as she often engaged in licentious dance, gesture, song, in addition to the physical act of sex. The seductive call of the prostitute-performer's body, a testament to her femininity, became blurred by the masculine street speak she practiced which subverted patriarchal standards for women as well as male desire. While their bodies were sexually desirable, their speech practices remained undeniably unladylike, a combination that broke from more polarized images of the woman slang speaker, such as the hypermasculine Owl in Sue's *Mysteries*, for example. This new corporal index attached to crude speech practices of characters such as Germinie and Nana, while pejoratively represented by male writers, introduces an element of embodied sociolinguistics to these works, as body and language become functions of one another as well as tools susceptible to manipulation in order to create more versatile images of gender that serve to undermine the male objectification of women.

In the nineteenth century, literary slumming was (and, to a degree, still is) a phenomenon that pervaded print culture and public discourse through a variety of formats: serials, novels, dictionaries, memoirs, and public debates, which served to infuse lower- and criminal-class culture into the culture-at-large. After the French Revolution, the desire of writers to construct the slang speaker as a literary figure not only meant an increased precision in the portrayal of spoken language over the course of the century but also the additional stylization of this highly embodied code as constructed through varying aspects of accent, pronunciation, gesture, mobility, and sexuality. This sociolinguistic evolution of slang within nineteenth-century French literature altered class lines and identities by expanding the nuances and possibilities between them. Most importantly, while this evolution in language underscores the initial tragic inability of the lower classes to represent their own language, the prominence and popularity of deviant characters in French literature eventually opened up their first opportunity for self-representation.

NOTES

1. "*[H]antées par le rebut de la population parisienne: forçats libérés, escrocs, voleurs, assassins y abondent [. . .]. Ce début annonce au lecteur qu'il doit assister à de sinistres scènes; s'il y consent, il pénétrera dans des régions horribles, inconnues; des types hideux, effrayants, fourmilleront dans ces cloaques impurs comme les reptiles dans les marais*" (Sue, *Mystères*, 35; English translation, 3). Apart from translated versions of Eugène Sue's *The Mysteries of Paris* and Victor Hugo's *Les misérables*, all English translations of French texts are my own.

2. "*Langage mystérieux, rempli d'images funestes, de métaphores dégouttantes de sang*" (Sue, *Mystères*, 35–37; English translation, 3).

3. These innovations made accessibility easier. This is not to say that the working classes in France did not have access to these texts. They generally had access through reading rooms (*les cabinets de lectures*), paper passing, word-of-mouth, especially during the first half of the nineteenth century. These works, apart from Sue's, whose narrative changed due to the high response from working-class readers, were destined for a bourgeois public. See chapter 3, "Slang as Language Politics."

4. "*Ces bas-fonds et ces gueux existent-ils vraiment?*" (Kalifa, *Les Bas-Fonds*, 17).

5. Ibid., 11.

6. "*[N]ée à la croisée de la littérature, de la philanthropie, du désir de réforme et de moralisation porté par les élites*" (Ibid., 17).

7. "*[U]n imaginaire homogène de la norme*" (Kalifa, *Crime et culture*, 10).

8. Gauthier, *Lire la ville*, 87.

9. Throughout this book I will refer to this dichotomy between the "lower" and "upper" classes. Although the divide between social boundaries is not so clear-cut, for me, this division places the nobility and the *haute bourgeoisie* in the upper-class stratum, whereas members of the working classes, criminal classes, and the poor fall within the category of "lower" class.

10. Pascale Gaitet, "From the Criminal's to the People's: The Evolution of Argot and Popular Language in the Nineteenth Century." *Nineteenth-Century French*

Studies, vol. 19, no. 2, 1991, pp. 231–46; Pascale Gaitet, *Political Stylistics: Popular Language as Literary Artifact*. London, Routledge, 1992; Nicolas Gauthier, *Lire la ville, dire le crime: mise en scène de la criminalité dans les mystères urbains*. Limoges, Presses Universitaires de Limoges, 2017; Andrea Goulet, "Apache Dancers and Savage Boxers: Criminal Choreographies from Les Mystères de Paris to The Wire." *Les Mystères urbains au XIXe siècle: circulations, transferts, appropriations*, edited by Dominique Kalifa and Marie-Ève Thérenty, 2015, Médias 19; Andrea Goulet, The Legacies of the Rue Morgue: Science, Space, and Crime Fiction in France. U of Pennsylvania P, 2016; Dominique Kalifa, *Crime et culture au XIXe siècle*. Paris, Perrin, 2005; Dominique Kalifa, *Les bas-fonds: histoire d'un imaginaire*. Paris, Éditions du Seuil, 2013; Claudine Nédélec, *Les Enfants de la Truche: la vie et le langage des argotiers, quatre textes argotiques (1596–1630)*. Paris, Klincksieck, 1998.

11. Agha, *Language and Social Relations*, 177.
12. Ibid.
13. As Agha explains, "A sociolect is a set of linguistic features that mark the social provenance of speaker along any demographic dimension, such as class, profession, gender, or age," whereas "a dialect is a special type of sociolect, the case where the demographic dimensions marked by speech are matters of geographic provenance alone" (Agha, *Language and Social Relations*, 134–135). For Agha, dialect or sociolect can index various speakers (Ibid., 135).
14. Ochs, "Indexicality and Socialization," 293.
15. Johnstone, "Locating Language," 31.
16. Eckhert, "Variation and the Indexical Field," 464.
17. Harvey, *Paris*, 24.
18. Ibid.
19. Ibid., 43.
20. Moreover, the "kaleidoscopic" identity of the criminal character means that he may find himself, albeit temporarily, in Parisian districts and social settings that do not index criminality. The criminal's ability to shape shift thus renders them analogous to a city in a constant state of identity crisis and change.
21. Bucholtz, "Word Up," 283.
22. Goulet, *The Legacies of the Rue Morgue*, 40.
23. Pike, *Metropolis on the Styx*, 183.
24. Koven, *Slumming*, 1; Ibid., 4.
25. Tannenbaum, "The Beginnings of Bleeding-Heart Liberalism," 493.
26. Gauthier, *Lire la ville*, 88.
27. Knight, *The Mysteries of the Cities*, 31.
28. Ibid.
29. Jullien, *Les Amoureux de Schéhérazade*, 28.
30. *Dans une capitale aussi populeuse que Paris, les mauvais lieux sont d'ordinaire en assez grand nombre; c'est là que tous les hommes tarés se donnent rendez-vous: afin de les rencontrer et de les surveiller, je fréquentais assidûment les endroits mal famés, m'y présentant tantôt sous un nom, tantôt sous un autre, et changeant très souvent de costume comme une personne qui a besoin de se dérober*

à l'œil de la police. Tous les voleurs que je voyais habituellement auraient juré que j'étais un des leurs. (Vidocq, Mémoires, 284)

31. Koven, Slumming, 9.

32. "Hanter de la Canaille, entretenir commerce avec de la Canaille." Dictionnaire de l'Académie française (1694), v.n. "S'encanailler," https://artflsrv03.uchicago.edu/philologic4/publicdicos/query?report=bibliography&head=s%27encanailler Accessed October 13, 2019.

33. Eighteenth-century dictionaries also emphasize the physical act of an encounter with the lower classes. Although the term *canaille* is used in most definitions, additional terms include *"petites gens"* or *"le bas peuple."* Neither the verb nor the substantive *canaille* appears in *argot* dictionaries in the nineteenth century. This reinforces the fact that slumming was an upper-class phenomenon, and not an activity that criminals and the working classes frequently engaged in.

34. Agha, *Language and Social Relations*, 146.

35. Ibid.

36. Agha, "The Social Life of Cultural Value," 231.

37. In sociolinguistic terms, a way of speaking or a word becomes "iconic" when it represents on a mass scale certain cultures, persons, and lifestyles. See Susan Gal and Judith Irvine, "Language Ideology and Linguistic Differentiation," in *Regimes of Language: Ideologies, Polities and Identities*, edited by P. Kroskrity. School of American Research, 2000, pp. 35–83.

38. For more on the use of French slang and popular language in the narrative voice, see Pascale Gaitet's work *Political Stylistics: Popular Language as Literary Artifact* (1992).

39. Halliday, "Anti-Languages," 570.

40. Ibid., 576.

41. Ibid., 575.

42. Ibid., 572.

43. Anti-languages can also be over-lexicalized, in which multiple synonyms for the same word exist. For example, there are higher numbers of French slang terms for "thief" (*pègre, cambrioleur, grinche, tireur, braqueur, cagou, orphelin, ami, ouvrier*) or "policeman" (*flic, cogne, rousse, sergot, raille, argousin, flicard, mouche, bec de gaz*) that appear before 1900. Halliday posits this because of "liveliness or humor, or in some cases, for the sake of secrecy" (570), all three of which can be found in nineteenth-century French criminal slang.

44. *Le Boulanger* (*le diable*), *malade* (*en prison*), *le sanglier* (*le confesseur*), *tante* (*homosexuel*).

45. Heller-Roazen, *Dark Tongues*, 31.

46. Ibid.

47. Merle, *L'Argot*, 31.

48. Cellard, *Anthologie*, 33.

49. *"La Coquille n'est pas un gang au sens moderne [. . .]. Il faut se la représenter comme une association professionnelle de truands astucieux et bien organisés, dispersée et diversifiée, dont les affidés, des spécialistes de tous les domaines de la*

délinquance, se 'repassent' [et sans doute se vendent] des renseignements et des services" (Cellard, 33).

50. Pechon de Ruby's *The Magnanimous Life of Dealers, Bandits, and Bohemians* (*La vie genereuse des Mercelots, des Gueux et Bohemiens*, 1596); Guillaume Bouchet's *Fifteenth Evening* (*La quinzième serée*, 1597); Olivier Chereau's *Jargon or the Language of Reformed Slang* (*Le jargon de l'argot réformé*, 1629); and his *Response and Complaint to the magnificent Godfather on the Jargon of slang* (*Reponse et complainte au grand Coesre sur le jargon de l'argot*, 1630).

51. "*Sorte de langage particulier & fait à plaire. Sorte de langage grossier qui ne peut être appelé un véritable langage*" (Richelet I, 413).

52. Richelet II, 62. In his sociolinguistic study of Parisian French, Anthony Lodge defines the *gueux* as, "Those who failed to settle and remained as transients [. . .] and viewed with deep fear and suspicion" (111).

53. Nédélec mentions several key texts from the eighteenth century that include slang: the play, *Cartouche, ou les voleurs, comédie* (1721), which was prohibited from the *Comédie française* because of its inclusion of slang; Alain René Lesage and d'Orneval's play *Les Pèlerins de la Mecque*, performed on July 29, 1726; and the article entitled, "Argot" by Vergy found in the re-edition of the etymological dictionary by Ménage (Nédélec, xxx).

54. "*Certain langage des gueux et des voleurs qui n'est intelligible qu'entre eux.*"

55. "*Cède de plus en plus la place à celui des classes vulgaires ou des professions spéciales*" (Sainéan, 6–7).

56. Kalifa, *Les Bas-Fonds*, 107–108.

57. Vidocq, *Mémoires*, 373.

58. "*Un tapis-franc, en argot de vol et de meurtre, signifie un estaminet ou un cabaret du plus bas étage*" (Sue, *Mystères*, 35; English translation, 3).

59. Sue, *Mystères*, 37; English translation, 3.

60. Balzac, *Splendeurs*, 519.

61. Ibid., 557.

62. Ibid., 578.

63. Found in Part III, Chapter 7 of *Splendeurs*.

64. Klein, *Le vocabulaire des mœurs*, 254.

65. As discussed in chapter 3, the popularity of serial novels released in installments in newspapers, coupled with cheaper means of printing and the reduction in newspaper subscriptions, ushered in a quadrupling of newspaper subscriptions before 1850. This increase, in addition to informal methods of newspaper access, speaks to the great increase in readers of these early works.

66. A "semiotic encounter" occurs when "a particular sign-phenomenon or communicative process connects persons to each other. (Even in the special case of face-to-face encounters it is not the fact of co-presence but the fact that one person's semiotic activity is audible and visible to another that creates the possibility of social interaction [. . .])" (Agha, *Language and Social Relations*, 10).

67. In a letter to French novelist Paul Meurice on August 28, 1853, Hugo expresses his personal distaste for serialized novels (Hugo and Meurice, 26). In a letter dated

October 12, 1865, Meurice warns Hugo of the damage that publishing *Les Misérables* could have on their newspaper *L'Évènement* (Ibid., 207).

68. Larchey published several versions from 1858 to 1889; however, here, I focus mainly on the sixth edition.

69. Bowles, "Alfred Delvau's Dictionaries," 218.

Chapter 1

Slang as Criminal Code

I swear to you that I tried to do what you told me. I have tried several times to speak to the ones who seemed the least evil, but if you only knew the way they spoke! What men!

—Eugène Sue, *The Mysteries of Paris* (1842–1843)

(*Je vous assure qu'afin de suivre vos recommandations, j'ai plusieurs fois tâché d'adresser la parole à ceux d'entre eux qui me semblaient moins criminels; mais si vous saviez quel langage! quels hommes!*)

The appearance of the criminal type in literature is hardly new to the literary landscape (French or otherwise) and can be dated back to the Middle Ages. However, the emergence of literary realism in the 1830s and 1840s presented a more sophisticated version of this character, one whose coded language, slang (*argot*) served as the primary means for writers, such as Eugène-François Vidocq, Eugène Sue, and Honoré de Balzac, to construct deviant figures from the Parisian underworld as well as a social identification for a bourgeois readership. In addition, the mass dispersion of these novels in serialized format meant that readers of all social strata gained exposure to "realistic" representations of life in present-day France. The effort to accurately portray the slang of the marginalized social and criminal classes became a staple of literary realism, thus distinguishing the "bad guy" characters of early nineteenth-century literature from those of the past.

Criminal characters in Vidocq's *Memoirs* (*Mémoires*, 1829), Eugène Sue's *The Mysteries of Paris* (*Les Mystères de Paris*, 1842–1843), and Honoré de Balzac's *Splendors and Miseries of Courtesans* (*Les Splendeurs et misères des courtisanes*, 1838–1847) serve as prototypes for this more complex, realistic version of criminality that relied so heavily on linguistic representation. In fact, language, as I argue, became the basis of this literary type and the main signifier of criminality for a bourgeois audience, as well as the defining mark for writers in terms of solidifying their personal credibility. Vidocq, Sue, and Balzac incorporated slang primarily as a means of building the foundation of criminal identity for a middle-class readership, and although slang's sociolinguistic associations changed throughout the century, depending on which social group adopted it, initially the introduction of slang within French literature became exclusively associated with society's villains. While literary critics, such as Claudine Nédélec and Pascale Gaitet, have analyzed the role of slang in French literature, I propose that reframing this analysis from a sociolinguistic perspective reveals not only linguistic changes that occurred over the course of the nineteenth century but significant artistic and social changes as well.

Slang, as indexical of criminals in nineteenth-century France, established the first indexical order of the language. Beginning with the nth degree and increasing in level (n+1st order, n+2nd order, etc.), indexical orders refer to degrees of cultural meaning attached to referential or non-referential signs, or indexes.[1] As Barbara Johnstone explains, these meanings become attached to certain linguistic forms when individuals are "told that they do, and they continue to share ideas about indexical meaning as long as they keep telling each other about them."[2] These orders do not supersede one another, but rather offer different (and sometimes competing) ideological interpretations of the indexes. For Michael Silverstein, the nth degree indexical order communicates a specific cultural ideology regarding appropriate indexical use of certain signs, or indexes. Therefore, indexes at the nth degree contain an "ethnopragmatic" usage, in that they contain a culturally recognized interpretation.[3] For example, the nineteenth-century word, *ouvrier*, which literally translates to "worker," was slang for "thief." At the nth order, the slang term, *ouvrier*, functions as a social classifier. At the n+1st order, *ouvrier* is the coded criminal term for thief that indexes a participant in criminal culture. And at the n+2nd order, *ouvrier* is the vernacular term for thief that indexes the misery and poverty of the working and criminal classes. Through the progression of the indexical orders, sociolinguistic processes may occur, such as "enregisterment," when linguistic forms are collectively recognized as a register, or as "iconization," when certain dialects, sociolects, or ways of speaking become representative of an entire culture or group of people. In terms of nineteenth-century French slang, its literary use indexes valuable social information concerning class and morality. While Vidocq, Sue, and Balzac incorporate criminal slang as a means of advertising their insider knowledge and attracting readers, at the same time, the writers must tactically outline their own social and moral positions as being noncriminal for their bourgeois audience.

This chapter explores nineteenth-century French writers' descents into the criminal underworld and their representations of slang, or their engagement in a sociolinguistic phenomenon that I term, *literary slumming*. In the early nineteenth century, one defined a "slum" as

> [a] street, alley, court, etc., situated in a crowded district of a town or city and inhabited by people of a low class or by the very poor [. . .] forming a thickly populated neighborhood or district where the houses and the conditions of life are of a squalid and wretched character.[4]

Within the literary realm, a fascination with the life of the lower classes, especially those considered dangerous, resulted in writers boasting of insider knowledge of an otherwise inaccessible world.[5] Slums, while part of a particular society, nevertheless remain contained within certain areas of a city. In a similar manner, French writers reflected a literary spatial containment for their representations of criminals, while occasionally playing on bourgeois fears of societal invasion.

Vidocq, Sue, and Balzac capitalized on the enticing nature of the workings of the Parisian underworld by showcasing it in their memoirs and novels as an extension of their own insider knowledge of criminal dealings. Their literary slumming constituted a cultural and social duality: on the one hand, it meant trading honorable subject matter for lowbrow topics that would attract the masses and make these writers a household name. A reduction in literary standards meant racy content, the use of non-Standard French, and works published via the press in serialized format. These novels became culturally analogous to the slums of the early nineteenth century, and interestingly, as explored in chapter 3, the majority of readers were bourgeois, not working class. On the other hand, literary slumming involved writers showcasing their ability to pass between society and anti-society, and therefore, their authority to accurately reconstruct the criminal realm within their novels.[6] In this manner, their bourgeois readers could vicariously partake in a slumming experience from the physical safety of their home. Identity-play, for the writer and his readers, constitutes the second part of literary slumming. The dual nature of the writer as verified members of both the French underworld and overworld presented new social possibilities for middle-class readers. By proving their indestructible moral character during their tour of exotic, forbidden social realms, writers who acted as guides, such as Vidocq, Sue, and Balzac, extend a similar moral immunity to their readers who can also experience, albeit via the imagination, social characterizations that are less rigid and more fluid than those constituted by society. Similar to *literal slumming*, the effect of *literary slumming* indulges upper-class desires to encounter foreign ways-of-life within the confines of the cityscape and ultimately reveals dormant yearnings by bourgeois readers for a class identity less confined by oppressive, societal ideals.

Within the representations of criminal anti-society, slang serves as an anti-language, that is, a variant "of one and the same underlying semiotic" (in this case, Standard French), even though they "may express different social structures."[7] Slang perverts Standard French words to accommodate its criminal users who seek to communicate in secret without having to invent an entirely new lexicon. As Daniel Heller-Roazen notes, languages used for a criminal purpose "constitute not so much secret languages [...] as secret uses of languages."[8] In this chapter, I analyze the ways in which Vidocq, Sue, and Balzac rendered slang as the primary index of criminal identity in the early nineteenth century. In terms of physical markers and social signs, slang was most useful to early nineteenth-century French writers as a means of representing social types, in that through specific speech habits, writers could easily communicate to the reader key social information regarding a character's moral barometer, which typically aligned with other qualities, such as their profession and physical appearance.

In spite of their indulgence in representations of the criminal underworld, Vidocq, Sue, and Balzac used several literary devices in order to distance themselves socially from their criminal subject matter, especially through their use of in-text codification; in other words, their use of italics, parentheses, footnotes, and glossaries distinguished the slang of their criminal characters from the Standard French of the upper-class characters, as well as from that of the bourgeois narrator. This demarcation highlighted the fact that slang was indeed different from the Standard even though the lexicon matched. The use of glossaries and footnotes to aid readers in their comprehension of criminal dialogue further emphasized the coded nature of the language and its relationship to Parisian society as an anti-language.

In line with the authors' use of such textual emendations, this chapter further reveals the ways in which slang served as linguistic scapegoat within the literary domain, becoming both representative of and conflated with other dialects and foreign languages. In spite of its pejorative connotations, in works by Vidocq, Sue, and Balzac the use of language as a means of class identification showcases the emergence of a more socially inclusive literary domain, one that valorizes criminal characters as much as, or perhaps even more so, than upper-class ones.[9]

CRIMINAL DESCENTS

For readers to fully engage in literary slumming, they first need a trustworthy guide who is well-versed in criminal dealings. Through their taboo tales of murderers and thieves, Vidocq, Sue, and Balzac establish themselves as privy to this knowledge firsthand, while at the same time convincing their readers of their bourgeois social standing. In spite of the risky nature of including such slang speech practices and the attention these representations brought to critics in the press, Vidocq, Sue, and Balzac explicitly condemn the use of slang in order to establish themselves on the same social (and thus moral) plane as their presumed audience, a literary device frequently utilized in literature in the seventeenth and eighteenth centuries following the restrictions on content and style set in place by the French Academy.[10] In ways similar to Pechon's condemnation at the end of *The Magnanimous Life*, Vidocq, Sue, and Balzac all critique both slang and its speakers. Nonetheless, these writers must engage in a delicate balancing act between convincing their readers of their moral integrity and their bonafide credibility as experts of the Parisian underworld. Like their criminal characters, Vidocq, Sue, and Balzac possess the ability to pass between society and anti-society, while revealing their insider knowledge of criminal life, including its secret language.

Vidocq's *Memoirs* launched a literary trend of representing criminals as real-life inhabitants of the city scene, along with cashing in on his insider knowledge that popularized police memoirs in the 1820s, even though two professional writers, Émile Morice and Louis-François L'Héritier, drafted *Mémoires*, and not Vidocq.[11] As Nicolas Gauthier notes, due to his unusual social trajectory, Vidocq's memoirs existed at the generic intersection between criminal and police memoirs.[12] The work experienced international success with audiences, appearing in translation and as various adaptations across Europe.[13] Gauthier posits Vidocq's memoirs as the first to establish a mythology around the criminal figure and his underworld, wherein the protagonist "tells his story but also offers a re-reading of History."[14] Vidocq's criminal mythos in early nineteenth-century France blurred the lines between fiction and reality, a characteristic that no doubt affected the subsequent representations of criminality in serial novels.

Within this competing version of History, Vidocq's stated goal was to unveil "the expedients of thieves, the signs with which one can recognize them [. . .], their behaviors, their habits, [. . .] their language and their dress."[15] Here Vidocq lists all of the "signs" to help the reader differentiate the "good" guys (i.e., upper-class Frenchmen and/or the educated who use Standard French) from the "bad" guys (i.e., lower-class, foreign, and/or uneducated people who use a nonstandard form of the language or a foreign language). Moreover, each of these non-referential indexes can be drawn from language alone. If a character speaks slang, the reader can make probable guesses about that character's profession, moral integrity, habits, and dress. Near the end of his autobiography, Vidocq validates the relationship between speech practices and social identity: "[T]herefore thieves have signs of recognition and a particular language. To possess this language, to be initiated to these signs, even if one is not of the same profession, is already a mark of their benevolence."[16] Vidocq reveals the value in knowing slang within the criminal community, and due to its closed nature, the acquisition of this anti-language entails a formal initiation into these organizations. Similar to Parisian society, criminal anti-society contains its own linguistic and cultural capital that contains value within the context of organized crime. Importantly, Vidocq's readers may find value in acquiring a familiarity with slang in order to possess the ability to identify real-life criminals. For the audience, there exists a direct correlation between language (slang) and social status (criminal), which served as the basis of this first indexical order. By considering the sociolinguistic evolution of slang language in early French works such as Vidocq's memoirs, one can better understand the larger artistic and social consequences that ensued as a result.

Although he came from a bourgeois family, Vidocq engaged in crime at a young age and spent his younger years going from one prison to another. His mastery of slang and his time spent as a cutthroat criminal granted Vidocq an air of authenticity, but also made him the most qualified candidate to instruct fellow writers on the ways of organized crime. As Dominique Kalifa notes, the originality of his memoirs is revealed in the "porosity" of the text itself, as it exists at a crossroads of the autobiographical, fictive, and judiciary.[17] One could argue, however, that this porosity came about in part from the appearance of different linguistic registers within the text, notably with Vidocq, as the narrator, and his use of Standard French and Vidocq, the criminal, and his use of slang. Although he based his memoirs mainly on his experience as an ex-criminal, Vidocq defines himself socially by explicitly condemning those he once associated with, as well as by distancing himself from his old lifestyle via language. In the initial "From Vidocq to the Reader" (*Vidocq au lecteur*), Vidocq explains that he employed a ghostwriter due to a broken arm, and, in spite of their literary styling, Vidocq affirms his correct usage of Standard French.[18] Despite the fact that Vidocq hired someone else to write his memoirs (which has been confirmed), the former criminal mastermind boasts of his impeccable French grammar, a quality that indexes someone from a bourgeois background who is educated, and thus morally sound. By adhering to linguistic norms, it is assumed that one adheres to other social norms as well. Although one could contest Vidocq's authenticity, especially given that he did not write the *Memoirs* himself, this preemptive claim advocates on behalf of his ability to write correctly, and therefore gives an initial presentation of Vidocq to the public as an upstanding bourgeois, and not a criminal lowlife.

To further plant himself firmly within this bourgeois social status, as well as to create separation between himself and the criminal world, Vidocq occasionally critiques the language of other characters within the narrative. For example, when he pretends to be a family's long-lost "Auguste Duval" and plots an escape via hospital, Vidocq finds himself on the run dressed as Sister Vidocq. A family living in a cottage takes him in for the evening, and Vidocq silently judges his host's surprisingly good French.[19] Again this commentary, while it appears within the narrative itself, contributes to the distancing between Vidocq and his subject matter via language. Although Vidocq has a positive analysis of his host's French, the fact that he comments on his language establishes Vidocq's role as a linguistic authority and places him in a superior social position as critic.

In addition to engaging in such linguistic differentiation in order to remove himself socially and morally from the criminals he describes, an older Vidocq claims that the fellow criminals whom he once partnered with were nothing but a means to an end. In an episode where Vidocq attempts to dig out of a prison in Lille with a fellow inmate, Desfosseux, a break in the narrative occurs in order for Vidocq to reassure his reader that under any other circumstances, he would not have associated himself with a person of such terrible repute.[20] Vidocq justifies his dealings with fellow criminals by portraying his situation as one of survival, as well as, again, by positing his accomplices as merely a means to an end. Later on, he confesses to developing a hatred of the criminal lifestyle, especially after having begun his criminal career at such a young age.[21] At this point, Vidocq's readers have witnessed his descent into criminality: he has stolen, conned law-abiding citizens, changed identities, and escaped from several prisons. He understands the internal mechanisms of criminal hierarchies, their coded language, and the French prison system. Vidocq has revealed ample secrets to his readers in an effort to prove himself as a reliable source. His weariness of the criminal lifestyle signals hope for a moral ascent, while keeping his readers intrigued to discover if his moral compass will guide him out.

At age twenty-four, he finds himself at Toulon prison in constant contact with some of the most horrific inmates. During this time, Vidocq feared his own moral and linguistic corruption, and tried with all his might to avoid adopting criminal slang.[22] Alas, his attempts at resistance are in vain as he quickly learns that slang is a necessary acquisition in the pursuit of liberty.[23] In Vidocq's experience, slang is such a foundational aspect of criminal life that it cannot be avoided, even if one wishes to escape the criminal game.[24] Following his conversion to private investigator, Vidocq becomes even more vocal about his disdain for criminal activity and creates a new life constructed around the destruction of evildoers. In his attempt to capture the notorious criminal, Saint-Germain, Vidocq vows to erase him, as well as others, from society.[25] This vow of destruction reassures bourgeois readers of Vidocq's social and moral transformation, which one could argue has culminated because his physical purging of his former comrades from society stands as the ultimate testimony to Vidocq's newfound role. In addition to revealing the ins-and-outs of criminal life, Vidocq takes the betrayal of his criminal peers one step further by publicly declaring war against them in his *Memoirs*.

In contrast, upon reading the opening chapter of Sue's *Mysteries*, a reader is immediately drawn into the Parisian underworld: "[W]e are going to attempt to depict some episodes from the lives of *French* savages who are as far removed from civilization as the Indians Cooper so vividly depicts. And these barbarians are all around us [. . .]."[26] This initial scene sets the tone for the reader's entrance into the criminal underworld. The narrator preemptively warns the reader, who may be unaware of what could possibly be born of such "episodes," of the descriptions referring to a barbarous people, a tribe of savages, in other words, non-Europeans. However, the twist is that this "biologically inferior" race of people is indeed European, and even populates the same society in which the middle-class reader resides. While coexisting in the same geographical area, these "barbarians" have created for themselves, in addition to their own language, a set of morals. Immediately, Sue establishes a connection between language, morality, and geography by characterizing this group of Parisian savages as first, inhabiting the same city as the reader; second, adhering to a different set of morals; and third, speaking an entirely different language, and a gruesome one at that. Although Sue exoticizes his criminal types more than Vidocq does, he nonetheless presents his readers with the makings of an anti-society with their own anti-language since these "savages" reside in the same city with their "mysterious language."

After the first paragraph, the narrator relates to a reader's possibly mixed feelings toward his scandalous subject matter by including himself in the reader's dilemma between loathing such literature and being oddly awestruck by it.[27] Sue's narrator apologizes on behalf of the setting in which these stories take place but also acknowledges the hope that "fearful curiosity" will outweigh any moral resistance to the subject matter. Nonetheless, the narrator feels obliged to warn his reader of the adventure that they are about to undertake, where they will no doubt catch a glimpse of this "infernal race" (*cette race infernale*).[28] Through these cautionary messages of the narrator, an acknowledgment of criminal characters in his text and the middle-class anxiety that might result, Sue absolves himself from any association with criminality by reassuring readers of his social standing as bourgeois. In addition, this reassurance acts as permission for the reader to engage in literary slumming: since the narrator identifies as middle class, and if he can implicate himself in this world of corruption and crime and emerge unscathed, then the reader may also vicariously indulge in this underworld as well. After all, the readers do not even come into direct contact with these ruthless barbarians.

In a further example of an author social distancing from a text's criminal content, in Balzac's *Splendors*, this occurs mainly in his chapter on slang entitled, "Philosophical, Linguistic and Literary Essay on Slang, Prostitutes and Thieves" (*Essai philosophique, linguistique et littéraire sur l'argot, les filles et les voleurs*). Unlike Vidocq and Sue, there are no preliminary warnings from the narrator about the dangers of exposure to criminal life and its language. In fact, slang does not even appear until after Lucien's arrest at the end of Part II. Nonetheless, Balzac does not fully condone its use, and neither does he fully condemn it; he simply presents it as useful information in order for the reader to be able to comprehend the actions of his criminal characters:

> The bizarre scenes that had to follow, everything would be intolerable and incomprehensible without a few explanations on the world of thieves and prisons, on their laws, their behaviors, and especially their language, whose ghastly poetry is indispensable at this part in the story.[29]

In the spirit of literary realism, Balzac depicts the social times in a semi-objective fashion. *Splendors*' portrayal of crime and criminals in early nineteenth-century Paris is neither an attempt at social reform nor an insider's guide to fighting crime. It is simply a *tableau de mœurs* (portrait of manners) in which the writer's personal stance remains slightly ambiguous. According to the narrator, the use of slang and the revelation of criminal habits merely serve a practical purpose: without exposure to certain aspects of criminal life, the reader would be disoriented, especially with regard to the criminals' language. While Vidocq and Sue tend to take explicit positions against criminal life and its language in order to reassure their reader, in contrast, Balzac does not indulge a perceived reader's desire to understand the author's moral orientation. In spite of this narrative difference, Balzac establishes his authority through the confident use of in-text definitions and footnotes that explain criminal systems and their language. In addition, the centrality of his notorious character, Vautrin, grants readers access to this anti-society through the lens of a criminal mastermind. The audience who may have encountered this character in previous works by Balzac can now participate in literary slumming via Vautrin with guidance from the narrator.

SLANG AND THE DANGEROUS CLASSES

The authors' attempts at separating themselves personally from slang and the social connotations embedded within it, however, did not work to undermine the associations that Vidocq, Sue, and Balzac established within their works between slang and specific social types. This association comprised the basis of the first indexical order and, in terms of literary slumming, permitted the writer and his readers to fully experience this anti-society and its anti-language. The monopolization of slang by criminal characters in works such as *Memoirs*, *The Mysteries of Paris*, and *Splendors and Miseries of*

Courtesans served as the primary means by which the reader identifies those characters as the "bad guys," and therefore allowed early writers both to showcase and exploit their insider knowledge of criminal life.

Revealing the extent to which language and social identity are related to one another, Vidocq's *Memoirs* was a leading text on criminal life and language. The memoir details the life of the former criminal mastermind-turned-chief of the "Security Brigade" (*la brigade de sûreté*) in Paris, and eventually private detective, while revealing the ins-and-outs of the criminal world. In the text, Vidocq's use of criminal slang also aided several writers of his day, including Victor Hugo, Sue, and Balzac, with their own representations of criminal characters. Although classified as a memoir, Vidocq's social conversion from the son of a lower-middle-class baker to France's most wanted criminal set off a trend of writers divulging aspects of the criminal world to a bourgeois audience. At the start of the autobiographical account, the reader witnesses the protagonist's gradual descent into hardcore criminality, beginning with a petty theft. During his time as a baker's apprentice in Arras, Vidocq begins stealing money from the counter, eventually seeking out the company of fellow criminals.[30] Vidocq's initiation parallels Pechon's earlier induction into an organization of thieving wandering merchants (*les mercelots*) in his work *The Magnanimous Life*, while reinforcing the image of criminal life as a closed circle. He even receives a name change when he tries to sell his family's silver engraved with "Vidocq" on each piece.[31] The adoption of a new name additionally marks Vidocq's sinister transformation, as well as the necessity of shedding one's former identity in order to become a bonafide criminal.

As Vidocq's *Memoirs* reveals closely guarded information regarding slang, criminal identity, and criminal networking, readers soon become immersed in this otherwise inaccessible anti-society, while Vidocq, the narrator, constantly reminds his audience of this privilege. While serving time at the Bicêtre prison, Vidocq comments on the closed nature of the criminal world, calling it a nation with its own language and ideologies; those unversed in slang, Vidocq explains, naturally stand as this nation's enemies.[32] Vidocq emphasizes language as the key to entering into this anti-society, as the coded language of the criminal simultaneously remains excluded from society while exclusive to its members, a phenomenon characteristic to anti-languages or any form of closed communication. In a scene where Vidocq is undercover, he identifies his surrounding company through their use of slang, and immediately knows that they are all *workers* (thieves).[33] At this point in the narrative, since several slang-speaking thieves have appeared, Vidocq has molded readers' expectations for criminal characters and their speech practices. His ability to identify his company due to their language thus parallels a reader's experience, who also comes to anticipate crooked characters based on their vocabulary and ways of speaking. Even though Vidocq consistently straddles the line between two social domains, the upper and lower classes, his alignment of language and social class throughout his memoirs works to develop the reader's sociolinguistic standards regarding speech and class. Vidocq's numerous anecdotes about criminal personas and the sometimes farcical situations in which he finds himself trying to evade capture coincide with consistent emphasis on criminal gestures, manners, and slang. Furthermore, from the position of narrator, Vidocq's language (or, more accurately, that of his ghostwriter's) mirrors that of his bourgeois readers. As he reflects on his sinister past, Vidocq does so using Standard French. This repetition and consistency cement the indexical relationship between speech and class for a nineteenth-century audience.

Similarly, Sue also makes the connection between speech and class, although he sometimes grossly misaligns them as well. Establishing the "city-mysteries" novels, a popular genre in Europe and the United States during the 1840s through the 1860s, from 1842 to 1843 Sue wrote *The Mysteries of Paris* for the French newspaper *Newspaper of Debates* (*Le Journal des débats*). As Paul Erickson notes, "these novels shared a concern with 'removing the veil' from the hidden operations of urban life" and "helps reveal the ways that popular writers, as well as elite thinkers, were coming to terms with the sudden increase in the size, density, and diversity of urban areas."[34] The novel tells the story of Rodolphe, a German aristocrat disguised as a fan painter, revealing the complex dynamics between the upper and lower classes within a rapidly evolving cityscape. Rodolphe can speak slang, and thus passes easily between society and anti-society, entangling himself with several criminal characters along the way. Throughout the novel, the reader encounters such characters as the Slasher, the Owl, the Schoolmaster, the Skeleton, Red Arm, the Big Gimp, and Gammy. Apart from Rodolphe, aristocratic characters (even evil ones) speak in Standard French, and Sue remains more-or-less consistent in establishing a relationship between social class and language.

Highlighting how slang-speaking characters in *Mysteries* are overwhelmingly criminal (other than Rodolphe, an aristocrat disguised as a worker), Sue juxtaposes the use of slang by the criminal class with the Standard French of other aristocratic characters. When the slumming aristocrats Tom and Sarah enter the White Rabbit tavern, their physical appearance reveals to the surrounding patrons that aristocrats such as themselves do not belong in shady establishments. In addition to their awkward demeanor, their use of language also seems out of place since the two characters speak in Standard French.[35] When Tom addresses the Slasher, a former-animal-slaughterer-turned-murderer, in the hopes of gaining information about Rodolphe, Tom's proper manner of speaking hinders their communication, as the Slasher must translate his slang into Standard French. When Tom asks about the identity of Red-Arm, the Slasher replies, "He fakes packing trunks," a response that bears repeating here:

Tom: I didn't understand what you said about Red-Arm. Rodolphe was leaving his place, surely?
Slasher: I told you that Red-Arm fakes packing trunks. [. . .]
Tom: What do you mean, he fakes packing trunks? What does that mean?
Slasher: Fakes packing trunks. He sells contraband goods. It seems you don't speak the lingo.[36]
Tom: My good man, I don't understand you.
Slasher: I am telling you that you don't speak slang like Monsieur Rodolphe.
Tom: Slang? said Tom, looking at Sarah in surprise.
Slasher: Come on, you guys are a couple of *mugs*[37] [. . .]. Well, since you don't speak this beautiful tongue, I'll tell you in plain French that Red-Arms is a contraband dealer.[38]

This interaction between Tom and the Slasher reinforces the correlation between class origin and speech practices; in other words, Standard French belongs to those of an educated, elite class, whereas non-Standard French, such as slang, belongs to the lower, dangerous classes who are detrimental to society: linguistically, morally, and socially. Socially powerful, the character Tom, who is from the privileged class, cannot recognize slang, which leads to a linguistic power shift. The character from the criminal class Slasher not only speaks slang but also holds a position of power, linguistically speaking, because he controls the information being relayed to Tom. Tom, despite his privileged social status, does not comprehend the slang terms, which, while further emphasizing his class background, makes it apparent to the reader that this is Tom's first visit to the White Rabbit, an establishment of ill repute. This scene is therefore an example of reverse cultural capital at work because the typically dominated class has become the dominant one. As Pierre Bourdieu explains, "Language is not only an instrument of communication or even of understanding but an instrument of power."[39] This reverse dominant class is further solely positioned within the context of an anti-society that contains its own agents and structures, which mediate the cultural value of their own kind of linguistic capital. Conversely, in the context of larger society, such slang has little-to-no value, except as an identifier of social degenerates. In a bourgeois-dominated society, in which culture, *in actuality*, is exclusive only to the dominant classes, the culture of Sue's anti-society is, in reality, only available "to those who are endowed with the means to appropriate it."[40] In a Bourdieusian sense, then, these "means" constitute societal clout and connection and formal education within society, as well as an appearance and speech practices that would encourage upward social mobility. In the context of an anti-society, these means also apply, albeit in a less institutionalized format, according to the system structures at play. In the criminal underworld, those "endowed with the means to appropriate it" possess the clout and connection with villains of higher ranking and an initiation into the criminal lifestyle through an acquisition of slang and an understanding of the criminal hierarchy and the French prison system. The means, much like the structures, of both society and anti-society mirror one another, thus a member of the French aristocracy, such as Tom, who is unversed in the ways of crime and with no knowledge of slang, holds little cultural capital in the context of this anti-society.

Between 1838 and 1847, around the same time Sue was publishing *The Mysteries of Paris*, Balzac wrote *Splendors* in serialized format for the French newspaper *The Press* (*La Presse*) as the follow-up novel to *Lost Illusions* (1837–1843), which tells the story of Lucien de Rubempré, a young man from the countryside who has high hopes of joining Parisian high society.[41] Through a series of failed and dishonest attempts at climbing the social ladder, *Splendors* begins with Lucien on the verge of committing suicide when the mastermind criminal Vautrin, also known as Cheats-Death (*Trompe-la-Mort*), who is based on real-life criminal Vidocq, approaches Lucien disguised as Spanish priest, Carlos Herrera. In order to use Lucien for his own gain, Vautrin draws the young man deeper into more financial and social problems.

The use of slang in *Splendors* does not appear often, however, until about halfway through the novel, following the protagonist's Lucien de Rubempré's arrest. After being accused of theft and murder, Lucien is taken to La Force prison, accompanied by Vautrin, who is disguised as the Spanish priest, Carlos Herrera. In the following chapter entitled, "Salad Basket" (*Le Panier à salade*), a slang term that refers to the police carriages used to transport prisoners, the narrator speaks explicitly about slang, marking it as a criminal code. In this manner, the narrator initiates his reader into the criminal anti-society of the Parisian prison. When the narrator describes how convicts transported in the Salad Basket head to the Courthouse (*Palais de Justice*) for their interrogation, he states that "in prison slang this is called *going to school*."[42] Throughout the story, the narrator continually prefaces the definition to slang terms with the phrase, "in prison slang" (*en argot de prison*). For example, the narrator states that

> in prison slang, the *sheep* is a snitch, who seems to be weighed down by some heavy affair, but whose proverbial skill is tricking others into thinking he is a *friend*. In slang, the word *friend* signifies, a thief emeritus [. . .] who wants to

remain a thief for the rest of his life, and who stays faithful *all the same* to the laws of *high crime society*.[43]

The slang terms and expressions that appear in Balzac's work frequently relate to criminal life and/or monetary exchange. See for instance:

Faces // Heads (of a coin) = francs // French francs[44]
La maison // the house = la Préfecture // Police headquarters[45]
Cheval de retour // Returning horse = un ancien forçat // an ex-convict[46]
Serré // packed in = mis en prison // put in prison[47]
Un cuisinier // a cook = un espion // a spy[48]
Terrer // to earth up = guillotiner // to guillotine[49]
Poisser nos philippes // to steal our change = filouter nos pièces d'or // to swipe our gold coins[50]
Abouler du carle // to cough up coin = donner de l'argent // to give money[51]
La Cigogne // the Stork = le Palais de Justice // Courthouse[52]
Cromper ma sorbonne // To save my Sorbonne = *sauver ma tête de la guillotine //* to save me from execution by guillotine[53]

In addition to the narrator's linguistic mediation and contextualization of slang within prisons, slang also appears, of course, in dialogue between criminal characters.[54] In one scene, Vautrin, again disguised as the priest Carlos Herrera, finds himself in prison and receives a visit from his aunt, Jacqueline Collin (also known as Asia), who is disguised as a marquise. During their interaction, they speak in slang in order to keep their conversation secret. When Monsieur Gault, the director of Conciergerie Prison, tells Monsieur de Granville, the Attorney General, of the marquise's visit to the Spanish priest, he comically states that no one could understand their conversation and assumes they spoke to one another in Spanish.[55] In another scene, when the hardcore criminal the Informer (*la Pouraille*) reveals to Vautrin the location of his gold, an exchange takes place that is peppered with slang. On occasion, Balzac provides translations in parentheses, but not always. For instance, in a scene during which the Informer refers to Vautrin by his real name "Jacques Collin," there are no translations provided (here, I provide my own in parentheses):

Informer: Here's the *ball* (the secret)! On that *baby doll* (theft/job), Ruffard, one of Bibi-Lupin's agents, went third man with me and Godet ...
Vautrin: Woolpicker?... cried Jacques Collin, using Ruffard's known name by the mob.
Informer: That's it. Those thugs ratted me out because I know their hideout and they don't know mine.
Vautrin: You are greasing my boots (You are preparing me to leave)! [...] said Jacques Collin

Informer: What?
Vautrin: Well, replied the *godfather* (criminal boss), see what one gets by putting all their confidence in me! [...]
Informer: You will always be our *godfather*. I will no longer keep any secrets from you, replied the Informer. My gold is in the *deep* (cellar) of Gonore's house.[56]

In this scene, a reader mainly needs to rely on context clues (in addition to Balzac's notes) in order to properly interpret the conversation between Vautrin and the Informer. Thus, thanks to Balzac's mediation between society and anti-society, the bourgeois reader has become privy to an otherwise secretive exchange. The frequency of dialogues in slang between criminals within *Splendors* therefore contributes to the establishment of an indexical relationship between slang and hardcore criminality, thus laying the foundation for the first indexical order.

The dynamic between society and anti-society also surfaces in *Splendors* via the narrator's commentaries. When discussing high-crime society (*la haute pègre*), the narrator compares it to the population of Saint-Germain, the Parisian district that traditionally housed French aristocracy. The narrator's description further paints this association of criminals as parallel to society's upper crust; however, instead of the richest nobles, it contains the top criminal bosses.[57] These aristocrats of the underworld had established a secret society known as the Society of the Ten-Thousand (*société des Dix-Mille*), whose members commit high-profile thefts.[58] The establishment of a criminal aristocracy that deals with high-stakes thefts further renders it akin to Parisian aristocracy in terms of being defined by money and exclusivity. As David Harvey notes in relation to Balzac's novels, "The guiding strings of power [...] lie within the credit system" and within bourgeois power structures, the same dynamic exists within the criminal social hierarchy.[59] In a like manner, when discussing prison life, the narrator states that convicts entrust their personal finances within a system that works like a bank.[60] While the establishment of a criminal social hierarchy and language corresponds to the social stratifications and standards French of society, in this instance Balzac introduces a newer aspect to that anti-society: a banking system which is overseen by Vautrin that allows for the circulation of monetary capital.

Nevertheless, Balzac's narrator softens his presentation of a criminal anti-society by positing it as a parody of Parisian society. Despite these social parallels, the anti-society is not a "real" society, according to Balzac's narrator. From a theoretical perspective, anti-societies form as a "mode of resistance" to society, and according to Halliday, these can be more nonviolent in their resistance or, conversely, overtly aggressive.[61] Anti-languages are the product of anti-societies, and although little is known about how they form, they often appear as relexicalized words from the language with the intent of communicating to exclude certain members of society. For Halliday, it is the anti-language, like language, that functions as a "reality-generating system" in order to construct the alternative world of the anti-society which functions in opposition to society.[62] In fact, the anti-language upholds the internal hierarchies that exist in the anti-society; it is the backbone of the anti-society. Thus, Balzac's treatment of criminal anti-society as a parody of society is not too far off, as the anti-society is the mirror image of the society, with the same structures and institutions that offer alternative social roles and values, and which also always involves a process of resocialization.

For instance, when describing fellow criminal Le Biffon, as a member of an elite criminal network, the narrator states that "these savages of high-crime society respect neither the law nor religion, nothing, not even natural history, of which the saintly nomenclature is, as one sees it, parodied by them."[63] From a theoretical perspective, Simon Dentith defines parody as "any cultural practice which provides a relatively polemical allusive imitation of another cultural production or practice" and explains that the playful "polemical" aspect is what distinguishes parody from imitation, travesty, or pastiche.[64] For Linda Hutcheon, parody "is doubly coded in political terms: it both legitimizes and subverts that which it parodies."[65] Thus, the criminal anti-society in Balzac's *Splendors* works as a parody of French society in which it mocks the agents, structures, and systems of society, perverting them within the anti-society. The counterparts of these agents, structures, and systems found within criminal anti-society imitate those of society as a critique (and as an ideological attack), not as praise in the form of imitation. The criminals' complete disrespect for the "law, religion, and even natural history" boils down to a parody of the intricate mechanisms that form these authoritative institutions, and through this parody, the narrator highlights the similarities between the two societies. Just as with the language of slang, these added aspects of organized crime work to subvert elements of upper-class society. For readers, then, the criminal becomes synonymous with the linguistic, moral, and social deformities that they create.

In each of their works, French authors Vidocq, Sue, and Balzac consistently associate slang with the criminal classes in order to condition their audience's social expectations regarding criminals and their speech practices. However, writers sometimes grossly misalign speech and representations of identity in order to call attention to the fact that certain social types have specific accents, lexicon, pronunciation, and registers. The result can be that a reader's awareness of language and social associations increases. In *Mysteries*, a disconnect occurs when characters from the criminal class use a language indicative of a person from an upper-class background and vice versa. For instance, at the beginning of the novel, Rodolphe intervenes in order to save Fleur from the Slasher, who is immediately struck by Rodolphe's ability to speak criminal slang: "But who are you, anyway? You speak the lingo like one of us."[66] Even though Rodolphe wears a disguise to appear working class, his otherwise effeminate appearance, a quality indexical of an aristocratic background, in this case, results in a mixed interpretation regarding his true social background.

A character in *Mysteries* whose entire identity is founded on the misalignment of class origin and speech is the Schoolmaster, a criminal who is named so due to his remarkable handwriting and high level of education.[67] In fact, during a meeting with Rodolphe, the Schoolmaster abandons his criminal garb in favor of a more bourgeois look: a green waistcoat and a hat.[68] In addition to a physical transformation, the Schoolmaster also undergoes a linguistic one, in which he drops his criminal slang for a more educated way of speaking.[69] According to the narrator, what's worse than the Schoolmaster's use of slang is his use of a language that indexes the French bourgeoisie, thus appearing to align him with a strong sense of morality. The Schoolmaster even corrects Rodolphe's grammar, a gesture that reinforces his role as learned criminal, while also undermining the reader's faith in Rodolphe's aristocratic education, not to mention questions the ability of the upper classes to maintain their social dominance in a post-Revolution era:

Rodolphe: Well, between you and I [. . .] he pointed out to me—
Schoolmaster: You mean, "between you and me"
Rodolphe: Well, you are up on your grammar.
Schoolmaster: The Schoolmaster, at your service.[70]

Correcting the aristocrat's grammar underscores the Schoolmaster's characterization as a learned criminal, while further revealing his linguistic superiority. The indexical misalignments that occur between the Schoolmaster's social status and his refined ways of speaking and dressing simultaneously indexes him as a person of an upper-class background as well as a person of strong moral integrity. Since bourgeois readers nevertheless remain acutely aware of the disconnect between the Schoolmaster's aristocratic air and his actual criminal lifestyle, this divide deepens the relationship that exists between certain manners of speaking and the people that the speech represents.[71] If criminals can become just as educated and refined as a person of upper-class standing, then their infiltration into society could potentially move beyond the Parisian underworld. Thus, the paradoxical relationships between appearance, class origin, and speech practices proves problematic to a bourgeois reader because of the appropriation of Standard French by a criminal who has not, in fact, undergone the necessary moral conversion. In this manner, Sue delineates such a contrast between character and class that the reader easily becomes aware of the topsy-turvy indexes at play and can therefore properly establish which language *should* go with which characters based on their class background.[72] Such an obvious switch in association between speech and class, albeit frightening, means that bourgeois readers may flex their acquired insider knowledge. Like the narrator, they, too, possess the ability to determine the language that corresponds to the appropriate social class and can discern when indexes no longer align. Within this context, their knowledge of slang permits bourgeois readers to engage in a kind of social porosity as they slip between society and anti-society, even if only within the realm of the imaginary; nevertheless, they may envision themselves as having different social personalities because of their linguistic access to the literary slums. Albeit a product of upper-class privilege, the expansion of social identity via subversive characters and nonstandard language in French literature ultimately contributes to the slow breakdown of class lines and the reimagining of more complex and nuanced social identities.

In contrast, in *Splendors*, a misalignment does not occur, but rather an overarching social ascent takes place for the criminal characters vis-à-vis their class status and profession. This transformation emerges in the form of a social mobility, as Balzac portrays certain institutions, such as marriage, as clearly middle-class. For example, when Prudence Servien (a.k.a. Europe) and Paccard, Vautrin's right-hand man, marry at the novel's end, Paccard proclaims that they are "bourgeois."[73] Later, Asia states that all of Vautrin's criminal gang will end up as "honest, bourgeois people."[74] Even Vautrin renounces his criminal lifestyle by the end of the novel, declaring himself buried with Lucien.[75] Eventually, Vautrin replaces Bibi Lupin as chief of the Security Brigade and hires his former Corsican lover, Theodore Calvi, to assist him.[76] Apart from the air of social mobility that Balzac advertises with his criminal characters, the indexical relationships between language, class, and morality stay consistent throughout the narrative. Nonetheless, a nineteenth-century bourgeois reader understands that such mobility should not take place. By grossly misaligning class status, profession, and language, Sue and Balzac emphasize these indexes even more so that their readers know a linguistic, social asymmetry is occurring. Interestingly, instead of undermining the relationship between speech and identity, this irregularity reinforces the correlation between slang and criminality. By engaging in this literary slumming, which constitutes the narrators' "firsthand" experience among the dregs of society, as well as the transgressive subject matter and the appearance of slang in literary works, bourgeois readers receive permission and the moral reassurance necessary to also take part. Through this vicarious voyage into the Parisian underworld, readers come to associate the use of slang as exclusive to criminality.

SLANG AS LINGUISTIC SCAPEGOAT

While Vidocq, Sue, and Balzac define slang as the coded anti-language of criminals through their reinforced representations of slang speakers as social delinquents, they also conflate slang with other nonstandard dialects, and even with other foreign languages. This conflation fed pervasive xenophobia among contemporary critics regarding the massive influx of "foreign" bodies into Paris.[77] Slang, as a social marker, could cover a wide range of identities, all which ultimately boiled down to being immoral at heart, resulting in a kind of linguistic scapegoating. The act of scapegoating involves the displacement of social problems onto those individuals and/or groups who make up vulnerable populations (ethnic, racial, and socioeconomic). For French writers portraying minorities and/or foreigners in early nineteenth-century texts, this politicized moral blame surfaces via the conflation of language, especially given the transgressive nature of incorporating slang into literary works at this time period. The decline in literary standards provoked bourgeois fears regarding their own social standing within society and the inability to control the infiltration and growth of "undesirable" persons within society.

In *Memoirs*, this linguistic conflation happens with regards to patois, as well as with portrayals of gypsy slang. When Vidocq meets a soldier in Picardy, he reveals that they spoke in the soldier's regional patois, and when Vidocq boards the frigate the *Muiron*, he speaks with the ship cook in the chef's provincial dialect.[78] The fact that Vidocq communicates in these regional dialects not only signals to the reader that he speaks more than one language, but it also places patois at the same social level as slang, since neither language is Standard French. Patois is also visually highlighted in the text in a similar manner to slang. For example, in a scene where Vidocq encounters a peasant woman, he is unable to understand all of her lexicon: "'Don't move, she said to me in patois; the surrounding area is full of *pine trees* (police officers) who were snooping in all directions.' I did know what she meant by the word *pine trees*, but I suspected that it did not apply to anything good."[79] In his interaction with the peasant woman, Vidocq cannot comprehend the exact meaning of the word "pine trees," but nevertheless recognizes that she is expressing something undesirable.[80] Here, a reversal of linguistic inclusivity occurs because Vidocq is no longer the one excluding people through criminal slang. Instead, the peasant woman's use of a regional dialect leaves him confused. A similar scene appears earlier on after a prison break when Vidocq meets two women while traveling through uninhabited lands who speak to the protagonist in an incomprehensible patois.[81] Due to Vidocq's explicit desire to avoid villages and rural areas, readers may assume that these two women are peasants. The fact that they work as farm laborers links a specific socioeconomic status with nonstandard forms of French, in other words, the lower classes. In these scenes, speaking patois is equivalent to speaking slang because it is a specialized form of French that only a small portion of the population speak; it is excluded from the Standard French, while only exclusive to a select few.

Concerning gypsies, or *les Romanichels*, after the reader discovers that Vidocq has joined a gypsy troop,[82] a conversation between Malgaret, a former officer of a draftee battalion, and Vidocq reveals the criminal reputation associated with this minority people:

Malgaret: [. . .] They are thieves!
Vidocq: Thieves! [. . .] What do you know about it?
Malgaret: That which you are going to know for yourself soon, if you want to follow me, because there is a big chance that we will not go far without seeing them *work*.[83]

Vidocq's shock upon discovering the true nature of the gypsies is ironic and places the criminal protagonist on the same social plane as the Roma people. Although Malgaret continues to explain in depth the seedy dealings of the gypsies, from a moral standpoint, Vidocq and his associate are the same: the criminal language they speak contains the same immoral connotations as the slang spoken by the gypsies. In describing them to Vidocq, it is almost as if Malgaret is describing his own criminal order. Malgaret states that it was at (Rasphuys) de Gand prison where he met two men of Roma origin and learned of their people, who practice dangerous trades and whose name changes depending on their geographic location.[84]

In this scene, Malgaret projects moral blame onto another social (and foreign) minority, while at the same time lumping them into the same social category as himself and his criminal brothers. The nomadic and professional nature of the Romas, according to Malgaret, seems to correspond perfectly to the criminal life thus described by Vidocq, as both wayfaring and contemptible. Again, the fact that by the end of Malgaret's rant Vidocq feels determined to avoid "such a dangerous society" would strike a middle-class reader as simultaneously comic and chilling; if a more dangerous band of social minorities exist in France, then a more extensive crime problem exists than formerly perceived.[85]

In terms of language, a linguistic conflation appears when the criminal animal doctor, Caron reveals to Vidocq that his mother was part of a *bande de Bohémiens,* or *Romanichels*, as they are called in a secret Bohemian slang.[86] Later, Vidocq is informed of a theft committed by Bohemians, and after learning that Caron and his gang are in Paris, Vidocq attempts to work with them in order to prove their guilt, but cannot help but be excluded linguistically.[87] Similar to criminal slang, the slang of the *Romanichels* is also strongly safeguarded from external members of their group. Having a coded language therefore enables the continuation of the organization and keeps illegal dealings hidden from outsiders. It also establishes a kind of linguistic standard between certain kinds of groups who use a coded language or a regional dialect versus those who communicate in a standardized form of the language. Essentially, not using the Standard French language automatically places one in a category of social (and criminal) otherness, while simultaneously guaranteeing that communication will not be streamlined.

In *Splendors*, the linguistic scapegoating of other languages onto criminal slang occurs with other Romance languages, as well as with the Baron de Nucingen's Jewish-Polish patois. In order to communicate with his former lover, Théodore Calvi, without Bibi-Lupin, the chief of the Safety Brigade (analogous to real-life Vidocq), overhearing them, Vautrin urges Théodore to speak Italian.[88] Like slang, Vautrin uses Italian in this scene in order to communicate secretly with a fellow criminal. In terms of use, the two languages become interchangeable: Italian might as well be slang and vice versa. To Bibi-Lupin and the surrounding prison guards, they are essentially the same thing and being used for the same purpose of perpetuating criminal activity. In another scene, Vautrin, disguised as the priest Carlos Herrera, receives a visit from his aunt, Jacqueline Collin (Asia), who is disguised as a marquise. During their interaction, they speak in slang that the prison director mistakes for Spanish. While Italian and Spanish, of course, do not possess the same negative connotation as slang, in the novel they are presented as criminal anti-languages.

In addition to slang's conflation with other Romance languages, Balzac further conflates it with the Baron de Nucingen's foreign Jewish-Polish dialect. In ways similar to Vidocq's pejorative portrayal of the Jewish hawker,[89] the Baron's patois contains strong anti-Semitic and racist undertones. Like the Jewish hawker, Balzac represents the Baron's Jewish-Polish patois phonetically. For example, upon seeing Esther for the first time at the Bois de Vincennes, the Baron screams for his coach driver, who is sleeping, to start driving, admonishing him for not doing an adequate job: "*Eef eyehahd brauht Chorge* (pronounced George) *eensted oft yoo, faht peast, hes woot haft beeter fount dis vohman.*"[90] Like slang, Balzac signals the Baron's patois through the use of italics with occasional explanations in parentheses. Additionally, Balzac uses a phonetic portrayal of the Baron's speech habits in order to parody them and includes scenes in which the supporting characters imitate the Baron's patois in order to render it more of a caricature than a realistic portrayal. When Vautrin attempts to trick Nucingen by using a fake Esther to seduce the Baron, the English woman mocks the Baron's way of speaking: "A little bit, my nephew, said the English woman who spoke French well. *But hoo ahr-yoo, yoo?* she said imitating Nucingen's way of speaking."[91] In a scene that takes place at the theater, Lucien finds himself in the presence of several aristocratic characters. Peyrade, disguised as the Englishman, Samuel Johnson, speaks French with an English accent, which prompts the courtisane, Esther, to compare Peyrade's French to that of the Baron's.[92] Balzac distinguishes Peyrade's anglicized French from Standard French in the same way as the Baron's patois: with italics and phonetic spelling. This scene thus serves as another example of the metalinguistic commentary that takes place within these kinds of works in which the narrator, as well as the supporting characters, freely pass judgments on others' unconventional speech practices. The fact that Peyrade is simulating an English accent, again, conflates the foreign with the nonstandard. When Esther announces in front of everyone that his French sounds like that of the Baron's, it incites additional comparisons such as the patois of Brittany versus that of Burgundy. There seems to be no distinction made on the part of the characters between different kinds of patois, or even the difference between a regional dialect and a foreigner speaking French with an accent; to the characters and the narrator, they seem to be one and the same. Interestingly, characters such as the Baron and Peyrade as Samuel Johnson, indeed speak Standard French, but they are not viewed as linguistic equals to the supporting characters who do not announce any obvious quirks in their speech habits. The blatant oddities of pronunciation of the Baron and Samuel immediately classifies them as social outsiders. The phonetic spellings that Balzac and Vidocq use in their respective narratives both stem from and simultaneously perpetuates pejorative ethnic and racial stereotypes. At the same time, it encourages the reader to engage in linguistic stereotyping as they read along; in some instances, even before the narrator announces the origin and/or social status of a certain character, readers can already infer what type of social figure they are due to their language. Essentially, slang speakers, in addition to other speakers of foreign languages and regional dialects, become synecdochal figures of marginalized ethnic, racial, and/or social groups. Regarding indexicality, by rendering foreign and minority languages analogous to slang, these writers create an indexical link between criminality and these languages which are now placed in the same indexical field as criminal slang, and thus contain the same immoral connotations by virtue of conflation.

Linguistic scapegoating in *Mysteries* does not occur, however, as it does in *Memoirs* and *Splendors*. Perhaps the Italian origins of bourgeois criminal, Polidori, serve as a kind of foreignization of the criminal type; however, he neither speaks slang nor comes from the criminal classes. Additionally, Rodolphe is not French, but German, which further complicates his role as moral savior. Cecily, the former wife of the African American doctor, David, is creole, speaks French and German (not slang), and figures as a temptress, but not necessarily as a criminal. In Sue's work, the alignment between class, language, morality, and ethnicity is not so clear-cut. The reader knows that Fleur is a prostitute and a slang speaker, even though she barely speaks a word of slang in the novel. She is also of noble (German) blood; however, she cannot escape her sordid past and dies in the end. With exception of Rodolphe, slang always implies criminality and immorality, whereas Standard French and foreign languages may or may not.

From a sociolinguistic perspective, criminal slang, while indicative of fears regarding the relationship between language, morality, and global power as expressed in public debates in France during the 1830s and 1840s, indexes a more expansive notion of criminality that may include ethnic and racial minorities, as well as foreigners. Vidocq, Sue, and Balzac play on this indexical relationship when their criminal characters disguise themselves as foreigners in which they alter their accents, gestures, and speech. Within these works, Standard French positions itself not only against slang as linguistically (and morally) superior but also against nonstandard dialects and foreign languages that writers conflate with criminal slang.

SLANG'S FIRST INDEXICAL ORDER

The nineteenth-century French writer's transgressive foray into the criminal underworld and his attempt at a realistic depiction marked a dramatic turn in the French literary tradition. Vidocq, Sue, and Balzac (in addition to others) simultaneously unveiled the ins-and-outs of this anti-society, while completely disregarding artistic standards of the time, especially vis-à-vis Standard French language. The in-text codification of slang terms and expressions through the use of italics, parentheses, footnotes, and glossaries, further demarcated the nonstandard language from the standard, while at the same time established a written codification of slang, a process that typically legitimizes language. As a result, a new kind of literary slumming came forth that exposed *en masse* a bourgeois public to more realistic and sophisticated depictions of French criminals that had previously remained foreign and inaccessible to them.

The cultural discourse generated at this time about the dangerous classes resulted in a cultural hegemony. Throughout their practice of literary slumming, French writers both appropriated and exploited criminal culture for monetary gain and personal fame. Even though similarities existed between the slang-speaking deviants who appeared in earlier works dating back to the fifteenth century, such as an initiation into the customs and codes of each criminal organization, for Vidocq, Sue, and Balzac, slang became the primary means of identifying the "bad guys" in a society that is undergoing a breakdown in social hierarchy. Across the centuries, slang continued to function as an anti-language; however, it became primarily an urban phenomenon in early French nineteenth-century works. For a bourgeois reader, criminal characters in *Memoirs*, *The Mysteries of Paris*, and *Splendors and Miseries of Courtesans* are recognizable through their speech practices, rendering language as a useful social identifier, as well as a key means of representing social types within the literary realm. The establishment of slang as an anti-language in these works becomes apparent several times through the juxtaposition of slang with Standard French within dialogue between characters of differing social strata.

In both *The Mysteries of Paris* and *Splendors and Miseries of Courtesans*, a constant tension exists between the criminal underworld and the customs and language of the upper classes. Due to their mastery of slang and infiltration of criminal life, Vidocq, Vautrin, and Rodolphe possess the ability to pass between society and anti-society undetected, principally due to language. In each work, the writers align speech and social class: those from the dangerous classes speak slang (with a few rare exceptions), while bourgeois and upper-class characters stick to Standard French, even if they engage in evil dealings themselves. In addition to the alignment of class origin and speech practices, writers can also misalign these two factors in order to reinforce the indexes at play. This technique is particular to Sue who emphasizes slang's association with the lower classes through the use of linguistic irony, in which characters from the criminal class use a language indicative of a person from a bourgeois background and vice versa. In any case, whether the language-class relationship is either aligned or misaligned, French readers in the early nineteenth century come to expect slang to be the language of evil, lower-class characters.

At the same time, this social descent via text that the writer simultaneously sanctions and condemns allows the reader to indulge in new identities as well. Vidocq, Sue, and Balzac socially exculpate themselves from their disreputable subject matter through an explicit condemnation of slang and/or of the evildoers themselves, in order to reassure readers of the authors' social orientation, which is indisputably bourgeois. In spite of the controversy surrounding each of these individual authors and their representation of a less-than-literary subject matter, the writers' acknowledgment of middle-class anxiety regarding the changing social scene and the massive population influxes occurring within the city also functions as a kind of social distancing from the criminal classes, while allowing readers permission to engage freely in literary slumming. The social orientation of the writers and their firsthand accounts of the criminal underworld create further an air of authenticity, while exoticizing the lower classes due to this newfound accessibility that was only available to the initiated before its mass dispersion via literature. The writer's insider knowledge of criminal types grants them a similar fluidity of identity witnessed in the criminal characters they write. Whether through firsthand experience, as in the case of Vidocq, or through the affirmations of the narrator as in the cases of Balzac and Sue, they flaunt slumming as a sign of their dual social identities. Although their primary identification with the middle and upper classes attempts to dilute their criminal associations, linguistic competencies grants them access to otherwise prohibited worlds.

Moreover, the wide-sweeping nature of this sociolinguistic phenomenon showcased the reverse cultural capital taking place in which the dominated culture establishes itself as the dominant one and vice versa. Slang further becomes synonymous with other "foreign" languages within the texts, and thus works as a linguistic scapegoat vis-à-vis the foreign and the nonstandard languages. Slang's fluidity in terms of the dialects and languages it indexes ultimately communicates one primary characteristic among "non-French" social types: immorality. By not using Standard French, one carries the brand of social Other and automatically possesses the motive of perpetuating crime and moral corruption. From a literary standpoint, the decision on the part of Vidocq, Sue, and Balzac, in addition to other writers, to include slang within memoirs, fiction, and dictionaries not only speaks to a collective need to identify and categorize those who threatened the social and national orders of France, that is, criminals and foreigners, but it also reveals a personal interest on the part of middle-class writers to cultivate aspects of criminal culture and create a literary demand for it. This space functions not only as a means of control and containment through identification and dispersion in the form of mass printed media but also as a site of cultural possibility for those who are simultaneously marginalized and misrepresented. While largely pejorative representations of criminals, foreigners, and the working classes appear in nineteenth-century French literature, it was nevertheless the vicarious literary slumming of middle-class readership that provided the social foundation necessary for the eventual self-representation of the lower classes.

NOTES

1. Within indexical orders exist indexes, or context-bounded signs which can be referential, that is, indexes that contribute to the literal meaning of the utterance like pronouns, or non-referential, that is, indexes that contain a social context within them such as choice of dialect, accent, gesture, slang, or pronunciation.
2. Johnstone, "Locating Language," 32.
3. Silverstein, "Indexical Order," 194.
4. "Slum, n.1." *OED Online*. September 2019. Oxford University Press. https://www-oed-com.sandiego.idm.oclc.org/view/Entry/182267?rskey=EYhjvo&result=1. Accessed November 24, 2019.
5. I use the term "lower classes" to refer to the working classes, the poor, and the dangerous classes.

6. Linguist M.A.K. Halliday defines an "anti-society" as "a society that is set up within another society as a conscious alternative to it" (570).

7. Halliday, "Anti-languages," 576.

8. Heller-Roazen, *Dark Tongues*, 37.

9. The expanding repertoire of socially varied characters corresponds to socialist movements such as Fourierism and Saint Simonianism, taking place in the early nineteenth century that mobilized on behalf of the working classes and women. Furthermore, works such as Sue's *Mysteries* elicited the interest of the working classes to such an extent that he decided to give his chapters an increasingly socialist slant in order to appeal to this demographic. Nonetheless, France's changing political front throughout the century does not imply a correlation to a more progressive literary landscape.

10. This targeted audience is subject to change as in the case of Sue. The unavoidable popularity of his work among the working classes influenced later installments of *The Mysteries of Paris*.

11. Kalifa, *Crime et culture*, 70–72.

12. Gauthier, *Lire la ville*, 51.

13. Ibid., 52.

14. "*[Il] propose son histoire mais offre aussi une relecture de l'Histoire*" (Ibid., 53).

15. "*Les expédients des voleurs, les signes auxquels on peut les reconnaître [. . .] leurs mœurs, leurs habitudes [. . .] leur langage et leur costume*" (Vidocq, *Mémoires*, 337). Vidocq emphasizes the power of signs several times within the narrative and, near the end of his *Memoirs*, he reiterates the power of these signs in reference to his own work undercover (Ibid., 455).

16. "*[A]ussi les voleurs ont-ils des signes de reconnaissance, et un langage particulier. Posséder ce langage, être initier à ces signes, lors même qu'on n'est pas du métier, c'est déjà un titre à leur bienveillance*" (Ibid., 531).

17. Kalifa, *Crime et culture*, 72.

18. Vidocq, *Mémoires*, 3. Within the narrative, Vidocq recounts a scene in which he becomes the assistant for a cattle dealer in Cholet after affirming his capacities to write, count, and keep records (Ibid., 119–20). Albeit vague, this is one of the few times that Vidocq explicitly refers to his capacity to write within the narrative itself. Upon returning to his hometown Arras, Vidocq finds work as a teacher with a local priest in which he makes his students "progress" more rapidly by writing out letters in pencil and having his pupils trace over them in pen (Ibid., 130).

19. Ibid., 115.

20. Ibid., 72.

21. Ibid., 118.

22. Ibid., 154.

23. Ibid., 154–155.

24. Later, Vidocq confesses that society is part of the reason that criminals cannot undergo proper reform (Ibid., 218). A similar sentiment is expressed by Vautrin, who is based on real-life Vidocq, in *Splendors* (Balzac, *Splendeurs*, 627).

25. Vidocq, *Mémoires*, 285.

26. "*Nous allons essayer de mettre sous les yeux du lecteur quelques épisodes de la vie d'autres barbares aussi en dehors de la civilisation que les sauvages peuplades si bien peintes par Cooper. Seulement les barbares dont nous parlons sont au milieu de nous [. . .]*" (Sue, *Mystères*, 35–37; English translation, 3).

27. Sue, *Mystères*, 37; English translation, 4.

28. Ibid.

29. "*[L]es scène curieuses qui devaient s'ensuivre, tout en serait inadmissible et incompréhensible, sans quelques explications sur le monde des voleurs et des bagnes, sur ses lois, sur ses mœurs, et surtout sur son langage, dont l'affreuse poésie est indispensable dans cette partie du récit*" (Balzac, *Splendeurs*, 515).

30. Vidocq, *Mémoires*, 8.

31. Ibid., 9. Vidocq provides more general commentaries on the adoption of criminal nicknames. For example, in a scene where he describes the formation of a criminal gang in the Parisian district (faubourg) Saint-Germain, the gang's leader, Constantin, goes by the name, "Antin," prompting Vidocq to explain that it is typical practice for tricksters to create nicknames based on the last syllable of their name (Ibid., 296).

32. Ibid., 87.

33. Ibid., 297.

34. Erickson, *Welcome to Sodom*, x–xi.

35. Sue, *Mystères*, 76; English translation, 44.

36. These footnotes appear in the original version of *Les Mystères de Paris* in *Le Journal des débats* (June 25, 1842): "That you do not speak slang" (*Que vous ne parlez pas argot*).

37. Sue's original footnote from *Le Journal des débats* (June 25, 1842): "Simple men" (*Hommes simples*).

38. *Tom: Je n'ai pas bien compris ce que vous m'avez dit sur ce Bras-Rouge. Rodolphe sortait de chez lui, sans doute?*
    Chourineur: Je vous ai dit que Bras-Rouge pastiquait la maltouze [. . .].
    Tom: Qu'est-ce que ça veut dire, pastiquer la mal. . . Comment dites-vous cela?
    Chourineur: Pastiquer la maltouze, faire la contrebande, donc! Il paraît que vous ne dévidez pas le jars?
    Tom: Mon brave, je ne vous comprends plus.
    Chourineur: Je vous dis: Vous ne parlez donc pas argot comme monsieur Rodolphe?
    Tom: Argot? dit Tom en regardant Sarah d'un air surpris.
    Chourineur: Allons, vous êtes des sinves [. . .] Eh bien, puisque vous ne parlez pas ce beau langage-là, je vous dis en bon français que Bras-Rouge est contrebandier [. . .]. (Sue, *Mystères*, 79; English translation, 46–47)

39. "*La langue n'est pas seulement un instrument de communication ou même de connaissance mais un instrument de pouvoir*" (Bourdieu, "L'économie," 20).

40. "*à ceux qui sont dotés des moyens de se l'approprier*" (Bourdieu, "Reproduction culturelle," 47).

41. On a personal level, Balzac disagreed with Sue's heavy socialist slant within *Mysteries* and instead favored the reestablishment of monarchism and Catholicism to

aid a degenerating society. Balzac's response to Sue's resounding popularity came about in his *Poor Relations* series (Bellos, 17).

42. "*En argot de prison, cela s'appelle aller à l'instruction*" (Balzac, *Splendeurs*, 356).

43. *En argot de prison, le* mouton *est un mouchard, qui paraît être sous le poids d'une méchante affaire, et dont l'habileté proverbiale consiste à se faire prendre pour un ami. Le mot ami signifie, en argot, un voleur émérite [. . .] qui veut rester voleur toute sa vie, et qui demeure fidèle quand même aux lois de la haute pègre.* (Ibid., 512)

44. Ibid., 169.
45. Ibid.
46. Ibid., 397.
47. Ibid., 522.
48. Ibid., 524.
49. Ibid., 529.
50. Ibid., 530. *Philippes* refers to coins with the effigy of Louis-Philippe I on the head of the coin.
51. Ibid.
52. Ibid., 532.
53. Ibid., 535. *Sorbonne* refers to the university in Paris; this term was used to mean "head" since criminals use their minds to "contemplate, reason, and guide crime." See the definition for "Sorbonne" in Alfred Delvau's *Dictionnaire de la langue verte: argots parisiens comparés* (1866).
54. Balzac's narrator offers partial reassurance to his reader by insisting that criminals that stem from the upper classes are extremely rare (Balzac, *Splendeurs*, 511).
55. Ibid., 592.
56. *Pouraille: Voici la balle! Dans le poupon, Ruffard, l'agent de Bibi-Lupin, était en tiers avec moi et Godet. . .*

    Vautrin: Arrachelaine?. . . s'écria Jacques Collin en donnant à Ruffard son nom de voleur.

    Pouraille: C'est cela. Les gueux m'ont vendu, parce que je connais leur cachette et qu'ils ne connaissent pas la mienne.

    Vautrin: Tu graisses mes bottes! [. . .] dit Jacques Collin

    Pouraille: Quoi?

    Vautrin: Eh bien, répondit le dab, vois ce qu'on gagne à mettre en moi toute confiance! [. . .]

    Pouraille: Tu es et tu seras toujours notre dab, je n'aurai pas de secrets pour toi, répliqua la Pouraille. Mon or est dans la profonde (la cave) de la maison à la Gonore. (Ibid., 562–63)

57. Ibid., 519.
58. Ibid., 520.
59. Harvey, *Paris*, 34–35.
60. Balzac, *Splendeurs*, 520.
61. Halliday, "Anti-Languages," 570.
62. Ibid., 574.

63. "*[C]es sauvages [de la haute pègre] ne respectent ni la loi, ni la religion, rien, pas même l'histoire naturelle, dont la sainte nomenclature est, comme on le voit, parodiée par eux*" (Ibid., 515).

64. Dentith, *Parody*, 9.

65. Hutcheon, *The Politics of Postmodernism*, 97.

66. "*[M]ais qui es-tu donc ? . . . tu dévides le jars comme père et mère!*" (Sue, *Mystères*, 42; English translation, 7). Fleur also remarks that Rodolphe appears and talks like the other customers at the White Rabbit (Sue, *Mystères*, 782; English translation, 859).

67. Sue, *Mystères*, 69; English translation, 36.

68. Sue, *Mystères*, 120; English translation, 93.

69. Sue, *Mystères*, 121; English translation, 93.

70. "*Rodolphe: Mais en se déduisant il m'a observé. . .*
    Maître: Il vous a fait observer. . .
    Rodolphe: Diable . . . vous êtes à la cheval sur la grammaire.
    Maître: Maître d'école, c'est mon état" (Sue, *Mystères*, 122; English translation, 95).

71. Although a correlation generally exists between class origin, language, and morality, it is important to note that slang's indexes in these texts do not exclude upper-class characters from moral deficiencies. Even though he was born into a bourgeois household, Vidocq still developed into a hardened criminal. Following his transformation, he explains that immorality can plague the upper classes as well (Vidocq, *Mémoires*, 336). He announces that one of the many objectives of his work is to reveal criminality at all levels of society (Ibid., 40–41). In *The Mysteries of Paris*, characters such as Sarah MacGregor, Polidori, and Jacques Ferrand arise from either an aristocratic or bourgeois background, yet they remain evil to the core.

72. In addition to misaligning class and language, nineteenth-century French writers also play with other indexes. For instance, in *Memoirs*, Vidocq misaligns the relationship between social class and morality. When describing the master thief Jossas, Vidocq emphasizes his uncharacteristic generosity. Another disconnect thus occurs between Jossas' success as a thief and his magnanimous disposition toward others (Vidocq does not specify whom exactly), and even the writer cannot reconcile Jossas' otherwise evil deeds with his generous ones, leaving it instead to the work of the "moralists" (Ibid., 141).

73. Balzac, *Splendeurs*, 612.

74. "*Honnêtes gens et bourgeois*" (Ibid., 613). A similar scene takes place in *Mysteries* when Nicolas Martial gives his younger siblings, Amandine and François, each a scarf. Their fascination with wearing the fabric in different ways prompts their older evil sister Calebasse to say that they look like "little rich kids" (*petits bourgeois* [Sue, *Mystères*, 673; English version, 736]).

75. Balzac, *Splendeurs*, 626–27.

76. Ibid., 640.

77. These fears also manifest themselves in generalizations made by writers. For example, Vidocq states that many serious crimes are the acts of foreigners (Vidocq, *Mémoires*, 531).

78. Ibid., 20, 159.

79. "'*Ne bougez pas, me dit-elle en patois; les environs sont remplis de* sapins *(gendarmes) qui furètent de tous côtés.' Je ne savais ce qu'elle entendait par ce mot de* sapins, *mais je me doutais qu'il ne s'appliquait à rien de bon*" (Ibid., 163).

80. A similar instance takes place during a deal between Caron and Vidocq's travel companion, Vidocq admits that he only partially understands what is being said because the exchange occurs in Flemish patois (Ibid., 45).

81. Ibid., 108–09.

82. Ibid., 46.

83. *Malgaret: [. . .] Ce sont des voleurs!*
   Vidocq: Des voleurs! [. . .] Qu'en savez-vous? . . .
   Malgaret: Ce que vous en allez savoir vous-même tout à l'heure, si vous voulez me suivre, car il y a gros à parier que nous n'irons pas bien loin sans les voir *travailler. . .* (Ibid., 48).

84. Ibid., 48–49.

85. In a later scene, Vidocq is trying to prove that master pickpocketer Hotot is guilty of an extensive pickpocketing scheme. In order to succeed, he employs the help of Hotot's Jewish servant, Graffré. Upon learning that Hotot is guilty, Gaffré says a word in Hebrew slang that Vidocq the narrator points out to his readers (Ibid., 405). The pejorative description of this term, which refers to a person blatantly guilty of a crime, also introduces an element of race to language and thus, the moral implications inherent in language. While this is the only time that Vidocq mentions Hebrew slang, the pejorative conflation of gypsies and Jewish people appears throughout the narrative. For example, he states that thieves who pocket jewels are mainly Jews or Bohemians who have learned this skill from their parents (Ibid., 534).

86. Ibid., 46.

87. Ibid., 464–65.

88. Balzac, *Splendeurs*, 551.

89. Vidocq, *Mémoires*, 444–45.

90. "*Zi chaffais âmné Chorche* (prononcez George), *au lier te doi, crosse pette, ils aurede pien si droufer cedde phâmme*" (Ibid., 112). My translation: "If I had brought George, instead of you, fat beast, he would have better known how to find this woman [. . .]" (*Si j'avais amené George, au lieu de toi, grosse bête, il aurait bien su trouver cette femme*).

91. "*Un peu, mon neveu, dit l'Anglaise qui parlait bien le français. Mais ki ed-dû, doi? fit-elle en imitant le parler de Nucingen*" (Ibid., 184). My translation: "But who are you, you?" (*Mais qui es-tu, toi?*).

92. Ibid., 301–2.

Chapter 2

Slang as Embodied Language

When in Paris, you meet a social type, it is no longer a man, it is a spectacle! It is no longer the moment of a lifetime, but an existence, several existences!

—Honoré de Balzac, *Splendors and Miseries of Courtesans* (1838–1847)

(*Quand, à Paris, vous rencontrez un type, ce n'est plus un homme, c'est un spectacle! ce n'est plus un moment de la vie, mais une existence, plusieurs existences!*)

Slang, in early French nineteenth-century works such as Vidocq's *Memoirs*, Sue's *The Mysteries of Paris*, and Balzac's *Splendors and Miseries of Courtesans*, becomes the primary identifier of the criminal type. As a non-referential index (i.e., a context-bounded sign) of criminality, this anti-language serves as the foundation of a more realist construction of the criminal figure compared to those in past centuries. Language, like clothing, gesture, and voice alteration, can simultaneously reveal and mask identities, and the criminal, as one witnesses in the aforementioned works, is a social figure whose entire livelihood depends on his ability to convincingly perform new identities through the manipulation of appearance and speech. As sociocultural linguist Mary Bucholtz points out, "[W]ithin discourse slang may be used to structure interaction and to produce emergent and temporary interactional identities."[1] Like the writer, whose talent Charles Baudelaire would later describe as his ability "at will, to be himself and an other," the criminal also possesses the privilege of inhabiting multiple identities, mainly through his manipulation of language, in addition to other non-referential indexes; the criminal is inherently a performer due to the nature of his trade which requires the capacity to deceive others and evade arrest (or worse).[2] This chapter continues the analysis of the criminal type in *Memoirs*, *Mysteries*, and *Splendors*, focusing specifically on the ways in which the realist construction of this literary figure relies on non-referential indexes such as appearance and physique, gesture and dance, as well as other forms of body language and speech, which ultimately served as social signs for the middle-class bourgeois reader, thus transforming the role of the audience members from passive receivers to active semioticians, or interpreters of signs and symbols.

In addition, in ways similar to a narrator, criminal figures in *Memoirs*, *Mysteries*, and *Splendors* present themselves as omniscient players on the Parisian stage. As master shape shifters, criminals and their convincing performances gain them access to all levels of the social hierarchy, a trope that can still be found in contemporary cinema, such as American con-artist films, *Catch Me If You Can* (2002), the remakes of the 1960 heist film, *Ocean's 11* (2001–2018), and *American Hustle* (2013).[3] Despite his ability to access varying social domains, the criminal figure can be found more regularly in certain geographic regions that become indexical of this social type and which serve as the backdrop of their embodied language, especially when they engage in risqué forms of dance or popular song. For sociolinguists, such as Mary Bucholtz and Kira Hall, the phenomenon of "embodiment" emerges from "a variety of semiotic practices that endow linguistic communication with meaning, from the indexicalities of bodily adornment to gesture, gaze, and other forms of movement."[4] The criminal's capacity in nineteenth-century French literature to change identities via language and the body played on collective bourgeois insecurities about who could be trusted. The role of the writer to decode, while offering his reader a way of identifying evil persons by using slang as a linguistic marker, thus became more significant. The uncanny characterization of the criminal as simultaneously having no identity and all identities frequently occurs in Vidocq's *Memoirs*, Sue's *Mysteries*, and Balzac's *Splendors*, in which the criminal's capacity to shape shift is facilitated through their appearance, language, and body. Although one may often believe the body to be peripheral to language, it is, in fact, essential to language. In addition to spoken slang, I argue here that the criminal characters also communicate an embodied slang composed of appearance, gesture, bodily movement, and licentious performances, such as in songs and dance.

EMBODIED SLANG AND THE CRIMINAL

In terms of the embodiment of slang, there are several aspects of the body that one can analyze that can communicate important ideology, such as voice, style, movement, and action.[5] In addition to spoken language, early nineteenth-century French writers engaged in a stylization of the criminal body that included various disguises which attempted to hide their imposing physiques and often abnormal facial features. Additionally, the criminal's propensity for reckless song and dance introduces an element of bodily performance that further constitutes an embodied slang. The criminal's body, gestures, and wild movements thus function as non-referential indexes that mark them as villainous, and coupled with their use of slang, contribute to a more comprehensive view of the first indexical order of criminal language in nineteenth-century France. As Bucholtz and Hall note:

> [L]anguage ideologies go beyond indexicality, readily enlisting an iconic dimension that links social categories to a bodily hexis that is imagined to be the source of socially marked linguistic forms or practices; iconicity thus positions language as a symptom of bodily disposition [. . .]. In other words, sociocultural beliefs about language rely on indexical iconization [. . .] an ideological process that rationalizes and naturalizes semiotic practice as inherent essence, often by anchoring it within the body.[6]

The analysis of embodied slang in relation to spoken slang further advances the iconization of slang language occurring in the n+1st order; at this stage, the speech itself becomes inherently symbolic of its speakers and takes on those same personality traits. Therefore, in the same way that contemporary Valley Girl speak is iconic of wealthy, dumb women from Southern California (and thus, those traits become imbued within the lexicon itself), nineteenth-century French slang contains innate meanings of immorality and villainy due to the pervasive reinforcement and diffusion of these lexical variants with a specific social type. Furthermore, the criminal body, as this chapter demonstrates, serves as a key component of slang's iconization process.

Importantly, a correlation between criminality and physique is one of the most notable aspects of the criminal type in nineteenth-century French literature. The grotesque physical attributes of early criminal types establish a foundation for what would later evolve into representations that are indexical of gender identity and/or sexuality. However, representations of slang speakers and their bodies in the 1830s and 1840s established a formulaic portrait of their social type, and especially of their language, which extended beyond spoken language to include the gestural and the physical. In general, male criminal characters in *Memoirs*, *Splendors*, and *Mysteries* are physically large and drawn with wide jaws and large heads, which are often marked by a sloped forehead or pointed nose. In terms of physiognomy in the nineteenth century, in 1876, Italian criminologist and physician Cesare Lombroso wrote *Criminal Man (L'Uomo Delinquente)*, a detailed analysis of criminals from various parts of Italy that argues in defense of criminal atavism. Through his observations, Lombroso presents what he considered to be fundamental physiognomic and personality traits of criminals (interestingly, these traits also align with the offspring of incest):

A resemblance to "savages" and people of the "colored races"[7]
Thinner than average body hair
A sloped forehead
A thicker skull
Smaller cranial volume
Large ears
A protruding jaw
Thick, curly hair
A close resemblance between the sexes (men and women)
Higher tolerance to physical pain (hence, their propensity for tattoos)
An underdeveloped moral sense
A dislike of work
A lack of remorse
Vanity
Narcissism
A disregard for the divine.[8]

While the early nineteenth-century French works discussed in this analysis predate Lombroso's findings by more-or-less forty years, they nonetheless tend to adhere to a similar notion of criminal atavism, which suggests that theories such as Lombroso's may have been extant decades earlier. Despite that, from a medical perspective, there are no actual links between Lombroso's outline and an association of physiognomy with criminality, what is most intriguing about the descriptions of criminals in the works of Vidocq, Balzac, and Sue is that the emphasis on such physical and emotional anomalies function to index criminal types in ways that work in harmony with their spoken slang. Even though the slang speaker's criminal physiognomy and overall physique nevertheless reside within the cultural imaginary as a physical manifestation of moral deficiency, in early nineteenth-century French novels, the bodily features and movements of the grotesque villain is the embodied language of his slang.

Therefore, for early nineteenth-century French writers, a person's physiognomy served simultaneously as a reliable social identifier and a text to be read within a network of "bodily semiotics."[9] In fact, in order to enlighten his readers, one of Vidocq's stated objectives in writing his *Memoirs* was to reproduce with accuracy criminal physiognomy.[10] As embodied slang, the criminal physique always exists in the realm of the monstrous. Vidocq begins his story by describing his abnormally colossal size and strength as a child.[11] In ways similar to Vidocq, the criminal character Saint-Germain also perfectly incarnates prescient theories behind physique and criminality, theories which would later appear in Lombroso's work on criminal physiognomy. For instance, Saint-Germain possesses a massive head with tiny eyes, and his hideous face, which is characterized by scars left from a smallpox outbreak, gives him the appearance of a hyena or a wolf, especially given his protruding jaw.[12] In Vidocq's physical profile of Saint-Germain's sidekick, Boudin, he states that the criminal's arched legs are a physical abnormality common among professional murderers.[13] The bodily traits of these criminal characters frequently involve an exaggeration of corporal features that are either enlarged, reduced, or severely deformed. Physically, these dramatizations of criminal bodies correspond to the elaborate personality features that the characters exhibit such as their propensity to lie, cheat, steal, and kill but also to their sexual and material hedonism that takes on a variety of forms. Significantly, one can interpret their hideous criminal forms as the physical incarnation of their speech; thus, their deformities, gestures, and movements importantly communicate information concerning criminal characters' social and moral standing in ways similar to their use of slang.

In *Mysteries*, malformed physiques appear for several criminal types, who generally derive their nicknames from a prominent deformity, thus creating a vast network of semiotic meaning to be read through the criminal body.[14] The variety of nicknames that appear for criminal characters such as the Slasher, Red-Arm, the Owl, the Schoolmaster, She-Wolf, Gammy, the Big Gimp, and the Skeleton represent an aspect of each character's personality and/or physical form.[15] For instance, the Slasher, or *le Chourineur* in French, received his unique nickname after a rage-filled attack on his soldier comrades. His obsession with butchery became the mark of his crime, as he wildly slit the throats of the Army troops in a veritable blood bath.

The son of Red-Arm, Gammy (*Tortillard*), not only resembles his father but also received his nickname due to his physical impairment.[16] The

Figure 2.1 "Tortillard." Illus. Honoré Daumier. *Les Mystères de Paris* by Eugène Sue. Vol. 1. Paris: C. Gosselin, 1843–1844.

incorrigible murderer, the Skeleton, received his nickname from his extremely thin physique.[17] While his fellow inmates resemble tigers, vultures, or foxes, the Skeleton's bony jawbone and unusually long neck give him the appearance of a snake. His lack of muscles, however, masks his unbelievable physical power and strength.[18] The Big Gimp (*Le Gros-Boiteux*), the Skeleton's accomplice, possesses a face similar to that of a bulldog.[19] The Big Gimp's sunken forehead, tiny eyes, drooping cheekbones, heavy jaw, and long teeth that look more like fangs make him appear as more of an animal than human.

Other criminal characters whose nicknames do not reflect a specific physical characteristic, such as the Schoolmaster and Red-Arm, are nevertheless equally

Figure 2.2 "Le Maître d'école." Illus. Charles Joseph Traviès. *Les Mystères de Paris* by Eugène Sue. Vol. 1. Paris: C. Gosselin, 1843–1844.

as hideous in appearance.[20] For instance, Sue describes the Schoolmaster as having white eyes without pupils, a severely scarred face, swollen lips from sulfuric acid burns, and removed nose cartilage that leaves two deformed holes as nostrils, all of which contribute to his nightmarish appearance.[21] His flattened forehead is like that of a tiger's; he has an unusually large head,

Figure 2.3 *"Bras-Rouge."* Illus. Honoré Daumier. *Les Mystères de Paris* by Eugène Sue. Vol. 1. Paris: C. Gosselin, 1843–1844.

broad shoulders, long, muscular arms, fat hairy hands, curved legs, and massive calves that announced his sheer strength. The Schoolmaster's Herculean build and facial features are also akin to those of a wild animal and remain so horrifying that the narrator cannot accurately describe them.[22] The character Red-Arm resembles a cross between a stone marten and a rat. His pointed nose, receding chin, bony cheekbones, and tiny black eyes communicate his deceptive ways.[23] The endless descriptions of freakish criminal bodies in *Mysteries* thus creates a physical portrait for this social type that, in ways similar to their use of slang, becomes iconic of their moral nature, as the body further encapsulates the criminal's "way of being."[24]

In *Mysteries*, women characters also adhere to the grotesque typology that characterizes the men and aligns with Lombroso's trait of female criminals having a close resemblance to the opposite sex. For example, the Owl, the female accomplice of the School Master, has only one eye, in addition to a hooked nose, thin lips, a protruding chin, and a mean face which explains her nickname.[25] Similarly, the narrator describes the She-Wolf, the former prison mate of Songbird, as a young, twenty-year-old girl who, along with her height, carried a very masculine build. According to the narrator, She-Wolf's unibrow hangs over her ferocious eyes, while her overall appearance creates a ghastly grin that resembles the wolf's toothy rictus.[26] Hardcore women criminals can be hardly differentiated from their male counterparts in Sue's novel, as they possess qualities of the opposite sex that index virility (large build, muscularity, exaggerated facial features, and bodily angularity), while physically resembling the animals after which they are named.[27] In *Splendors*, the narrator describes both Vautrin's aunt, Asia, and Esther's service maid, Europe, as hypermasculine. Asia possesses a hideous face and resembles a monkey while Europe appears worn by evil even though her own corruption seems limitless.[28] In *Splendors*, general comments on criminal physiognomy, in addition to character descriptions that reinforce certain physical defects of criminal types, contribute to an indexical relationship between language and body. A similar relationship is shown as underlying criminal song and dance, one that would evolve over time to express certain gender or sexual inclinations.

Notably, whenever linguistic practices and embodied language do not align in Sue's novel, the "semiotics of style" become difficult for readers to interpret.[29] For instance, one of the reasons that the character Rodolphe is tough to socially classify for the other characters is because of the peculiarity of his face.[30] Although he speaks criminal slang and dresses like a fan painter, his pale complexion, big brown eyes, nonchalant gait, and white elegant hands are instead the physical traits of an aristocratic man. While, linguistically, Rodolphe resembles a criminal, his physique remains perplexing for characters such as the Slasher. Although he is unaware of Rodolphe's true origins as the grand duke of Gerolstein, the Slasher nevertheless notices a semiotic gap between Rodolphe's use of language, dress, and physical appearance. While the narrator informs the reader that Rodolphe is between thirty- and thirty-six years in age, his "svelte" and "perfectly proportioned" build do not, however, seem comparable to the muscular grandeur of the Slasher. In fact, Rodolphe's physiognomy makes him difficult to categorize socially:

> [His physiognomy] combined the strangest contrasts. His features were regular and beautiful—too beautiful for a man, perhaps. His pale, delicate complexion, his large, burnt-orange irises that were ringed with blue in eyes that were almost always half closed, his nonchalant bearing, distracted gaze, and ironic smile all seemed to betoken a blasé man whose constitution was, if not broke, at least weakened by the aristocratic excesses of an opulent life.[31]

Rodolphe's effeminate beauty, pale skin, big eyes, and nonchalant demeanor index a man bored by the excesses of aristocratic life—not a working-class fan painter. The contrasts are so remarkable that the duke's affected mannerisms and physical beauty do not align with the hardened faces of the regulars at the White Rabbit Inn.[32] Ultimately, Rodolphe's physical appearance betrays his attempts at masking his true social identity, as his use of slang appears odd to the patrons of the White Rabbit Inn whose criminal appearances necessitate such speech. To contrast the misalignment even more, Sue addresses the linguistic irony in an exchange between the Slasher and Rodolphe. After their introduction, the Slasher playfully refers to the fan painter as "my lord" (the double irony of this title is not lost on readers).[33] By addressing Rodolphe as a lord, the Slasher thus highlights a misalignment between Rodolphe's physiognomy and his speech practices. Rodolphe's sharply contrasting physical appearance and linguistic practices ultimately encapsulate opposite ways of being.[34]

Unlike Vidocq and Sue, Balzac typically shies away from extensive detail of criminal physique, preferring instead to provide more general descriptions of his criminal characters, while acknowledging the importance of physical markers that embody such types as the prostitute, the thief, the murderer, and the ex-con. Occasionally, however, the text gets quite specific, providing a physical correspondent of criminal linguistic practices. For example, when describing the physical build of Vautrin's former lover Théodore Calvi, the narrator states that the young man possesses a strength that one would consider desirable if it was not for his arched eyebrows and sunken forehead, which gives him a menacing appearance.[35] Additionally, his lack of muscle movement is coded as indicative of the Corsican people and their quickness to anger and even kill.[36] While Balzac is specific about the kinds of physical features Calvi possesses, he further makes these a product of ethnicity; Calvi's negative physical and personality traits thus become conflated with a non-Gaulois people. Coupled with the explicit sexual relations between two men, Balzac introduces a more sophisticated bodily representation than Sue and Vidocq, one which incorporates ethnic origin and same-sex desire as elements of the body that communicate moral deficiency and criminality in ways analogous to their coded slang.

The description of Vautrin's physical appearance occurs in an earlier novel by Balzac, *Le Père Goriot* (1834), which introduces the criminal mastermind as exceptionally muscular and strong, as well as red-headed, a common trait of moral and sexual debauchery in European literary and religious traditions. In *Splendors*, however, the text does not relay much detail concerning Vautrin's physiognomy or physique. Nevertheless, in one scene, his black wig falls to reveal a bald head, transforming Vautrin into a corpse-like figure.[37] Similar to his lover Calvi, Vautrin's embodied slang goes beyond grotesque appearance to include more subversive bodily aspects, such as his sexuality.[38]

The monstrous appearance of villainous men and women in early nineteenth-century French works that sometimes borders on the fantastical reveals that same physical indexes applied to both. It would not be until after 1850, with the development of the prostitute in naturalist literature, that women criminals could embody indexes of femininity and masculinity, or even queer identity, thus raising the complexity of their physical profile. However, the consistency with which writers such as Vidocq, Sue, and Balzac employ bodily features as the physical incarnation of linguistic practices (and thus of good or evil) results in characters' physique and physiognomy as useful non-referential indexes for bourgeois readers. In addition, based on appearance, a nineteenth-century reader could accurately infer that these gruesome characters were also slang speakers. The layering of multiple indexes such as language, appearance, dress, and performance are what ultimately stylize and constitute the first indexical order of the realist criminal type in a way that the sociolinguistic concept of "iconization" arises in which spoken and embodied language become representative of their ontology.

The hypermasculinized (and sometimes animalized) appearances of both male and female criminals in nineteenth-century French literature has less to do with individual gender identity than it does with perceived inherent criminal traits that served as identity markers for the bourgeois reader. The lack of commentary on sexual preference in these novels in terms of the women criminal characters further dissociates their masculine features from their sexuality, and instead categorizes physiognomy as a physical testimony of hardcore criminality as well as an embodied version of slang. Additionally, masculinizing women, rather than feminizing men, may have been more acceptable to nineteenth-century audiences in the same way that actresses were permitted to play male roles, but not vice versa. Nevertheless, the standardization of a code of criminal appearance among French writers in the early nineteenth century points to representations of physiognomy and physique that was polarized by gender. Vidocq, Sue, and Balzac notably further designate a black-and-white dichotomy between the body and morality that writers such as Hugo, Edmond and Jules de

Goncourt, and Zola would begin to nuance in later works. Not only would a deformed body serve as a significant index of immorality for middle-class readers, in addition to an embodied version of their linguistic practices, but it would also transform into a site in which categories of sex and could be systematically undone.

THE EMBODIMENT OF SLANG AS CRIMINAL DISGUISE

In *Memoirs*, *Mysteries*, and *Splendors*, criminal characters often take on additional names and personas for the purpose of disguise. Such disguises contribute to a visual stylization of the criminal body that is analogous to the stylization of their slang speech (such as accent, lexicon, and pronunciation). For instance, Vidocq adopts completely new identities, such as Duval, but also adopts new last names such as "Rousseau," "Comte de B . . . ," and "Blondel."[39] He even creates fake wrinkles and dons some fancy duds in order to pass as a bourgeois gentleman.[40] Vidocq uses several disguises while he is in Arras to see his dying father, and poses as an Austrian soldier claiming to speak German.[41] He also pretends to be a Jewish hawker, and then a German servant, in order to trick jewel thief, Moiselet.[42] Following a moral conversion and his advancement up the social hierarchy, Vidocq nevertheless possesses the ability to alter his identity in order to access both upper- and lower-class milieus through disguise. As a detective, Vidocq discusses the extent to which Parisian criminals accepted him as one of their own:

> I presented myself so well, on the inside as well as on the outside, nothing leaked out; the thieves that knew me held me as one of their best mates, others considered themselves lucky to be able to show me their secrets, either for the pleasure of talking with me, or sometimes to consult me.[43]

Vidocq's claim does not portray him as a mere acquaintance of these criminals, but rather as a trusted associate of organized crime. Due to the believability of his disguises, the thieves reveal their darkest secrets to him, occasionally with the intention of soliciting advice. The intimate bonds Vidocq forms as a result of his credibility in disguise appear to be more the result of the visual cues derived from his appearance, mannerisms, and language, rather than his ability to pull off large-scale heists. These non-referential indexes communicate to Vidocq's interlocutors both of his social identity as well as his professional capability and expertise.[44]

Interestingly, in Sue's *Mysteries*, the use of disguises is a typical feature of upper-class characters, rather than lower-class ones. For instance, Rodolphe, who Karl Marx famously compared to Haroun-al-Rachid, the disguise-loving caliph from *A Thousand and One Nights*, hides his true identity by dressing as a worker (as does his right-hand man, Sir Walter Murph, who appears as a mysterious coal merchant).[45] And the criminal schemer Father Polidori takes on the identity of Cesar Bradamanti, an Italian dentist, and at the request of the evil notary Jacques Ferrand, Polidori also undertakes the role of Dr. Vincent in order to poison Louise Morel.[46] Rodolphe's evil ex-wife, Sarah, dresses as a man while frequenting the Lapin-Blanc,[47] and the Slasher disguises himself as a man with a blue cap (*au bonnet bleu*) in order to rescue the son of Madame Georges and the Schoolmaster, François Germain, from prison.[48] Nevertheless, Sue does not indulge in bourgeois anxiety vis-à-vis criminal transformations, thus avoiding the use of linguistic fluidity as a means of social fluidity, with the exception of Rodolphe, who Sue positions as morally superior to the other characters in the novel. Rodolphe thus passes from society to anti-society (thanks to his mastery of slang) in pursuit of eradicating evil people from the city, which therefore justifies his speech in the eyes of the reader.

In spite of the lack of linguistic variation in *Mysteries*, in Balzac's *Splendors*, linguistic and bodily practices go hand-in-hand to form one cohesive vision of French slang. As Bucholtz and Hall note:

> In styles, linguistic and embodied practices align to produce a culturally meaningful whole (even if the assemblage of features exploit semiotic dissonances between established stylistic meanings). Thus the semiotics of style includes all dimensions of language as well as material and embodied resources of self-presentation, which together yield ideologically cohesive semiotic packages available for interpretation by others.[49]

This stylistic cohesion renders Balzac's take on the criminal shape shifter more sophisticated; a new identity is not simply a costume change, but rather includes several nuanced features, such as accent, language, and gestures, all of which are embodied features that contribute to the criminal's eventual iconization in the literary world. Notably, the character Vautrin can mask his true identity because of the way he speaks, which is a frightening prospect for a bourgeois reader. At the same time, readers are aware that these languages do not particularly belong to Vautrin but rather only to the characters he plays.[50] In contrast, for Balzac, speech practices go beyond a simple one-to-one correspondence between language and social type; for several characters in *Splendors*, the linguistic repertoire of criminals (and even honorable characters) functions as a part of the mechanisms of embodiment that include physiognomy, appearance, mobility, and movement. Together, these mechanisms contribute to a coherent entity that make up a form of slang.

GENDER-BENDING AS EMBODIED SLANG

In the case of Balzac and gender-bending, there exists a linguistic complexity when it comes to the stylization of the slang speaker. In addition to disguise and language, an even more complex interpretation emerges that relates to the criminal's gender-bending tendencies. Although the criminal's slang directly communicates his social standing, a feminized image of the male criminal occurs frequently in early nineteenth-century French texts, wherein cross-dressing and/or resembling a woman functioned as characteristic features of both male criminal masterminds and detectives in disguise. By the 1840s, this parodied image of the male criminal accomplished through his clothing segued into more complex constructions of gender for both male and female criminal characters that included physique, speech practices, and in some cases, sexual orientation. The evolution of the representation of criminal characters from merely that of cross-dressing to several added aspects made for a highly complex, stylized gender profile, one that added to the overall embodiment of his secret anti-language.[51] The evolution of the criminal figure from Vidocq to Balzac reveals a progression in gender fluidity that moves from parody to an index of sexuality, features of the body that work in conjunction with spoken slang. The inclusion of evil characters, like Vautrin, whom Balzac included as a main player in several novels and portrayed as overtly engaging in male-male sex, marked the introduction of same-sex relations, which was a key component of his character development.[52]

The occurrence of the cross-dressing male criminal in the early nineteenth century was, in many ways, an extension of farcical and theatrical cross-dressing dating back to the Middle Ages, which could denote immorality, but did not necessarily serve as embodied slang like the drag of early nineteenth-century French criminals.[53] Records of transvestite men appear in the early medieval period, although, in reality, the authorities did not condone this behavior.[54] In addition, a woman disguised as a man was viewed as more socially acceptable than a man disguised as a woman. As Keith Busby notes, instances of women posing as men occur with greater frequency in French Medieval literature.[55] Katie Normington mentions that in tales where women pretended to pass as men, they often did so in order to advance their social circumstances.[56] In the context of Arthurian romance and the *fabliaux*, Busby adds that, in some cases, women disguised as men, further allowed the women to retain their position of power within the relationship.[57] For example, in the *fabliau*, "Long Butthole Berengier" (*Berengier au long cul*), the wife of a lazy knight decides to impersonate a knight to maintain an outside dalliance. While instances of men imitating women in Greek mythology, such as Thetis dressing her son Achilles as a girl in order for him to avoid capture or death, would have been familiar to writers of French Arthurian romances and *fabliaux*, the trope of the transvestite man remained quite uncommon in the premodern French literary tradition.⁵⁸

Amusingly, throughout his memoir, Vidocq tells of several instances in which he cross-dresses like a woman in order to escape arrest. His penchant for dressing in drag serves as an additional layer of embodiment, not only due to its frequency but also due to the striking juxtaposition between his masculine physique and his feminine dress. For example, upon deserting the Army, Vidocq finds himself without papers and is arrested in Lille wearing a woman's clothes, while running from a jealous husband.⁵⁹ In another scene, after a recent prison escape, the police catch Vidocq, who claims he is Auguste Duval, a deserter of the frigate *Cocarde*.⁶⁰ In order to verify his identity, the police bring Vidocq to a detention facility where he happens to meet an old friend of Auguste's. This close friend reveals to Vidocq that Auguste is dead, but that he can help Vidocq pass as him. Upon meeting Auguste's parents, Vidocq succeeds in convincing them that he is their son, but due to Auguste's status as a deserter, Vidocq must await trial at a prison in Brittany, France. After being held for fifteen days, he decides to escape by drinking tobacco juice, ending up in the hospital. With the help of a former prisoner-turned-nurse, Vidocq procures the habit of Sister Françoise, a nun who lives at the hospital:

> Around two in the morning, I indeed saw [the nurse] arrive with a package containing a dress, guimpe, tights etc. that he had taken from sister's bedroom while she was at mass. All of my nine roommates slept deeply; I passed nonetheless through the ward in order to get ready. What gave me the most trouble was the headgear; I had no idea the way in which to arrange it [. . .]. Finally *Sister Vidocq's* look was achieved.⁶¹

This short description of Vidocq's preparation as Sister Françoise provides several seemingly unnecessary details to the reader concerning the different accessories of his outfit, and even the result of the entire "look." Although highly comical, the inclusion of Vidocq's trouble with the ensemble itself makes one wonder why the author felt the need to detail so carefully this act of transformation from man into woman, other than to create a humorous scene concerning the obstacles particular to skilled criminals.⁶² In addition, the emphasis on Vidocq's large physique at the beginning of the memoir raises a question about why Vidocq would defer to dressing as a woman in order to escape.⁶³ The need to fully immerse oneself within a social role, like that of the nun (an ironic choice), validates the criminal's cross-dressing.⁶⁴ In addition to providing comic relief, cross-dressing as a woman becomes an acceptable part of the male criminal identity, and ultimately allows for more subversive elements of their identity to be developed in literature, such as their sexuality. However, in terms of fiction, the cross-dressing of virulent male criminals perhaps functions more as an acceptable form of gender-play for the bourgeois reader because it ostensibly exists as a professional necessity in order to carry out their evil schemes via access to a variety of social domains, and ultimately, to escape authority.[65]

The answer may be that these theatrical, farcical aspects to Vidocq's misadventures are part of a literary tradition for scheming characters that dates back to the Middle Ages, and one that is especially epitomized in the seventeenth century in the work of Molière.[66] Despite Vidocq's reasons, as Bucholtz and Hall reveal, "[T]he stylistic meaning of a linguistic variant cannot be determined in isolation; instead, stylistic analysis requires examination of the place of specific semiotic forms within a wider system of social meaning."[67] By considering his propensity for women's dress and accessories, together with his gargantuan build and foul language, readers of Vidocq's *Memoirs* receive a portrait of the criminal slang-speaker that is not only highly stylized but also linguistically comprehensive. If readers can "read" the many elements that make up criminal language, such as accent, fashion, lexicon, physiognomy, physique, and bodily movement, their overall communicative competence of this elusive social type advances. Slang, therefore, extends beyond the spoken word into several embodied realms that also contribute to its delivery and meaning.

Despite several occurrences of cross-dressing in Vidocq's *Memoirs*, there is, however, a noticeable decline in the instances of male cross-dressing in French literature by the 1840s. In Sue's *The Mysteries of Paris* criminal disguises abound; however, gender lines are not blurred with costume (other than the exception of one female aristocratic character, Sarah, who dresses as a man as part of a criminal scheme).[68] In *Splendors*, criminal cross-dressing occurs, albeit less frequently than in Vidocq's work. When male cross-dressing does take place in *Splendors*, it is explicitly linked to male-male sex, introducing a new element of embodiment vis-à-vis the criminal slang speaker. For example, when police nab the young Corsican criminal Theodore Calvi, who is the former lover and protégé of criminal mastermind, Vautrin, as well as a seasoned thief, he is disguised as a woman in the midst of a big theft.[69] In ways similar to Vidocq, the narrator describes Theodore as physically imposing, making readers wonder why dressing in women's clothing would be the first choice as a criminal disguise. Perhaps, as in earlier works, Balzac uses Theodore's cross-dressing to create a comedic effect or as an intertexual nod to Vidocq and others. This scene also serves to showcase the social complexity of the high-profile criminal figure. Notably, with Balzac's *Splendors* a shift occurs that combines the parody of criminal cross-dressing with taboo sexuality.

Figure 2.4 "Saint Jerome in a Woman's Dress." *Belles heures de Jean de France*, commissioned by Jean duc de berry, circa 1409.

Throughout the novel, the sexual preferences of criminal mastermind, Vautrin, is explicitly mentioned. In one scene, the criminal, Silk Thread (*Fil-de-soie*), refers to Theodore as Vautrin's "aunt"—a slang term for men who engage in sex acts with other men.[70] Additionally, the narrator explains how Vautrin, on his way to Corsica to see Theodore, runs into Lucien de Rupembré, a young man from the countryside who had failed

Figure 2.5 "Thomas Seyton et la comtesse Sarah." Illus. Edouard de Beaumont. *Les Mystères de Paris* by Eugène Sue. Vol. 1. Paris: C. Gosselin, 1843–1844.

to make it in Parisian high society, and who is now on the verge of suicide. The narrator states that Vautrin abandons his devotion to Theodore in that moment in order to worship a "new idol."[71] At the end of the novel, Vautrin threatens to reveal to the public sensitive letters from two noblewomen to Lucien, proclaiming that women stand as the inferior sex and can only obtain beauty when they look like men.[72] Compared to villains in Vidocq's *Memoirs* and Sue's *Mysteries*, in *Splendors* there exists a salient sexual component to the criminal figure. He remains a performer of multiple identities, but now he has a reputation as sexual deviant. Balzac's added complexity to this literary type results in a sexually fluid persona who is, at times, gender-ambiguous. Thus, in *Splendors*, Balzac presents a more complex criminal character; the novel's relationships between psychopathy, sexuality, femininity, and criminality establish a newer view of gender and sexual fluidity associated with the male criminal that was not present in Vidocq's earlier *Memoirs*. Although cross-dressing still occurs, it is now presented as merely a part of the profession. However, the undertones of what would have been considered taboo sexuality appear to exist as part of a compromised morality inherent in the criminal type. Much like the ideological variability of slang, the criminal possesses social, gender, and sexual mutability as well.[73] However, unlike his predecessors, Balzac actively ties transvestism to sexuality and lifestyle, thus rendering this detail more than merely part of the criminal profession but also as a combined index of same-sex relations, sexual deviancy, and male criminal identity, all of which constitute his "slang."

SLANG AS EMBODIED CRIMINAL PERFORMANCE

Despite Sue's conservatism in terms of criminal role-playing, overall, the ability for his characters to change identity functions as a requirement for adept criminals; in this sense, the criminal identity positions itself as highly performative. From their mannerisms to their speech practices, and even through their clothing, the author stylizes every part of their physical body, transforming it into slang incarnate. Ultimately, these "linguistic and embodied practices align to produce a culturally meaningful whole (even if the assemblage of features exploits semiotic dissonances between established stylistic meanings)."[74] In addition to practices of identity performativity via disguise, the author renders the criminal's identity as "performative" in another sense: through his performance of licentious song and dance. These performances, like the criminal's various outfits and impersonations, also figure into his inherent identity that, albeit theatrical, serve as the foundation for what will evolve into performances linked to gender stylization, language, and agency that will eventually appear in French naturalist works, especially in terms of the characterization of the prostitute.

For instance, when Vidocq and the criminal animal doctor Caron (a.k.a. Christian) travel across Brussels, they enter into a destitute house to discover a group of people smoking, drinking, and engaging in other licentious behaviors.[75] In the background, the two hear bizarre songs accompanied by a tambourine that resembles a funereal chant.[76] They notice a woman in the middle of the room wearing a turban and dancing in a wildly sensual manner.[77] In a similar scene, upon leaving Nantes, Vidocq comes to a town decimated by war, finding the remaining side of a wall that once was a hostel. In front of the wall, he witnesses soldiers dancing to the sound of the church organ with women who were forced into prostitution due to the war.[78] The seedy house and disintegrating wall that Vidocq describes indexes the kinds of persons frequenting them (criminals, prostitutes, gypsies, and soldiers), the language they use, along with the music and obscene dance.

The presence of the obscene dance known as *le chahut* (literally translates as "the ruckus"), a precursor to the Cancan, appears in both Vidocq's and Sue's works. Through the literary representation of *le chahut*, Andrea Goulet analyzes the relationship between deviant language and bodies within "a spacial imaginary" with "a dance that became linked in the popular imagination to the Can-can and to criminal slang."[79] In the *Dictionnaire de la danse* (1895), Gustave Desrat provides the following definition for *chahut*: "One gave this name to a sort of epileptic dance or of *delirium tremens*, which is to dance what slang is to the French language; as Delvau would say, it's the green tongue of choreography."[80] The *chahut* was thus a type of dance indexical of the lower and criminal classes and served as the corporal equivalent of slang. If the criminal par excellence had a linguistic code, they also had a bodily one that indexed the same savagery, violence, and social deviance. As Goulet notes, "by the start of the July Monarchy, *le chahut* had been linked to criminality in the cultural imagination."[81] When this dance appears in French literary works, it is generally connected to prostitutes and sexual licentiousness, thus serving as an embodied index of immorality. In *Memoirs*, Vidocq witnesses the *chahut* at tavern Guillotin:

> Men or women, everyone there was smoking while dancing, the pipe passed from mouth to mouth, and the most pleasant gallantry that one could make to the nymphs who came to this meeting place, spread their charms in the postures and attitudes of the indecent *chahut*.[82]

Vidocq describes the *chahut* as being so indecent that even the peace officers and detectives present did not intervene.[83] Instead, the authorities remain to the side in order to avoid any physical contact. While the bodies of the "deviant" dancers remain contained within the tavern Guillotin, when the soldiers dance with the prostitutes in front of a decimated wall it suggests that the infiltration of such bodies into the public domain results in the unraveling of civic authority. The threat of anarchy looms as Vidocq reveals the high corruptibility factor even among upstanding members of society, especially those who are trained to protect and serve. This scene reveals the ways in which the sensual movement of the criminal body functions in ways analogous to slang: those who come into contact with criminals, even the most righteous members of society, are not exempt from contamination. Although slang serves as the primary identifier of the dangerous classes in early nineteenth-century French works, Vidocq further plays on his readers' fears via dance, which he expressly links to a kind of sexual promiscuity. This early example of embodied sociolinguistics becomes full-fledged in naturalist novels after 1850, in which vulgar gestures and sexually suggestive movements serve as key indexes of the prostitute.

A similar appearance of the *chahut* occurs at the end of *Mysteries* when the Slasher is encircled by a carnivalesque celebration for mid-Lent at the southern limits of Paris. As he is overtaken by a crowd of people dressed in old masquerade costumes on their way to the public execution of two women, a scene of chaotic revelry erupts. The Slasher hears the dancehall music and, while attempting to move through the crowds of criminals and deviant women, he views from the outside an underground room filled with musicians where drunk men and women "were lustily dancing the mad and obscene dance called the Cancan."[84] The Slasher's visceral disgust heightens when he observes the crowd applauding two couples for their vulgar movements and language.[85] The relationship between gestures and words evoked in this scene thus establishes an indexical connection between obscene forms of dance and vulgar ways of speaking. Even though the Slasher also speaks slang, his moral evolution over the course of the narrative, as well as the narrator's description of his ironic repulsion toward the dangerous classes, temporarily excuses him from this particular social association.[86] He notably avoids direct contact with the dancers, remaining separate by virtue of the building itself. And as he gazes into the interior space from the safety of the exterior boulevard, he also mirrors the voyeuristic gaze of Sue's readers, who are able to absorb valuable social information concerning the deviant dance from the safety of their home.

For a reader, the character of the Slasher functions as a go-between for the licentious music, bodily movements, and language which takes place in an underground room on the edges of Paris, a physical site that aligns with a reader's indexical expectations. In addition, the Slasher may also be an interlocuter, which falls in line with conventions of Classical art, with which the audience would have been familiar. The presence of the *chahut* dancers aligns with their location, offering not only social context to the reader but also linguistic context. While describing the uninhibited bodies of the dancers south of the Parisian city center, Sue's narrator simultaneously demarcates the area as one of anarchy and crime. Additionally, in conjunction with the portrayal of the carnivalesque dance, the narrator conducts a dance between interior and exterior space.

When the narrator reveals the identity of one of the *chahut* dancers to be the criminal known as the Skeleton, a lack of space in the underground room prompts the criminal to mobilize the other dancers to the exterior space of the boulevard where they successfully penetrate the crowd.[87] While, for the most part in French literature of the period, criminal characters tend to remain in their designated geographical areas, early nineteenth-century writers, however, do not shy from threatening criminal invasion of the readers' geographical and social spaces: Harvey acknowledges the growing "porosity of boundaries and traffic" that does not "diminish the fierce struggle to limit access and to protect interiors from the penetration [. . .] by unwanted others into interior spaces."[88] And the moral condemnation surrounding transgressed boundaries in *Mysteries*, as Goulet remarks, "can be seen as a desire for containment—the containment of chaos, the channeling of violence, the taming of the more troublesome elements disrupting France's national body."[89] The bourgeois desire to control disorderly bodies that engage in licentious forms of dance requires restriction "for 'proper' dance stays within its (social and spatial) limits."[90] While Sue emphasizes the inherent performative nature of criminal bodies through their *chahut* dance in the streets, playing on bourgeois fears of complete moral and physical disorder, he nonetheless keeps their lawlessness contained to the outskirts of Paris. Reckless bodies and specific places become indexical of the criminal type, but they also never exist outside the matrices of bourgeois hegemony in early nineteenth-century French novels. Sue's representation of the *chahut* dance far from the city center, and in the context of public festivities, shows lower-class disorder within its prescribed domain of order, that is, an urban region designated for crime and a festival-like celebration which permits degrees of social tomfoolery, such as drunkenness, transvestism, and sexual indecency.

In addition to licentious dance, songs containing slang and the vernacular also play an important role in the embodied language of the criminal type, serving as a powerful social identifier that would evolve into an index of lower-class misery, such as in Victor Hugo's *Les Misérables*, and later, into an index of sexual promiscuity related to women performers, such as in Zola's *Nana*. Vidocq provides several instances in which criminals break out in slang songs mid-narrative. For example, the author describes the sunset as the hour that brought about songs in prison, recounting a specific performance by a convict who has been to prison before (known as in criminal slang as *un cheval de retour*) who sings among the drunken cacophony of his fellow inmates.[91] While, in this particular instance, Vidocq does not provide notation for the song's slang terms and expressions, he does provide footnotes that include translations.

As the night begins to wind down at tavern Guillotin, a fellow secret agent Riboulet begins to sing a slang ballad.[92] Mid-song, the prostitute Manon la Blonde interrupts Riboulet's fourteen slang verses, adding an additional eight verses.[93] Vidocq describes the professional thief, Winter de Sarre-Louis, as "the author of a series of songs, very popular amongst convicts, who viewed him as their Anacreon."⁹⁴ Again, Vidocq provides footnoted translations of the slang, while simultaneously linking subversive song to subversive language, and therefore to the criminal type.⁹⁵ The song entitled "Air : de l' 'Heureux pilote'" is five verses long and tells the story of a criminal who robs a bourgeois man while his lover steals money from a boutique:

While scampering about
A big Mister topnotch
Wanting to turn out,
Flashes his gold watch
After the dance,
Creeping behind him on the streets,
I stun him in a trance,
I grab him by the shirt piece,
I nab his watch, his shoes, and his pants,
Then I scrammed from the police.⁹⁶

This excerpt from Winter's ditty contains at least one slang term in every line. The lyrics to this song, in addition to others, appear in full within the narrative, disrupting the main story of the text. The stories told in most of the criminal songs that appear in Vidocq's memoir often tell the tale of crime gone awry and the judicial consequences of these actions, such as imprisonment or death. In some cases, like in Riboulet's song, the lyrics point out the cyclical character of crime and punishment and that, in spite of the tragedy that befalls society's delinquents, criminals everywhere will continue to scheme.

In addition to such performances in taverns, slang songs serve as an integral feature for the spectacle of public executions, highlighting the criminal's inability to suppress his hysteria even among the general population. Similar to the portrayal of the prostitute in naturalist novels, the criminal is also able to transform both private and public spaces into his personal stage. Vidocq describes the spectacle of convicts heading to the scaffolds to be hanged, noticing the delight of certain prisoners and the "licentious songs" (*chansons licencieuses*) they sing on their way to the gallows.⁹⁷ Whether held in interior or exterior spaces, the association between criminality, slang, and reckless song and dance is made clear throughout Vidocq's memoirs. In addition, the reprisal of Riboulet's refrain in Hugo's *The Last Day of a Condemned Man* "[embeds it] in a social context linking it to a particular social type, as well as to certain emotions, even though these associations seem semantically arbitrary."⁹⁸ For instance, upon hearing the sweet melody of a young girl's song from his prison cell, the lamentable tune's prurient content inspires within the condemned man "a visceral disgust."[99] Although linguistically similar, the function of Hugo's *Lirlonfa* differs from that of Riboulet's:

> Despite not knowing the melody, the tone of the song differs based on the context; unlike Ribolet's upbeat drinking song, Hugo's Lirlonfa is a somber lament outside prison walls and is not so much a proleptic warning as it is a tale of misery. Its similarity to Vidocq's Lonfa malura in addition to its use in a criminal context further strengthens the Lirlonfa's association with criminal bodies [. . .]. Despite its cryptic meaning, the refrain [. . .] expresses a different emotion whilst remaining associated with criminals.[100]

However, in Sue's *Mysteries*, the spectacle of prostitution becomes synonymous with song. For instance, at the beginning of the novel, prostitutes populate a dark Parisian street and sing in the doorways of their brothels. Fleur-de-Marie gets her slang nickname, "Songbird," from her heavenly singing. Compared to the convict, the prostitute's performance is more subdued and less hysterical in nature, albeit just as dangerous. The figure of the femme fatale (or as they were known in the late nineteenth century, "Vamps," which is short for vampires), such as Zola's Nana, becomes fully realized in French literature of the fin-de-siècle and uses public performances in cabarets and theaters to play with notions of femininity in relation to male desire. Thus, when compared to the wild performance of Vidocq's Manon la Blonde, this new woman-of-the-night wields her siren's song in order to lure socially powerful men into a downward spiral of moral corruption while simultaneously questioning nineteenth-century ideas as to what behaviors, dress, and speech constituted a woman.

In terms of such moral degeneration, the aural and bodily spectacles that take place within the novels *Memoirs*, *The Last Day of a Condemned Man*, and *Mysteries* function as corporal forms of the speech practices linked to marginalized social groups. In a previous article, I noted that "the act of singing alludes to the transgressive nature of the criminal body. Like the dissonance [. . .], it is a body that disrupts even when physically confined."[101] Recklessly improvised song and dance in public places therefore become synonymous with the spoken slang of the criminal persona in early nineteenth-century French literature and an essential component of this identity that would create a space for the questioning of gender and sexual conventions in later works. The kinds of performances that Sue and other French writers, such as Hugo, associate with criminals are both public and private, but often times verge on the bestial and hysterical. With their sexually suggestive gestures and movement, in addition to their loud singing, screaming, and crying, the criminal figure emerges as an anti-artist whose primordial desires can become physically manifested at any given moment, resulting in a total liberation of the unconscious, which would have been a terrifying, albeit appealing, image for bourgeois readers whose social class revolves around the systematic repression of biological and psychological yearning. These criminal figures thus morph into perverted physical hallmarks of the oral traditions of centuries past, who, if left unrestrained, threatened the unraveling of dominant middle-class ideology.

THE ICONIZATION OF THE CRIMINAL

The literary creation of the criminal type in early French nineteenth-century realist works emerged out of a list of common bodily traits such as performance, appearance, dress, physique, and language, all characteristics that served as the basis of this social type within the collective bourgeois imaginary. The reading of these indexes transforms these works into a semiotic exploration on the part of the audience. In the minds of the middle-class nineteenth-century reader, this criminal code generally indexes a gruesome physiognomy and physique, a propensity for sexual deviancy implied in their licentious song and dance that would later become fully realized post-1850 with the slang-speaking prostitute and the multiple identities and squalid physical locales that the slang speaker frequents. The descriptions of criminal physical and linguistic traits communicate a perceived biological barbarity and inferiority that represents a social Darwinism, predating the late nineteenth-century studies by Lombroso on criminal atavism. In addition to transgressing linguistic boundaries, criminals transgress gender, moral, physical, and sexual boundaries as well, and in order to control and contain them, an appropriation and then a reappropriation of their identities must take place.

These "barbarous" Europeans reside in specific Parisian districts and frequent similar establishments of disrepute; the characters that participate in villainous dealings communicate in slang in a physical location that is befitting of such speech such as brothels, taverns, criminal hideouts, and prisons. In contrast, nature marks a Rousseauian space of morality and thus romanticized linguistic purity, especially in Sue's *Mysteries* where slang does not appear in the scenes that take place at Rodolphe's farm in Bouqueval, except when our criminal characters leave their urban dwellings to carry out their sinister plans in the countryside.[102] The overwhelming presence of sexually suggestive dance and slang songs in these seedy criminal sites further reinforces the relationship between bodily and social chaos. Like physical place, bodily movements embody the same indexes as spoken slang that relate to a certain moral state as well as a certain social status.

Luckily, for nineteenth-century readers, the spectacle of slang never actually infiltrates respectable social spaces, although the threat of invasion remains ever present. In the end, the upper classes are the only ones who can successfully appropriate lower-class spaces, while the perceived dangerous classes can never fully reside in these spaces reserved for those of a higher social (and ostensibly moral) status due to their being marked by their language and appearance which reveals them as criminal. Furthermore, the criminal's embodied language in the form of disguise and cross-dressing, in addition to licentious dance and song, firmly establishes spoken slang as the speech of the dangerous classes. From a sociolinguistic perspective, it is during this first indexical order that iconization occurs thanks to this literary representation that is simultaneously bodily and linguistic. As the next chapter will show, the press became the medium through which these representations reached both literate and illiterate audiences, thus securing slang as a criminal code in the minds of the collective.

NOTES

1. Bucholtz, "Word Up," 285.
2. "*Qu'il peut à sa guise être lui-même et autrui*," from Baudelaire's prose poem "Les foules." See English translation, "Crowds," 21.
3. Multiple identity changes are arguably a common characteristic of the detective, a figure who serves as the criminal's social counterpart in literature and film.
4. Bucholtz and Hall, "Embodied Sociolinguistics," 173.
5. Ibid., 174.
6. Ibid., 178.
7. This quality listed by Lombroso reveals the blatant racism that existed in theories of criminal atavism and Social Darwinism of the period, which suggested that people of certain racial identities could be compared to criminals or inferior beings. Unfortunately, these theories also propelled other tragic acts of white supremacy in the nineteenth century such as colonialism.
8. Lombroso, *Criminal Man*, 91.
9. Bucholtz and Hall, "Embodied Sociolinguistics," 174.
10. Vidocq, *Mémoires*, 338.
11. Ibid., 7–8.
12. Ibid., 291–92.
13. Ibid., 292.
14. At the beginning of the novel, the narrator explains that criminals can derive nicknames from some physical deformity or feature (Sue, *Mystères*, 37; English translation, 3).
15. Sue also uses name changes in order to signal internal transformation. This is especially true of Fleur, who, at the beginning of the novel, is known as "Songbird"

(*la Goualeuse*) and then *Fleur-de-Marie* (slang for "Virgin Mary"). While in prison, the narrator and characters refer to her as "Songbird" yet occasionally use *Fleur-de-Marie*. During their time at Rodolphe's country home, supporting characters only refer to her as "Marie." And at the end of the novel, she receives a new name: "Princess Amélie."

16. Sue, *Mystères*, 134; English translation, 108. See figure 2.1.
17. Sue, *Mystères*, 942; English translation, 1042.
18. Sue, *Mystères*, 943.
19. Sue, *Mystères*, 950; English translation, 1051.
20. See figures 2.2 and 2.3.
21. Sue, *Mystères*, 73, 281.
22. Here, again, is an attempt to mirror the internal judgments of Sue's readers in order to reaffirm his moral stance vis-à-vis the criminal classes. Sue, *Mystères*, 73; English translation, 40.
23. Sue, *Mystères*, 133–34; English translation, 108.
24. Woolard, "Why *dat* now?," 438.
25. Sue, *Mystères*, 73; English translation, 40.
26. Sue, *Mystères*, 578; English translation, 628.
27. Nicolas Gauthier typifies these women criminals in city-mysteries as "hors séduction" or excluded from male desire (*Lire la ville*, 163). See chapter 6 of this book, "Slang as the Language of Whores."
28. Balzac, *Splendeurs*, 100, 102, 206.
29. Bucholtz and Hall define the "semiotics of style" as "all dimensions of language as well as material and embodied resources of self-presentation, which together yield ideologically cohesive semiotic packages available for interpretation by others" ("Embodied Sociolinguistics," 180).
30. Sue, *Mystères*, 46; English translation, 11.
31. *[Sa physionomie] réunissait les contrastes les plus bizarres. Ses traits étaient régulièrement beaux, trop beaux peut-être pour un homme. Son teint d'une pâleur délicate, ses grands yeux d'un brun orangé, presque toujours à demi fermés et entourés d'une légère auréole d'azur, sa démarche nonchalante, son regard distrait, son sourire ironique, semblaient annoncer un homme blasé, dont la constitution était sinon délabrée, du moins affaiblie par les aristocratiques excès d'une vie opulente.* (Sue, *Mystères*, 46; English translation, 11–12)
32. Sue, *Mystères*, 44; English translation, 10.
33. Sue, *Mystères*, 5; English translation, 16.
34. For the most part, Sue provides several more details concerning the physical descriptions of hardcore criminals, in contrast to those with ambiguous moral tendencies (e.g., Fleur and the Slasher) or middle-class villains such as Polidori and Jacques Ferrand. As Goulet remarks, the Slasher's athletic build, red hair, and tan skin (a characteristic of convicts) are undermined by his honesty and sensitivity ("Apache Dancers," 31). The Slasher's former nickname, "Albino" (*l'Albinos*), reflected his physiognomy due to his flaxen hair and reddish eyes which have faded over time (Sue, *Mystères*, 66; English translation, 33). While his physical traits reveal his propensity for murder, the Slasher's commitment to moral reform softens the brutality

of his appearance in relation to more hardened criminals (Sue, *Mystères*, 45; English translation, 10). Polidori, however, resembles Judas Iscariot in appearance because of his red beard; however, like the Owl, he has green eyes and a hooked nose (Sue, *Mystères*, 214; English translation, 202). In fact, Polidori's physiognomy is so striking that Rodolphe suspects Cesar Bradamanti was Polidori in disguise (Sue, *Mystères*, 224; English translation, 214). Similarly, Jacques Ferrand, the evil notary, possesses peculiar physical features: he is unusually hairy, with faint eyebrows, a flat face with a short, flat nose and thin lips (Sue, *Mystères*, 500; English translation, 534). His teeth are black and rotten, and his negligent personal hygiene makes him naturally dirty, with his nails covered in dirt and a body odor like a goat. In these descriptions, Polidori's and Ferrand's evilness manifests through their physical appearance and lack of personal hygiene, and not their language. In the bizarre physical peculiarities of these middle-class villains, Sue showcases the downright hideousness contained within the physiognomies of hardened criminals who have no interest in moral reform. These characters' appearances further embody the look and manners of the slang speaker for the middle-class reader, which serve as invaluable class and moral identifiers.

35. Bazlac, *Splendeurs*, 552.

36. "*Qui les rend si prompts à l'assassinat dans une querelle soudaine*" (Ibid.).

37. Ibid., 93. Bourgeois characters in both *Père Goriot* and *Splendors* are able to identify Vautrin due to bodily markings. For example, in *Père Goriot*, Mademoiselle Michonneau (later Madame Poiret), a former tenant of the boarding house run by Madame Vauquer, where Vautrin also resided, identified Vautrin as Jacques Collin due to the markings "T.F." on his shoulder. In *Splendors*, Bibi-Lupin's examination of Vautrin's body reveals a scar on Vautrin's left arm, immediately implicating him. Soon after Bibi-Lupin's assessment, Madame Poiret comes to the prison to confirm his identity (Ibid., 426–28).

38. In terms of the virile criminal physique and sexuality in Balzac's *Le Père Goriot* (1834), Richard Berrong discusses the lack of key physical identifiers that Balzac's principal criminal character Vautrin contains, such as effeminacy, that would generally be linked to same-sex relations in the collective imaginary in the nineteenth century. For Berrong, this suggests that Balzac actively challenged cultural perceptions of the body and sexuality in order "to convince his readers that same-sex oriented men did not necessarily have to fit society's effeminate stereotype" (58). While Berrong argues that Balzac contextualizes his criminal character within a judgeless society due to the supporting characters' lack of comments on Vautrin's sexuality, perhaps Balzac's critique resides in the presence of a character who is a sinister villain, therefore further critiquing Vautrin's innate immorality as a psychopathic criminal, rather than as a man who engages in sexual acts with other men.

39. Vidocq, *Mémoires*, 34, 38, 178.

40. Ibid., 319.

41. Ibid., 173, 176.

42. Ibid., 442–43. Vidocq's ability to change identities and play so many roles occurs so frequently that he even begins to believe his own deceptions (Ibid., 38). The

extreme measures that Vidocq takes in order to deceive others results in a destabilization of his core identity. Criminal acting can be so convincing, even to the criminal himself, that it sometimes results in a permanent delusional state.

    43. *Je m'arrangerai si bien, qu'au-dedans comme au-dehors, rien ne transpirait; les voleurs de ma connaissance me tenaient pour le meilleur de leurs camarades, les autres s'estimaient heureux de pouvoir m'initier à leurs secrets, soit pour le plaisir de s'entretenir avec moi, soit aussi parfois pour me consulter.* (Ibid., 286)

    44. During a dinner with a prostitute with connections to a criminal gang in the Saint-Germain district (*faubourg*), Vidocq discloses to his readers that his dress, body language, and spoken language communicated to her that he was a thief (Ibid., 297).

    45. Sue, *Mystères*, 76.

    46. Ibid., 515.

    47. Ibid., 76.

    48. Ibid., 988.

    49. Bucholtz and Hall, "Embodied Sociolinguistics," 180.

    50. Vautrin is not the only character to take on a several identities throughout the course of the narrative. Criminal and police types alike constantly take on different personas in order to gain access to certain social milieus. In one scene, Vautrin's aunt Jacqueline Collin (a.k.a. Asia) dons a blonde wig, makeup, and clothes dressed like an aristocratic lady from the Saint-Germain district in order to make contact with Vautrin in prison (Balzac, *Splendeurs*, 402). She later poses as her friend, the clothing vendor, Madame Nourrisson, also known as Madame Saint-Estève, in order to meet with the Duchesse of Maufrigneuse and Madame de Sérisy (Ibid., 408–10). Even later in the novel, when she dresses as Madame de San-Esteban, Asia seems like a woman with a habit of pretending (Ibid., 557). Throughout the novel, a reader typically encounters many identities within one character, a staple feature of criminal types that early nineteenth-century French writers commonly emphasized within their works. For instance, Esther's service maid Prudence Servien is first introduced to the reader as *Europe*, and then *Eugénie*. In addition to Vautrin, another notorious ex-con known as Dannepont has several nicknames and disguises (Ibid., 514), and the convict Sélérier goes by four names: *l'Auvergnat, le père Ralleau, le Rouleur,* and *Fil-de-Soie* (Ibid.). With each new name, presumably comes a completely new (or stolen) identity. Even the "good" guys in Balzac's narrative engage in masking their true identities with both costumes and different ways of speaking. The undercover spies, Peyrade and Contenson, appear in several disguises throughout the story, such as a member of the upper-middle class and a former merchant, a Mogul and a mulatto servant, a broker and a baggage boy (Ibid., 168, 269, 273). Peyrade's protégé, Corentin, also takes on several different identities such as Monsieur de Saint-Estève, an elderly valet known as Monsieur de Saint-Denis, a sick old man, and a traveling salesman (Ibid., 286, 311–12, 329, 341). Importantly, for these characters, language plays an integral role in their ability to change identities. When Peyrade attempts to pass himself off as an English millionaire, he does so mainly because of his mastery of English (Ibid., 268). However, language can also betray his identity: When Peyrade learns that his daughter has been kidnapped his southern French accent comes out, thus revealing his true identity to Vautrin and the other (Ibid., 328).

51. In terms of gender and identity, the inherent theatricality of criminal characters, expressed through their penchant for cross-dressing, disguise, singing, and dancing, does not completely align with Judith Butler's notion of gender performativity as "a stylized repetition of acts" ("Performative," 519). In the portrayals of criminality in realist French literature, "the gendered self [is] prior to its acts" (Ibid., 520); this was a performance that was simply viewed as part of the profession, as compared to a radical gender performativity, and ultimately created a space in which to deconstruct and expand social categories in nineteenth-century France.

52. Although highly pejorative in terms of representation, one can trace the increasing emergence of gender and sexually fluid characters within French literature from the early nineteenth century onwards that would later transform into visions of performativity that aligned with Butler's definition as "the stylization of the body" that produces the "allusion of an abiding gendered self" for its audience ("Ibid.," 519).

53. As Julie Coleman explains, in French medieval mystery plays, men typically played a variety of women characters from the Bible (30).

54. Normington, *Gender and Medieval Drama*, 57.

55. Busby, "'*Plus acesmez qu'une popine*,'" 45.

56. Normington, *Gender and Medieval Drama*, 58.

57. Busby, "'*Plus acesmez qu'une popine*,'" 45–46.

58. Busby explains that the episode of Achilles' cross-dressing would have been well-known to a Medieval audience since it had been retold within various works throughout the Middle Ages such as Statius' *Thebaid*, the *Gesta Romanorum*, Ovid's *Ars Amatoria* and *Metamorphoses*, and *Ovide moralisé* (Ibid).

59. Vidocq, *Mémoires*, 30.

60. Ibid., 110.

61. *Vers deux heures du matin, je le vis en effet arriver avec un paquet contenant robe, guimpe, bas, etc., qu'il avait enlevé de la cellule de la sœur, pendant qu'elle était à matines. Tous mes camarades de salle, au nombre de neuf, étaient profondément endormis; je passai néanmoins sur le carré, pour faire ma toilette. Ce qui me donna le plus de mal, ce fut la coiffure; je n'avais aucune idée de la manière de la disposer [. . .]. Enfin la toilette de sœur Vidocq est achevée.* (Ibid., 113)

62. Busby explains that in premodern French works, cases of male cross-dressing "are not presented as manifestations of a sexual inclination or lifestyle but rather as a means of disguise which enables authors to develop their narrative structures and at the same time to generate comedy" (45). Thirteenth-century French fabliaux such as Douin de Lavesne's *Trubert* and tales such as Raoul de Hondene's *Meraugais de Portlesguez*, *Floire et Blancheflor*, *Claris et Laris*, and Robert de Blois' *Floris et Lyriopé* include men impersonating women in ways that propel the narrative, add comedic and entertainment value, and contribute greater complexity of character perspective (Roberts, 84–85). Similarly, the motives behind Vidocq's inclusion of several cross-dressing scenes probably align more closely with the aforementioned reasons than as commentaries on his sexuality or gender identity. It would not be until the late nineteenth century when cross-dressing practices would constitute acts of "perversions" within the French medical community. Parisian doctors known as the *aliénistes* studied cases of clothing fetishism, which included transvestism. See Jann

Matlock's "Masquerading Women, Pathological Men: Cross-Dressing, Fetishism, and the Theory of Perversion, 1882–1935."

63. *Mémoires*, 7–8. The farce continues as "Sister Vidocq" leaves the premises, escaping through the countryside. Along the way, he/she asks two different people for directions and runs into a priest who addresses him as "my dear sister" (*Ma chère sœur* [Ibid., 114]). He then spends time with the priest, accompanying him to mass and dining with him afterward. Throughout these encounters, there is no word from Vidocq (as narrator or character) concerning the believability of his outfit, thus a reader can safely assume that in spite of his large build, these townspeople believe in Vidocq's disguise, which suggests that perhaps Vidocq's original concern with appearance had to do with his "passing" as a woman. Despite his rationale for cross-dressing as a means to evade prison, there is a noticeable lack of moral judgment surrounding the disguises. In fact, donning a woman's clothes simply seems to be part of the job of a criminal.

64. Specific instances of men posing as nuns were even more rare. In Heldris de Cornuälle's thirteenth-century *Roman de Silence*, a man posing as a nun is found among Queen Eufeme's attendants, and it may be possible that historical records of similar events inspired Vidocq's ecclesiastical cross-dressing scene. Gregory of Tours tells of an impotent man who was discovered living dressed as a woman at St. Radegund's convent in Poitiers, France in 590 (Partner, 17). In Jean de Berry's book of hours, entitled *Belles heures de Jean de France* (c. 1409), an illustrated depiction of Saint Jerome dressed in women's clothing rushing to Matins can be found. See figure 2.4. As an act of vengeance, prankster monks replaced Jerome's habit with the dress in an effort to humiliate the saint. As Simon Dentith explains, intertextuality can inform practices of parody and a reader's ability to discern between the degrees of intertextuality can help them discern between degrees of parody. Whether more general or specific, parody "is based [. . .] on the intertextual stance that writing adopts" (Dentith, 9). Allusions to medieval texts or Molière in Vidocq not only serve as a literary nod to the precursory works on morality and human nature but they also elicit the theatrical portrayal of criminal characters taking on new identities, oftentimes in very farcical manners. Language plays a significant role with regards to Molière's social typifying and identity shifting; in several of his works, he manipulates the speech habits of certain characters in order to better portray them socially. Even if his representation is blatantly caricatured, it is just as subversive all the same.

65. In his study on transvestism in nineteenth-century French theater, Lenard Berlanstein analyzes the acceptability for French audiences of certain kinds of cross-dressing on the stage from the eighteenth century to the late nineteenth century, mainly women dressed as men, as this did not undermine patriarchal authority for the bourgeoisie. He argues that this tolerance for female actresses to dress as men coincided with views on the body and sexuality (351). As Michel Foucault theorizes, the social repression of sexuality, which began in the seventeenth century and progressed alongside the development of capitalism and a bourgeois society, resulted in a discourse on sex that was more institutionalized in nature (25–27). With regards to men, in the late eighteenth century, it remained common for actors to play female roles; however, by the nineteenth century, audiences no longer accepted men in dresses, as

audiences viewed this as a threat to patriarchal norms. Frequently, in the text, Vidocq comments on the theatrical nature of criminality and one's ability successfully to perform a new identity (*Mémoires*, 455).

66. The intertexual influence of Molière abounds in Balzac's work as well. References to Molière appear frequently in *Splendors*. See Balzac, *Splendeurs*, 267, 346, 399, 438.

67. Bucholtz and Hall, "Embodied Sociolinguistics," 180.

68. See figure 2.5.

69. Balzac, *Splendeurs*, 546.

70. Ibid., 529.

71. "*nouvelle idole*" (Ibid., 500).

72. Ibid., 601.

73. Coupled with Vautrin's open sexual preferences for other men, Balzac also maternalizes his main criminal character. Despite his resemblance to a corpse, his ghastly physiognomy, and sociopathic nature, the narrator frequently describes Vautrin as a mother figure (Ibid., 93, 502, 507, 597).

74. Bucholtz and Hall, "Embodied Sociolinguistics," 180.

75. Vidocq, *Mémoires*, 46.

76. Ibid.

77. Ibid.

78. Ibid., 119.

79. Goulet, "Apache Dancers," 25–26.

80. "*On a donné ce nom à une sorte de danse épileptique ou de delirium tremens, qui est à la danse proprement dite ce que l'argot est à la langue française; comme le dirait Delvau, c'est la langue verte de la chorégraphie*" (Desrat, *Dictionnaire de la danse*, 72).

81. Goulet, "Apache Dancers," 86.

82. "*Hommes ou femmes, tout le monde y fumait en dansant, la pipe passait de bouche en bouche, et la plus aimable galanterie que l'on pût faire aux nymphes qui venaient à ce rendez-vous, étaler leurs grâces dans les postures et attitudes de l'indécente chahut*" (Vidocq, *Mémoires*, 375).

83. Ibid.

84. "*se livraient avec emportement à cette danse folle et obscène appelée le chahut*" (Sue, *Mystères*, 1146–47; English translation, 1280–81).

85. Sue, *Mystères*, 1148; English translation, 1281.

86. Sue, *Mystères*, 1147; English translation, 1280–81.

87. Sue, *Mystères*, 1148–50.

88. Harvey, *Paris*, 43.

89. Goulet, "Apache Dancers," 36.

90. Ibid., 38.

91. Vidocq, *Mémoires*, 93–94.

92. Ibid., 377.

93. Ibid., 378–79.

94. "*L'auteur d'une foule de chansons, fort en vogue parmi les forçats, qui le regardent comme leur Anacréon*" (Ibid., 456).

95. Perhaps the most subversive kinds of song of the nineteenth century took place within the *goguettes*, or "*sociétés chantantes ouvrières*" that gathered regularly in cafés and were prohibited by the government due to their promotion of certain political views (Pillet and Thérenty, 9). While describing his investigation of Raoul, a winemaker and the organizer of *goguettes* in his Parisian cabaret at the city limits near Rochechouart, Vidocq includes a long footnote on dangers of these anti-Monarchy groups (*Mémoires*, 479).

96. "*En faisant nos gambades*, /
Un grand messière franc /
Voulant faire parade, /
Serre un bogue d'orient. /
Après la gambriade, /
Le filant sus l'estrade, /
D'esbrouf je l'estourbis, /
J'enflaque, sa limace, /
Son bogue, *ses* frusques, *ses* passes, /
J'm'en fus au fouraillis" (Ibid., 456–57).

97. Ibid., 143. As I have written in an article elsewhere, Riboulet's ballad reprise at tavern Guillotin includes the nonsensical refrains, *Lonfa malura dondaine* and *Lonfa malura dondé*, which "disrupts and propels the narrative at the same time, in ways similar to Riboulet's song within *Memoirs*" (Smith, 42). The refrain "expresses regret and misfortune whilst proleptically warning the reader of an inevitable fate for thieves, and its repetition as the story unfolds associates it with criminals and their predicament" (Ibid.).

98. Ibid.
99. Ibid.
100. Ibid., 43.
101. Ibid.
102. Even though Sue demarcates the country as a space in which Standard French appears, in her pastoral novels (*les romans* champêtres), such as *La Mare au diable* (1846), *François le Champi* (1847), *La Petite Fadette* (1848), and *Les Maîtres sonneurs* (1853), George Sand presents a glorified representation of country life and, more particularly, countrified dialects such as patois *berrichon*. Her tasteful use of patois in these novels reveals a rejection of standard literary forms, and even expresses a preference for more "primitive" dialects over the legitimate language in order to present the reader with a more realistic portrayal of country folks.

Chapter 3

Slang as Language Politics

That which is angelic under one form becomes without a doubt diabolic under another. In this way, morality would be a question of form.

—Louis Desnoyers, *Le Siècle*
(September 1847)

(*Ce qui est angélique sous une forme devient sans doute diabolique sous une autre. Ainsi, la moralité serait une question de forme*)

In his *Memoirs*, Vidocq tells the tale of an unnamed scholar who pays the narrator a surprise visit. Before inquiring into the scholar's reason for seeking out the now redeemed Vidocq, the former criminal reflects on his notoriety within the literary community:

> Since I published Memoirs, [the erudite] came to my home until the grammarians arrived to offer to teach me French, on the condition that I would teach them slang. Maybe they were philologists? Anyways, the erudite came to my house; what did he want from me?[1]

This anecdote, which initially unveils Vidocq's inner monologue, reveals a meeting of the minds between the criminal mastermind and the honorable man of letters, who presents Vidocq with a book in Latin on the great pedagogue Godefroid, a historian of thieves.[2] Although an unlikely source, Vidocq, and other verified criminals possessed a linguistic expertise and insider knowledge of a forbidden lifestyle that bourgeois writers sought out in order to perfectly replicate it within their oeuvre. Vidocq's story monologue thus reveals the linguistic and social exchange that occurred between the respective representatives of high- and low-brow culture, one that engendered vehement public debates mainly concerning the merits of the use of slang language in French literature.

This chapter explores the literary descent of nineteenth-century French upper-class writers into the 1830s–1840s underworld (*les bas-fonds*), a concept that I refer to as "literary slumming," and its political, sociocultural, and linguistic implications. This literary slum was characterized by the views of critics who found serial novels (*les romans-feuilletons*) to be lowbrow due to their form and content. However, in the main, these critics' disdain arose from the fact that these works permitted middle-class readers to vicariously participate in a lifestyle that attracted them, but which was one that was also threatening their own social positioning. As this chapter further argues, in addition to the establishment of a literary slum and slang's first indexical order, the use of criminal culture and the language of slang by bourgeois writers reveals a cultural appropriation that ultimately contributed to the iconization of the slang speaker. However, in addition to consistent representations of embodied and spoken slang in French literature, the diffusion of these portraits to readers occurred via the press. Without continuous reinforcement between linguistic variants and their social meanings, indexicality (and consequently, iconization) of a specific social type cannot occur. French newspapers, as a new form of mass media, successfully exposed literate and illiterate audiences to these characterological figures and thus, ensured the iconization of slang's first indexical order, that is, the slang speaker as a hardened criminal.

Notably, however, as the creation of this literary slum was taking place, a reverse cultural appropriation was also occurring; in other words, literary slumming constituted both top-down and bottom-up processes in which (1) the upper classes appropriated lower-class culture, language, and space, while (2) the lower classes invaded upper-class culture and space (and occasionally adopted Standard French). Recognition of this upper-class literary appropriation, and in particular, the lower-class reverse appropriation, occurred in nineteenth-century France through public and critical debates on the merits of serialized literature in newspapers, especially in terms of the serials' marginalized characters and their use of non-Standard French and slang. This metalinguistic critical commentary not only revealed and shaped collective societal definitions about what constituted literature but also interrogated the identities of various social types contained within that literature, in particular, criminal characters. Although the character of the criminal in French literature can be found in texts dating back to the fifteenth century, the extent to which a French bourgeois public was exposed to criminal characters in literature in the nineteenth century was unprecedented.

In this manner, the nineteenth century marks an especially unique moment in French literary history in which marginalized social types were suddenly key characters in novels, memoirs, and plays, while their (rather homogenized) characterization was reaching thousands of readers. The blurring of lines between reality and fiction by early writers, such as Eugène Sue, Honoré de Balzac, and Eugène François Vidocq, ultimately crafted the characters of "the criminal," "the worker," and "the bourgeois," constructions that heavily relied on portraying the characters' speech practices. These authors' desires to instantiate and define such social categories undoubtedly raises questions in terms of authenticity. This chapter, however, is not concerned with whether a characterization was authentically that of a criminal, a working-class person, or a bourgeoisie. Instead, this chapter focuses on how these social categories emerged through serialized literature and the public debates surrounding its merits, which served both to reflect and inform the social discourse on different social types. In particular, the role of newspapers, in catalyzing the iconization of slang as speech inherently representative of the criminal type, not only brought about a relaxing of literary standards in terms of content and format but also, in a move toward increased democratization, created social categories that became ever more nuanced, rather than clearly defined.[3] Even though the readers of these works were predominately middle class, the popularity of serials, such as Sue's *The Mysteries of Paris*, reached illiterate audiences as well who, through word-of-mouth, gained exposure to slang speakers. According to Barbara Johnstone, sociolinguistic occurrences such as indexicality (and one could say iconization, as well) form simply due to being told that these meanings exist.[4] In nineteenth-century France, the press' ability to reach beyond the literate population meant that they could continue to reinforce the indexical connection between linguistic variants of slang and its criminal meaning.

The growing interconnectivity between the French press and the literary world culminated in the serialized novel and its placement at the bottom, or *rez-de-chaussée* (ground floor), of the newspaper. Nevertheless, the popularity of serialized literature corresponded not only with innovations in printing but also literary content. In order to establish their larger reputation in the popular sense, upper-class writers thus began to experiment with representations of criminal and working-class characters within their works. These representations of criminals and the working class, as discussed in chapters 1 and 2, relied on particular characteristics, such as language, performance, physiognomy and physique, as well as dress; however, a social separation between the dangerous criminal and working classes becomes increasingly intertwined in early nineteenth-century French novels and memoirs.

The upper-class appropriation and construction of lower-class culture for mass consumption further ignited public concerns regarding what was perceived as a link between the degradation of literature and the increasing democratization of society. The more readers who had access to these works, which exposed immoral content to potentially vulnerable readers such as the uneducated lower classes and women, the higher the risk for the cultural downfall of France's artistic domains. Therefore, a study of the relationship between literacy and crime in nineteenth-century French literature sheds light on the social identity of readers of early serialized works as well as the ways in which the upper classes monopolized this construction and consumption of lower-class culture. Thus, in early nineteenth-century France language in literature emerged as not only a social marker but also a moral one. Therefore, this analysis of the various public arguments that circulated around the 1840s in France shows that the use of slang in serialized novels functioned as a language that was bounded by class stereotypes, and thus certain moral stereotypes as well. The delicate relationship between language, class, and politics, especially with regards to the middle class at the end of the eighteenth century, provides greater insight into the serious threat that slang in literature posed for both French bourgeois critics and politicians. Slang, it was feared, threatened to unravel the dominant ideology, as it was not just a language but also metonymy for deviant bodies that, in their upward trajectory, could eventually weaken a bourgeois hegemony.

Through an analysis of the various debates that arose in the 1830s regarding what Sainte-Beuve calls "industrial literature" (*la littérature industrielle*), it becomes apparent that the break in literary conventions, such as content, format, and style, intensifies in the early nineteenth century. Aristocratic and bourgeois critics such as Sainte-Beuve, Paul Gaschon de Molènes, Alfred Nettement, Arthur de Gobineau, Louis Desnoyers, and Benoît-Marie Chapuys-Montlaville notably argued both for and against the mass production of serial novels, which included debates on the use of criminal language, slang (*argot*), in literary works. Underlying these public dialogues, the efforts to eradicate slang and other forms of non-Standard French from literature reflected a larger desire to further eliminate so-called "criminal" bodies from society. Through a discursive unpacking of these debates, this chapter argues as well that the innovations in newspaper production and distribution, while nevertheless aiding in the democratization of literature, ultimately worked to break down the polarizing social connotations that slang had carried up to that point as well as laid the foundation for the emergence of a new social indexical order in the second half of the nineteenth century.

LANGUAGE POLICY IN NINETEENTH-CENTURY FRANCE

As discussed in both Prologue and chapter 1, slang as a nineteenth-century literary phenomenon inserts itself into an extensive ideological network of linguistic politics that date back to the sixteenth century. In the late eighteenth century, an attempt to eliminate popular and regional dialects from the Ancien Régime took effect. In fact, efforts to unify the country via language had commenced even earlier with the Ordinance of Villers-Cotterêts (1539), which called for the use of French instead of Latin in official contracts and legislation. However, these efforts did not gain intensity until much later. As Renée Balibar and Dominique LaPorte report, a common language was not required under the Ancien Régime, and, in fact, threatened the power of the aristocracy.[5] Until the eighteenth century, French was the language of the monarchy. Through collective efforts on the part of the middle class, French eventually became the language of administration, paving the way for the rise in bourgeois power. As Michel de Certeau et al. note, following the Revolution of 1789 two main linguistic issues surfaced:

> On the one hand, to explain to the inhabitants of the countryside the meaning of the new laws in a language known to them—that is to say, translate; on the other hand, to elaborate on a policy of language politics.[6]

These official attempts to standardize French within the rural areas of the country were met with the obstacles of communicating with inhabitants who only spoke in a regional dialect or patois. Anthony Lodge points out that before any sanctioned efforts were made to implement Standard French across the nation, dialects, patois, and other minority languages had not been vilified to the same extent in the past.[7] Therefore, French authorities knew that to achieve such a massive undertaking, a more systematic approach was needed to reeducate the masses in order to unite the country under one language.

In terms of these efforts, on August 13, 1790, the Abbé Grégoire circulated a questionnaire on patois, collecting responses from August 17, 1790, to January 12, 1792, after which he eventually compiled his "Report on the Necessity and the Means of Eliminating Patois and Universalizing the Use of the French Language" (*Rapport sur la nécessité et les moyens d'anéantir les patois et d'universaliser l'usage de la langue française*). The questionnaire itself is made up of forty-three questions which reveal

> two fields of analysis: one looking at the language, which is from the eighteenth century depiction of society (questions 1 to 28); the other field, complementary, has for objective instruction and its opposite, prejudices (questions 31–37 and 38–40).[8]

Grégoire's investigation reveals a study that is both linguistic and ethnographic, as well as political, in that the use of French by ideological state apparatuses, such as the Catholic Church and schools, became a means for the bourgeoisie to gain political influence over the aristocracy and the working classes.

These early efforts to purify the French language through the elimination of patois and other regional dialects, of course, masked larger sociopolitical desires, reflecting bourgeois beliefs on nationality in relation to collective mores and global influence. By the time nineteenth-century slang entered the political and literary arena, the stage had been set by the pre-Revolutionary efforts of the bourgeoisie to unify the language in the name of political advancement. However, as Renée Balibar and LaPorte argue the rise of the middle class could not have overtaken the monarchy under the Ancien Régime without the participation of the lower classes:

> It is a characteristic particular to the French bourgeois revolution to have not been able to achieve their rights and their class aspirations without other oppressed classes recognizing the rights and the aspirations similar to theirs. In other words, *without it ceasing to be bourgeois*, the bourgeois French revolution *did not conduct itself in the name of the bourgeoisie, but in the name of the people*. And yet, it is precisely in this general domination realized in the name of general rights of society that is in play in the interest brought by the bourgeoisie to the linguistic question, an interest represented at the political level in a bourgeois language policy.[9]

Following the French Revolution, it goes without saying that the Royal Court no longer had the same influence over Paris: population increases gave way to a breakdown in social hierarchy, as well as the deterioration of a feudal class system, and thus the inability to categorize people by birth created a lack of social control that incited panic.

In terms of such fears, the sudden appearance of the underrepresented social types of criminals and the lower classes in nineteenth-century French literature reveals an ambivalent mix of fear and fascination that occurred for the literate public, as well as a collective attempt to represent social minorities for their sake, rather than attempts at self-representation by these minorities themselves. These representations of the slang speaker both reflected and perpetuated the social discourse of the time as being from the criminal and lower classes. However, within the collective imaginary of slang speakers who communicated in their own criminal code, there existed a temporal divide between that which was modern, in other words, literate and written, and that which was archaic, or illiterate and oral.

SLANG AND THE PRESS

The critics of slang in the public debates reinforced the bourgeois fears surrounding the polyphony of new urban inhabitants that threatened the social stability of France. Certainly, slang was a frightful language for the bourgeois reader. In no other time in France's history had slang appeared with such frequency in written works. Its original purpose as a secret criminal code meant that illiterate speakers were maintaining and spreading a purely oral language. Attempts at containment came in the form of codification (i.e., slang dictionaries) and/or exposure via serials, accompanied by moral warnings. Accompanying and catalyzing this linguistic phenomenon were several other factors that contributed to slang's mass circulation such as the invention of the steam-powered printing press, cheaper newspaper subscriptions, the popularity of the serialized novel, and a newfound interest in criminal life. Despite warnings from writers, slang's growing popularity in serialized novels was met with resistance from critics who thought the use of criminal language perpetuated crime and immorality. Slang thus became the linguistic scapegoat of the public as well as a substitute for the dangerous persons who could not be so easily identified and removed from the city. Politicians and literary critics pointed the finger at different causes for these literary transgressions, and thus they advocated various methods to prevent such language from infecting conventional upper-class institutions even further. Unfortunately for them, the increase in literacy rates meant the democratization of education not only for the morally sound but also for the morally unsound.

The public interest in the criminal world in early nineteenth-century France was due to several factors. In 1810, Napoléon had established the French Penal Code, which outlined various criminal offenses and their corresponding punishments. Following the Revolution, France saw the modern development of police forces consisting of three main divisions: (1) state civilian police, (2) civilian municipal police, and (3) state military police.[10] The evolution of new police organizations made law enforcement in nineteenth-century France a greater part of public life, and therefore more prevalent in the reporting of the press. Although often sensationalized, this mass media coverage not only made crime seem more widespread but also contributed to the collective imaginary concerning criminals and their way-of-life. As Dominique Kalifa explains:

> [Crime in various media] allows of course to give access and social visibility to crime, but it also contributes to diffusing a homogenous imaginary of the norm, of common perceptions and shared from tolerable and the intolerable [. . .]. As a social product, crime only defines itself in relation to rules, values, and collective feelings that a society gives.[11]

French newspapers were instrumental in establishing a sense of shared societal norms among a mass readership that engaged in the reading of weekly serials in order to experience the dealings of evil characters and their heroic counterparts. In addition, the formal reports of crime granted readers real-life events that corresponded more-or-less to the assaults, murders, and thefts appearing in their favorite books. These readers made up what Asif

Agha calls a "speech chain network," in other words, the receivers of shared messages.[12] Within a speech chain, it is not imperative for members to know or even be aware of one another; it is simply the transmission of "symbolic values" to its network of members. The press became the medium through which this speech chain formed, by rendering the norms of "right" and "wrong" as uniform within the collective imaginary.

While representations of criminal life permeated the press and literature, the social "rules, values, and collective sentiments" (*règles, valeurs et sentiments collectifs*) accompanied representations of crime within the press, while slang constantly evoked the moral and national detriment these shifts had on society. According to Lodge, the linguistic diversity in Paris and other French cities masked a "fundamental orderliness" of shared biases and opinions on language variation.[13] Additionally, the ritualization of reading newspapers and their circulation seemingly implicated readers in what was happening, as Alain Vaillant states: "The rumination of the same news, day after day, seems to plunge the newspaper reader into the same reality of things, in such a way that it ends up conflating the real world, clearly unknowable, and the represented world."[14] This blurring of reality and fiction contributed to the mass conceptualization of marginalized social types:

> The public—that of Eugène Sue, for example—is thus submerged in a universe where the broadcasted representation of the real and the narrative fiction are inextricably mixed and constitute together a kind of second nature which, in return, predetermines its relationship to the world and in which we are from now on all immersed.[15]

The creation of this literary realm that was partly reality and partly fiction came about through what Marc Angenot terms the "social discourse" (*le discours social*), or the collection of discursive artifacts that arise from a wide-range of sources and media and that generate a collective imaginary regarding certain aspects of society, in addition to generating

> topics and 'themes' that circulate from one sector to another, but also distinctive characteristics and idiosyncrasies, sources of a 'not yet said' which would remain unspeakable if it was not able to emerge as distinctive forms within a totality.[16]

Therefore nineteenth-century French serial novels, dictionaries, and memoirs in which slang appeared both contributed to and perpetuated a social discourse on criminals and working-class types, in addition to communicating key social information on non-slang speakers such as the aristocracy and the haute bourgeoisie. This social discourse informs the fictive utterances of would-be criminals that appear in a variety of French texts throughout the nineteenth century that are intertextually in "dialogue" with one another over time. These utterances, while wholly informed by the circulation of a hegemonic belief regarding society and its members, simultaneously serve to promote a collective imaginary regarding the upper crust of society.

This growing use of slang in literary works did not go unnoticed by critics, thus coinciding with the use of slang in literature was a debate that became deeply intertwined with the question, *what is literature?* Although the influence of certain regulatory institutions, such as the French Academy and the Catholic Church, was still strong in the nineteenth century, writers were nevertheless adapting to the sociopolitical atmosphere by inserting topics and styles of writing that were judged to be nonconventional. Vaillant explains that around the 1820s, a paradigm shift took place in the minds of writers, one that corresponded to the innovations happening in the press. Before this time, writing was based on a culture of rhetoric that dated back to antiquity, with the primary objective of a writer to announce and convince their reader of their personal opinion: "Based on this conception of language, there stems a moral and a philosophy, which closely links the discourse—all discursive production to its subjective origin."[17] However, in the early nineteenth century, a narrative discourse began to replace this subjective discourse as an attempt to depict life as it was. The writer's role thus morphed from moralizing didact into that of storyteller "who knows how *to tell* the world to his readers"; the narration thus served the double function of presenting the world as it actually was, while veiling the opinions of the writer himself.[18] This shift from "moralizing didact" to "storyteller" occurred in both fiction and nonfiction (memoirs and dictionaries), as well as coincided with the emergence of the genre of literary Realism and its later outgrowth at the end of the nineteenth century, Naturalism. Seeking to depict the world as it is meant that the narrator or lexicographer needed to expand their social terrain and create a literary product that was more panoramic in nature. And in order to be sufficiently grounded in reality, these new works demanded a certain degree of social inclusivity.

In terms of employing linguistic speech practices that were inclusive as well as viewed as "criminal-like" or "low-class," there were many reasons why writers would include slang in their works. First, given its dangerous origins, this way of speaking might seduce more readers, thus boosting the fame and income of the author. Second, there was a desire to contain a seemingly uncontainable portion of the population by revealing their "true" way-of-life. Third, there was the desire to make sense of the vast urban changes taking place within a short amount of time via social (and linguistic) categorization. Fourth was the desire to have an original literary angle. In spite of the main factors for watering down previously instituted literary and linguistic conventions, an element of danger still existed for these writers. The open political atmosphere under Louis XVIII and the Charter of 1814 was quick to dissolve under the July monarchy. The September laws of 1835 placed heavy restrictions on views and drawings in the press that offended the monarchy, and in June of 1848 the *cautionnement*, or a deposit granted to the state by newspapers as a kind of political collateral, was reimposed onto newspapers. This tense political atmosphere created risks for anyone who was addressing forbidden topics. At the same time, such tension beckoned writers to address the political, social, and urban changes taking place. Combined with the rising public interest in criminal life and the concurrent shifting role of the writer, the more open political atmosphere created the perfect moment for writers to abandon literary conventions and to begin expanding the possibilities of literary content and form.

INNOVATIONS IN THE PRESS AND THE DEMOCRATIZATION OF LITERATURE

For what was viewed by many as a form of linguistic contamination, innovations in the press were, in part, to blame. For instance, the format of the newspaper itself had transformed at the beginning of the nineteenth century to accommodate literary works. In 1799, when the *Journal des débats* came under the direction of Louis-François Bertin and his younger brother, Pierre Louis Bertin, they introduced the serialized novel in the *rez-de-chaussée*, the bottom section of the pages of the newspaper. Initially, serialized writing was nonpolitical and included critiques that were varied in nature.[19] This variety led to a journalistic space that consisted of "a polyphonic universe where all kinds of discourse [came] in succession and respond to each other often through the means of multiple signs of complicity."[20] Due to its multipurpose nature, the *rez-de-chaussée* naturally accommodated the emergence of the serialized novel, a new genre that was beginning to define itself as not only sensational but also, in many ways, shocking.

Unlike other newspapers of the time period, the *Journal des débats* escaped censorship under Bonaparte's decree on January 17, 1800, to eliminate sixty of seventy-three French newspapers already in existence and prevent the creation of any further newspapers. The serialized format, while initially used for interesting cultural knowledge, continued in its existence in the *Journal des débats*, eventually evolving to accommodate fiction. Prior to this, newspapers had housed a strong political purpose.[21] It was not until 1829 when the *Revue de Paris* and the *Revue des deux mondes* began publishing short stories by popular writers, or as Lise Dumasy-Queffélec notes, that the *rez-de-chaussée* became more literary.[22]

A drop in newspaper subscription prices for *La Presse* and *Le Siècle* by respective and rival editors Émile Girardin and Louis Desnoyers in 1836 from eighty francs to forty francs allowed for increased sales, and thus a greater democratization of readers. The effects on the number of newspapers printed were astounding. In 1803, eleven Parisian newspapers in circulation printed 36,000 daily copies. In a span of eighty-four years from 1830 to 1914, the number of newspapers printed daily in 1803 had increased by 60 percent, with 145,000 copies in 1845, and more than a million copies between 1845 and 1870. By the second half of the nineteenth century, prices for single-copy sales were reduced to one *sou*, while there was a quadruple increase in newspaper copies (about 600,000 newspapers were sold for this reduced fair). While most newspapers came out of Paris (by 1914, there were about eighty daily Parisian newspapers), such increases also occurred in smaller towns. From the around 3,000 copies that had been produced daily under Napoléon Bonaparte, by mid-century these had increased to 60,000. By 1870, the number of copies was 350,000.[23]

While local towns also produced their own newspapers, the distribution of major Parisian newspapers went beyond the city limits, and thus innovations in transport also contributed to a wider exposure to serial novels, as well as various sociolects, or the languages that index social origin. The postal service in France reigned over newspaper distribution until 1870, increasing the value of newspaper prices, as well as limiting delivery to places in which *La Poste* existed.[24] In spite of some limitations, the delivery of Parisian newspapers was more expedient than ever. By 1814, it only took thirty-four hours for a delivery from Paris to Lyon, and by 1830 only three days to Bordeaux, four to Marseille, and about one week to smaller urban centers.[25] As Vaillant asserts, it was the explosion of innovation in industries related to printed media around the 1830s that accounts for the development of mass culture; the establishment of a media network (*un système médiatique*), in addition to public reading establishments, such as reading rooms (*les cabinets de lecture*); and that provided the industrial, cultural, and social environment in which slang and other unsavory portrayals of society could circulate, even among readers who were not newspaper subscribers; in other words, the working classes.[26] This expansion of the media network during the early nineteenth century, while seemingly unregulated in terms of the content, makes up the major part of a discursive total that is, in fact, a social discourse. According to Angenot these separate discourses, while seemingly disconnected, are actually organized under a unifying hegemonic order or "a complex set of prescriptive rules of diversification of spoken expressions and of cohesion, of coalescence, of integration."[27] Interestingly, this network of "prescriptive rules" becomes more evident in the public debates on serial novels and the use of slang in literature as a meta-discourse that reflects collective anxieties and ideas regarding social class and notions of the French nation-state. It is through these debates, then, that a clearer picture surfaces regarding the bourgeois ideology that governed the social discourse via this more democratic, mass media network.

THE MORAL DEBATES BEHIND THE *QUERELLE DU ROMAN-FEUILLETON*

As an immediate response to these innovations happening in the press, a quarrel emerged on the merits of what Charles Augustin Sainte-Beuve called "industrial literature" (*la littérature industrielle*). Early critics involved in the "dispute of the serialized novel" (*la querelle du roman-feuilleton*), which took place from 1836 to 1848, first attacked or defended the moral nature of the genre before addressing the dangerous properties of slang. This critique against the serialized novel was in part due to its fabrication, the mass production of which created suspicion concerning motives that were more economically, rather than artistically, based. The collaboration between newspapers, authors, and editors led to a kind of cookie-cutter literature, or standardized plots and forms, in which certain aspects of the serialized narrative and structure appeared over and over, thus establishing these elements as a tried-and-true formula.

As Umberto Eco acknowledges with regard to Sue's *Mysteries*, the plot structure is "sinusoidal," meaning that, unlike the traditional curved plot construction of other texts in which tension culminates and then releases leading to the dénouement, Sue's text contains multiple curves that repeat the same culmination and release pattern throughout the storyline.[28] Eco states that

> *Les Mystères de Paris* is no longer a novel but a series of montages designed for the continual and renewable gratification of its readers. From here on Sue is no longer concerned with obeying the laws of good narration and [. . .] introduces into it certain convenient artifices [. . .].[29]

Kalifa notes further that, in addition to a riveting, repetitive narrative, these popular novels contained a significant amount of discourse:

> This mastery of the story is often accompanied by the elimination of too many apparent traces of utterance. It is better that the events tell the story themselves, in a functional dynamic and everything tightens towards the flow of the story. Evolving in this incredibly black-and-white ideological universe, the characters

are often reduced to allegorical roles, even down to anthropomorphized concepts (the Avenger, the Bad Guy, the Victim), apt to prove the most absolute identification.[30]

Sue's desire to write a best-selling series had the additional effect of typecasting social types through derivative indexes such as appearance and speech, and as Kalifa notes, these types became so reductive that they were allegorical (and I would add, thanks to their slang, iconic). The literary strategies that Sue used to seduce his readers, such as riveting plotlines and the consistent suspension of narrative closure, went hand-in-hand with the creation of character types that were meant to translate for readers in real life. From this perspective, the repetitive features that indexed the literary criminal type, especially slang, transformed the role of the writer, whose new medium was the press as interpreter of present-day reality.

Within this evolving genre of the serial that was both journalistic and literary, as well as aural, the role of the writer thus evolved alongside his work. Like the journal itself, he became a composite figure: novelist, journalist, and storyteller. As the reader's tastes evolved, so did the writer's capacity to satisfy his public:

> What the newspaper reader wants, it is not to read a novel, but to *hear* a story *told* by the author who, like the storyteller in the salon or by the corner of the fire, knows all the techniques to retain their attention: the rapidity of the story, the recourse of the dialogue, the irony, or on the contrary, the poignant and the speculative, etc.[31]

Indeed, one of the driving forces of the serialized novel was its capacity to seduce the masses (as well as to rake in profits), but as a result of this formulaic characterization, a bourgeois anxiety developed regarding the readers' capacity to discern between high and low culture.

In 1839, Sainte-Beuve penned his "On Industrial Literature" (*De la littérature industrielle*) which appeared in the *Revue des Deux Mondes*, wherein he condemns the inherently immoral nature of these novels, focusing mainly on the corrupt motivations behind their production. An overall degeneration in newspaper ethics, such as editors forging author names to attract readers, authors including superfluous words, and using explicitly prohibited and vulgar topics to make more money, not only contributed to the degeneration of literary standards but also branded the serialized novel as the new get rich quick scheme of the century. In addition to two types of literature, "honorable literature" (*la littérature honorable*) and "industrial literature," Anthony Glinoer points out that there were also two types of publishing when it came to books (as opposed to the serialized novel). The first contained the overall objective to "create a public for writers" (*créer un public pour les auteurs*), while the second aimed to "create writers for a public" (*créer des auteurs pour un public*). The former corresponded to honorable literature, and the latter corresponded to industrial literature.[32] These changes taking place within the press and publishing companies were in part due to complicity between writers, editors, and even illustrators. Notably, Balzac's essay "On the Current State of the Bookstore" (*De l'état actuel de la librairie*) expressed an opposition to the hierarchy of bookstores that called for the mediation of printers and papermakers, and thus led to higher prices and taxes on the work itself. Like the division of editors that Glinoer addresses, Balzac also comments on the overall trend of intermediaries entering the scene to profit from book production. For the celebrated author, "finally, it is necessary to only obtain one volume that makes itself exactly like bread, and sells itself like bread, so that there is no other intermediary between the writer and the consumer than the bookstore."[33] For some nineteenth-century French critics and writers, however, literary form mattered just as much as content and held a certain moral weight. The gimmicky style of the changing aspects of the content, mediums, and production of literature, while providing every author the opportunity to gain fame in print form, radically destabilized the identity of writers and the definition of French literature itself that had been so neatly defined in the seventeenth century.

The role of a book's presentation also could not be discounted. The more honorable publishers that Glinoer cites generally produced texts with ornamental covers and illustrations. Illustrators then became associated with specific writers, and editors, who were seeking the same kind of literary glory as the writers themselves, or who took a chance on unknown poets, while writing up contracts for established writers based on future projects.[34] Another kind of editor, those who specialized in industrial literature, typically focused on the production of two types of literature: (1) plays (as in vaudeville comedy and melodrama) and (2) novels. Their texts were not neatly ornamented, but rather were known for "a presentation deprived of care, of volumes hastily composed."[35] The new layouts and emphasis on serialization in certain newspapers therefore corresponded to publishing houses that privileged quantity over quality. In the first half of the nineteenth century, serial novels were just as abhorred in the newspaper as they were in printed book form. The physical quality of the books published as serials is an important aspect of literary slumming, which constitutes the inclusion of vulgar content and language, as well as the substandard format of these novels that, by French convention, rendered them "slummy."

For Sainte-Beuve, the purpose of the industrial writer was no longer to write for writing's sake, but rather to write for living's sake (*vivre en écrivant*), and this was turning every man into *un homme de lettres*. It is this democratization of the writer that, according to the critic, constituted an industrial literature, in addition to a combined lack of artistic talent and moral integrity: "With our electoral and industrial traditions, everyone, at least one time in their life, will have had their page, their discourse, their *toast*, will be an *author*."[36] In contrast, it was honorable literature that belonged to a small, artistically—and morally—inclined elite; and it was only in restoring glory to the artistically—and morally—deserving would a remedy come about and conquer this industrial "evil."[37] As critic Paul Gaschon de Molènes lamented only a few years later, the democratization of the writer was simply an artistic degeneration: "By degrading art, one renders it accessible to all [. . .] since storytellers descend into the street, everyone has their story to tell."[38] The popularity and rise of serialized literature, in fact, meant a simultaneous democratization of the reader *and* the writer, a phenomenon that was increasingly linked to concerns about the degradation of literary art.

SLANG AND BOURGEOIS FEARS OF THE DANGEROUS CLASSES

In the first half of the nineteenth century, as one may have already surmised, there was rarely an agreement for the inclusion of slang-speaking characters in literature between literary critics, politicians, and writers. Oftentimes, they either wholeheartedly condemned their use, or they recognized criminal characters in terms of metaphor, stating that the characters had some poetic value, but unfortunately it was not enough to merit a place in the literary world. This growing concern between morality and style corresponded to the rapid, increased production of these novels as well as to their content. In July 1842, journalist and critic Alfred Nettement issued his response to Sue's *Mysteries* in his "Letters to a Young Woman of the World on *The Mysteries of Paris*" (*Lettres à une jeune femme du monde sur les Mystères de Paris*). These letters appeared in *La Gazette de France* and vehemently attack the immoral nature of Sue's work. According to Nettement, since neither style nor morality is present within *Mysteries*, these cannot possibly account for the work's popularity. Instead, as he writes, Sue's work should be likened to a public execution "that everyone can watch from the comfort of their home."[39] Although brief in his anti-slang stance, Nettement is clear in his view that such language does not belong in literature and carries no stylistic worth. For him morality and style inform one another, and thus Nettement establishes an important precedent in the realm of linguistic prescriptivism that his contemporaries develop further in regard to serial literature, as well as its morality, use of slang language, and global influence.

While Nettement stands against the production of serial novels, and especially the use of slang, some critics did not completely condemn the circulation of serialized literature among a growing reading public. On October 29, 1844, diplomat and writer Arthur de Gobineau published his "Essays of Critique. *Esther, Splendor and Miseries of Courtesans*, by Mr. Balzac" (Essais de critique. *Esther, Splendeur et misères des courtisanes*, par M. Balzac) in *Le Commerce*. At the beginning of his argument, Gobineau acknowledges the changes taking place within the literary world and suggests that it is time to accept them "since clamors of critiques could not stop the triumphs of this new arrival."[40] He states further that the democratization of reading is not solely the product of mediocre literature, but rather that this expresses a desire for both education and truth:

> Today, the number of readers has grown inordinately. Everyone reads and wants to read a lot [. . .]. This thirst for reading does not have for one sole motive an inert curiosity; Certainly it is the desire to learn that hides itself underneath, and the need no less strong to pursue the confirmation of ideas that preoccupy the mass of our population today.[41]

The readers Gobineau refers to made up a portion of the population that was not well-educated due to their socioeconomic status, and who were therefore more susceptible to false ideas. Nevertheless, the undiscerning reader, while still vulnerable, can use this low-quality literature to develop their taste for more sophisticated works. Therefore, instead of interpreting the democratization of readers as an infringement on bourgeois territory, Gobineau presents it as a latent craving for social enlightenment as well as an opportunity for the lower classes to undergo social refinement. According to Gobineau, for this portion of the population that lacks discipline and cannot appreciate great literary works due to their child-like ignorance, the serialized novel functions as an intermediate literature that helps them to become more intellectually evolved. Therefore, through the use of fiction, science can slowly be introduced to these "child readers" (*lecteurs enfants*) without scaring them off:

> Add to this that a people sidelined is very voluntarily a child that throws away the book when the subject becomes too serious, and boredom stems from that. The serialized novel thus plays, in some ways, in this moment of our social existence, the role of perfected alphabet book and embellished in engraved images. There will come a day, perhaps, where education will come to an end; so these elementary books will be rejected with disdain; one will no longer regret their faults, because one will not longer need their qualities, and they will have filled their office which was to initiate gently into the world a multitude of ideas up

until then profane, and became avid probably to enter further before the temple, and to arrive to the veritable sanctuary.[42]

This intermediary role of the serialized novel, however, according to Gobineau, will inevitably render the genre obsolete as elitist ideology begins to heal the lower classes that have been viewed as less intellectually evolved, and therefore infantilized for their literary preferences. For Gobineau, then, the democratization of education will also help to cure the public of this vulgar pastime of reading serial novels and open their eyes to quality writing instead. Notably, his use of religious imagery, "temple" and "veritable sanctuary," in the last sentence highlights the strong moral connotations associated with different genres of literature of the period. For those who have been enlightened, "true" literature resides on high, both socially and morally. The use of such metaphors suggests that a certain conversion process must first take place, and that there exists a "chosen people" who can deem precisely what is "good" literature in terms of its aesthetic quality and moral nature. For Gobineau, the critique of the serialized novel can be replaced by praise; in fact, in addition to guiding the masses to better reading material, he asserts that another benefit is the development of moral soundness.

After his claims on the long-term effects of reader preferences, Gobineau delves into an analysis of Balzac's character, the courtesan, Esther, from *Splendors*. Because of Esther's own conversion process as a "courtesan purified by love" (*courtisane purifiée par l'amour*), Gobineau believes that such a positive portrayal of a prostitute can have a redemptive effect on readers, inspiring them to engage in philanthropic work in order to save certain women.[43] Although Gobineau advocates the educational and cultural advantages of reading serialized literature, his defense nevertheless masks an underlying motive to eventually eradicate it.[44] He does not support the value of this genre in and of itself but rather seeks to accept the current situation, while drawing what possible good may come from it in an attempt to preserve the dominant ideology while simultaneously destroying the serialized novel's promotion of lower-class values. Despite his overall disapproval, Gobineau's argument contains a drastically different tone from that of Nettement and Sainte-Beuve's concerning industrial literature. Gobineau does not deny the changes taking place in the literary world, but rather relies on the hope that the popularity of serial novels is only a temporary phenomenon. Nonetheless, Gobineau's recognition of its advantages, such as acting as a gateway literature to uneducated classes as well as a platform to encourage philanthropy, reveals a slight undoing of many of the all-condemning critiques on the "so-called" merits of serialized literature that had circulated before.

In terms of the serial novel's use of criminal language, perhaps the most notable back-and-forth debate to take place on the merits of slang occurred between the senator Baron Benoît-Marie Chapuys-Montlaville and writer-journalist Louis Desnoyers in 1847. In 1843, 1845, and 1847, the Baron Chapuys-Montlaville gave three different discourses at the Chamber of Deputies. In his critique of serial novels, Chapuys-Montlaville called for the elimination of tax stamps on periodicals stating that due to these burdensome taxes, newspapers were turning to serial novels to stay afloat. In terms of language, Chapuys-Montlaville posits slang as a "mutilation" of this "beautiful French language" (*belle langue française*):

> This French language, so beautiful in its simplicity, so clear, so well organized, the language of works of art of the human spirit, that of science and diplomacy, this language destined perhaps to become universal, how is it treated by these romantic adventurers? [. . .] [O]ne disrupts it, one exaggerates it, one adds new words, sonorous, but empty, and without respect for public modesty, one tries to introduce it into the dictionary of prison slang. It is the same with literature as with language: taste gets lost, classical traditions disappear, and one hears veritable princes of French intelligence misspeak. One mocks Racine and Molière, and one debases the old glory of our literature.[45]

Chapuys-Montlaville's anti-slang stance reflects elitist ideology on literary languages that was deeply entrenched in French culture. As sociolinguist Deborah Cameron notes with regard to prescriptivism, which generally refers to "those forms that are most conservative, elitist and authoritarian," those who have "mastered" linguistic norms (all of which are arbitrary) "often contribute to a circle of exclusion and intimidation, as those who have mastered a particular practice use it in turn to intimidate others," especially with regards to writers, linguists, and literary critics.[46] While critics such as Nettement and Chapuys-Montlaville certainly engaged in good old-fashioned prescriptivism, all of the aforementioned nineteenth-century critics also engage in what Cameron terms "verbal hygiene," or the attempt to establish a kind of linguistic "norm" about "how language ought to work."[47] Linguistic normativity could take several forms: it could be the elimination of certain speech practices or words like slang, or it could be the laissez-faire attitude of letting language "be" without trying to purge it of undesirable characteristics. Both approaches figure as an attempt to produce a normative ideology in terms of how language should be. In the case of slang, attempts at "controlling" linguistic norms are simultaneously attempts at "controlling" a certain social type (the criminal and working classes) as well as their linguistic and moral infiltration into upper-class domains (whether it be artistic or political ones). In contrast, rules on correct grammar and punctuation usage can serve as an overarching norm with regards to *all* speakers. While these speech practices can index upper-class, educated men, women, or children, correct grammar and punctuation are not simply the speech practices of a particular type but are, in theory, the standard for all types. Slang, however, in the first half of the nineteenth century, was the language of only the dangerous classes, and thus never the linguistic standard.

Critics of serialized literature positioned themselves as authorities on literary standards and language, thus engaging in and feeding a "circle of exclusion and intimidation."[48] Part of the need to publicly denounce the immoral content within work containing criminal language stems from the development of an additional "circle of exclusion and intimidation," one in which lax standards and criminal codes abounded within the sacred literary space of upper-class writers. Whether or not the slang that French writers appropriated was authentic, the fact remains that the upper classes were both "excluded" and "intimidated" by the dangerous classes and their ability to communicate in secret. In this sense, the pen that writers such as Sue, Balzac, Hugo, and Vidocq wielded was far more threatening than the actual slang speakers who were not even able to write their own language. The arguments that critics such as Chapuys-Montlaville and Nettement present are therefore twofold: first, they attack the slang speakers (prostitutes, criminals, workers) who really exist, but who further exist as part of a collective imaginary (and are thus mainly constructions in ways similar to how Kalifa discusses the criminal underworld). Second, the critics attack the writers who gave voice to these social deviants as they were contributing to the ostensible elimination of France's literary and linguistic glory, an act which reflects much larger fears concerning France's power in a global context. In order to combat both concerns, upper-class critics waged a war on undesirable language through the elimination of nonstandard codes and dialects therefore creating an illusion of control over their perceived artistic domains such as literature, over lower-class bodies, and ultimately, over the sociopolitical trajectory of the French nation-state.

In response to the critiques of Chapuys-Montlaville, writer-journalist Louis Desnoyers issued counter-responses that appeared September 1847, in *Le Siècle*, a political and literary newspaper that promoted French republicanism. Concerning language, Desnoyers attempts to broaden the definition of slang in order to neutralize the negative connotations associated with the word. He further accuses Chapuys-Montlaville of using his own slang in the form of political jargon.[49] Desnoyer's last installment on September 29, 1847, consistently pokes fun of Chapuys-Montlaville's use of this "beautiful French language" in order to reveal his opponent's own linguistic imperfections. When Chapuys-Montlaville blames serial novels for the demise of bookstores, stating that "good books" can no longer be found there apart from "a few eminent works" (*quelques ouvrages éminents*), Desnoyers accuses the baron of being wholly unaware of the slew of excellent writers to appear in the last fifty years such as Chateaubriand, Lamartine, Dumas, Hugo, and George Sand, among others.[50] Chapuy-Montlaville's lax usage of the qualifier "a few" to describe the books that are reader-worthy provides Desnoyers with a second means of attacking his opponent's own less-than-perfect use of French. Albeit a stretch in comparison to the transgressive nature of slang expressions, at the very least, Desnoyers nevertheless makes it clear that members from all class milieus speak an imperfect French that can contain jargon. His added mention of sixteen contemporary writers and politicians who experienced success in their respective lifetimes is Desnoyers' attempt to present early nineteenth-century works as works of value precisely due to their popularity—whatever the reasons for their popularity, these writers had an impact on the evolution of French literature and politics. Desnoyers tries to defuse his opponent's attack by suggesting that the appearance of these new words of slang are not as threatening as they appear: they are either merely fleeting, new expressions or useful acquisitions. Thus, to neutralize slang's negative connotations, Desnoyers avoids any reference to the prison slang that Chapuys-Montlaville explicitly mentions, opting instead to spin his own response to be one that favors both variety and creativity, while, at the same time, undermining his opponent's idealized vision of pre-Revolutionary French literature.

Attempts at abating the perceptions of slang as harmful through the presentation of various paradigm shifts regarding language and literature thus becomes Desnoyers' main rhetorical strategy. Within the larger debate on serialized literature, he stands out as one of the few who is wholly in defense of its production and circulation. Whether motivated by his own interests as literary director of *Le Siècle* to promote the publication of serial novels, or by a personal belief on the merits of contemporary fiction, Desnoyers nevertheless presents an interesting contrast to his fellow critics. Although, given his profession, Desnoyers' defense obviously contains economic motivations, it still represents a slow unraveling of French literary standards through public attempts at redefining what is literature. Desnoyers's sardonic approach seeks to reorient the mind of the reader and those of his opponents: by positing slang as a jargon, as in a set of technical terms that circulate among a closed group of people, as opposed to a criminal language, Desnoyers not only extracts the negative social characteristics associated with slang but also effectively evacuates any underlying moral associations.

SOCIAL TYPES AND THE SLANG SPEAKER

The use of class distinctions (the dangerous classes, the working classes, the common people, and the bourgeoisie) by critics within the debates surrounding deviant bodies and dangerous language reveals how a nineteenth-century public clung to a kind of eighteenth-century typology in order to feel more in control of the political, social, and urban instability plaguing the nineteenth century.[51] Ironically, the efforts to separate classes neatly into categories evolved into a social mixing of the working and dangerous classes, which could even be set separately within class categories themselves. As Kalifa argues in terms of crime fiction of the nineteenth century, writers established a basic sociology between the lower and upper classes in order to better highlight their opposition and tension. In addition to the distinctions made between the lower and upper classes, the seemingly simple categorization and opposition between the elites (*les élites*) and the criminal classes (*la pègre*) became even more polarized through their association with specific regions of the urban topography.[52] The wealthy could be found in the most luxurious districts of Paris, while criminal foes haunted the city's subterranean network of catacombs and sewers, as well as the aboveground bars, brothels, poorhouses, and prisons. Social types of the nineteenth century were not only assigned to wide-sweeping categories, they were also simultaneously confined and defined by their geographical dwelling. Consequently, such expansive social classifications created not less but rather increasing, social and moral ambiguity.[53]

In actuality, these social categories were, of course, much more nuanced, as well as risked being conflated. Instead of one "working class" (*classe ouvrière*) that existed in the nineteenth century, Jean-Michel Gourden states there existed several "working classes" (*classes ouvrières*) that consisted of a wide range of workers, including artisans that made up their own internal hierarchy. The dawn of the Industrial Revolution in France, originally a product of eighteenth-century England, had seen the replacement of men by machines. With the establishment of factories came inhumane work conditions, long hours, and the expectation that factory workers were forced to carry out their duties in sync with the machines themselves; soon enough these "laborious classes, became 'dangerous classes,' they haunted the city."[54] This social breakdown between the criminal and working classes surfaced in both fiction and nonfiction, mainly through the positioning of slang as the language of both classes as well as from the propensity of criminal characters in novels to dress as workers. For example, at the beginning of *Mysteries*, Sue presents slang speaker, Rodolphe, dressed as a fan painter. Similarly, *Les Misérables*' Marius spots former convict Jean Valjean dressed as a worker[55] and several times throughout the narrative, Hugo makes reference to Valjean's workers' clothes.[56] When Valjean arrives at Montreuil-sur-Mer as Father Madeleine, the narrator states that "his clothes, manners, and turn of phrase were those of a mere laborer,"[57] and near the novel's end, a sickly Valjean musters up the strength to don his "old workeringman's gear."[58] Hugo's Éponine, the girl of the people par excellence, dons workers clothes as well; this representation functions to give Éponine a certain mobility within the narrative, and given her family's criminal dealings as well as her own tendencies to hustle and manipulate other characters, her clothing further conflates the line between criminal and worker.[59] As Louis Chevalier notes with regards to Balzac's oeuvre, over time

> criminality was now described [. . .] as no longer merely an appanage of those giants of crime to whom Balzac devoted his main attention, but an emanation from the popular masses as a whole; not something exceptional, but something ordinary and genuinely social.[60]

Within the literary realm, French writers thus began to render their portrayals of criminals and criminal activity much more socially ambiguous: linguistically—and morally—speaking, the class lines became blurred between criminals and workers; however, in general, a lower social status still meant a predisposition to crime, and therefore to speaking slang as well.

Similarly, the bourgeoisie was just as difficult to define. In his discourse presented to the Chamber of Deputies in 1847, French politician Louis-Antoine Garnier-Pagès acknowledged the complexities in pinpointing who was bourgeois, stating that even those of the bourgeoisie could not identify themselves as such:

> The representatives of the bourgeoisie knew themselves as bourgeois, the majority of them however would not have had the idea to present themselves as such and no one would have been able to neither count the bourgeoisie nor to characterize the bourgeoisie.[61]

Criminals and workers were therefore not the only social classes to face conflation. As Adeline Daumard notes, the petite bourgeoisie was often mistaken for the common people (*le peuple*) and vice versa. The difference, according to Daumard, could be found in the quality of their life; and the working classes should be more fittingly referred to as the working-class bourgeoisie (*bourgeoisie populaire*) due to the instability of their resources.[62] David Martens discusses further the ambiguity of the noble class following the Revolution stating that "[I]n the nineteenth century, in France, the nobility seems, certainly, a thing of the past, but of a past which continues to haunt the present as a long-lasting concern."[63] Whether bourgeois, criminal, or working class, attempts at establishing concrete social categories increasingly obscured class lines, while nevertheless widening the possibilities within these broader categorizations. Literature, especially serial novels, provided the ultimate medium for diffusing such social representations that were comprised of key characteristics that soon became both staples and indicators of class status. In the case of the criminal characters, their slang and body language, and the public's newfound exposure to these via newspapers led to the iconicization of this character type. However, over time, the boundary between criminal and working class began to dissolve, which eventually established new collective ideologies concerning the use of slang and its speakers.

SLANG SPEAKERS AND LITERACY

Within these critical debates on slang in nineteenth-century-serialized novels, there exist clear indexical relationships between language and literary genre as well as a variety of social characteristics that lend insight into the creation of a collective societal fear of the "dangerous classes." Moreover, fears about the susceptibility of certain readers (the working class and women) to the novels' immoral content and language prompted further concerns. Despite such warnings from critics, however, these works were popular and in high demand. In terms of a relation between morality and literacy in nineteenth-century France, A.R. Gillis discusses the correlation between literacy rates and crime. In a study based on data from the "General Committee of Administration on Criminal Justice" (*Comité général de l'administration de la justice criminelle*) and the *Annuaire Statistique* from 1856 to 1914, Gillis found that in spite of the rise of public education in France, formal schooling did not have a desired impact on crime rates. In fact, Gillis discovered that "crime is substantially reduced by including literacy in the equations."[64] At the onset of the French Revolution, less than 50 percent of men and 27 percent of women possessed functional literacy.[65] By the late-nineteenth century's drastic reforms in public schooling, in addition to the rise of print culture and the mass production of cheaper reads, the majority of men and women had the ability to (at least) sign their names to official documents.[66] Even before the Revolution of 1789, urban areas had higher literacy rates than provincial ones, and one could also establish then a positive correlation between an advanced level of literacy (the ability to read and write in Standard French) and a person's social and professional status. From 1879 to 1880, Louis Maggiolo, the overseer of the Academy of Nancy, conducted a study on literacy with the help of nearly 16,000 instructors across the country. Through the tallying of signed marriage contracts, Maggiolo proposed a physical division of France that separated it into two regions, with the north and east being more literate than the south and west. However, according to Lyons, "[t]his simple dichotomy [. . .] tended to ignore the urban, literate Midi, the southern crescent, already mentioned, which ran from Bordeaux to the Mediterranean and up the Rhône valley."[67]

Although Maggiolo's study tends to be overly reductive, his attempt to trace literacy rates geographically in the late-nineteenth century echoes a similar desire of lexicographers to map the geographical locations of slang speakers.

Nevertheless, in nineteenth-century France most working-class men and women did not possess the advanced reading and writing skills that would allow them to read and/or write unassisted. Those who came from a typically illiterate class milieu were better versed in the oral traditions of the time that had evolved over the nineteenth century. In the late eighteenth and early nineteenth century, the "winter vigil" (*veillée d'hiver*) was a common practice in rural areas, occurring in the evening after completing the day's work. While there were variations of this practice, in general, the vigil contained the same formulaic elements: following the day's work, the practical need for light and warmth motivated a gathering of community members, typically in a barn or stable, which included storytelling, dancing, and courtship activities, although not necessarily all three.[68] According to Lyons, since these were communities rooted in an oral tradition, the information on the vigil comes principally from clerical and personal records. In the nineteenth century, clergymen, however, condemned this practice as "immoral" in an effort to maintain their own political power within the community, creating propaganda that branded the vigil as a kind of communal orgy where one could indulge in alcohol and other licentious pursuits. The attempt to completely eradicate the practice did affect its longevity, however, and although the winter vigil faded out by the end of the nineteenth century as efforts to suppress it took effect and the emergence of the café-cabaret gained popularity among the working class, the vigil is one of the many oral traditions that characterized rural, working-class culture. The Catholic Church's condemnation of the practice reveals how the unrestrained nature of popular, oral cultures threatened the reinforcement of bourgeois ideology; thus, these were traditions that needed to be harnessed and controlled in order to maintain existing ideological state apparatuses, such as the Church and the French Academy, as well as the standard of civic order.

Gillis notes that the boom in literacy rates during the nineteenth century were due partly to the establishment of public education, especially between 1836 and 1886 when France experienced huge population increases. This rapid rise in population deepened the gap between those who were educated and those who were not, having severe social effects on the minority:

> [I]lliteracy and the absence of formal education would have limited not only individuals' capacity to interact with others, especially in organized contexts but their level of employability as well. The disadvantages of illiteracy would have become both concentrated and intensified in this subpopulation.[69]

The widening of the literacy gap suggests a greater disposition toward violent crimes for the illiterate, as this gap not only rendered them less employable but also significantly diminished their social status in the eyes of others therefore alienating them even more. Similar to speech practices, the ability to read and write contributes to what Bourdieu refers to as a "system of social differences which are both classified and classifying, ranked and ranking, [and] mark those who appropriate them."[70]

The statistics presented by Gillis assert that the hardened criminals and corrupted members of the working classes were not the primary readers of serialized literature. Judith Lyon-Caen points out that even with the reduction in newspaper subscription prices, typically, those who could afford them were of higher social strata:

> The newspaper is a costly entity, that only a tiny minority can acquire [. . .]. 40 francs rests a considerable sum, when a primary school teacher makes 500 francs a year, a low-grade clerk or a qualified worker in Paris between 800 and 1000 francs.[71]

Anthony Glinoer attempts to define the readership of industrial literature as *le peuple* (the common people):

> And yet, of whom or of what does one speak of around 1830 when it is no longer a question of 'People' as an allegory but of 'people' as a category of readers? Essentially, of the working, urban middle classes, if not Parisian: the doormen and doorwomen, maids, office employees, and members of all professions who assume a permanent contact with privileged social groups. The proletariat, the peasantry, and even the artisans are almost nearly completely absent from collective representations of the literary readership, for the good and simple reason that the majority of them are illiterate.[72]

Glinoer's notion that the working classes, including artisans and peasants, could not read and therefore were not included in this nebulous readership known as *le peuple* serves to define them socially as prone to crime, especially when one considers Gillis' findings. This confusion between social boundaries when referring to the dangerous class becomes even more understandable if one considers the gaps and limitations of certain social groups. From a linguistic point-of-view, there is a web of indexical complexity that functions in parallel with a social conflagration between social status, literacy, and criminality. In the first half of the nineteenth century, then, slang as the language of criminals could now connote a whole host of people from differing class backgrounds. The slang speaker could be a worker or a cutthroat criminal roaming the streets of Paris. This conflation of the working classes with the dangerous class not only inspired collective fears regarding who the slang speaker may be, but it also further reveals how a language became representative of the deeper fears surrounding the increasing number of new and "foreign" inhabitants within the city.

This is not to say that serial novels were completely inaccessible to minority readers. Aside from the potentially immoral motivations behind its production, the rate at which newspapers and publishing houses produced popular literature meant a lack of control over who read this literature, as well as when and how it circulated. Its successful reception among readers therefore underscores the potential danger of a passive consumer as well as a loss of agency. In addition to the criminal and working classes, there was also a psychological stereotyping that occurred as well about readers of recreational literature, especially with readers of the serialized novel. Those readers were thought to be both submissive and infantile in nature; they could neither judge for themselves quality literature nor did they possess the capacity to analyze the content of what they read. In the eyes of critics, then, this readership would just blindly adhere to whatever ideology was being touted, while also presenting as a potential source of civil unrest.

For the Catholic Church, as well as the bourgeois public, in addition to lacking basic reading and writing skills, the working classes (and women) lacked the capacity to distinguish good books from bad. Starting with the Bourbon Restoration in 1814, the desire of the bourgeoisie and the Catholic Church to control what and how the working classes and women read intensified all the way through the Third Republic. The principal fear was that an "incorrect" reading could breed revolutionaries, and thus the Church ran an aggressive campaign to combat the circulation of bad books as well as anti-Christian Enlightenment thought, taking extreme measures throughout France, such as *auto-da-fé*.[73] The low literacy rates and attempts to thwart the circulation of unfavorable texts, however, did not mean that neither workers nor women managed to acquire reading and writing skills. These minority readerships were typically self-taught with the help of family or community members:

> The education of the autodidact was, by definition, intermittent and incomplete, constantly sacrificed to the family's economic needs. Erratic attendance made it difficult for teachers to impart learning as a cumulative process. Formal schooling was far less important for the apprentice reader than the informal networks of relatives, neighbours, priests, and benevolent employers who took time to assist the debutant reader. The home and the local community remained important sources of the educational process.[74]

The minority of working-class intellectuals who could read and write, thanks to informal learning methods, familiarized themselves with the canonical literature of the time.[75] As Christine Haynes explores, the transformation of the publishing industry in nineteenth-century France directly affected readers. Specifically, Haynes cites the law of 1866, which allowed publishers to maintain the rights of a writer's work fifty years after the writer's death.[76] She explains that this law "initiated a new 'high monopoly' regime" since publishers tended to produce more costly editions of novels; this meant that the lower classes could only afford "cheap reprints of classic texts."[77] However, their consumption and imitation of traditionally "bourgeois" literature did not affect their class identity. Although they depended culturally and intellectually on the bourgeoisie, the lower classes remained committed to their own social milieu, while nevertheless expressing a selectiveness and introspection in terms of the kinds of literature they consumed. As a matter of fact, they tended to consume readings that were less recreational and more socialist and political in nature:

> But what did other autodidacts read in their dedicated pursuit of self-culture? To some extent, they accepted advice to concentrate on utilitarian reading, together with knowledge of uplifting canonical works. Many of them felt that purely recreational fiction was a waste of their time. Their responses to self-improving literature, however, were not uniform. Although they often read the same books, it is not always possible to predict what they thought of them. Workers conducted their own dialogue with the texts they acquired, and searched for answers to problems arising from their own experience of life and work.[78]

There were many formal and informal means from which these underrepresented readers benefited.[79] The founding of two working-class newspapers *La Ruche populaire* (1839) and *L'Atelier* (1840–1850) signals a literary demand for and by the working classes; moreover, the emergence of reading rooms in the 1820s, and even informal methods such as "paper-passing," or when a reader finished their newspaper, they simply "passed" it along, exposed this minority readership to literature that was more recreational than functional. The existence of reading rooms in cities and towns contributed to the widespread circulation of books and newspapers, and although the content varied depending on the city or town, it did offer passers-by with the opportunity to read. According to Françoise Parent-Lardeur, the newspaper industry played a significant role in the development of the reading room since subscriptions were costly, while nevertheless in high demand by readers. As a result, newspaper circulations in France increased as more and more reading rooms appeared:

> It is certain, however, that the most solidly established reading rooms, as with the most precarious ones, assured along with cafés a public diffusion of the press. Through them, the newspaper infiltrated every neighborhood.[80]

Others collectively shared a subscription in order to afford the fees.[81] In terms of public libraries, their main function until the late nineteenth century was to preserve books, rather than to lend them to the public, an act that seldom occurred, and especially not to readers of a lower social milieu.

While bourgeois and Catholic critics feared for the passive, uneducated worker, these working-class intellectuals, in a kind of reverse cultural appropriation, were changing the face of France's reading public as well as its literature. As Christopher Prendergast points out:

> Indeed a large number of people probably had no direct acquaintance with [*The Mysteries of Paris*] itself, either as active readers or passive listeners, but had heard it talked about in the hum of daily urban conversation, and themselves came to form opinions of its significance [for instance, how many of Sue's semi-literate correspondents appealing for help had actually read the novel?].[82]

While they were perhaps not the intended readership, French writers could not ignore the positive reception from a growing working-class public, and therefore those writers (such as Sue) began to mold their narratives according to the demands of this new demographic. Curiously, a romanticized vision of the common people started to surface in literary works that were still largely intended for a literate, bourgeois, population such as *Les Misérables*, and even historical works like Jules Michelet's *The People* (*Le Peuple*, 1846).

It was not until the late nineteenth century that most of the working classes and women acquired advanced literacy. This shift was due mainly to reforms in education that came about in the second half of the nineteenth century. Also, in 1892, the ten-hour workday came into effect, which permitted the worker more time for other leisurely pursuits such as reading. Women further gained more social mobility as they entered the white-collar workforce, an opportunity that encouraged the development of their reading and writing skills. Finally, the reformative measures that took place in the late nineteenth century introduced a new market of readers that opened the doors for a literature that was actually "for and by the people."

However, during the first half of the nineteenth century this readership had yet to reach full democratization, as only a small percentage of the lower classes possessed the ability to sign their name, and an even smaller number could demonstrate advanced reading and writing skills. Despite the weak literacy rates among the working classes and women, social minorities were still exposed to successful serialized literature of the times. The reading rooms, collective readings, paper-passing, and even overhearing public discussions on popular works such as *The Mysteries of Paris* did not leave the lower classes completely in the dark. In fact, the democratization of literature was so hotly contested in the *querelle du roman-feuilleton* precisely because more people from a variety of backgrounds were participating in the same literary experience. Furthermore, this expanded exposure to embodied and spoken slang as a criminal language to audiences of all literacy levels meant that iconization could occur at slang's first indexical order. Even though the literary experience was changing due to the industrial innovations that allowed for the production and distribution of a greater volume of works, which, in turn, transformed the objectives of some writers from art to that of monetary gain, what is most particular about reading culture in the nineteenth century is that it was a collective, social experience. The controversies surrounding serial novels and slang in literature thus speak to a larger phenomenon: that of a collective of readers from all social milieus who participated in the same narrative from which they received specific ideas about the other classes. The public critical discussions on the merits of literary format and content not only presented themselves as a means of social containment and control, but they also work to expand and include members of the lower classes both on and off the page. Consequently, a growing sphere of worker-poets such as Charles Poncy, Jules Vinçard, Savinien Lapointe, in addition to others, began to develop within popular culture.[83] And despite efforts to categorize, the mixing of the criminal and working classes in fiction and nonfiction increasingly obscured class boundaries, thus allowing for more social expansion.

SLANG AND THE EXPANSION OF IDENTITY

The critical discourses discussed in this chapter surrounding the serialized novel and its use of slang in nineteenth-century France serve as authoritative texts that both reinforced and perpetuated collective ideas about criminals and criminal language. In the 1840s, when these polemics took place, slang simultaneously signified a specific social class—the "dangerous" class, which referred mainly to criminals, but could also include working-class types. The pejorative representation and conflation of criminals and working-class types worked to create a literary space, or slum, that functioned as a site of cultural hybridity, as well as cultural appropriation, creating both social and artistic possibilities for marginalized persons from the encounter between the dominant and dominated classes. The critiques of slang in the press highlight the ways in which this dangerous language existed within the context of class typology, and therefore moral typology. While attempts at social categorization were made on the part of writers, especially in the first half of the nineteenth century, these classifications could never adequately function as an effective way to socially harness the lower classes. Nonetheless, slang language became a particularly significant "marker" of social and moral deviance, and through its exposure to a bourgeois public, this anti-language also gradually climbed the ranks in terms of social importance—in other words, to speak criminal slang was to be against the betterment of society.

Therefore, through their public discourse, critics and politicians could seemingly educate a collective army of readers to avoid the use of slang because it was not only detrimental to an individual's morality, but to the continued success of the nation as well. In terms of Bourdieu's theory of cultural capital, the symbolic power of language and its ability to signal social status, as well as capital, not only becomes even more apparent in the debates on slang and its literary use in nineteenth-century France but also reveals a linguistic shift that was taking place. Slang, and its mounting popularity in literary works, thus signal a breakdown in the rigid prescriptivism of the past, while perhaps a growing collective desire for greater social fluidity, or democracy, via language.

For instance, Vidocq's works advertised a certain authenticity as well as the possibility of social mobility through writing. Additionally, the popularity of certain works among the working classes, such as *Mysteries*, not only signaled to writers that their readership extended beyond their own social circle, but that minorities were making their own attempts at literary production. The worker-poets (*les poètes ouvriers*), a small minority that was often excluded among their peers, wrote poems that were less canonical and more "an extension of the oral culture which they inherited."[84] Autobiographies by workers, and later by demimondaines

> fulfilled an inner need. Autobiography was a step in the process of defining one's identity, both as an individual and as a member of a group or class. The act of writing itself brought greater self-knowledge and self-assertion.[85]

I would add, here, that their act of writing, albeit by a small portion of the working classes, also brought them greater social validation throughout the course of the nineteenth century, something which did not become fully visible until the twentieth century.

Leaving questions of authenticity behind, whether or not these unconventional writers, such as Vidocq, actually wrote their own works, the fact that a minority of people claimed that they were from a lower social stratum and still pursued literary endeavors signaled a larger shift in notions of authorship, readership, and literature itself. As Kalifa asserts, the images of criminals and their world created as a result "an immense intertext [. . .] of which the repetition creates a culture and a community of readers at the same time."[86] Texts deemed inferior because of their format and content were the slums of the literary world, while composed of a composite of cultures that formed the figure of the social lowlife. And like the actual physical slums of the bustling metropolis, the serialized novel was a site the upper class could frequent as well as appropriate in the name of a greater social and moral good. However, it was also a site in which fluid identities were possible, including for the writer. This significant debate on the serialized novel in the first half of the nineteenth century thus sets up the foundation for writers in the second half of the century to give greater consideration to the meaning of slang and its aesthetic value, especially as metaphor.

NOTES

1. *Depuis que j'ai publié des Mémoires, il est venu chez moi jusqu'à des grammairiens pour m'offrir de m'apprendre le français, à condition que je leur enseignerais l'argot. Peut-être étaient-ce des philologues? Quoi qu'il en soit, l'érudit vint chez moi; que me voulait-il?* (Vidocq, *Mémoires*, 512)
2. Ibid., 513.
3. Kira Hall and Ayden Parish explain that indexes differ from icons in that "indexical links are based in existential connections, rather than arbitrary cultural convention (*symbol*) or similarity of qualities *(icon)*" (2).
4. Johnstone, "Locating Language," 32.
5. Balibar and LaPorte, *Le français national*, 36.
6. "*[D]'une part expliquer aux habitants de la campagne le sens des lois nouvelles dans une langue connue d'eux—c'est-à-dire traduire; d'autre part élaborer une politique d'instruction politique*" (De Certeau et al., 12).
7. Lodge, *A Sociolinguistic History*, 101.
8. "*Deux champs d'analyse: l'un regarde la langue, qui est au XVIIIe siècle peinture de la société [questions 1 à 28]; l'autre, complémentaire, a pour objet l'instruction et son envers, les préjugés [questions 31–37 et 38–40]*" (De Certeau et al., 18).
9. *C'est une caractéristique propre de la révolution bourgeoise française de n'avoir pu faire triompher ses droits et ses aspirations de classe sans que les autres classes opprimées reconnaissent ces droits et ces aspirations comme les leurs. En d'autres termes, et sans qu'elle cesse pour autant d'être bourgeoise, la révolution bourgeoise française ne s'est pas faite au nom de la bourgeoisie, mais au nom du peuple. Or c'est précisément cette domination générale réalisée au nom des droits généraux de la société qui est en jeu dans l'intérêt porté par la bourgeoisie à la question linguistique, intérêt représenté au niveau politique dans une politique bourgeoise de la langue.* (Balibar and LaPorte, 84–85)
10. Emsley, "A Typology of Nineteenth-Century Police," 36.
11. *[Le crime dans les médias différents] permet bien sûr de donner au crime accès et visibilité sociale, mais il contribue aussi à diffuser un imaginaire homogène de la norme, des perceptions communes et partagées du tolérable et de l'intolérable [. . .]. Produit social, le crime ne se définit qu'en fonction des règles, des valeurs et des sentiments collectifs que se donne une société.* (Kalifa, *Crime et culture*, 10)
12. Agha, *Language and Social Relations*, 67.
13. Lodge, *A Sociolinguistic History*, 122.

14. *"[L]e ressassement des mêmes nouvelles, jour après jour, semble plonger le lecteur du journal dans la réalité même des choses, en sorte qu'il finit par confondre le monde réel, évidemment inconnaissable, et le monde représenté"* (Vaillant, 17).

15. *Le public—celui d'Eugène Sue, par exemple—est ainsi immergé dans un univers où la représentation médiatisée du réel et la fiction narrative sont inextricablement mêlées et constituent ensemble une sorte de seconde nature qui, en retour, prédétermine son rapport au monde et dans laquelle nous sommes désormais tous plongés.* (Ibid., 20)

16. *"Des topiques et des 'thèmes' qui circulent d'un secteur à l'autre, mais aussi des particularités et des originalités, sources d'un 'pas encore dit' qui demeurerait indicible s'il ne pouvait émerger comme formes distinctives au sein de la totalité"* (Angenot, 2).

17. *"De cette conception du langage, il découle une morale et une philosophie, qui lient étroitement le discours—toute production discursive—à son origine subjective"* (Vaillant, 14).

18. *"Qui sait raconter le monde à ses lecteurs"* (Ibid., 15).

19. "It was the *Journal des débats* which inaugurated this usage in 1800, and the vocation of the serialized novel was reserved for critique for a long time. One finds, in fact, book reviews, summaries of plays, fashion trends, popular science—a mix of old popular culture from almanacs and of 'scholarly' knowledge from reviews" (*Ce fut le* Journal des débats *qui inaugura cet usage, en 1800, et la vocation du feuilleton resta longtemps critique. On y trouve en effet de la critique de livres, des comptes rendus de théâtre, des bulletins de mode, de la vulgarisation scientifique—un mélange de l'ancienne culture populaire des almanachs et de la culture 'savante' des revues* [Dumasy-Queffélec, 5]).

20. *"Un univers polyphonique où se succèdent, et se répondent souvent aussi au moyen de multiples signes de connivence, tous les types de discours [. . .]"* (Thérenty and Vaillant, 97).

21. See Alain Vaillant's "Invention littéraire et culture médiatique au XIXe siècle" in *Culture de masse et culture médiatique en Europe et dans les Amériques 1860-1940*, edited by Jean-Yves Mollier, Jean-François Sirinelli and François Vallotton, PUF, 2006, pp. 11–22.

22. Dumasy-Queffélec, *La Querelle du roman-feuilleton*, 6.

23. Lyon-Caen, "Lecteurs et lectures," 29.

24. Judith Lyon-Caen points out that there were 1,775 postal establishments in France in 1820, 1,975 in 1830, and 3,010 in 1845 (30–31).

25. Lyon-Caen, "Lecteurs et lectures," 31.

26. For Martyn Lyons, mass culture is not synonymous with popular culture. In fact, "[M]ass culture drove out popular culture, borrowing from it, and occasionally absorbing it, but essentially relegating it to a quaint survival in a mass age" (Lyons, *Reading Culture*, 61). Additionally, for Kalifa, the term "mass culture" is riddled with ambiguity: "One does not know if it designates the whole of society or only the working classes, if it indicates an origin or a destination" (*[O]n ne sait si elle désigne l'ensemble de la société ou les seules classes populaires, si elle indique une origine ou une destination* [*La Culture de masse*, 3]). Nonetheless, Kalifa acknowledges the

innovations in the press industry from 1839 onward as the initial entrance into the "Age of the Masses" ([*l'âge des masses*] Ibid., 5).

27. "*[Un] ensemble complexe des règles prescriptives de diversification des dicibles et de cohésion, de coalescence, d'intégration*" (Angenot, 16).

28. Eco, "Rhetoric and Ideology," 560; Even within the narrative, Sue's narrator recognizes the use of a certain plot design in order to keep the storyline interesting and to gratify the reader (Sue, *Mystères*, 362–63; English translation, 373).

29. Eco, "Rhetoric and Ideology," 560–62.

30. *Cette maîtrise du récit s'accompagne souvent de l'effacement des traces trop apparentes d'énonciation. Mieux vaut que les événements se racontent d'eux-mêmes, dans une dynamique fonctionnelle et toute tendue vers l'aval du récit. Évoluant dans un univers idéologique fortement manichéen, les personnages sont souvent réduits à des rôles allégoriques, voire à des concepts anthropomorphisés [le Vengeur, le Mal, la Victime], aptes à prouver l'identification la plus absolue.* (Kalifa, Culture de masse, 35)

31. *Ce que veut le lecteur du journal, ce n'est pas lire un roman, mais* entendre raconter *une histoire par un auteur qui, comme le conteur de salon ou de coin du feu, connaît toutes les techniques pour retenir l'attention: la rapidité du récit, le recours au dialogue, l'ironie ou, au contraire, le pathétique et le spéculaire, etc.* (Thérenty and Vaillant, 106)

32. Glinoer, "Des Éditeurs," 20.

33. "*[i]l faut enfin obtenir qu'un volume se fabrique exactement comme un pain, et se débite comme un pain, qu'il n'y ait d'autre intermédiaire entre un auteur et un consommateur que le libraire*" (Balzac, "De l'état actuel," 667).

34. Glinoer, "Des Éditeurs," 21.

35. "*Une présentation dépourvue de soin, de volumes hâtivement composés [. . .]*" (Ibid., 24).

36. "*Avec nos mœurs électorales, industrielles, tout le monde, une fois au moins dans sa vie, aura eu sa page, son discours, son prospectus, son* toast, *sera* auteur" (Dumasy-Queffélec, 31).

37. Ibid., 41.

38. "*[E]n abaissant l'art, on le rend accessible à tous [. . .] depuis que les conteurs descendent aussi dans la rue, tout le monde a son histoire à conter*" (Ibid., 181).

39. "*Que chacun peut voir de chez soi*" (Nettement, *Études critiques*, 325).

40. "*Puisque les clameurs de la critique n'ont pu arrêter les triomphes de ce nouveau-venu*" (Dumasy-Queffélec, 88).

41. *Aujourd'hui, le nombre des lecteurs s'est démesurément augmenté. Tout le monde lit et veut lire beaucoup [. . .]. Cette soif de lecture n'a pas pour seul mobile une inerte curiosité; bien certainement c'est le désir d'apprendre qui se cache là-dessous, et le besoin non moins vif de poursuivre la confirmation des idées qui préoccupent aujourd'hui la masse de notre population.* (Ibid., 88–89)

42. *Ajoutez à cela qu'un peuple sur les bancs est un enfant très volontaire qui jette le livre lorsque le sujet devient trop grave, et que l'ennui en sort. Le roman-feuilleton joue donc, en quelque sorte, à ce moment de notre existence sociale, le rôle*

d'un abécédaire perfectionné et orné d'images en taille-douce. Il viendra un jour, peut-être, où l'éducation s'achèvera; alors ces livres élémentaires seront rejetés avec mépris; on ne déplorera plus leurs défauts, parce qu'on n'aura plus besoin de leurs qualités, et ils auront rempli leur office qui était d'initier doucement au monde des idées une foule jusque-là profane, et devenue avide probablement d'entrer plus avant dans le temple, et d'arriver au véritable sanctuaire. (Ibid., 89–90)

43. Ibid., 93–94.

44. Other writers, like Gobineau, expressed a similar attitude toward the serialized novel and questioned its longevity. In 1853, writer Hippolyte Castille also adhered to the belief that it acted as an intermediary literature whose utility was fixed as readers evolved intellectually: "The usefulness [of the serialized novel] is not contestable in the past; it formed generations of superficial readers, without a doubt, but which passed the taste and the need of reading within the habits. When the serialized novel goes out or transforms, there will remain a population of readers to whom it will be permitted to offer several ideas [. . .] like laments and almanacs, the serialized novel will have its purpose" (*L'utilité [du roman-feuilleton] n'est pas contestable dans le passé; il a formé des générations de lecteurs superficiels, sans doute, mais qui font passer dans les mœurs le goût et le besoin de la lecture. Quand le roman-feuilleton se sera éteint ou transformé, il restera un peuple de lecteurs à qui il sera permis alors d'offrir quelques idées [. . .] comme les complaintes et les almanachs, le roman-feuilleton aura eu son utilité* [Castille, 333]).

45. *Cette langue française, si belle dans sa simplicité, si claire, si bien ordonnée, la langue des chefs-d'œuvre de l'esprit humain, celle de la science et de la diplomatie, cette langue destinée peut-être à devenir universelle, comment est-elle traitée par ces aventuriers romantiques? [. . .] [O]n la bouleverse, on la surcharge, on ajoute de mots nouveaux, sonores, mais vides, et, sans respect pour la pudeur publique, on essaye d'introduire dans le dictionnaire l'argot du bagne. Il en est de la littérature comme de la langue: le goût se perd, les traditions classiques disparaissent, et on l'entend médire des véritables princes de l'intelligence française. On se moque de Racine et de Molière, et on profane les vieilles gloires de notre littérature.* (Dumasy-Queffélec, 109–10)

46. Cameron, *Verbal Hygiene*, 12.

47. Ibid., 8.

48. Ibid., 12.

49. Dumasy-Queffélec, *La Querelle du roman-feuilleton*, 127.

50. Ibid., 151.

51. Before the emergence of the writer-journalist in the 1820s, writers had placed less emphasis on the realistic depiction of the external world, focusing more on "psychological introspection, on the model of works by Rousseau, Madame de Staël, or Benjamin Constant" (*L'introspection psychologique, sur le modèle des œuvres de Rousseau, de Mme de Staël ou de Benjamin Constant* [Vaillant, 19]). The trend of realist works, notably a reaction to the inventions of photography and film, that coincided with innovations in the press and publishing houses spurred a mélange of attempts at reproducing an objective view of reality in the fiction of French novels in ways that sought to fabricate particular ideas about the people and groups that made

up the bustling metropolis. Indeed, one of the complexities surrounding social and linguistic representation is defining these social categories.

52. Kalifa, *Crime et Culture*, 41–42.

53. This tendency for social generalization on the part of critics and writers plays into the nineteenth-century interest in social "types" and physiologies. As Valérie Stiénon notes, the blurring between medical and social categorizations in the nineteenth century led to medical categorization was even less scientific and more paradigmatic (22–23). Moreover, the "science" behind studying a person's exterior characteristics was further used to define their artistic and/or literary representation (Ibid., 26). The nineteenth century's obsession with reducing people to "types" did not actually fix social categories into place, but instead contributed to an "imaginary reconstruction renewed incessantly. It has to do less with categorizing pre-existing types to give them some order, than to surrender to the creative multiplication of types and of sub-types like as many means of being in the world and being in society" (*reconstruction imaginaire sans cesse renouvelée. Il s'agit moins de classer des types préexistant pour y mettre de l'ordre, que de se livrer à la multiplication créative des types et des sous-types comme autant de modes d'être-au-monde et d'être-en-société* [Ibid., 130]). These social types and sub-types, such as slang speakers, created further a new kind of Otherness that comprised persons of the same nationality and of the same society (Ibid., 260). For Stiénon, the physiologies were less about exploring or controlling the social order, but rather existed to highlight social contrasts that produced a comedic effect, like caricatures (Ibid., 131). However, the act of categorizing and classifying is inherently an act of containment and control through that of ontological definition. As Marie-Ève Thérenty outlines, "The nineteenth century, and particularly the 1820s–1840s, was the great age of taxomony [. . .]. All of these typologies which are in general written by men of letters, allow, by establishing a grammar book of the world, to render it readable" (*Le XIXe siècle, et singulièrement les années 1820–1840, est la grande époque de la taxinomie [. . .]. Toutes ces typologies, qui sont en général écrites par des littérateurs, permettent, en établissant une grammaire du monde, de le rendre lisible* [Thérenty, *Mosaïques*, 186]). Nonetheless, a categorical name contains an endless list of characteristics, both real and imagined, that make up the image of a person or thing; however, this person or thing also exists within the context of a distinct sociohistorical perspective. This, in turn, renders "readable" that which may not be completely apparent. As Thérenty suggests, through typology, writers establish a social grammar that facilitates the recognition of a person's moral distinction in addition to their social one, distinctions that had become distorted in the wake of revolution, urbanization, and industrialization. Early works such as Louis Prudhomme's *Descriptive and Philosophical Journey through Old and New Paris* (*Voyage descriptif et philosophique de l'ancien et du nouveau Paris*, 1814), the collections *Paris or the Book of the One-Hundred and Ones* (*Paris ou le livre des cent-et-un*, 1831–1834), *The French As Portrayed by Themselves* (*Les Français peints par eux-mêmes*, 1840–1842), and *The Devil in Paris* (*Le Diable à Paris*, 1845–1846) attempt to define the cultural, social, and urban atmosphere in order to create a sense of totality and control concerning the constant creation of new social types in the mid of fluctuating political regimes and grand-scale urbanization. These works, known

as "panoramic literature," according to Walter Benjamin, contributed to a collective imaginary vis-à-vis social class: "When the writer gave himself to the market, he was looking around himself like in a panorama. A particular literary genre conserved his initial attempts to orient himself. That is panoramic literature" (*Quand l'écrivain s'était rendu au marché, il regardait autour de lui comme dans un panorama. Un genre littéraire particulier a conservé ses premières tentatives pour s'orienter. C'est une littérature panoramique* [Benjamin, 55]).

54. "*Classes laborieuses, devenues 'classes dangereuses', ils ont hanté la ville*" (Gourden, 6).

55. Hugo, *Les Misérables*, 1002; English translation, 601.

56. Hugo, *Les Misérables*, 1197; English translation, 726.

57. "*Il n'avait que les vêtements, la tournure et le langage d'un ouvrier*" (Hugo, *Les Misérables*, 239; English translation, 135).

58. "*Vieux vêtement d'ouvrier*" (Hugo, *Les Misérables*, 1911; English translation, 1170). Hugo's narrator plays with the origins of Valjean's clothing and even playfully suggests that he stole them from a dead worker (Hugo, *Les Misérables*, 423; English translation, 250).

59. Hugo, *Les Misérables*, 1403, 1540; English translation, 855, 940.

60. Chevalier, *Laboring Classes*, 77.

61. "*Les représentants de la bourgeoisie se savaient bourgeois, la plupart d'entre eux pourtant n'auraient pas eu idée de se présenter comme tels et personne n'aurait été capables de dénombrer les bourgeois ni de caractériser la bourgeoisie*" (qtd. in Daumard, xi).

62. Ibid., 254–55.

63. "*[A]u XIXe siècle, en France, la noblesse semble, certes, chose du passé, mais d'un passé qui continue de hanter le présent à la façon d'un enjeu vivace*" (Martens, 10).

64. Gillis, "Institutional Dynamics," 1312. Gillis acknowledges that other factors such as the final adjustment to the French penal code in 1863, which reduced the severity of some crimes, as well as "[c]hanges in population composition, industrialization, the economy, and general quality of life could reasonably be expected to be correlated with both literacy and crime and contribute to their association" (Ibid., 1316).

65. "Functional literacy" refers to one's capacity to sign an official document. With regards to the acquisition of reading and writing abilities, the major reformative measures included the Guizot Laws of 1833 that mandated primary education for boys in every commune, the Falloux Law of 1850 that mandated primary education for girls in every commune and the Jules Ferry Laws in the 1880s that mandated free, secular primary education for both boys and girls (Lyons, *Readers and Society*, 6–7).

66. Ibid., 1.

67. Lyons, *Reading Culture*, 52.

68. Lyons, *Reading Culture*, 139. The work and storytelling that occurred could also happen simultaneously, not necessarily in succession (Ibid., 143).

69. Gillis, "Institutional Dynamics," 1309.
70. Bourdieu, *Language and Symbolic Power*, 56.
71. *Le journal est un bien cher, que seule une infime minorité peut acquérir [. . .]. 40 francs demeurent une somme considérable, quand un instituteur gagne 500 francs par an, un petit employé ou un ouvrier qualifié à Paris entre 800 et 1 000 francs.* (Lyon-Caen, 30)
72. *Or, de qui et de quoi parle-t-on vers 1830 quand il est question non plus du 'Peuple' comme allégorie mais du 'peuple' comme catégorie de lecteurs? Essentiellement, de la 'bourgeoisie populaire' urbaine, sinon parisienne: les portiers et les portières, les femmes de chambres, les employés de bureau et les membres de toutes les professions qui supposent un contact permanent avec les groupes sociaux privilégiés. Le prolétariat, la paysannerie et même l'artisanat sont à peu près complètement absents des représentations collectives du lectorat littéraire, pour la bonne et simple raison qu'ils sont très majoritairement analphabètes.* (Glinoer, "Classes de textes et littérature industrielle," 9)
73. *Auto-da-fé* is a medieval Spanish term that translates to "act of faith" and refers to the public punishment of a heretic, such as death by burning.
74. Lyons, *Reading Culture*, 113.
75. According to Lyons, working-class intellectuals did not read a lot of fiction, and read mostly classical seventeenth-century literature, eighteenth-century enlightenment philosophy, especially Rousseau and Voltaire, and nineteenth-century writers who were vocal about workers' rights, especially Victor Hugo (Lyons, *Reading Culture*, 125–26). The poetry they produced was also closer to popular song in resemblance: "Their poetry, however, was often an extension of the oral culture which they inherited, and which survived in popular song [. . .]. French worker-poets might prefer local languages which were closer to popular usage [. . .]. Poetry was closer than prose to popular oral tradition, and it found ready outlets in nineteenth-century newspapers" (Ibid., 128).
76. Haynes, *Lost Illusions*, 236.
77. Ibid., 237.
78. Lyons, *Reading Culture*, 125.
79. Advanced literacy rates of workers and women generally came about in a nonconventional fashion, either from autodidacticism or education from clergy or family members. Literacy also varied by profession: "Professional groups such as lawyers and clerics were highly literate and were likely to own their own libraries. Lower down the scale, shopkeepers and craft workers were more literate than domestic servants or unskilled labourers. Well-integrated Parisians tended to have a greater reading ability than recently arrived migrants from the countryside" (Lyons, *Readers and Society*, 5).
80. *"Il est certain, toutefois, que les cabinets de lecture les plus solidement établis, comme les plus précaires, assuraient avec les cafés une diffusion publique de la presse. Par eux, le journal pénétrait dans tous les quartiers"* (Parent-Lardeur, 110).
81. Thérenty and Vaillant, *1836*, 27.
82. Prendergast, *For the People by the People?*, 89–90.

83. For an in-depth study of working-class writers in nineteenth-century France, see Bettina Lerner's, *Inventing the Popular: Printing, Politics, and Poetics*. New York: Routledge, 2018.

84. Lyons, *Reading Culture*, 128.

85. Ibid., 132.

86. "*[U]n immense intertexte [. . .] dont la répétition fonde à la fois une culture et une communauté de lecteurs*" (Kalifa, *Crime et Culture*, 39).

Chapter 4

Slang as the Language of Misery

The thieves' language knows how to yield to the demands of poetry; this poetry, it is true, does not make itself noticed neither by an extreme elegance nor by a richness in rhyme; but, on the other hand, it neither lacks energy nor originality.

—Eugène-François Vidocq, *Les voleurs: physiologie de leurs mœurs et de leur langage* (1836)

(*Le langage des voleurs sait aussi se plier aux exigences de la poésie; cette poésie, il est vrai, ne se fait remarquer ni par une extrême élégance, ni par la richesse de ses rimes; mais, en revanche, elle ne manque ni d'énergie ni d'originalité*)

Prior to 1850, stereotypes of criminals and their use of slang established the first indexical order for its representations in French literature. From a sociolinguistic perspective, slang, as a secret criminal code, was used by writers such as Eugène Sue, Honoré de Balzac, and Eugène François Vidocq in order to render their characterizations of criminals more realistic, while simultaneously reaping literary acclaim and monetary success. As Philippe Dufour explains, the "philological novel" of the nineteenth century included great canonical French novelists such as Stendhal, Balzac, Gustave Flaubert, Victor Hugo, and Émile Zola whose discourse around language sought to uncover unconscious social ideologies within words.[1] Unlike the epistolary novels of the eighteenth century that valorized idiolects, the ethnolinguistic works of these "polyglots," as Dufour so aptly terms the aforementioned writers, "represent a battle of the sociolects" and sought to explain rather than just imitate.² These men, as outlined in chapters 1 through 3 of this book, discarded correct usage of French in favor of an oral language style as "linguistic homogeneity" equaled implausibility, a sign of artistic ineptitude in nineteenth-century France.³

In his earlier works *The Last Day of a Condemned Man* (*Le dernier jour d'un condamné*, 1829) and *The Hunchback of Notre Dame* (*Notre dame de Paris*, 1831), Victor Hugo also included representations of criminal characters that adhered to earlier stereotypes as well as used slang as criminal code. For instance, in *The Last Day of a Condemned Man*, Hugo explores the psychological unraveling of a man twenty-four hours after his being condemned to death. Narrated in the first person, the story focuses on the condemned man's interior thoughts, as well as the criminal characters surrounding him during his time in two Parisian prisons, Bicêtre and Conciergerie. While the use of slang functions as a necessary signifier of the criminal persona in *Last Day*, in this work Hugo notably creates a new application of slang which reflects the misery of a young girl who uses it to sing a lament. Hugo's use of slang in this work does not detract from his main objective, however, because rather than intended as an insider's glimpse into criminal life, *The Last Day of a Condemned Man* is instead a commentary on the death penalty.

Two years after the publication of *Last Day*, in *The Hunchback of Notre Dame* (1831), in Book II, Chapter Six, "The Broken Jug," Hugo presents the medieval poet Pierre Gringoire who finds himself surrounded by deformed, sickly beggars in the Court of Miracles, after which he is taken to a cabaret and presented to the king of Argot Kingdom, Clopin Trouillefou, who seeks to punish the poet by hanging for stepping into the "argot kingdom without being an argot speaker."⁴ In an initiation scene into the Argot Order, Gringoire affirms, "I consent. I am a thief, a slang speaker, a free citizen, a beggar, everything that you will want."⁵ Later, following his failed attempt at stealing a mannequin's purse, without ringing any of the bells attached to it, the bohemian Esmeralda saves Gringoire from death by marrying him. Criminal slang in dialogue is used throughout the chapter, while the poet's fate remains uncertain until the end. This experience of the slang speaker in *The Hunchback of Notre Dame* echoes the plot trajectories created by earlier fifteenth-century writers such as François Villon, Pechon de Ruby, and Guillaume Bouchet, in which characters are inducted into a highly structured, secretive criminal order made up of beggars and thieves.

Although Hugo subverted literary conventions through his representations of slang in several of his works, he executed this differently from his contemporaries, as he refused to publish in a serialized format, prioritizing aesthetics over pulp. Nevertheless, Hugo's distinction was fully realized with the publication of *Les Misérables* (1862). In this epic novel, the representation of criminal slang and its speakers elevates the status of this anti-language in French literature through the use of a legitimate genre as well as a revamping of earlier criminal stereotypes into more nuanced, moral characters, while glorifying the misery of the lower classes as a social mission ripe for Christian salvation. Contrary to Balzac, whose essay "Philosophical, Linguistic, and Literary Essay on Slang, Prostitutes and Thieves" (1847–1848) presented crime as a product of nature that went against the civilized state and slang as a refusal of society's language, Hugo's essay "Slang," which was published a few months after, refutes Balzac's claims, stating that crime and slang *are* products of the society.[6] As Guy Rosa notes, Hugo's use of slang as the language of misery

> allows [him] to evoke slang in terms so close to those of Balzac that they seem borrowed from him—same animality, same dangerous violence—, but to draw from them completely different consequences, depending on whether misery is the source or synonym of crime.[7]

In her study on the modern composition of Victor Hugo's oeuvre, Judith Wulf examines Hugo's poetic use of nonstandard languages and states that representations of language in realist French works, such as those of Balzac, typically prioritized a technical analysis over "sentiment and emotion."[8] Wulf additionally comments on Hugo's authorial position as that of a poet, "rather than of historian, politician or even philosopher."[9] Unlike his contemporaries, his self-designated purpose was "to elaborate on writing that appeals to passions in order to inscribe sensitivity into its usages."[10] In addition to a play-on-words and his use of puns, Hugo embraces the stylistic challenge of eternalizing slang and rendering it universally sublime.

Hugo's emphasis on the poetic aspects of slang rendered the language worthy of highbrow literary works, even if it was to his linguistic detriment. The contrast in Hugo's treatment of slang was notable even to fellow writers of the time period. For example, in a letter dated July 1862 to Edma Roger des Genettes, Flaubert critiqued Hugo's *Misérables* for a lack of discernment between the characters' speech: "As for their conversation, they speak very well, but all of them *the same*."[11] In spite of obvious stylistic differences between Hugo and his contemporaries in their representations and overall literary presentations of criminal slang, Hugo attempts to poeticize, even at the risk of appearing too linguistically uniform, that gruesome language which was deemed and treated in a manner wholly unpoetic by the likes of Vidocq, Sue, and Balzac.

In an effort to exploit the true literary potential of this anti-language, Hugo dedicates an entire chapter of *Les Misérables* to the paradoxical quality of this "abject idiom."[12] In the novel, the narrator transforms over the course of the narrative from being a guide, or *interlocuteur*, of the Parisian underworld to an advocate for the common people, adopting what Dufour terms an "eloquence of the tribune."[13] In addition to speaking on behalf of an oppressed portion of the population, Hugo reveals the ways in which the "the monstrous could be divine."[14] Building upon previous indexes of the criminal type, *Les Misérables* reveals the emergence of a second indexical order in which criminals are victims of social circumstance, and as a consequence, enveloped in misery. *Les Misérables* thus outlines a markedly different indexicality from earlier ones that charts a transformation of the criminal from social deviant to social victim. An analysis of this complex work reveals the invention of a new indexical order of slang based on those previously established by earlier writers.

The emergence of a second indexical order occurs in *Les Misérables* in three notable ways: first, the representation of the criminal type has even stronger associations with the working classes, thus introducing a strong sociological component. As evidenced in Chapter 2 of *Les Misérables*, characters of various degrees of criminality, such as Jean Valjean and Éponine, wear worker's garb. The term *misérables* ("the miserable ones") refers to the masses afflicted by poverty, disease, suffering, and crime and functions as a reminder of the source of their criminal activity, the poverty which begets their misery (*la misère*). Even certain slang terms affiliated with destitution and class status housed criminal meanings. For example, the words "orphan" (*orphelin*), "alms giver" (*aumonier*), and "worker" (*ouvrier*) were all slang terms for "thief." Hugo's novel thus marks a shift in focus from the inherent immorality of criminals to the social circumstances which engender immoral behavior.

Second, Hugo's criminal types function within a narrative which is propelled by the Christian story of Jesus Christ's sacrifice for the redemption of all in the New Testament. Within the larger context of a Christian narrative, social status no longer serves as the primary marker of honorable and dishonorable persons. Rather, in the tradition of Enlightenment thought, it is the collection of actions, behaviors, and the thoughts of each individual which serves as the barometer of moral judgment, a judgment that considers social circumstances through the lens of the Christian tradition of compassion. The introduction of this Christian component therefore contrasts the nature of Hugo's literary slumming with that of other writers. For Vidocq, Balzac, and Sue, slang remains a dangerous language, while, in contrast, Hugo's narrator implores readers to spend time among these dregs of society in order to experience firsthand their horrific language.[15] He likens the sewers to the intestines of Paris and states that this is the physical site where slang and its speakers are fostered.[16] Therefore, the idea of slang as the language of misery offers a contrasting view of literary slumming than what went before, as, in

Les Misérables, the use of slang becomes an impetus for liberal pity, while awakening an urge to be a savior, rather than merely evoking the middle-class contempt or voyeurism of its earlier uses.

Third, in terms of aesthetics and style, Hugo presents a highly poetic text which illuminates the metaphorical value of slang as well as his own talent for constructing metaphors. The descriptions of criminal types, and especially their language, testifies to Hugo's ability to take a distasteful topic and elevate it into the realm of the sublime through his use of poetic devices, such as metaphor, repetition, internal rhyme, alliteration, assonance, and consonance, in order to construct an aesthetically pleasing work. This elevation of the criminal type and their language to the realm of the divine using poetic literary devices, as well as the inclusion of classical elements, alters the role of slang in literature. Instead of serving as a means of social identification (in the hopes of social eradication), Hugo's slang functions to reveal the language's creative potential (while showcasing the literary talent of the writer) in terms of the lower classes, thus, in this case, slang is meant to expose the social issues related to poverty. The linguistic genius of Hugo lies in his ability to showcase slang's poetic value, while still maintaining it as a language of the dregs of society. Hugo therefore creates a paradoxical vision of the slang speaker and their language as symptoms of larger sociological problems, while revealing their humanity.

SLANG'S SECOND INDEXICAL ORDER

In *Les Misérables*, Hugo offers new definitions of slang. As Louis Chevalier remarks, "The history of thieves' slang is dwelt on at far greater length than contemporary examples of it."[17] The images that Hugo evokes not only reinforce preexisting indexical associations with the slang, such as the thief plotting a heist, the convict plotting his escape, a language born of shadows, and the physical deformation of words through the branding of the executioner, which transforms the language into a metonymic equivalent for its speaker, but it also provides an opportunity for the writer to flaunt his literary genius by crafting vivid metaphors that communicate an elevated aesthetic from otherwise vulgar language and subject matter.

In Part Four, Book VII, entitled, "Slang," Hugo's narrator artistically transforms this dangerous language into a platform for a discourse on poetic language. To contextualize the language for his audience, Hugo presents the potential origins of slang in the chapters entitled "Origins" and "Roots." He begins the chapter, "Origins," by defining slang for his reader as both a nation of people and a language, both defined by their thieving natures.[18] As with earlier works, such as Olivier Chereau's *Jargon or the Language of Reformed*

Slang (*Le jargon ou langage de l'argot reformé*, 1630), Hugo aligns slang with both a people and a language: it is the thieves that steal, and the words that are stolen from Standard French.[19] In *Les Misérables* the role of slang as metonymical substitute for the criminal is not only more apparent than in works by Vidocq, Balzac, and Sue, but its metonymy further contributes to the poetic styling of slang in the text. In "Roots," Hugo emphasizes the parasitical quality of this dangerous language as well as its capacity to feed off Standard French.[20] Thus, slang is an anti-language that mirrors the social role of the criminal, the main character of an anti-society that exists within society. Like a shape shifter, slang continually hides itself among the standard terms and phrases that already exist, while manipulating and perverting these words in order to render both their meanings and existence criminal.

In addition to emphasizing slang's capacity to pervert standard French, Hugo's narrator makes it clear that the slang of which he speaks is not jargon, but rather the language of the Parisian underbelly and thus, the "language of misery."[21] The narrator's initial definition of "true" slang introduces elements of the language which correspond to those of Vidocq, Balzac, and Sue, as an inferior speech practice infused with immoral implications. Unlike some dictionary entries in the second half of the nineteenth century that attempted to position criminal slang as jargon, Hugo remains adamant concerning the indexical relationship between immorality and slang. Even though Hugo does not mention criminality explicitly, certain adjectives he uses to describe the language ("ugly," "underhand," "treacherous," "venomous," "cruel," "sleazy," and "vile") could serve to index criminal dealings, and thus the lower classes. In addition to addressing slang's vulgarity, Hugo introduces a new association with the language, that of misery, which he likens to a disease.[22] The *Dictionary of the French Academy* (1835) defined "misery" (*misère*) as: "An unfortunate state, an unfortunate condition, extreme destitution, a deprivation of necessary things for living."[23] Slang, as a language of misery, and not simply criminal code, presents its speakers as victims of circumstance who are so impoverished they lack basic necessities. The notion of slang as the language of shadows further refers to a lurking indexical of the criminal type, while acknowledging the lack of compassion for those who are poverty-stricken. Even though they are people who chose to cast themselves outside of society's gaze in order to conduct their sketchy dealings, they are also persons who society casts aside without reflection. Hugo's narrator calls the resistance to slang a social irresponsibility, likening it to a surgeon who refuses to examine a gruesome medical condition.[24] In *Les Misérables* a sociological element of slang thus emerges as it transforms into a phenomenon that is simultaneously linguistic, literary, and social, in ways which radically shift the intentions of slang speakers as well as their motives for acquiring the language. In the case of the criminal, slang requires an initiation in order to communicate in secret with other criminal members, whereas, in contrast, the misery-afflicted character speaks slang as a byproduct of extreme poverty. In the tradition of the Enlightenment thinkers, Hugo's use of medical metaphors further serve to create a distance between the inspector and the disease, as he posits collective social change as the solution to misery and its symptoms.[25] Within a growing capitalist society, this remedy calls for involvement from privileged members of society to eradicate social bias followed with efforts to analyze the social plights of the less fortunate, ultimately to save them.

A TWIST ON THE CRIMINAL TYPE

For Hugo, the French term *peuple* represents a fusion between the criminal and working classes. Unlike Vidocq, Vautrin, and the ensemble of evildoers in *The Mysteries of Paris*, characters such as Jean Valjean, Fantine, Cosette, Éponine, and Gavroche engage in crime due to their life circumstances; however, they express guilt over their actions, while demonstrating their capacity for generosity and reform throughout the novel. Certain criminal characterizations, such as physical appearance, geography, the connection between language and social class, and performance, remain either absent in *Les Misérables* or are barely emphasized. This is mainly because Hugo diffuses criminal qualities across both physical and social boundaries. On occasion, Hugo offers up details that function as means of social identification; for example, when Valjean blows out his candle with his nose, in the manner of a prisoner, Hugo's main objective is not to present the ways in which a reader can identify these evildoers to prevent them from destabilizing bourgeois values.[26] Instead, Hugo sets *Les Misérables* apart from previous works by presenting criminality as a product of larger social issues as he reinserts Christian values into the dynamics between poverty, immorality, and criminality. In doing so, (1) he transforms the overarching narrative and literary context of slang and its speakers; (2) introduces a second indexical order that builds upon elements of the first indexical order; and (3) transforms the notion of slumming as a means of social investigation to rescue the lower classes, rather than, as earlier writers, as a form of class exoticization.

Hugo maintains the indexical relationships between language, morality, and social status, while simultaneously nuancing them through the blurring of physical and moral boundaries. For example, the speech-place barriers that Vidocq, Balzac, and Sue demarcate within their respective works become more ambiguous in *Les Misérables*, as criminal slang pervades all of Paris. While Hugo recognizes the role of the Parisian underground (in particular, the sewers) in perpetuating this language, he rarely gives detailed descriptions of districts in which this language finds itself.[27] Overall, Hugo does not designate certain areas as the haunts of slang speakers, and although he acknowledges the relationship between slang and the Parisian underworld, he emphasizes slang's lack of physical containment through the mobility of his criminal characters which contain much more moral complexity than the slang-speaking criminal characters of Vidocq, Balzac, and Sue. The image of the *misérables* contains elements of the criminal (as well as the destitute and working classes), which both softens their moral polarization and further corresponds to an indeterminate geographical location. The psychological complexity of characters such as Valjean, Fantine, Cosette, Gavroche, and Éponine lends itself to a physical fluidity due to their lack of extreme social categorization.[28] In *Les Misérables*, the Christian tenants of compassion and forgiveness scaffold the moral examination of lower-class characters, rendering their transgressions as part of an ethical whole which includes their thoughts, motives, and life circumstances. An example of this is when Gavroche encounters a beggar girl of thirteen or fourteen years old who is outgrowing her skirt; he informs her that when the length causes bodily indecency, that is, nudity, then she must acquire a new skirt.[29] Instead of condemning the girl, Gavroche's reaction is one of sensitivity when he laments the girl's lack of undergarments and gives her an item of clothing.[30] Rather than disgust at the girl's indecency, Gavroche displays enormous generosity toward her, handing her the wool scarf around his neck. It is this type of paradigm shift which transforms previous representations of the slang speaker; while evil characters still exist, such as Thénardier, the other lower-class characters in *Les Misérables* stand out as victims enveloped in misery, in other words, social circumstances which place their actions within a morally gray zone. This impoverished existence, along with the Christian plot arc that transforms Valjean into the ultimate antihero, bolsters the image of the common people as figures of suffering as well as divine veneration, rather than social degeneration and crime.

The emergence of a second indexical order, however, does not undo the first indexical order. As Kira Hall and Ayden Parish explain:

> As subjects are embedded in multiple networks simultaneously, their actions may have varying meanings within these social systems. These differing *indexical orders* (Silverstein 2003) construct a range of possible linkages between forms and meanings, as the agents constructed in one indexical order are presupposed yet also created anew in another as new contexts and new forms of meaningful action become possible.[31]

The elements of the criminal type that are present in Vidocq, Balzac, and Sue remain in portrayals of this figure after 1850, however, with slight modifications.[32] In contrast to the work of these earlier writers, *Les*

Misérables contains traditional images of the slang speaker as well as novel ones which position this figure as a product of social misery. Thus, in terms of traditional images, the use of slang as a coded anti-language remains. For instance, the four members of the criminal gang *Patron-Minette* use slang to communicate in secret.[33] While on his way to help bust Thénardier out of jail, Brujon exclaims, "What a good night for a getaway!"[34] Once Thénardier has escaped, he witnesses the four men speaking slang:

> The first man was saying, low but distinctly: Let's beat it. What're we coolin' our 'eels in this 'ole *icigo* for?'[35]

> The second replied: It's pissing down fit to put out the devil's bonfire. The cops are onto us, to boot, and there's a gunner on the lookout. We're gonna get ourselves put back in the slammer killin' time 'ere *icicaille*.'[36]

The slang terms that Hugo includes in this initial dialogue are not invented, but rather belong to the criminal lexicon in circulation and appear in the major slang dictionaries of the nineteenth century.[37] Typically, Hugo does not use italics to demarcate slang terms; however, this is not the case when the narrator provides commentary, especially in the chapter on slang. He also includes occasional translations in footnotes. Although his brief vignette of criminal language more or less aligns with those found in Vidocq, Balzac, and Sue, Hugo further provides a brief etymological breakdown of the slang used by the two criminals.[38] Due to the distinction between the two terms *icigo* and *icicaille*, Thénardier can identify Brujon as a "prowler of the barriers" (*rôdeur de barrières*), and Babet as a "junk dealer at the Temple" (*revendeur au Temple*). This subtle detail distinguishes a seemingly standard dialogue between criminal types from those of previous works. In *Les Misérables*, Hugo differentiates between contemporary slang and ancient slang (*l'ancien argot*), by consistently revealing the terms that come from the slang of Antiquity.[39] It is this subtle difference that allows Thénardier to use slang as a social identifier among criminals, while, at the same time, it establishes a relationship between slang and the era of Classical Antiquity, an association which further infuses slang with literary value. In addition to the inclusion of this subtle linguistic feature, the narrator reveals that Thénardier identifies Montparnasse by his lack of slang.[40] Montparnasse's linguistic peculiarity resembles previous indexical inversions, such as that of the Schoolmaster in *The Mysteries of Paris*, as his use of Standard French corresponds to other bourgeois traits, like his interest in nice clothes.[41] Unlike the Schoolmaster, Montparnasse fails to obtain the same level of dress as a bourgeois man. Despite his obsession with fashion, his redingote remains tattered and worn, a sign which is further indicative of his status as a failed bourgeois, whereas the Schoolmaster's power resides in his ability to pass as a member of the upper middle class (at least both in appearance and linguistically). In addition to his interest in fine clothing, the narrator describes Montparnasse's physical appearance as more effeminate than masculine.[42] This mix of paradoxical details not only defies the indexical expectations but also, as Chevalier notes, devalues the believability of the four-man gang that ran the Parisian underworld from 1830 to 1835.[43] The similarities between Hugo's text and previous works are subtly undermined by the inclusion of these details: the difference between contemporary and ancient slang, as well as criminal gang members who neither speak slang nor succeed in appearing bourgeois. The three remaining members of the gang also possess a mix of features that are traditionally considered to be criminal, in addition to features that are atypical of the criminal type; for instance, Gueulemer resembles a low-class Hercules due to his height, incredible strength, and chiseled body.[44] He has the physical strength that characterizes the criminal types of Vidocq, Balzac, and Sue; however, by reframing Gueulemer's appearance in the tradition of mythology and the physique of a Greek god, Hugo restores a literary dignity to the representation of this social figure. Additionally, Babet is thin and shrewd, pulls teeth for money, but also reads the newspaper, which the narrator describes as exceptional given his class status.[45] Claquesous possesses neither a name nor, on occasion, a body, as he sometimes takes on the appearance of a ghost who disappears and reappears at will.[46] Even Hugo's general description of the four men enters into the realm of the mythological: "[T]hey were a sort of single four–headed mystery thief working Paris."[47] Thus, both slang and the slang speaker in *Les Misérables* emerge as chimeric figures, possessing elements of the past as well as the present; they are simultaneously gruesome and glorious. It is, of course, not by accident that these criminal dialogues and descriptions occur right before Hugo's chapter on slang, and therefore serve as a precursor to the writer's discourse on slang's poetic devices.

In line with their physical appearance, in Hugo's work the slang speaker also uses a variety of disguises in order to gain greater access to certain social milieus (mainly bourgeois); however, the use of costumes does not occur as frequently as in previous works. There is also a noticeable lack of aristocratic characters compared to *The Mysteries of Paris* and *Splendors and Miseries of Courtesans*. Within the narrative, two characters in particular undergo several identity changes. First, following the Bishop's gesture of mercy, Valjean relocates to the coastal town *Montreuil-sur-Mer*, where he adopts the persona of a businessman, becoming known as Monsieur Madeleine, and is elected town mayor. The collapse of his secret life as Madeleine leads him to Paris with Cosette. While on the run in the city, he climbs over a convent wall and finds Fauchelevent, whom Valjean had previously saved from a fatal horse and cart accident. Fauchelevent claims Valjean as his brother "Ultime," so that he can stay at the convent with Cosette. Unlike Vidocq, Vautrin, and the band of scheming characters in *Mysteries*, Valjean's new identities exist on murky moral grounds: he is evading arrest and re-imprisonment but does not use the guises as means to carry out thefts or murders. In fact, the ultimate criminal shape shifter in *Les Misérables* is not Valjean, but rather Thénardier, who hides his identity only to trick people of the lower and middle classes, not the aristocracy. At the novel's end, when Thénardier tries to blackmail Marius for money by offering up Valjean's identity, Marius, who is already aware of Valjean's past, recognizes the multiple identities of Thénardier, who presents himself under the alias of Thénard.[48] Thénardier takes on several identities throughout the narrative in order to fulfill his criminal intentions, and Hugo builds upon previous indexes of the criminal shape shifter; however, he illuminates the role of poverty as responsible for propelling criminal acts. Marius' accusation of "beggar" directly invokes money as the motivation for Thénardier's evil schemes. Even though this character exploits others without guilt, he still resembles the Condemned Man for which crime has become a byproduct of socioeconomic injustice.

Another alteration to the index of criminal disguise is a crime-by-association element that emerges in characters that aid villains in feigning an honest identity. Hugo's narrator describes a Jewish man who built a successful business on disguising criminal lowlifes as respectable citizens.[49] This man, known as the Changer (*le Changeur*), engages in his own criminality by acquiring bourgeois clothing for social delinquents.[50] While, in this specific case, there is a clear anti-Semitic element to the Changer and his financial motives, at the same time, there is also a criminal system of disguises which descends into the realm of Balzacian theatricality.[51] These disguises link the slang speaker to criminality, as discussed in chapter 2. They are master shapeshifters, using both language and costume to cover their tracks, a trope still widely used in narrative and cinema today. At the same time, the shapeshifter index present in *Les Misérables* differs slightly, in that the use of disguise to carry out criminal acts stems from poverty, or, as in the case of the bourgeois, Changer, it serves as a nod to a society motivated by capitalism. The motivation for crime becomes increasingly socially and morally complex in Hugo's work because it ultimately stems from an economic lack that can affect characters of all social backgrounds.

In terms of class nuance, the workers garb that Valjean, Éponine, and Gavroche don contributes to a newfound mixing of the criminal and working classes, which are, however, both destitute. The role of social mobility as advertised in Vidocq's *Memoirs*, as well as in Sue's *The Mysteries of Paris* and Balzac's *Splendors and Miseries of Courtesans*, notably does not factor into the storyline of *Les Misérables*. Disguises might buy more material wealth; however, they do not buy the air of upper-class status, an aspect that embodies the deterministic philosophy of literary Naturalism. While Hugo establishes certain characters as shape shifters, in the case of Valjean, his moral conversion following Muriel's compassion alters the motivation of his shape-shifting. Although the use of disguises to mislead another is a dishonest act, Valjean uses his disguises to conduct good deeds, thus muddying the moral waters of the act. The most notable of Valjean's disguises is his transformation into Monsieur Madeleine, an identity that stems from the desire to leave behind his criminal life rather than to continue it. Valjean's adoption of a more honest persona emerges throughout the text when supporting characters refer to Valjean as "bourgeois." When Montparnasse, the leader of a criminal gang in Paris, tries to mug Valjean, Gavroche witnesses their interaction; however, he does not immediately identify them. From Gavroche's perspective, Valjean's silhouette resembles that of a middle-class gent.[52] Later, when Montparnasse tells Gavroche of his encounter with Valjean, Montparnasse also describes him as bourgeois.[53] Gavroche addresses Valjean directly as "Bourgeois" in addition to other nicknames such as "Monsieur Thingummyjig" and "citizen."[54] When Valjean arrives as Monsieur Fauchelevent along with Cosette to see Marius, the doorman immediately notes Valjean's nice clothes, referring to him as an "upstanding bourgeois."[55] Throughout *Les Misérables*, there exist indexes of the classic criminal type, such as disguise, language, and physique; however, these indexes come loaded with new complexities that build upon previous representations, thus laying the foundation for a second indexical order to surface. The slang speaker is thus presented as not purely criminal, but rather only the product of the unfortunate social circumstances that create such moral intricacies.

THE SLANG SPEAKER AS POET

Another innovation on the criminal type which emerges in Hugo's work is the image of the slang speaker as poet. As Wulf acknowledges, Hugo was drafting *Les Misérables* around the same time that Karl Marx was formulating his theories on the proletariat; however, unlike Marx,

> the liberation of the miserable ones occurs by a more fundamental revolution, that which will permit them to have access to their own production tool and their history, that is to say, language.[56]

The poetics of slang comes to fruition in the character of Gavroche.[57] While Valjean is able to read and write, abilities he acquired in prison at forty years old,[58] Gavroche "remains the unforgettable incarnation of popular speak, with his gift for invention, which breaks ordinary language and the manners of thinking that suit it."[59] When the eldest child of Thénardier happens upon two orphan children, he transforms their interaction into a linguistic spectacle, which elicits metalinguistic commentary from the narrator. First, the use of assonance and consonance characterizes this chapter. Gavroche, in what sounds like modern-day rap, addresses the brothers using a wide variety of slang terms for "kids" that all begin with the letter *m*: "moutards" (1283, 1295), "momacques" (1283), "mômes" (1285), "momignards" (1286, 1296), "momichards" (1291), and "mioches" (1297).[60] When Gavroche runs into Montparnasse, the gang member warns Gavroche of an approaching police constable by using alliteration:

> Listen to what I tell you, boy, if I was out in the square with my *digger* and my *dagger* and my *dug*s and you were to lavish ten sous on me I wouldn't mind singing for my supper, but it's not Mardi Gras yet. (My emphasis)[61]

The narrator explains that Montparnasse's words had a peculiar effect on Gavroche, and later reveals its coded meaning to alert Gavroche of the policeman's presence.[62] Montparnasse's use of consonance to protect his friend triggers the narrator's commentary:

> That syllable *dig*, not voiced on its own but artfully combined with other words in a sentence means: *Watch out, we can't talk freely*. There was as well in Montparnasse's sentence a literary beauty that was lost on Gavroche. "My digger, my dagger and my dugs" was a slang phrase from the Temple quartier that signifies *my dog, my knife, and my wife*, and was very much in use among the clowns and the commedia dell'arte red-tails of the *grand siècle*, when Molière wrote and Callot drew.[63]

In this explanation, the narrator likens slang to a kind of magic "talisman" that contains mysterious powers, while also highlighting several poetic aspects of Montparnasse's saving phrase. The repetition of the word *dig* (and its variants) creates a consonance (the narrator refers to it as "assonance"). This, in addition to its combination with additional words in the sentence, results in an artistic mixing of [d] and [g] sounds. The narrator also translates Montparnasse's enigmatic sentence for the reader, which asserts the narrator's role as a linguistic and social mediator between the lower and upper classes. Unlike the reader, the narrator possesses a special knowledge of criminal slang, and thus occupies an authoritative role. Additionally, this kind of revelation on the part of the narrator reinforces the authenticity of the writer himself. Finally, this passage places a larger emphasis on the inherent creativeness, and even literariness, present within Montparnasse's warning. Due to the artistic mixing of the words and the use of poetic devices, such as repetition and consonance, an aesthetic beauty emerges from the sentence (one that is lost on Gavroche). At the same time, the narrator reveals that the three "d" words Montparnasse repeats come from ancient slang (*l'argot du Temple*), a detail that further reinforces Hugo's overall objective in establishing a relationship between nineteenth-century criminality and the artistic glory of times past. The brief reference to Molière and Jacques Callot reminds the audience of the romanticization of artists that occurs over time.[64] In spite of the contentious reputation of these artists, Hugo presents them as innovators for their respective time periods. While evoking their genius, Hugo highlights the fact that present-day glorification can erase the memory of past resistance to artistic innovation, and the presentation of criminal slang as poetic (to the extent that canonical French writers used it as well) reinforces Hugo's goal in attempting to restore literary dignity to both slang and the slang speaker.

Throughout this chapter, Gavroche extensively uses slang expressions and terms without any highlighting by the author (italics, parentheses, footnotes, etc.) and/or translations. The representation of his street speak without any kind of textual marker, apart from the occasional commentary from the narrator, gives the language a fluidity that further mirrors Gavroche's physical fluidity as he wanders through the streets of Paris. As Karen Masters-Wicks writes, Gavroche's role is one of linguistic mediator as he "provides an equalizing spectacle for the grotesque and the sublime, in that he brings reciprocity between the language of hardened criminals and helpless street dwellers."[65] This fluidity, defined by an orality created through phonetic spellings and the repetition of certain sounds, gives Gavroche, according to Dufour, "a new eloquence, different from that elevated one of the Friends of the ABC or of Gillenormand, heir to the classical art of conversation."[66] Throughout the description of his journey with the two orphan kids through the Marais to his housing in the elephant statue near the Gare d'Austerlitz, Gavroche seemingly talks to everyone he encounters along the way, peppering his speech with funny terms. When they come across a girl in the street, Gavroche cannot help but address her as "Mamselle Back-of-a-Bus."[67] Gavroche's use of the Latin term *Omnibus* in the original French version to refer to the young girl alludes to the democratization of the literary space as one that includes all, in addition to the growing democratization of public space thanks to the many urban innovations taking place in Paris, especially those in transportation technology that included the horse-drawn omnibus. While it is unlikely that Gavroche has an understanding of Latin, this allusion speaks to the ever-present changes occurring in both urban and literary Paris.

In addition to the slang terms *merlan* and *angliche*, Gavroche uses terms that appear to be invented. When the eldest of the two boys explains that his mother was going to bring them to look for blessed box tree twigs for Palm

Sunday, Gavroche replies with "Neurs."[68] *Neurs* appears to be an abbreviation of another slang term (*goupineurs, nonneurs, monseigneurs*?) However, the narrator does not define it. When the youngest boy chimes in to explain that their mother lives with Mamselle Miss, Gavroche responds with another one-word answer: "Tanflûte."[69] Similarly, the narrator does not provide any explanation, and the term does not appear in any slang dictionaries. Despite the occasional linguistic idiosyncrasies, Hugo weaves in terms and expressions which do belong to the criminal lexicon. When Gavroche witnesses the baker cutting up the brown bread, he refers to the bread as a "rock-hard black dodger," in other words, black bread.[70] Once safely inside the elephant statue, Gavroche begins to initiate the two boys into the world of slang. When Gavroche tells them to blow out the candle because he cannot afford to keep it burning during the night, the eldest remarks that leaving a candle burning is a fire hazard to which Gavroche responds: "We say heat up the stew."[71] Later, he encourages them to go to sleep, employing slang terms, while also translating and instructing the two boys.[72] Gavroche fulfills a role that is as much paternal as it is pedagogical. Once inside the elephant statue, he begins to initiate the two boys into the language by correcting their use of Standard French with the corresponding slang term. Moreover, slang's role changes, as it is no longer the coded language of crime, but rather the translated language of misery. Gavroche's motive in looking after the two boys, despite his own destitution, stems from a desire to protect them. His linguistic instruction is combined with his fatherly instincts to feed and house them. Hugo's emphasis on compassion marks a paradigm shift as well as the establishment of a new indexical order: slang as the language of misery which invites pity and mercy. This new association between slang and social injustice marks the emergence of a second indexical order, one that appeared thanks to the earlier brandings of the language by writers such as Balzac and Sue.

In addition, the phonetic spelling of the title "mademoiselle" (*mamselle*) introduces an aural dimension to Hugo's characters. While linguistic realism is present in previous works, such as Balzac's *Splendors*, in *Les Misérables* a lack of parody surrounds phonetic spellings. The imitation of characters' accents implies supplementary features, such as mannerisms and physical appearances.[73] The importance of phonetics occasionally surfaces in other characters, as well. For example, the narrator explains that Valjean's name, the same as his father's, was once *Vlajean*, most likely a contraction of *Voilà Jean*.[74] The homophonous nature of Valjean's name, as well as homonymic (*Jean = gens* = "people"), highlights the centrality of aurality within Hugo's text. In order to uncover the layers of meaning, it is necessary to experience them aurally. In addition to communicating valuable social information regarding the characters' identity, speech practices in *Les Misérables* also contain literary mechanisms that relate specifically to the spoken word, such as homonyms and homophones, but also alliteration, assonance, and consonance. When Gavroche stops at a bakery to buy bread for himself and the two young boys, he notices the baker cutting an unbleached loaf of bread (*pain bis*), which prompts Gavroche to ask, "Whathahellsat?"[75] which subsequently invites an explanation on the part of the narrator.[76] The narrator, due to his authoritative position on language, reassures his reader that Gavroche's question, the pronunciation of which reduces six syllables to three, is neither an Eastern European language nor the "savage cries" of indigenous people. The narrator transcribes the phonetic spelling into Standard French and, surprisingly, it is a question that the reader asks daily: "What the hell is that?" A similar phonetic spelling occurs again when Gavroche reveals to Montparnasse that he lives in an elephant.[77] In response to Montparnasse's shock, Gavroche retorts, "Whaddovit?"[78] Again, this phonetic spelling segues into the narrator's metalinguistic commentary on this odd spelling of "What of it."[79] The bizarre spelling of a common question is because this pronunciation is only spoken, never written. Like the first example, Gavroche's question reduces a five-syllable question to two, and the abbreviations, in addition to the phonetic spellings, help to recreate Gavroche's accent in written form. The presentation of slang as an aural language is therefore not meant to retract from its literariness, but rather to earmark it as a new poetic form, one that is both spoken and now written out phonetically in its spoken form.

Despite this attempt to represent oral speech on the page, the narrator warns the reader that a written text can never fully capture the pronunciation of a character. For example, when attempting to recreate Javert's accent, the narrator includes a disclaimer at the end stating that the police inspector's tone resembled the roar of an animal.[80] By describing Javert's command as resembling a roar, rather than human speech, the narrator aligns a nonstandard pronunciation with animal sounds, suggesting it as a biologically inferior way of speaking. Additionally, the narrator recognizes the limitations of the written word in accurately translating the oral version onto the page. No spelling can relay the true pronunciation to the reader. A similar instance occurs when Montparnasse cries out "Kirikikiou!" to Gavroche from outside his elephant abode, which the narrator explains is a coded call to signal the young boy.[81] Like Gavroche's questions, *Whathahellsat* and *Whaddovit* (*Keksekça?* and *Kekçaa?*), Montparnasse's cry repeats the sound [k], which resembles the sound of the French rooster (*Cocorico!*), giving his special call an onomatopoeic feel. The fact that it resembles an animal sound (Hugo says that only a parakeet could recreate it) puts it on the same biological level as Javert's roar: Montparnasse's language is no longer in the realm of human language, but rather resembles an inferior form of communication found in the animal kingdom. The substandard nature of Montparnasse's cry elicits a similar commentary from the narrator regarding the phrase's oral nature;

the spelling he gives of the cry (*Kirikikiou!*) barely does it justice in terms of representation. It seems for Hugo's narrator that the closer a word is to a sound, the more difficult it is to translate it onto the written page. In any case, the attempt to restore a sense of poetry to a traditionally oral, popular language using poetic devices such as alliteration, assonance, consonance, and repetition, distinguishes *Les Misérables* as representing a break from previous depictions of criminal slang.

While Gavroche's speech embodies the poetry of the popular, it further includes an element of performance in the form of popular song. To preface Gavroche's working-class songs (*chansons populaires*), Hugo includes background information on the role of songs in prison. He describes a holding cavern where convicts en route to a prison in Toulon stay until their delivery; to pass the time in their tomb-like purgatory, they sing slang songs to cope with the hopelessness of their situation.[82] The use of song as a coping mechanism aligns the affliction of prisoners with that of those suffering from severe destitution.[83] Gavroche represents an extension of the prisoner's misery, and typically sings while walking through the city. In one scene, he waves a pistol, while singing a short verse, on his way to war.[84] The war that Gavroche is going off to wage refers both to the insurrection within the story as well as a literary war.

After mentioning that Gavroche's gun does not have a cock (and is therefore useless), the narrator launches into a commentary on the young Thénardier's use of song and questions its origins, suggesting that perhaps Gavroche is the creator of his own tunes.[85] Gavroche thus becomes the antithesis of the writer through his intimate connection with song and the aural rather than the written. At the same time, he functions as a mirror image of the writer through his impromptu creation of songs.[86] His songs accompany his jaunts through Paris as the chaos of the crowds begins to heighten. Within these popular songs, Gavroche adds his own "babble,"[87] and the cacophony of the war-torn metropolis begins to harmonize, revealing Gavroche as "a gamin of letters."[88] Through Gavroche's experience of urban discord, Hugo establishes a relationship between the aural and the written. By contributing his own musical styling to the disarray of voices and yells that define the Parisian landscape, Gavroche inhabits the same creative role as the writer, except aurally, in order to collect the dissonant parts and harmonize them into a whole. Throughout the narrative, Gavroche inhabits this role, and even dies singing[89]:

> One bullet, though, better aimed or more treacherous than the others, ended up hitting the will-o'-the-wisp-child [. . .]. [H]e lifted up both arms in the air, turned his head to where the bullet had come from, and began singing:
> I fell from the air,
> That's the fault of Voltaire,

> Nose in gutter, though,
> That's the fault of— [90]

Before he can finish his verse, a second bullet kills Gavroche. The act of dying as he sings seals Gavroche's role as a symbol of the relationship between the popular and the poetic, especially given the AABB rhyme scheme and the reference to two major French Enlightenment philosophers.[91] In the mid of the insurrection, song emerges as a metaphorical light in the dark in the same way that song both united and comforted the prisoners awaiting deportation. Gavroche's songs represent the dawn of a new poetry, one that emerges from the streets and is as fleeting as Gavroche's sudden death. This nonconventional use of rhyme, in addition to the use of a nonstandard form of French, marks a shift in poetic conventions of the nineteenth century. The lack of literariness inherent in popular song is the exact quality from which its creative potency is derived. The task of recognizing its potential to innovate poetic norms rests on the shoulders of the writer, whose role is to draw forth the poetic devices at work within the language by showcasing them through his own genius, while attempting to translate an otherwise oral, ephemeral language onto the written page.

REMAKING MISERY IN *LES MISÉRABLES* (1862)

In *Les Misérables*, Hugo casts misery as the source of this dangerous language, seemingly taking a page from the origin narrative of Pechon de Ruby's *The Magnanimous Life of Dealers, Bandits, and Bohemians* (*La vie généreuse des mercelots, gueuz et boesmiens*). However, unlike Pechon whose first-hand account of derelicts and other wandering untouchables errs on the side of farcical, Hugo's portrayal of errant criminal types contains strong Biblical undertones that recast this figure as morally acceptable for a bourgeois audience. The most apparent of these undertones is the story of Jean Valjean himself, who embodies the figure of the Christ. Following his spiritual reformation, Valjean's role as the sacrificial lamb mirrors that of Jesus' sacrifice for the sins of mankind, and throughout the novel Hugo employs different synonyms for God in order to emphasize Valjean's divinity. During the insurrection of June 5, 1832, led by the Friends of the ABC (*les amis de l'A B C*), the narrator describes Valjean as the person who exposes himself on the battlefront in order to save the injured since he possesses an angelic omnipresence.[92] After Marius learns that Valjean saved him at the barricade, in his mind the convict undergoes a Christ-like transfiguration.[93] This notion of criminal redemption is not new to Hugo's work, and also appeared in earlier works: Vidocq renounces his villainous ways to ascend socially as the head of the national police in Paris; The Slasher, Fleur, and other characters join Rodolphe to stop criminal wrongdoing; and Vautrin's social and moral trajectory imitates that of Vidocq's. However, the difference between criminal redemption in *Les Misérables* versus the earlier works is that the slang speaker serves as a complex mix of the criminal and working classes who are deeply afflicted by poverty. As Pascale Gaitet notes, "The misère [. . .] is the indeterminate area between criminals and *peuple*, the area through which the language of one infiltrate the other and that, according to Hugo, may be widening."[94] Misery becomes the common thread linking the dangerous and working classes together, a thread that contains its own language of expression—slang, "further signaling to the reader the lack of an adequate vocabulary in the normative literary language to describe, or fully comprehend, the atrocity of that which has no name, 'la misère.'"[95] The psychological aspect of lower-class suffering showcases the moral dilemmas that arise out of necessity as well as the capacity for the slang speaker's Christ-like redemption is not present in earlier works.

The character that best exemplifies this complex moral landscape is Jean Valjean. From a physical point of view, Valjean seemingly corresponds to past representations of the criminal man. While, at times, he appears as a grotesque figure, one that resembles criminals in early nineteenth-century literature, Valjean had a bizarre physiognomy that presents him as simultaneously meek and severe.[96] He is misery incarnate, possessing a stocky, average build, and is somewhere between forty-six and forty-eight years old.[97] When he arrives at Bishop Muriel's residence, the narrator describes him as evil in appearance.[98] He possesses the strength of four men, and neither laughs, speaks, nor shows emotion in general; the bishop senses that there is something monstrous in him.[99] Following Muriel's act of grace, Valjean becomes more aware of moral boundaries. This glimpse into Valjean's conscience, as well as his internal struggle between good and evil, casts away moral binaries, presenting instead a more complex version of criminality. The narrator states that Valjean is not inherently bad, but that prison life had changed him and then launches into a philosophical discussion on whether or not human beings are inherently good and/or divine.[100] This digression works both as a reconsideration of any initial judgments of the former convict and aligns social worthiness with divine worthiness, not class status.[101] In this context of a Christian morality, original sin places everyone on the same moral playing field, giving greater weight to a lifetime of actions, intentions, and motivations that only God can witness in their entirety.[102] This analysis of the slang speaker through a religious lens greatly differentiates it from representations before 1850. Hugo introduces questions regarding the nature of man in order to contextualize the moral underpinnings of his lower-class characters. This resituating of criminality, and certainly of language, within a more socially noble context of Christian morality as well as a Biblical narrative, elevates Hugo's use of so-called vulgar topics to the realm of the spiritual, whereas with Vidocq, Balzac, and Sue, these topics remain a physical reminder of the moral threat these subjects pose to the righteous upper classes. From this perspective, the act of slumming also changes with *Les Misérables*, as it becomes much less a form of upper-class indulgence and identity play, and more of an investigation into social injustice, pity, and salvation.

Far from the realm of parody, Hugo transforms misery into a symptom of larger social issues, as well as a sign of greater alignment with Christ. As Claudine Nédélec points out, the portrayals of the poor and criminal in *The Magnanimous Life* explicitly goes against Christian orthodoxy.[103] Throughout the narrative, Pechon presents these unfortunate souls as caricatures of human suffering, and, at the end of his story, he explicitly condemns their lifestyle in order to socially remove himself from the very people whose communities he so eagerly joined. This distancing and condemnation still occurs in Hugo's work; however, it does not occur by using parody, but rather through the narrator's explicit denunciation of slang and the slang speaker as criminal. These negative portrayals co-exist with classical references from antiquity that characterize the criminal type and his language, and thus elevate them to a status worthy of highbrow literature. Starting with the highest exemplar of the Word, the Bible becomes Hugo's means of transforming common people (*le peuple*) from laughable to laudable.

SLANG AS METAPHOR

The condemnation of slang and the social distancing that takes place in early nineteenth-century French literature did not undermine the recognition of the inherently poetic nature of the language. Although the acknowledgment of slang's metaphoric qualities culminates with Hugo's *Les Misérables* (1862), in earlier works, Balzac, Vidocq, and Sue recognize the dormant literariness within this criminal code and take advantage of the metaphorical quality that characterized this anti-language. As aforementioned, anti-languages index an "alternative social reality," and to quote Halliday, "it is this metaphorical character that defines the anti-language. An anti-language is a metaphor for everyday language."[104] Writers, especially Balzac and Sue, were aware of the disconnect between slang as indexical of criminals and its metaphorical capacity to describe the world.

In the opening chapter of *Mysteries*, Sue's narrator prepares his reader for the journey they are about to undergo and describes criminal language as brimming with metaphors.[105] As Dominique Kalifa points out, Sue's reference to Cooper's *The Last of the Mohicans* and Native Americans is a literary motif that occurred in works before 1850, stating that "the association between the savages of the Old and New World came about very naturally."[106] This comparison appeals to bourgeois exoticism and feeds their fascination with Parisian barbarians, in other words, the dangerous classes. Although grotesque, Sue's mention of criminal metaphor, a natural byproduct of slang, alludes to its inherent poetic value that would not be fully celebrated by writers until Hugo's epic novel. Throughout *Mysteries*, Sue frequently comments on slang's metaphorical ability to elicit horrific images. In one instance, the narrator comments on Songbird's nickname, *Fleur-de-Marie* ("Flower of Mary"), which is slang for the Holy Virgin:

> If only I could make my reader understand my surprise at encountering such a name amid the constant stream of foul language in which the words that signified theft, blood, and murder are even more hideous and frightening than the hideous and frightening things they represent. Here was a metaphor, a sweet bit of poetry, so tenderly pious: Fleur-de-Marie! [. . .] What a peculiar contrast, what a strange accident of faith! The inventors of this appalling language had also risen to the level of sacred poetry.[107]

In this example, even though the slang words themselves are more gruesome than the actions they depict, the narrator recognizes slang's poetic value, and the images that this anti-language conjures have the potential to appeal to readers on an aesthetic level, which suggests that, even if it stems from the dregs of society, slang is nevertheless literary. Sue also introduces a religious aspect to the language: the name *Fleur-de-Marie* is slang for the Virgin Mary, the quintessential figure of female purity and holiness. The pious poetry inherent in the term recalls another famous Mary from the Bible: Mary Magdalene, the reformed prostitute who becomes a devoted follower of Jesus.[108] Within Fleur's slang name, a strange paradox unfolds in which holiness and moral purity coexists with criminality and immorality.

In addition to commentary, Sue showcases the metaphorical nature of slang through a brief conversation between the Slasher and an adolescent named Fishhook:

Slasher: Hey, Fishhook, are you still downing the hard stuff?
Fishhook: You bet! I'd rather starve and wear old rags that go without putting liquor in my gullet or tobacco in my pipe.[109]

In this brief exchange, slang expressions and terms such as "to do the tortoise" (*faire la tortue*) and "philosophers" (*philosophes*), meaning "shoes," infuse otherwise banal actions and objects with a sense of playfulness and creative possibility. Although Fishhook is speaking about his preference for drinking hard liquor and smoking, these nonsensical slang expressions mask the underlying poverty and immorality of the character, introducing a kind of innocent inventiveness akin to that of a child's. In this dialogue, Sue reveals slang to be a creative, inventive language, even if the words and expressions refer to vulgar acts.

Unlike Vidocq's *Memoirs* and Sue's Mysteries, in *Splendors*, Balzac highlights slang's metaphorical nature through the introduction of new literary associations. Midway through the novel, the narrative is interrupted with his essay on slang in which the narrator attempts to prepare the reader for forthcoming scenes:

> Therefore, before any comment on the language of the Greeks, of crooks, of thieves and murderers, called *slang*, that literature has appropriated with much success [. . .]. Perhaps to the astonishment of lots of people, there is no language more energetic, more colorful than that of the underworld [. . .]. Each word of this language is a brutal image, inventive or terrible [. . .]. Every word is savage in this language [. . .]. And what poetry! [. . .] What vivacity in these images! *Playing dominoes* means to eat; how else do hunted men eat?[110]

The description of slang as a language teeming with ghastly images coexists with its creative potential. The juxtaposition between the establishment of slang as a "brutal image" containing "vivacity" gives a reader the impression that there are two different narrators speaking: one who voices the moral irresponsibility of including such a language in a literary text, and another who praises the poetic nature of this criminal language and its potential to enrich a literary text. This opposition between content and form creates slang's inherent paradox, which Hugo elaborates on in *Les Misérables* as a response to Balzac. Despite the vulgar images these expressions conjure, the metaphorical aspect of the terms contributes stylistically to the text, thus rendering it more literary in the classical poetic sense. Balzac's essay emphasizes this paradox of slang—the fact that it is simultaneously both anti-literary and literary, thereby creating the potential for a literary space in which slang can appear without condemnation.

Contrary to Balzac, Hugo argues that slang, a language that is simultaneously a literary and social phenomenon,[111] merits analysis precisely because it stands as the symptom of larger social issues. However, the question regarding its inclusion in literary works unveils a deeper purpose for the language, and inquiries into the utility of slang allude to a second function that this dangerous language contains: the potential to elevate literary style.[112] Although he represents slang as "the word made convict,"[113] unlike his predecessors, Hugo exploits the language in order to showcase his own poetic genius. In addition to being the language of misery and of shadows, slang contains the ability to liberate the unconscious because it is the language that cries and laughs.[114] Unleashed within this emotional liberation is the carnivalesque:

> [I]t is in essence an over-sized spectacle, which simultaneously captivates and repulses the crowd [. . .]. Slang's impact on the reader is thus confrontational; it presents a mirroring of 'acceptable' words, in the form of a spectacle, as well as poeticizing them (taking them out of the everyday context and giving them a more profound meaning).[115]

This spectacle therefore becomes the platform for the writer to tap into the emotional subconscious and present the sublime via the grotesque through unconventional manipulations of a criminal language in order to convey a divine poetry.

In "Roots," Hugo posits metaphor as one of the etymological explanations for certain slang terms that undergo an evolution from their raw state into a more poetic one.[116] Following this preemptive attempt to assuage a reader's criticism, Hugo relies on metaphor to emphasize the horror of this language, comparing words to the crab's claw and a bloody eye that infuse phrases with a notable vitality.[117] From here, the audience is permitted to enter into the realms of the mythical and the fantastic. Beastly animals abound as the writer attempts to find an appropriate imagery that adequately expresses the horror inherent within the language. The language that Sue once described as "a mysterious language, full of morbid imagery and metaphors steeped in blood" comes to fruition in *Les Misérables*.[118] These initial images of slang that Hugo presents contain animal references that could be found in the bestiaries of the Middle Ages: a claw (*une griffe*), a bloody eyeball (*un œil éteint et sanglant*), and a crab's claw (*une pince de crabe*). The mythical imagery linked to slang and Hugo's execution of metaphor culminates at the end of "Roots" when he laments the plight of the *misérables*[119]:

> O poor thinking of the down–and–out! Alas! Will no one come to the rescue of the human soul in this shadowland? Is its destiny to wait forever there for the mind, the liberator, the towering rider of the pegasuses and the hippogriffs, the fighter the color of dawn who descends from out of the blue between two wings, the radiant knight in shining armor of the future? Will it always call out in vain for the lance of light of the ideal to rescue it? Is it condemned to the horror of hearing Evil approaching through the denseness of the abyss and glimpsing, closer and closer to it, beneath the hideous water, that draconian head, that great maw chomping on foam, that serpentine undulation of claws, swellings, and rings? Must it stay there, without a glimmer of light, without a glimmer of hope, delivered up to that awful approach, dimly sniffed out by the monster,

shaking, frantic, wringing its hands, forever chained to the rock of night, somber Andromeda, white and naked in the darkness!"[120]

This concluding paragraph of the section overflows with poetic mechanisms. The presence of internal rhyme that overlaps with alliteration/assonance/consonance (all italicized below) characterizes the entire passage:

1. *Ô pau*vre *pe*ns*ée* des *mi*sérables! Hélas! Perso*nne ne* viendra-t-il *au* secours de l'*â*me hu*maine* dans cette *ombre*? (Repetition of sounds [o], [e], [m], [n], and [p]).
2. *Sa* de*stinée* e*st*-elle d'y *att*endre *à* jamais l'e*sp*rit, le libérat*eur*, l'*immens*e chevauch*eur des* pé*ga*ses et d*es hi*ppogr*iffes*, le comb*att*ant coul*eur* d'*a*urore qu*i* d*es*cend de l'*a*z*u*r entre deu*x a*iles, le r*a*d*i*eux cheval*i*er de l'*a*venir? (Repetition of sounds [a], [s], [e], [t], [i] and [z]; Repetition of –eur ending).
3. App*ella*-t-*elle* tou*jou*rs *en* vain à *s*on *s*ecour*s la lan*ce de *lu*mière de *l'*idéa*l*? (Repetition of sounds [l], [u], [ã], [i], and [s]).
4. E*st*-*elle* condam*née* à *en*ten*d*re *v*enir *é*po*u*v*ant*able*m*ent dans l'*ép*aisseur du *g*ouffre *le* M*al, et* à *entre*v*o*ir, de *p*lu*s en p*lu*s* près d'*elle*, *sou*s l'*eau* hideuse, ce*tte t*erre draco*nienne, cett*e gueu*l*e mâcha*nt l'*écume, *et* ce*tte* ondula*tion* serpe*n*te*n*te de *g*r*iff*es, de *g*on*fl*ements et d'a*nn*ea*ux*? (Repetition of sounds [m], [n], [l], [e], [v], [u], [p], [s], [t], [o], [ã], [õ], [f], [g], and [r]).
5. *F*au*t-il* qu'*elle re*s*te l*à, *sans* u*n*e *l*ueur, *sans* espoir, livr*ée* à ce*tte* approche *f*ormi*d*able, vaguem*en*t *fl*air*ée* d*u* mon*s*tre, *f*rissonna*nte*, échevel*ée*, se *t*or*d*a*nt les* bras, à jamais e*n*ch*a*înée au ro*ch*er *de la n*uit, sombre Andromède *bl*an*ch*e *et n*ue dans *l*es *t*én*è*bres! (Repetition of sounds [t], [l], [s], [ã], [r], [f], [e], [ʃ], [n] and [d]).

The poetic techniques of repeating certain sounds and the presence of internal rhyme also become heightened by the poetic symbolism that Hugo uses to describe the *misérables*. Exclamations such as "*O*" and "*Alas!*" serve as sanctioned poetic expressions of affliction, and thus establish the tone for Hugo's concluding paragraph which treats an inherently un-poetic subject (the poor) as intrinsically sublime. Again, instead of defining the subject in socially divisive terms, Hugo simply speaks of "the human soul in this shadowland," descending into poetic and mythological symbolism. In fact, the symbols that Hugo evokes straddle the line between the mythological and the Christian. Regarding the salvation of these condemned souls, Hugo introduces the image of a savior who takes on several forms: the spirit, the liberator, the rider of Pegasus and the hippogriff, the fighter, and the radiant knight of the future. The figure of the savior, as well as creatures like the hippogriff and the monster that lives beneath the depths of the sea, is the figure found in Greek mythology and the Book of Revelation.[121] Other figures, such as Pegasus and Andromeda, remain exclusive to Greek mythology. The symbolic association (in the case of Andromeda, equivalence) of these figures with nineteenth-century criminal outcasts represents a completely new perspective and representation of the slang speaker. By inserting these figures and their social plight into biblical and mythological contexts, Hugo looks to Classical Antiquity in order to recast the criminal character into a more literary light. What once incarnated physical and moral filth now finds itself a symbol of sacredness, the sublime, and creative potential precisely because of the aesthetically superior language and images used to represent their social circumstances. This return to Classical Antiquity further provides Hugo the opportunity to display his poetic prowess that can transform even the most un-literary topics into works of art. By virtue of being a language, slang possesses the potential to transform a text into poetry.[122] Through his ornate metaphors, Hugo suggests that it is not so much a question of legitimate language as it is of talent on the part of the writer. In order to render criminality more literary, Hugo contextualizes the *misérables* and their language in the tradition of a narrative that is both classical and religious. From Vidocq to Hugo, the subject matter remains the same; and yet, in *Les Misérables*, the disconnect between the style (*la forme*) and the content (*le fond*) deepens not only through Hugo's refusal to pen a serial novel but also through his refusal to describe the topic at hand in any way unworthy of the highest literary aesthetics. By transfiguring criminal slang and the slang speaker of Vidocq, Balzac, and Sue into symbols of human suffering and humility, Hugo's characters become glorious vestiges of both antiquity and Christianity. Moreover, the romanticization of the lower echelons of society does not excuse the gruesome lifestyle and language they speak. In fact, in the same way that Hugo is able to merge images of Christianity, mythology, and science, he is also able to merge the people's glory with their ghastliness in order to construct a more morally nuanced vision of the *misérables*.

THE AESTHETICS OF SLANG

The use of slang in *Les Misérables* stands as testimony to the belief that the horrific merits analysis because of the larger social issues it masks as well as its creative power. Like Montaparnasse's secret cry, Hugo's use of slang stands not as a literary talisman the writer is meant to keep secret, but rather it is meant to be used in the name of a higher literary objective. Hugo's restyling of the tropes found in Pechon, as well as in Vidocq, Balzac, and Sue, realigns the common people with the marginalized figures that Jesus valorizes in the

New Testament, and especially in the Beatitudes.[123] Both poverty and misery in *Les Misérables* serve as markers of Christ, while criminal acts are merely products of these social diseases, rather than as means of spreading evil for evil's sake. As Hugo recontextualizes the slang speaker within a Christian tradition, he simultaneously recontextualizes slang into a Classical tradition. References to Greek mythology and works from antiquity abound throughout the novel, especially with regard to the criminal figure. In addition, the inclusion of scientific and medical images as an extensive metaphor for the *misérables* and their language results in a strangely chimeric work that unites a patchwork of ideologies into one seamless text which preserves traditional images while simultaneously perverting them.

Slang's second indexical order thus emerges in three ways: first, Hugo presents the slang speaker as more morally, as well as psychologically, complex, further nuancing the lines between the criminal and the working classes. Second, the inclusion of both a Christian story plot arc and a reframing of the perspective through which the audience views slang speakers renders the presentation of the criminal type as morally ambiguous, while elevating them to the level of the divine. Values such as pity, mercy, and sacrifice become the hallmarks of figures of destitution in *Les Misérables*, and unlike Pechon, who did not exhibit the Christian values in his account of the beggars and thugs (*les gueux*), Hugo fills a gap in earlier works by shifting the collective lens toward these social untouchables from one of condemnation to one of compassion. Third, the elevation of the slang speaker as a figure of the Christ alters the role of slang itself in literature, thus marking a prominent indexical shift in which slang's second indexical order emerges. The literary slumming before 1850 arises from a horror-fascination with the criminal classes, while indulging a bourgeois voyeurism in order to peer into the normally inaccessible lives of thieves, murderers, and prostitutes. Although a sentiment of class superiority remains, in contrast, Hugo's literary slumming contains far less disdain for the "barbarians" overtaking Paris, while speaking more to social privilege and the duty of the upper classes to rescue the less fortunate lower classes. The slumming in *Les Misérables* therefore has less to do with an exoticization of slang speakers and more with a call to help them.

Subsequently, Hugo's emphasis on the poetic devices inherent in slang allow him to showcase his talent through the literary exploitation of these devices. Slang's main role is no longer a means of social identification, but rather allows the writer to achieve greater poetic heights. The revamping of the image of the slang speaker and slang through its association with higher images and literary mechanisms provides the foundation for the writer's own poetic license. What results is a *mise-en-abyme* of metaphor: a language that is intrinsically metaphorical provides the starting place from which the writer can craft his own ornate metaphors. While Hugo preserves earlier indexical associations and extends metonymical relationships between slang and its speakers, he simultaneously elevates both the grotesque and sublime in the language of the criminal and lower classes to the divine.

NOTES

1. Dufour, *La Pensée romanesque*, 23.
2. Ibid., 135; "Représente l'affrontement des sociolectes" (Ibid., 19).
3. Ibid., 121.
4. "*Le royaume d'argot sans être argotier*" (Hugo, *Notre-Dame de Paris*, 168).
5. "*Je consens. Je suis truand, argotier, franc-bourgeois, petite flambe, tout ce que vous voudrez*" (Ibid., 171).
6. Balzac's essay appears as a chapter in the last part of *Splendors and Miseries of Courtesans*, which appeared in the newspaper, *La Presse*, from April 13, 1847 to May 4, 1847. The first version of Hugo's essay dates from winter 1847–1848.
7. "*Elle permet à Hugo d'évoquer l'argot en des termes si proches de ceux de Balzac qu'ils lui semblent empruntés—même bestialité, même violence dangereuse—, mais d'en tirer des conséquences toutes différentes, selon que la misère est cause ou synonyme du crime*" (Rosa, 156).
8. Wulf, *Étude sur la langue romanesque*, 465.
9. "*Plutôt qu'en historien, en homme politique ou même en philosophe*" (Ibid., 11).
10. "*élaborer une écriture qui fasse appel aux passions, afin d'inscrire la sensibilité dans les usages*" (Ibid., 467).
11. "*Quant à leurs discours, ils parlent très bien, mais tous de même*" (Flaubert, *Correspondance*, vol. III, 236).
12. "*Idiome abject*" (Hugo, *Les misérables*, 1328; English translation, IV.7.i, 806). My citation of the page numbers, for example: (IV.7.i, 806), refer to Part IV, Book 7, Chapter I, page 806 in the English translation by Julie Rose.
13. "*L'éloquence de la tribune*" (Dufour, 277).
14. "*Le monstrueux pouvait être divin*" (Hugo, *Les Misérables*, 1766; English translation, V.4.i, 1083).
15. Ibid., 1328; English translation, IV.7.i, 806.
16. Ibid., 1683; English translation, IV.7.iv, 1030.
17. Chevalier, *Laboring Classes*, 91.
18. Ibid., 1327; English translation, IV.7.i, 805.
19. Hugo, *Les Misérables*, 1333; English translation, IV.7.i, 809.
20. Hugo often compares slang to a parasite (Hugo, *Les Misérables*, 1337, 1339; English translation, IV.7.ii, 811, 813).
21. "*[L]a langue [. . .] de la misère*" (Hugo, *Les Misérables*, 1329, 1331; English translation, IV.7.i, 806–807).
22. This "pustulous vocabulary" (*vocabulaire pustuleux* [Hugo, *Les Misérables*, 1328; English translation, IV.7. i, 806]) stems from a "social consumption" (*phthisie sociale* [Hugo, *Les Misérables*, 1350; English translation, IV.7.iv, 821]) which Hugo

calls "misery" (*la misère* [Hugo, *Les Misérables*, 350; English translation, IV.7.iv, 821]). In Julie Rose's translation, she uses "destitution" instead of misery.

23. "*État malheureux, condition malheureuse, extrême indigence, privation des choses nécessaires à la vie.*"

24. Hugo, *Les Misérables*, 1329; English translation, IV.7.i, 806.

25. Ibid., 1352; English translation, IV.7.iv, 822.

26. Ibid., 128; English translation, I.2.v, 7.

27. Hugo's chapter entitled, "The Dregs" ("Le Bas-Fond") in Part 3, Book 7, focuses less on the relationship between language and place, and more as a platform from which Hugo can showcase his talent for metaphor.

28. This nuanced moral image is also present in Sue's work, however, not to the same effect: characters such as Fleur-de-Marie and the Slasher, who undergo an internal transformation, end up dead or killed off in the end. In *The Mysteries of Paris*, neither bloodline nor repentance can redeem one's past actions.

29. Hugo, *Les Misérables*, 1284; English translation, IV.6.ii, 779.

30. Ibid.

31. Hall and Parish, "Agency," 3.

32. Some criminal characters, such as Montparnasse, a member of the four-man criminal gang *Patron-Minette*, recall earlier criminal figures. Like the Schoolmaster in *The Mysteries of Paris*, Montparnasse uses a disguise in order to meet up with a recently escaped Babet. When Gavroche runs into him in disguise, he is shocked at Montparnasse's middle-class coat and glasses that give him the appearance of a doctor (Hugo, *Les Misérables*, 1288; English translation, IV.6.ii, 781). At the end of Montparnasse's cane, the handle reveals a detachable knife, a trick that elicits Gavroche's admiration for having the idea to disguise his knife in bourgeois fashion (Hugo, *Les Misérables*, 1289; English translation, IV.6.ii, 782). The figure of the criminal disguised as a respectable bourgeois can be found throughout literary works in the nineteenth century.

33. The narrator explains that *Patron-Minette* is also a slang term (Hugo, *Les Misérables*, 995; English translation, III.7.iv, 597).

34. "*Quelle bonne sorgue pour une crampe!*" (Hugo, *Les Misérables*, 1311; English translation, IV.6.iii, 796). Hugo includes this translation in a footnote: "*Quelle bonne nuit pour une évasion!*" (Ibid.).

35. Hugo's translation: "*Allons-nous-en. Qu'est-ce que nous faisons ici?*" (Ibid., 1317; English translation, IV.6.iii, 800).

36. Hugo's translation: "*Il pleut à éteindre le feu du diable. Et puis les gens de police vont passer. Il y a là un soldat qui fait sentinelle. Nous allons nous faire arrêter ici*" (Ibid.); "*Le premier disait bas, mais distinctement:*

— *Décarrons. Qu'est-ce que nous maquillons icigo?*

Le second répondit:

— *Il lansquine à éteindre le riffe du rabouin. Et puis les coqueurs vont passer, il y a là un grivier qui porte gaffe, nous allons nous faire emballer icicaille?*" (Ibid.).

37. In the section entitled, "Roots," Hugo lists etymologies stemming from Spanish, Italian, English, German, Latin, Scottish, Basque, and Celtic (Hugo, *Les Misérables*, 1338; English translation, IV.7.ii, 812). In the early twentieth century,

Lazare Sainéan revealed that the list of slang terms that Hugo analyzes in this passage do not belong to the lexicon of the criminals in the nineteenth century, and they certainly do not appear in the dialogue between criminal characters in *Les Misérables* (296–97). Additionally, these terms do not appear in the major slang dictionaries of the time. As Sainéan explains, these terms are not criminal slang and have nothing in common with any "living variety of French" ("*variété vivante du français*" [Ibid., 297]).

38. "*Ces deux mots, icigo et icicaille, qui tous deux veulent dire ici, et qui appartiennent, le premier à l'argot des barrières, le second à l'argot du Temple, furent des traits de lumière pour Thénardier*" (Hugo, Les Misérables, 1317; English translation, IV.6.iii, 800).

39. Ibid.
40. Ibid.
41. Ibid., 993; English translation, III.7.iii, 596.
42. Hugo, *Les Misérables*, 993-994; English translation, III.7.iii, 596–97.
43. Chevalier, *Laboring Classes*, 92.
44. Hugo, *Les Misérables*, 991; English translation, III.7.iii, 595.
45. Ibid., 991–92; English translation, III.7.iii, 595–96.
46. Ibid., 992–93; English translation, III.7.iii, 596.
47. "*[C]'était une sorte de mystérieux voleur à quatre têtes travaillent en grand sur Paris*" (Ibid., 994; English translation, III.7.iv, 597).
48. Ibid., 1921; English translation, V.9.iv, 1178.
49. Ibid., 1915; English translation, V.9.iv, 1174.
50. Ibid., 1915–1916; English translation, V.9.iv, 1174.
51. Ibid., 1916; English translation, V.9.iv, 1174.
52. Ibid., 1242; English translation, IV.4.ii,754.
53. Ibid., 1289; English translation, IV.6.ii, 782.
54. "*Bourgeois*" (Ibid., 1560; English translation, IV.15.ii, 951); "*Monsieur Chose*" (Ibid., 1561; English translation, IV.15.ii, 952); "*citoyen*" (Ibid., 1562; English translation, IV.15.ii, 952).
55. "*Bourgeois correct*" (Ibid., 1793; English translation, V.5.iv, 1098).
56. "*La libération des misérables passe par une révolution plus fondamentale, celle qui leur permettra d'avoir accès à l'outil de production d'eux-mêmes et de leur histoire, c'est-à-dire la langue*" (Hugo, *Les Misérables*, 552).
57. Hugo even titles his chapter, "Some Insights into the Origins of Gavroche's Poetry — Influence of an Academician on this Poetry" (*Quelques éclaircissements sur les origines de la poésie de Gavroche. Influence d'un académicien sur cette poésie* [Hugo, *Les Misérables*, 1443; English translation, IV.11.i 879]).
58. Ibid., 139; English translation, I.2.iii 64 and I.2.vii, 76.
59. "*Reste l'inoubliable incarnation du parler populaire, avec son don d'invention, qui casse le langage ordinaire et les manières de penser qui s'y assortissent*" (Dufour, 284).
60. These page numbers refer to the French edition.
61. *Écoute ce que je te dis, garçon, si j'étais sur la place, avec mon dogue, ma dague et ma digue, et si vous me prodiguiez dix gros sous, je ne refuserais pas d'y*

160   Chapter 4

goupiner, mais nous ne sommes pas le mardi gras. (Hugo, *Les Misérables*, 1291; English translation, IV.6.ii, 783)

62. Ibid.

63. *Cette syllabe dig, non prononcée isolément, mais artistement mêlée aux mots d'une phrase, veut dire: – Prenons garde, on ne peut pas parler librement. — Il y avait en outre dans la phrase de Montparnasse une beauté littéraire qui échappa à Gavroche, c'est mon dogue, ma dague et ma digue, locution de l'argot du Temple qui signifie, mon chien, mon couteau et ma femme, fort usité parmi les pitres et les queues rouges du grand siècle où Molière écrivait et où Callot dessinait.* (Ibid., 1292; English translation, IV.6.ii, 784)

64. Karen Masters-Wicks cites the works of Callot and his depictions of the grotesque as highlighting Hugo's theories on the grotesque and its relationship with the sublime (7).

65. Ibid., 96.

66. "*Une nouvelle éloquence, différente de celle, soutenue, des amis de l'ABC, ou de celle de Gillenormand, hériter du classique art de la conversation*" (Dufour, 284).

67. "*mamselle Omnibus*" (Hugo, *Les Misérables*, 1283; English translation, IV.6.ii, 778).

68. Translation: "'You don't say'" (English translation, IV.6.ii, 780); "*neurs*" (English translation, IV.6.ii, 1285).

69. Hugo, *Les Misérables*, 1286; English Translation: "'I'll be blowed'" (IV.6.ii, 780).

70. "*Du larton brutal*" (Hugo, *Les Misérables*, 1287; English translation, IV.6.ii, 780).

71. "*[O]n dit riffauder le bocard*" (Ibid., 1303; English translation, IV.6.ii, 791).

72. Ibid., 1304; English translation, IV.6.ii, 79.

73. The narrator states that gestures accompanied Gavroche's songs (Ibid., 1566; English translation, IV.15.iv, 955).

74. English translation, IV.6.ii, 1290.

75. "Keksekça?" (Hugo, *Les Misérables*, 1286; English translation, IV.6.ii, 780).

76. Ibid., 1286; English translation, IV.6.ii, 780.

77. Ibid., 1290; English translation, IV.6.ii, 782.

78. "*Kekçaa?*" (Ibid.; English translation, IV.6.ii, 783).

79. Ibid; English translation, IV.6.ii, 783.

80. Ibid., 413; English translation, I.8.iv, 244.

81. Ibid., 1307; English translation, IV.6.ii, 793–94.

82. Ibid., 1343; English translation, IV.7.ii, 816.

83. Ibid.; English translation, IV.7.ii, 816.

84. Ibid., 1444; English translation, IV.11.i, 880.

85. Ibid.

86. An interaction between a sergeant for the National Guard (*sergent de ville*) and Gavroche exemplifies the young Thénardier's ability to infuse certain words with new meaning, in a similar way that Hugo does vis-à-vis slang. In one scene, Gavroche uses the term *bourgeois* as an insult against the sergeant (Hugo, *Les Misérables*, 1568; English translation, IV.15.iv, 956). Like certain slang terms,

Gavroche twists the positive connotations of the term *bourgeois* by explicitly referring to it as an insult (the lower-class equivalent of "lout" [*voyou*]). From the reader's point of view, to be bourgeois implies not only a certain financial, educational, and linguistic superiority but also a moral superiority. Gavroche's inversion of the term to playfully represent a pejorative word for someone of the middle class establishes the analogy that *lout is to the lower classes as bourgeois is to the middle classes*, thus making them social equivalents through this clever reversal of the word's social meaning. Similarly, the ways in which a writer employs a term can alter the social meaning it carries.

87. "*Gazouillement*" (Ibid., 1444; English translation, IV.11.i, 880).
88. "*un gamin de lettres*" (Ibid.).
89. As he wanders through the streets of Paris, Gavroche discovers that the isolation of the night provides the perfect opportunity for song (Ibid., 1564–65; English translation, IV.15.iv, 954). Again, his rhymes declare a figurative war on the traditional conventions of literature.
90. *Une balle pourtant, mieux ajustée ou plus traître que les autres, finit par atteindre l'enfant feu follet [. . .]. [I]l éleva ses deux bras en l'air, regarda du côté d'où était venu le coup, et se mit à chanter:*
   Je suis tombé par terre,
   C'est la faute à Voltaire,
   Le nez dans le ruisseau,
   C'est la faute à . . . . (Ibid., 1634; English translation, V.1.xv, 998–99)
91. The last word of the last verse is "Rousseau."
92. Hugo, *Les Misérables*, 1676; English translation, V.1.xxiv, 1027.
93. Ibid., 1933; English translation, V.9.iv, 1186.
94. Gaitet, "From the Criminal's to the People's," 239.
95. Masters-Wicks, *Victor Hugo's Les Misérables*, 90–91.
96. Hugo, *Les Misérables*, 105; English translation, I.2.i, 55.
97. Ibid., 99; English translation, I.2.i, 51.
98. Ibid., 117; English translation, I.2.iii, 63.
99. Ibid., 142; English translation, I.2.vii, 78–79.
100. Ibid., 139; English translation, I.2.vii, 77.
101. Ibid., 1332; English translation, IV.7.i, 809.
102. Ibid., 990; English translation, III.7.ii, 595.
103. Nédélec, *Les Enfants de la Truche*, XXI–XXIV.
104. Halliday, "Anti-Languages," 572, 578.
105. Sue, *Mystères*, 35–37; English translation, 3.
106. "*L'association entre les sauvages de l'Ancien et du Nouveau Monde se fait alors très naturellement*" (Kalifa, *Les bas-fonds*, 124).
107. *Pourrons-nous faire comprendre au lecteur notre singulière impression, lorsqu'au milieu de ce vocabulaire infâme, où les mots qui signifient le vol, le sang, le meutre, sont encore plus hideux et plus effrayants que les hideuses et effrayantes choses qu'ils expriment, lorsque nous avons, disons-nous, surpris cette métaphore d'une poésie si douce, si tendrement pieuse: Fleur-de-Marie?* (Sue, *Mystères*, 45; English translation, 11)

108. This comparison becomes more in apparent in the chapters of *Mysteries*, in which supporting characters only refer to Fleur as *Marie*.

109. "*Chourineur: Eh! Barbillon, tu pitanches donc toujours de l'eau d'aff ? Barbillon: Toujours! J'aime mieux* faire la tortue *et avoir des* philosophes *aux* arpions *que d'être sans eau d'aff dans l'*avaloir *et sans* tréfoin *dans ma* chiffarde" (Sue, *Mystères*, 48; English translation, 13).

110. *Donc, avant tout un mot sur la langue des grecs, des filous, des voleurs et des assassins, nommée l'*argot, *et que la littérature a* [. . .] *employée avec tant de succès* [. . .]. *Disons-le, peut-être à l'étonnement de beaucoup de gens, il n'est pas de langue plus énergique, plus colorée que celle de ce monde souterrain* [. . .]. *Chaque mot de ce langage est une image brutale, ingénieuse ou terrible* [. . .]. *Tout est farouche dans cet idiome.* [. . .] *Et quelle poésie!* [. . .] *Quelle vivacité d'images!* Jouer des dominos, *signifie manger; comment mangent les gens poursuivis?* (Balzac, *Splendeurs*, 515–16)

111. Hugo, *Les Misérables*, 1329; English translation, IV.7.i, 806.

112. Ibid., 1332; English translation, IV.7.i, 808.

113. "*Le verbe devenu forçat*" (Ibid., 1344; English translation, IV.7.ii, 817).

114. The title of Part IV, Book 7, Chapter iii, is "Slang that Cries and Slang that Laughs" (*Argot qui pleure et argot qui rit*).

115. Masters-Wicks, *Victor Hugo's Les Misérables*, 94.

116. Hugo, *Les Misérables*, 1339; English translation, IV.7.ii, 813.

117. Ibid., 1328; English translation, IV.7.i, 806.

118. "*Mystérieux, rempli d'images funestes, de métaphores dégouttantes de sang*" (Sue, *Mystères*, 37; English translation, 3).

119. The term *misérables* with a lower case "m" refers both to the poor and the common people.

120. *Ô pauvre pensée des misérables! Hélas! personne ne viendra-t-il au secours de l'âme humaine dans cette ombre? Sa destinée est-elle d'y attendre à jamais l'esprit, le libérateur, l'immense chevaucheur des pégases et des hippogriffes, le combattant couleur d'aurore qui descend de l'azur entre deux ailes, le radieux chevalier de l'avenir? Appellera-t-elle toujours en vain à son secours la lance de lumière de l'idéal? Est-elle condamnée à entendre venir épouvantablement dans l'épaisseur du gouffre le Mal, et à entrevoir, de plus en plus près d'elle, sous l'eau hideuse, cette terre draconienne, cette gueule mâchant l'écume, et cette ondulation serpentente de griffes, de gonflements et d'anneaux? Faut-il qu'elle reste là, sans une lueur, sans espoir, livrée à cette approche formidable, vaguement flairée du monstre, frissonnante, échevelée, se tordant les bras, à jamais enchaînée au rocher de la nuit, sombre Andromède blanche et nue dans les ténèbres!* (Hugo, *Les Misérables*, 1344–45; English translation, IV.7.ii, 817)

121. In the Book of Revelation, which describes the return of Jesus and the restoration of his kingdom, images of mythical creatures and prophetic saviors pervade the entire text: "Around the throne, and on each side of the throne, are four living creatures, full of eyes in front and behind: the first living creature like a lion, the second living creature like an ox, the third living creature with a face like a human face, and

the fourth living creature like a flying eagle. And the four living creatures, each of them with six wings, are full of eyes all around and inside" (Revelation 4:6–8).

"I looked, and there was a white horse! Its rider had a bow; a crown was given to him, and he came out conquering and to conquer" (Revelation 6:2).

"When he opened the fourth seal, I heard the voice of the fourth living creature call out, Come! I looked and there was a pale green horse! Its rider's name was Death, and Hades followed with him; they were given authority over a fourth of the earth, to kill with sword, famine, and pestilence, and by the wild animals of the earth" (Revelation 6:7–8).

"And I saw a beast rising out of the sea, having ten horns and seven heads; and on its horns were ten diadems, and on its heads were blasphemous names. And the beast that I saw was like a leopard, its feet were like a bear's, and its mouth was like a lion's mouth" (Revelation 13:1–2).

122. Hugo, *Les Misérables*, 1336; English translation, IV.7.ii, 811.
123. Book of Matthew 5:1–12.

Chapter 5

Slang as the Language of Parisians

And so slang goes on decomposing and recomposing itself endlessly; a murky and swift labor that never stops.

—Victor Hugo, Les Misérables (1862)

(*Aussi l'argot va-t-il se décomposant et se recomposant sans cesse; travail obscur et rapide qui ne s'arrête jamais*)

In the late sixteenth century, the wandering misfit Pechon de Ruby found himself in the midst of various criminal organizations, uninitiated and unaware of the mysterious languages they spoke. In one account, he details encounters with members of the Argot Order at the Châtaigneraie fair:

> At the Châtaigneraie fair near Fontenay, where I was accosted by all the *Pechons, Blesches & Coesmelotiers hurez* in order to know if I knew the profession and all: asking me the word and the ways of the ceremony, it was my turn to enter into this profession & to pay the dues after the fair ended: because they knew that I didn't know anything, that is to say that I understood neither the language nor the ceremonies.[1]

Pechon's unexpected induction into the Argot Order necessitated his acquisition of their secret criminal code, a language completely foreign to the naïve protagonist. This account, like many others in circulation from the sixteenth century onward, reveals the perspective of the uninitiated outsider, while ultimately reflecting an analogous mindset of bourgeois readers in nineteenth-century France, who were eager to undergo a similar induction into the exclusive brotherhood of thieves and murderers, albeit a vicarious one. Instead of physical encounters between criminal recruiters and new members, as in Pechon's experience, readers relied on the work of slang lexicographers who beckoned their audience to immerse themselves in the forbidden language of society's untouchables.

As it made its literary début in the early nineteenth century, the slang language used by the socially marginalized, such as criminals, prostitutes, the uneducated working classes, and poor orphans, indexed both a moral and social decline. As slang became more prevalent in both popular and highbrow literature over the course of the century, it further became the language of working-class Parisians due to the influence of print and newspaper industries on the dissemination of such social representations, as well as writers' more empathetic representations of speakers of slang. This new indexical order, in fact, emerged with the publication of Victor Hugo's *Les Misérables* (1862), wherein speakers of slang were now working class, not simply hardened criminals. In addition to serial novels, several successful nonfiction genres that also contained slang, such as the dictionary, exposed an upper-class audience to lower-class speech practices, as, in response to high consumer demand in the second half of the century, several editions of slang dictionaries were published. Given low literacy rates as well as the literary preferences of the working classes of the period, the readership of these slang dictionaries was predominately middle class.

Due to their power to codify language in relation to written norms, dictionaries function as authoritative references.[2] In his study on English dictionaries, Phil Benson argues that, while they may appear to be both exhaustive and objective, dictionaries are instead ethnocentric in nature. From a political perspective, then, dictionaries therefore define the boundaries of what constitutes correct speech. In the context of nationalism or imperialism, these serve as powerful weapons in their ability to marginalize "peripheral" cultures, offering only a narrow worldview.[3] The act of including certain words, while excluding others, "is thus linked to social and ideological practices beyond the dictionary."[4]

In 1694, as part of the standardization efforts that began in the seventeenth century, the French Academy released its first official dictionary containing a list of acceptable French words and their definitions. The Academy's regular publication of dictionaries worked in conjunction with the additional standardization efforts made by Abbé Grégoire in the late eighteenth century.[5] These standardized dictionaries fulfilled both nationalistic and imperialistic objectives of the elimination of regional or foreign dialects in order for the State to maintain control over its people. In contrast, in the case of slang dictionaries, which were mainly focused on Parisian vernacular in the second half of the nineteenth century, their function markedly differed from the Standard French dictionaries, which were truly ethnocentric in nature.

Despite the influence of monolingual Standard French dictionaries, nineteenth-century slang dictionaries subverted both the linguistic and literary conventions already established in France, and therefore altered the linguistic landscape. As Anthony Lodge notes, "Since the standard language *is* the language, it is only when an innovation has succeeded in modifying the norms of the standard that a significant language change is deemed to have occurred."[6] The popularity of these alternative reference works in the second half of the century thus suggests a crumbling of the strict prescriptivism which is imposed through what Louis Althusser termed the "ideological state apparatuses," such as the Church and schools, therefore revealing the emergence of linguistic innovation through the modification of linguistic and literary conventions.[7] Moreover, it can be argued that slang dictionaries expressed much more than a need to communicate and impose a new political ideology as, in their own way, these dictionaries were a continuation of the encyclopedic goal of the eighteenth century in which classification equaled comprehension. As Benson claims, dictionaries should be viewed as "a historically situated form of discourse through which certain linguistic communities have come to represent their languages of themselves and others."[8] In other words, all dictionaries, even those that transgress linguistic standards, operate as a semiotic endeavor which expresses a desire both to determine and redefine social meaning.

The invention of this social meaning falls into the hands of the makers of dictionaries, as even though lexicographers may not view their work as "a process of representation," the nature of dictionary-making entails "a process of description" within the confines of culturally imposed constraints that may give the impression of "'accuracy' and 'objectivity.'"[9] Slang dictionaries published in nineteenth-century France thus reveal the ways in which lexicographers built on previous works, while striving to achieve more "accuracy" than their predecessors. However, unlike standard dictionaries, the accuracy of slang dictionaries relied on the firsthand experience of the lexicographer as one who, in earlier versions, slums linguistically, and later as *flâneur*, or one who cultivates his content directly from the milieus of an eclectic mix of Parisian streets and neighborhoods. The representative aspect of slang thus takes on new dimensions as the writers of dictionaries altered slang's indexical associations with their definitions, presented detailed origin stories to readers, and, near the turn of the nineteenth century, determined the ways in which slang must be performed by its speakers.

In the analysis of the five dictionaries that follow, I first explore the indexical shift in the social connotations associated with the various nineteenth-century French terms for slang, such as *argot*, *jargon*, and *langue verte*;

and second, I trace the corresponding shift in the type of literary slumming in which these lexicographers engaged. I argue that slang dictionaries both reinforced and altered the social connotations of the language, thus aiding in the sociolinguistic concept of enregisterment, or the process through which dialects and sociolects becomes socially recognized as a register by a community.[10] In other words, as Lodge explains, dialects and sociolects, which deal with "inter-speaker variation" and correspond to levels of "communicative isolation," convert to registers which pertain to "intra-speaker variation" and correspond to the variety of applications that one single speaker may execute with their language.[11] This conversion takes place through a series of social processes, and as Lodge acknowledges, there is a correlation between "the registers a person has access to" and "his place in the social structure."[12] When spoken languages become written ones, they then become enregistered, and in the case of French slang, the register pertains to a social class, such as the criminal and working classes, or a geographic location, or, as in this case, Paris.[13] Both the codification and publication of slang in dictionaries throughout the nineteenth century, and especially after 1850, indexically linked the speech forms, or slang words and expressions, to social class, as well as to geographic identity—the Parisian urbanite. The codification of slang's criminal codes and its subsequent rebranding as Parisian vernacular was ultimately mainstreamed into the Parisian language, while it further diffused the immorality associated with slang into society. Moreover, not only did slang dictionaries both codify and popularize slang, they also determined the performance of the language that involved bodily gestures as much as accent and delivery.

The dictionaries analyzed in this chapter date span the course of the nineteenth century: Eugène-François Vidocq's *Thieves: The Physiology of Their Ways and of Their Language* (*Les voleurs: physiologie de leurs mœurs et de leur langage*, 1836); Lorédan Larchey's *The Eccentricities of the French Language* (*Les excentricités de la langue française*, 1859);[14] Alfred Delvau's *Dictionary of Green Tongue: Comparative Parisian Slang* (*Dictionnaire de la langue verte: argots parisiens comparés*, 1866); Lucien Rigaud's *Dictionary of Parisian Jargon: Ancient and Modern Slang* (*Dictionnaire du jargon parisien. L'argot ancien et l'argot moderne*, 1878); and Jules Lermina and Henri Lévêque's *Thematic French-Slang Dictionary* (*Dictionnaire thématique français-argot*, 1897). While several more slang dictionaries appeared over the course of the century, including a dictionary published in 1844 as a lexical companion to Eugène Sue's *The Mysteries of Paris*, I focus primarily on these due to their market success.[15] In my analysis, I illuminate codification practices such as the classification, definition, and organization of slang terms within these dictionaries, including philological explanations, dialogues, and visual demarcation of the terms by italicization.

In addition, I discuss the literary and literal slumming that took place at the end of the early modern through the modern periods, as well as the ways in which these practices mainstreamed elements of transgressive subculture through a blurring of class boundaries and the immoral connotations associated with slang. Unlike the debates concerning literary conventions in the dispute of the serialized novel, in which opponents of the genre believed that democratization equaled degradation, instead, in the second half of the nineteenth century lexicographers equated democratization with cultural progress. I therefore reveal the ways in which slang's transformation into a mainstream vernacular becomes its enregisterment in popular dictionaries. Finally, I trace the incorporation of an embodied stylistics within slang dictionaries, in which French lexicographers in the late nineteenthcentury focused on the importance of inhabiting the role of the slang speaker through additional non-lexical indexes, thus revealing a higher degree of proficiency in the knowledge of slang by middle-class readers.

PART I: THE MEANING OF SLANG

From the late sixteenth until the late nineteenth centuries, lexicographers sought to contextualize slang socially in order to enlighten their audience about its origins, uses, meanings, dangers, and advantages. The establishment of these indexes over the course of several centuries imbued the term *argot* (slang), with a variety of social and geographical implications. *Argot* simultaneously indexed a criminal order (with a capital A), a social type (criminal, working class, and trendy Parisian, in that order), a region, and a sociolect (*argot*, with a lower-case a). Thus, in addition to compiling a list of slang words and their definitions, lexicographers further sought to present readers with both an origin story and a detailed explanation on the emergence of the language. Their desire to expand upon slang's history was often coupled with an account of the lexicographer's firsthand experience with the language in order to prove the authenticity of the dictionary itself as well as to reshape the role of the lexicographer as part compiler and part storyteller (in ways similar to a novel writer).

Although slang dictionaries and glossaries were not new to the literary landscape, there had been a boom in consumer demand for these works, especially in the latter part of the nineteenth century. Precursors to these works included Pechon de Ruby's glossary of merchant jargon in his text *The Magnanimous Life* (1596), written in the French vernacular,[16] in addition to Guillaume Bouchet's *Fifteenth Evening* (1597). Bouchet, a well-read printer and bookseller from the Poitevine region, situates his text within a wider literary scope than *The Magnanimous Life*, by referencing the anonymous author's *The Farce of Master Pathelin*, Rabelais, Erasmus, Machiavelli, Plutarch, Plato, and Aristotle. Bouchet also includes a wide vocabulary, ranging from the vulgar to the erudite. As Claudine Nédélec points out, the sheer volume of the *Evenings* demanded a competent reader.[17] Instead of a formal conclusion, Bouchet's text ends with a two-page long list of jargon and their standard equivalents.[18] The list of words that he compiles is neither alphabetical nor thematic which has the effect of giving it an oral quality. The most formative slang dictionary to appear prior to 1789 was Olivier Chereau's *Jargon or the Language of Reformed Slang* (*Le jargon ou langage de l'argot reformé*, 1630), a detailed work on different criminal organizations composed of Bohemians and wanderers that further includes a jargon dictionary of their language. Like Pechon, Chereau defines *argot* as the language of criminal organizations, such as the merchant order (*la Mercerie*), whose meetings and recruitment were held at fairs in Niort, Foutenay, and the Poitou province. Chereau's work provided the foundation for several lexicographers in the nineteenth century, such as Eugène François Vidocq and Lucien Rigaud. The earlier compilations of jargon laid the foundation for the later indexical relationship between criminality and slang, as well as the iconization of slang's first indexical order in novels, memoirs, and reference works. These early foundational texts greatly influenced dictionary writers in the latter half of the nineteenth century not only in terms of lexicon but also the varied format of the dictionary itself, which often included examples of dialogues, plays, and songs.

One of the earliest slang dictionaries of the nineteenth century was Eugène-François Vidocq's *Thieves: The Physiology of their Ways and of their Language* (1836). In *Thieves*, Vidocq includes a nonalphabetical slang-French dictionary, where, in this context, the term *argot* refers strictly to the coded slang used by criminals.[19] As Pascale Gaitet points out, Vidocq distinguishes his slang terms by both the criminal type and their geographic origin because "[a]t this point in time, argot is more fragmented than it was originally, and not yet linked to the capital, as will be the case later in the century."[20] Vidocq consulted earlier works, such as Chereau's *Jargon* and François Villon's jargon ballads I–XI, and thus his dictionary includes a variety of paratext, including letters written by thieves, slang songs, and a dialogue between criminals.[21] This ex-con's motive for publishing a slang dictionary had been the success of his memoirs, explaining that it was the opportune moment for him to "depict thieves as they are in reality, with their vices and their qualities," rather than simply teach the "dandies" and "society women" criminal words.[22] Like his memoirs, Vidocq's dictionary contributes to an iconization of slang as the language of thieves, prostitutes, and murderers. As discussed in chapter 1, the building of what Agha terms, "characterological figures," or when registers become indexically connected to the activities and identities that they sustain, in relation to the criminal identity, occurred mainly in the beginning of the nineteenth century through the mass publication and diffusion of serial novels and memoirs about crime in Paris.[23] Even though Vidocq's supposed objective was to reveal this secret code in order to crack down on crime, personal profit, and fame were more likely his main motivating factors for the publication of *Thieves*.[24] In order to rid society of evildoers, Vidocq attempts to portray the criminal identity as accurately as possible via their language:

> I believed that knowledge of their language would serve best as a means to get to know them, which is why that which was initially only a study of habits became a Dictionary of the argot language that was as complete as possible.[25]

The indexical relationship between slang and criminal identity that writers reinforced at the beginning of the century contributed to slang's iconization, and the dictionaries that appeared around the same time also contributed to this process, in addition to beginning the process of slang's enregisterment. In her analysis of Pittsburghese, Johnstone elaborates on the how's and why's of enregisterment, stating that physical appearance, written works, and images "help link linguistic form and social identity," while "particular junctures in the lives of individuals and the histories of communities" promote the enregisterment of speech practices.[26] In the early nineteenth century, the codification of slang as criminal code and its mass diffusion in serial novels and memoirs, coincided with profound social and urban changes in Paris, and thus laid the historical groundwork for its later enregisterment and indexical evolutions.

The association between language and identity altered in the second half of the nineteenth century as writers and lexicographers reappropriated criminal subculture through a process that Alfred Delvau refers to as "bourgeoisification." Slang dictionaries produced during this time notably did not seek to eliminate unsavory language and its speakers from French culture and society. Instead, a new wave of linguistic branding emerged as the strong indexical ties between slang and criminality began to loosen, just as *argot* endured a rebranding as a Parisian jargon found within all classes. As a result, the earlier immoral connotations associated with slang were neutralized. Whereas the early dictionary writers, such as Vidocq, attempted to lessen the contentiousness of their subject matter by hiding behind a mask of morality, later writers flaunted their innovative use of slang.

Published over twenty years after Vidocq's work, Lorédan Larchey's *The Eccentricities of the French Language* (1859) marks a shift from previous definitions that defined *argot* as the slang of criminals. In his dictionary, Larchey attempts to reframe slang as a kind of technical jargon found within most speech communities. His work influenced several lexicographers in the second half of the nineteenth century, including Alfred Delvau, Lucien Rigaud, and Charles Virmaître.[27] Larchey's dictionary is ordered alphabetically, and its entries often include derivatives, examples, and quotes; however, he avoids etymological explanations. Ten editions of Larchey's dictionary appeared within a twenty-year span, with his sixth edition displaying a new title: *Historical, Etymological, and Anecdotal Dictionary of Parisian Slang* (*Dictionnaire historique, étymologique et anecdotique de l'argot parisien*, 1872). This new title reflected his attempt to render the connotations of *argot* less taboo. The former title *The Eccentricities of the French Language* (1859) is broader in scope, whereas the latter 1872 title *Historical, Etymological, and Anecdotal Dictionary of Parisian Slang* advertises a narrow scope of study which is geographically centered, while further highlighting the shifting role of the dictionary writer as storyteller through its use of anecdotes. In other words, the dictionary writers' focus on Paris feeds the myth surrounding the city as a site of creation, modernity, and transformation:

> If I qualified my dictionary as *Parisian*, it is from the point of view of language, as with any other, Paris is the great meeting place. There, all of the new words are produced or converge: those of the prison like those of sports, those of the bedroom like those of the workshop, those of the barracks like those of the halls of the Assembly, those of the market like those of the university, like those of journalism [. . .]. Paris alone owns the privilege to let these terms die or to give them life, because Paris makes words trendy as it does with hats.[28]

For Larchey, Paris becomes a site of both linguistic encounter and production, functioning as the reigning authority on current trends, including the evolution of language. The transient, ephemeral nature of the city-dwellers, in addition to the population's sheer size and diversity, is inevitably mirrored in their language, an effect that further marks Paris as not only linguistically prolific but also avant-garde.

Announcing his conception of *argot* as encompassing a broader social language, Larchey asserts that

> a lot of people imagine that slang is only the language of thieves. The truth is that its domain is a lot bigger. Its etymology is proof of that. ARGOT derives (at least for us) from the old word *argue*, and does not only signify (like *argutie* which has the same origin): ruse, finesse, and subtlety. *To speak argot*, is to use the subtlety of language. Nothing more [. . .] The *Précieuses* used it like thieves did. Everybody has their slang.[29]

Here, Larchey's break from previous lexicographic works signals an ideological shift concerning the number and types social groups that slang indexes.

This shift corresponds to post-1850 urban changes such as alterations in the city's physical infrastructure and a population boom. As Johnstone explains, such fluxes in population mobility "often gives rise to new ways of speaking enregistered with new contexts for their use."[30] By broadening slang to connote any *sociolect* (a technical language particular to a specific speech community), Larchey extracts the negative associations from the word, allowing it more universal application. Jean-René Klein posits this neutralization as a phenomenon that occurred specifically in the second half of the nineteenth century: "Under this new terminology, it is the concept of slang that gets diluted: *eccentricities of the language, green tongue, Parisian slang, Parisian language, Parisian jargon* constitute in a way 'synonyms' covering a rather indistinct notion."[31] Therefore, no longer is the slang of society's degenerates infecting the upper classes; instead, it is reflective of the infinite number of social types and sub-types that populate Paris. As a result of this linguistic melting pot, slang's previous moral associations become equally muddled. Since the social background of slang speakers varies, the degenerate morality previously associated with the criminal and working classes can no longer be pinned down on one speech community. Moreover, even though dictionaries suggest that its chosen words imply an agreement on meanings by an entire community, Benson acknowledges that this is not the case: "Class, gender, ethnicity and political opinion are four of the factors that have been identified as determining the degree to which dictionary users are likely to recognize themselves in the dictionary."[32] Slang dictionaries written by middle-class lexicographers thus fostered an indexical rewiring between language and social groups. Nevertheless, these works were not intended for slang users, such as the lower classes, but rather only for bourgeois readers, thus indicating a collective bourgeois interest in Parisian subculture which was combined with a class agenda of both linguistic and cultural appropriation.

In his *Historical, Etymological, and Anecdotal Dictionary of Parisian Slang*, Larchey includes a section entitled, "The Seven Elements of Slang" (*Les sept éléments de l'argot*), in order to provide his further linguistic analysis of what constitutes *argot*, wherein he discusses etymologies, word modifications, and substitutions, phonetics, play-on-words, and foreign imports. The influence of Old and Middle French, in addition to the use of foreign words, thus signals slang as a language of creative interpretation, rather than one of creation itself.[33] This new twist on a familiar lexicon further highlights the evolutionary quality of language as well as neutralizes slang's criminal connotations that were so pervasive in the first half of the nineteenth century. In Part IV of his dictionary, entitled, "Its Relationship with Ways of Life" (*Ses rapports avec les mœurs*), Larchey addresses the fact that slang possesses social indexes: "In slang more than any other language, certain terms characterize an order of ideas, habits, and instincts."[34] Through an analysis of the number of synonyms for several words, Larchey acknowledges previously held notions regarding slang speakers as arising from the criminal classes, along with the degenerate moral connotations this indexed by default. However, he then transitions from these earlier indexes to contemporary indexicalities; in other words, those that involve the working classes:

> In all fairness, however, one would know to treat with an absolute severity the popular element that serves as the basis of the preceding observations. How would the common people pride themselves on the finesse within their language? [. . .] If one does not want to be shocked by the rustic nature of this form, the study on Parisian slang will make them discover, to the most eminent degree, certain qualities of color.[35]

Through his social shift of slang's connotations from the dangerous to the working classes to Parisians more generally, thus marking slang as a language indexical of Parisians, Larchey further includes slang's previous immoral associations as well. Stating that his motivation in creating such a work is the need to know "that which is said" (*ce qui se dit*), rather than "that which has to be said" (*ce qui doit se dire*), Larchey seeks to provide a depth of knowledge that would satisfy the standards of ancient, classical, and contemporary authors.[36] In addition to giving slang respectable origins, Larchey further brands it as fashionable; in this manner, he commodifies slang differently from his predecessors who had instead emphasized its taboo factor. Larchey thus acknowledges both the universalization of the language and its ability to extend to various social strata. Whereas the lexicographer of the past touted his descent into the Parisian underworld, braving where no soul would dare go in order to expose this secret criminal code, the lexicographer of the second half of the nineteenth century boasted of broader social access, thus transforming his position from someone who goes slumming to that of *flâneur* in order to flaunt what was one of the hottest linguistic trends of the modern era. The lexicographers who followed Larchey fulfilled a role much like the one he established: they acknowledge slang's universalizing quality, as well as the language's capacity to simultaneously index both the criminal classes and all Parisians. Thus, despite its origins as a subversive language, in the latter half of the nineteenth century, slang transforms into a wide urban trend marked by both its literary and cultural richness.

The evolution of the lexicographer in the second half of the nineteenth century into a storytelling *flâneur* who rebranded slang as Parisian jargon further included the language's ability for subversion. One such lexicographer, Alfred Delvau, an unconventional, outspoken journalist from a bourgeois background notably used his dictionaries as a weapon against the censorship implemented by Napoléon III during the Second Empire. Delvau's *Erotic*

Modern Dictionary (*Dictionnaire érotique moderne*, 1864) was, in fact, so contentious that it could not be published in France, initially making an anonymous appearance in Belgium before finding its way across the border.[37] Once established in France, the dictionary became an instant success, and Delvau's anonymity as "a professor of Green Tongue" (*un professeur de Langue Verte*) allowed him to evade arrest.[38] His dictionary is ordered alphabetically, with each entry containing a quote from noted authors, such as Villon, popular songwriters (Béranger), anonymous songs, Arabic songs, anonymous persons, medieval farces, and Delvau himself. The extent to which he references classical French literature was, as Brett Bowles asserts, an ingenious attempt at destabilizing canonical French literature.[39] In his introduction, Delvau states that the creation of such a dictionary emerged from necessity. In addition, he lauds the power in speaking authentically, while condemning the hypocrisy of the Academy. As its title implies, the *Erotic Modern Dictionary* focuses specifically on sexual jargon, a subject matter that then was just as marginalized as its speakers.[40] For Delvau, in spite of society's exclusion of what it deemed untouchables, integration was as inevitable for them as it was for their language. While the sociopolitical mindset of the day did not favor the inclusion of subcultures and nonstandard languages, especially given the extreme censorship under Napoléon III, Delvau nevertheless designates himself as the caretaker of abandoned expressions and words left for dead at the foot of the Academy's doors. His dictionary is thus the self-proclaimed orphanage in which they shall be housed, until the realization that "that which is spoken must be written, and everything must be spoken" manifests itself in the sanctioned dictionaries and literary works of regulatory institutions.[41] The *Erotic Modern Dictionary* thus stands as Delvau's attempt at subverting centuries of linguistic prescriptivism through his revealing of an overtly risqué topic.

Two years following the publication of his *Erotic Modern Dictionary* (1864), Delvau released the *Dictionary of Green Tongue: Comparative Parisian Slang* (1866). This work, while contentious, was not nearly as scandalous as his *Erotic Dictionary* had been, which helped Delvau escape prosecution a second time.[42] This dictionary contains nearly seven thousand entries and classifications for various types of Parisian slang and was an immediate consumer success. In the *Preface*, Delvau presents an even broader definition of the term *argot* to include any technical language spoken by any specialized group. He breaks the term down into two sub-divisions for his readers, referring to the English words, *cant* and *slang*, as analogous terms: "Cant is a particular slang; slang is general. Thieves especially speak the first one; everyone in Paris speaks the second one."[43] Delvau's use of the English *cant* to refer to criminal codes further merges the earlier definition of *argot* with a foreign word, therefore allowing *argot* to undergo a redefinition as Parisian jargon. Through a re-enregisterment of the term *argot*, writers and lexicographers could now expand the content of their works to extend beyond criminal culture in order to encompass a more panoramic perspective of Parisian society.

Both the emphasis on urban life and the rebranding of slang as the language of Parisians that came about with lexicographers such as Larchey and Delvau continued well into the nineteenth century. In 1878, Lucien Rigaud published his *Dictionary of Parisian Jargon: Ancient and Modern Slang*, a dictionary that echoes similarities to its predecessors.[44] Arranged alphabetically, the entries are occasionally contain quotes from various sources. In this work, Rigaud refers to the term *argot*, in a more democratic sense, locating it geographically in Paris. In addition, he lists the various professional jargons, citing the books he consulted, and emphasizing the speech habits of the working classes.[45] Moreover, in the title, Rigaud introduces a temporal demarcation between *ancient argot* and *modern argot*, a distinction that that had already occurred in earlier works; however, one that earlier lexicographers had never given much treatment. In the late-nineteenth century, lexicographers' attempted to render the term *argot* as indexical of a multitude of speech communities and social types by neutralizing its former association with both the criminal classes and declining morals.[46] Rigaud thus includes the earlier term *jargon*, in addition to the contemporary one *argot*, using them interchangeably in his definition:

> Parisian jargon is a strange language, free from appearance, sometimes somber and brief, sometimes full of imagery and enjoyable, sometimes masked like Arlequin, like him it is dressed in bits and fragments, who runs in the streets and is recruited in the street, in prisons, in shops, in the boutique, at the counter, in the workshop, in the barracks, in school, at the theater, in the homes of artists and literary types, bankers and charlatans. Every caste, every public sector possesses its own jargon. From the thief to the diplomat, from *Lacenaire* until *Talleyrand*, everyone speaks more or less slang.[47]

As Rigaud suggests, slang ran freely in the streets, invading every nook and cranny of the city, and every social class; it could be neither captured nor controlled. The democratization of *argot* by authors and lexicographers in the second half of the nineteenth century was partly a subversion of linguistic hegemony, and partly a marketing strategy to make money. However, it is also a capitulation to that fact that, in any age and society, language is an evolving entity that cannot remain in a fixed form; it is susceptible to the changes of the times, and thus resisting it would be to resist the fluxes of society.

In his dictionary, Rigaud gives a philological overview of slang, analyzing the various theories on its etymology, temporally locating "primitive argot" (*l'argot primitif*) as the slang of the fifteenth century.[48] The use of the word "primitive" to qualify earlier representations of the language suggests an evolution as well as supports the more neutral social connotations that the term indexes in the late nineteenth century. By establishing this distinction, Rigaud creates an indexical distance between the slang of the past and that of the modern day, reassuring his reader that "primitive slang" was the language of less-evolved human beings—biologically, intellectually, morally, and therefore linguistically. This temporal distinction between slang of the past and the modern day further functions as a re-enregisterment that introduces new social contexts to the language.

Despite this clarification, Rigaud nevertheless firmly places slang within the realm of the scholarly. Although slang had been a language of criminals, its existence had also been entirely dependent on grammarians and scholars, known as *Les Archisuppôts*, who created, taught, and modified the language in order to preserve the secrecy of the Argot criminal order. Rigaud traces a brief geographical evolution to accompany the social one that began after the publication of Chereau's *Jargon* which, according to Rigaud, led to the decline of the language due to the inability of criminals to make reforms.[49] The exposure of the secret language to authorities had amounted to a dispersion of the Argot Order that further made the maintenance of the language more difficult, while also causing those who were in charge of its preservation ("the most intelligent") to pursue more lucrative endeavors. Rigaud proposes his own theory on the matter, however, asserting that a lack of imagination, in addition to a lack of prospective criminals worthy of the order, were the reasons behind the decline of slang's linguistic maintenance.[50] From this point of view, the migration of slang into the hands of the nineteenth-century lexicographer seemed both natural and inevitable.

Nevertheless, slang's association with academia does not dissipate in the late nineteenth century. Rigaud makes clear that slang's home has been the literary world ever since Villon:

> François Villon spoke this tongue and left some curious specimens of it, among others some ballads whose meaning is not easy to grasp. Later, slang counted for numerous lexicographers who tried to track it in its evolutions. It drew writers; and, presently, the novels of Balzac, Eugène Sue, and Victor Hugo greatly contributed to spread this trend amongst the public. Today who is the novel manufacturer who is assured of success if he will not look for his hero in the shadowy world where the slang language is everyday currency [. . .].[51]

Here, Rigaud acknowledges the profound role that contemporary authors played in terms of the public exposure to, as well as a fascination with, slang. This was a two-way street, as the public's reception of slang dictionaries undoubtedly influenced the language's pervasiveness in literature, a fact that Rigaud acknowledges when he states that the inclusion of criminal codes and a depiction of the urban underworld guaranteed the market success of any novel. In addition, the simultaneous undermining and reinforcement of regulatory institutions that was present in Delvau's work appear in Rigaud's as well in the form of a call to create a "Chair of Modern Argot," a move that would "render a great service to French humanities [. . .] because the majority of our writers are behind fifty years on slang as it is spoken presently."[52] The unifying theme among later lexicographers is the recognition of a literary revolution that will permanently alter the bourgeois literary landscape. The Academy's refusal to officially sanction less "literary" speech practices would be a refusal of modernity itself, as the rate at which languages transform, disappear, and reappear calls for slang's preservation:

> All of this forms a considerable whole. Taken in its entirety, Parisian jargon is so varied, it makes up such a large number of words and expressions, every day its potential grows so much that one wanted to follow it step by step, it would be necessary, each year, to devote to it a glossary in the care of forty academics of a new kind, and forty academics would hardly suffice for this work, if they wanted to omit any expressions that show up incessantly.[53]

The constant evolution of slang words and expressions demands the rigorous (and perhaps impossible) task of harvesting, organizing, and enregistering the lexicon in written form. A linguistic effort of this largesse would necessitate a greater effort on the part of lexicographers than the creation of a standardized dictionary. The reason that Rigaud emphasizes the enormity of this task is to valorize the work of the slang lexicographer in relation to that of the writers of Standard French. At the same time, in line with previous slang dictionaries, Rigaud crafts his own origin story, one that writes him into slang's ongoing history as the rightful keeper of both its maintenance and continuity. Moreover, the alteration of the definition of *argot*, as well as its social and moral connotations over the course of several decades in the nineteenth century, reveals a newly democratic view of what was formerly a criminal language, a newer social perspective which became deeply rooted in its geographical location of the city of Paris.

PART II: THE CITY AS SOURCE

Unlike nineteenth-century writers who flaunted their real-life descent into the lower-class milieu by slumming in districts frequented by the criminal and working classes, slang lexicographers affirmed their authenticity instead through a social wandering, or *flânerie*, into all districts of Paris. They thus functioned as both secret observers and mediators of slang, while their presence designated them as a kind of cartographer of linguistic boundaries, both literal and figurative. In their works, these dictionary writers often marked out geographical pockets where slang had migrated, as well as where it currently resided. Linguistic boundaries corresponded to physical boundaries that further corresponded to social boundaries. By delineating these linguistic frontiers, slang lexicographers both constructed and deconstructed the language through their detailed accounts of the language's etymological, geographical, and social origins, which indexed for a nineteenth-century reader the social background of the speakers, in addition to their professional, physical, and moral makeup. The linking of slang to Paris that occurred in slang dictionaries after 1850 re-enregistered this former criminal code not only in a specific place but also as a specific social identity.

The geographical makeup of slang in early dictionaries aligned with the physical boundaries outlined in early novels. In both genres, novelists and lexicographers mapped the poor, criminal, and working-class districts, or slums, as sites where slang speakers resided. For instance, Vidocq's experience as a criminal granted him clear insider knowledge of the language. Following his professional conversion to an agent, his task was to frequent "all of the evil places of the interior and its surrounding areas,"[54] and thus he spent time in Paris' "places of ill-repute" (*endroits mal famés*), which were mostly "outside city limits" (*hors barrière*).[55] Through his fraternization with criminals as well as his ability to pass himself off as "one of them" (*un des leurs*), Vidocq became an omnipresent figure within the city: "I was everywhere, I knew everything."[56] This access to forbidden social spaces, however, is a dangerous undertaking. Nevertheless, figures such as Vidocq constituted a rare social type who had been initiated into the criminal hierarchy and could thus "pass" as criminal, even after their conversion in order to infiltrate spaces inaccessible to bourgeois readers.

Like Vidocq's ubiquitous knowledge of the streets of Paris, in his *Dictionary of Parisian Jargon*, Rigaud cites various Parisian haunts that were not particular to one social milieu, but rather to several:

> We have collected, with care, and from a little bit everywhere, elements of this book: from the street, the workshops, the barracks, the theater, the most gay and sinister places; we wanted to hear the high and low criminal classes speak, and we have rummaged through a little bit of every world, every corner and nook of society, and from all of these strictly prohibited words, there is not a single one that was not the object of intense examination.[57]

For Rigaud, it was the democratization of these social and geographical spaces that was paving the way for a "literary revolution,"[58] as the language of the streets would inspire the new wave of writers to come. The geographical positioning of Delvau's *Dictionary of Green Tongue* also widens from the criminal underworld and ghettoes to encompassing the entire city of Paris. In fact, several dictionary writers, including Delvau, flaunted their work as that of linguistic *flâneurs* in order to compile a comprehensive list of terms. Those who did not conduct the appropriate fieldwork became targets of critique, such as Larchey and his *Historical Dictionary*, which focuses on Parisian slang but contains no mention of whether he obtained his material from the streets.[59] For this, Larchey's work was openly denounced by Delvau: "His mistake was not to have gathered these orphans here from the street, but from books [. . .]."[60] It was therefore imperative for the reputation of the lexicographer, as well as the authenticity of the dictionary, to outline sensory experiences within the city because doing so revealed the firsthand work of the dictionary-maker, demonstrating that his word lists were indeed both contemporary and socially varied.

Delvau emphasizes that the *Dictionary of Green Tongue* centers geographically on Paris, a place that exists as its own entity, beyond even the country itself: "In France, one perhaps speaks French; but in Paris, we speak slang, and a slang that varies from one district to another, from one street to another, from one floor to another."[61] Specifically, Delvau cites la Rue Saint-Antoine in the fourth arrondissement of Paris, a main road that runs from Place de la Bastille, a historical site that is emblematic of revolution, to the Marais, a quarter in Paris that once housed Parisian nobility. The physical connection between these two districts symbolizes a social connection between the old aristocracy in the Marais, who metonymically represent Standard French and their institutionalized measures to "purge" society of undesirable speech practices, and the revolutionaries of Place de la Bastille, who metonymically represent the rise of the lower classes, including their language and culture which had been deemed "nonstandard." The second street that Delvau cites is la Rue Neuve-Bréda, which today is la Rue Clauzel in the ninth arrondissement in the quartier Saint-Georges, an area of Paris that has a reputation as being distinctly bohemian, artistic, and literary as well as a well-known area for street prostitutes. In making this geographical reference, Delvau acknowledges the creative potential of slang as well as the avant-garde attitude that characterizes this area that allows for artistic evolution. He further provides an extensive list of more general places where slang can be found: a painter or a worker's workshop, literary bars or cabarets, or any place where there exists an encounter of a variety of social classes. His list reveals a widening of class associations with slang as well as an overall diffusion of slang within the public domain, in addition to underscoring the inherent link between physical location and linguistic innovation.

The deviations in language between physical spaces mirror the complexities and variations of the city's inhabitants, which, in terms of slang's sociolinguistic evolution, Delvau acknowledges. For instance, he states that a handful of slang words and expressions are the production of prison life. He also offers an interesting description of the physical journey that a word takes on its path to "bourgeoisification," which is an inventive way of referring to the process of mainstreaming that slang was undergoing: "One could be surprised too, and rightly so, to see attributed to this working-class language a bunch of words that come from the lexicon of the labor camp, prison, and evil places."[62] Delvau even traces the precise trajectory a slang expression has as it travels from the prison to the mouth of the working-class Parisian:

> An expression slips from the withered lips of the convict, not in the labor camp, where it is prohibited for good people to go, but in a cabaret, in a Parisian street, where it is prohibited for rogues to spend time and where they all rush over like hornets to a honey cake: ten pairs of ears gather the expression and ten mouths repeat it—without cleaning it up. It makes its way from workshop to workshop, from neighborhood to neighborhood until the day when, falling in its turn from the lips of a drunk, into a literary café or an artsy brasserie, it is thus collected by a curious listener, by some watchful flâneur, who finds it emphatic and original, and who spreads it here and there—so much so and so well that, finally it enters into an article, then into a book, and then into general circulation.[63]

Delvau's description of slang's physical voyage throughout the urban landscape emphasizes the indexical evolution of a language previously identified as the speech of the criminal classes. When considering the sociolinguistic changes surrounding French slang from the late Renaissance to the late nineteenth century, the linguistic process that Delvau details is, in fact, enregisterment. He describes to his readers the slow transition this primarily oral language makes through the various class milieus, as it starts from the bottom and works its way up the social hierarchy, until it makes its way into the privileged hands of the male writer or lexicographer, who possesses the talent, but more importantly the social standing, to adapt this criminal anti-language to written form. Through this codification of criminal anti-language via writing, and especially its compilation in dictionaries, slang became officially recognized as a linguistic register in nineteenth-century France.

The urban innovations taking place during the second half of the nineteenth century, along with soaring population increases, spurred greater interaction between people of all social backgrounds. While the fairs and marketplaces of the Loire Valley were once the centers of organized crime, Paris now ruled as the hub of urban crime. Following the wide-sweeping changes instituted by Napoléon III during the Second Empire, overseen by

Georges-Eugène Haussmann as the Prefect of the Department of the Seine, the encounter between persons of all classes became a daily norm. In his in-depth analysis of the structural changes that took place in Paris at this time, historian David Harvey explains that "[Haussmann's] investments covered not only a new network of roads but also sewers, parks, monuments, and symbolic spaces, schools, churches, administrative buildings, housing, hotels, commercial premises, and the like."[64] The opening up of public spaces and the construction of wide boulevards, coupled with a higher concentration of people, forced linguistic encounters as well. Due to these urban innovations, including the development of modern police forces, criminals could no longer maintain their linguistic code so easily, as both adoptions and adaptations by dominant social classes were bound to take place. For Delvau, it seemed that the working classes, including artists and artisans, were the most susceptible to the influence of criminal slang on their own speech practices.[65] In spite of this trajectory, it is ultimately up to the lexicographer, characterized as a vigilant wanderer, who possesses the artistic inclinations to see beyond the vulgarity of slang expressions in order to guide them into the literary domain for a middle-class readership to adopt. This "watchful *flâneur*" visits all Parisian districts, both public and private spaces, in order to transform the earlier slumming of his predecessors into a desired modern practice.

Within the list of people and places that he mentions, Delvau also includes the host of social limitations bounded by class. The site in which the interaction between criminals and "honest people" takes place is an open, free-flowing space, while the enclosed environments of the prisons and work camps neither permit the interaction between persons of opposing moral views nor the interaction between differing languages. This containment serves to prevent both moral and linguistic corruption but also occurs to the detriment of linguistic, and by extension, artistic evolution. This argument that physical and social boundaries work as an impediment to creative progress, and not a catalyst of it, represents a radical paradigm shift in French attitudes toward art.

In *Dictionary of Green Tongue*, as *flâneur*, Delvau's approach is more socially removed. At several points in the Preface, Delvau boasts of his time spent on the streets of Paris as a source of authenticity for his dictionary:

> [I] have walked past so many times the intersections and the universities of the city we call Lutèce, that I have picked their stem and collected on their native dunghill all the words for my Dictionary, all the bizarre terms, all the picturesque expressions which find themselves accumulated there [. . .].[66]

Like flowers gently picked from a field, Delvau harvests words and expressions from different districts of Paris. The factor of danger ever-present in the slumming of earlier works is not emphasized, and even though *flânerie* involves both effort and mobility, it is mostly presented as a leisurely activity. From his wanderings, Delvau cultivates material for an "unpublishable" book due to its obscene content,[67] while his newfound lack of social division between city districts and its resulting democratization of the urban space encourages linguistic encounters and evolutions.[68] The redesign of Paris' interior space under Haussmann resulted in "powerful effects on Parisian economy, politics, and culture"[69] which included, as Catherine Nesci notes, the designation of places in the city that were not particular to either gender or class background "such as churches, dance halls, brasseries, literary or artistic salons, theaters on the Boulevard du Temple, exhibition rooms, balls, department stores, [and] train stations" in addition to specific events such as "revolutions, public celebrations, [and] Carnival [. . .]."[70] The increased traffic flow between Parisian districts, as well as the consequential creation of social sites that encouraged contact between the upper and lower classes, served to push slums to the periphery of the city. From a perspective of spatial relations, the slumming that characterized early nineteenth-century works naturally evolves in tandem with the urban transformations taking place after 1850. With the democratization of certain places, as well as easier access to Parisian districts, Delvau's depiction of the acquisition of slang words as an effortless city jaunt corresponds to the newfound sense of the city as "a world of speedup and rapid compression of space relations."[71] With larger roads, better lighting, increased accessibility, and the emergence of a capitalist society, Haussmann gentrified the once forbidden quartiers of the criminal underworld and working class ghettoes, allowing for a modern relationship of writers with the city space and its inhabitants. Because of his time spent on the streets of Paris, Delvau traverses both physical and linguistic boundaries, while the city itself becomes the most significant, immediate creator of an inherently ephemeral phenomenon: a democratic evolution of language.

PART III: PERFORMANCE AND SLANG

Throughout the nineteenth century, another significant evolution concerning the performance of slang emerges within dictionaries. As Agha points out, vocabulary that indexes social stereotypes may expand to include other stylistic features of speech such as bodily gestures and behaviors, material accessories, and pronunciation.[72] By the mid-to-late part of the nineteenth century, dictionary writers insisted upon the need to showcase the delivery of slang through the speaker's voice and body. In terms of enregisterment, Johnstone explains that "[a] person who uses a particular form while looking a particular way can link the linguistic form to the look."[73] Whether by a direct explanation of this delivery, or by the inclusion of examples, usually in the form of dialogues and songs, lexicographers began to expand the indexical cues beyond the lexicon itself to include the physical body.

Earlier compilations, such as Chereau's dictionary, *Jargon or the Language of Reformed Slang* (1630), included a dialogue between two slang speakers (*Argotiers*), *Le Malingreux* and *Le Polisson*. This dialogue introduced a theatrical aspect to Chereau's work, as it not only contextualized jargon for readers in terms of conversation but also echoed the same elements of farce from stories in the Middles Ages in which the criminals were transformed into victims. The fact that Chereau frames slang in a theatrical way helps audiences better to comprehend the terms found in *Jargon* as well as indulges the lexicographer's desire to create both an origin narrative and a social context. Additionally, within the narrative Chereau inserts popular slang songs about the different members of the Argot Order, while including their enemies. Through approaching his explanations with dialogue, storytelling, and popular song, Chereau shows readers how slang was performed, and, at the same time, he illuminates the fact that slang is a language that *must* be performed for a literate audience that is excluded from the demographic in which slang circulated.

Such performative showcasing continued in nineteenth-century slang dictionaries. For instance, Vidocq includes theatrical dialogues in *Memoirs* and *Thieves*.[74] Notably, meta-theater is further included when Vidocq, who is disguised as a criminal, volunteers to play himself in a play called "Vidocq defeated."[75] As this performative aspect of slang developed over the century, it culminated in the embodied indexicality present within Jules Lermina's and Henri Lévêque's *Thematic French-Slang Dictionary* (1897). Their dictionary is alphabetical with each entry numerated and includes related idiomatic expressions and/or maxims and proverbs. The last sixty pages of the dictionary include an index of slang terms also arranged alphabetically and includes page numbers that reference the entries found in the French-slang section of the dictionary. In the Preface, Lermina and Lévêque present several of the same aspects of slang as their predecessors. For instance, they cite slang's ephemerality as the principal reason for its difficulty, especially when it comes to learning slang, and they characterize it as the most difficult language to learn (in fact, it is never fully knowable).[76] They situate slang geographically in Paris, while promoting the language as universal.[77] These aspects of the *Thematic French-Slang Dictionary* are ones that lexicographers in the second half of the nineteenth century had already enregistered. Nonetheless, a few distinct differences within Lermina and Lévêque's work distinguish it as a revolutionary slang text, as well as one that reveals the drastic ideological changes that had occurred since the earlier dictionaries of the 1830s. For instance, the objective of the *Thematic French-Slang Dictionary* is as follows:

Our ambition is higher. We noticed that the people of the world were greatly eager, under the pretext of artistic airs, to speak slang. Without discussing this trend—of which we are not judges—at the very least we wanted to provide to these ambitious folks the means to speak purely and boldly this language that they hardly speak and that they ruin with ghastly mistakes [. . .] Thanks to this dictionary, each one will know how to translate their impressions into the language of pimps and prostitutes.[78]

In the late nineteenth century, speaking slang is no longer specifically indexical of the criminal and working classes, but now also refers to artists, the bohemian lifestyle, and a liberal mindset, while indexing an overall Parisian trendiness. Lermina and Lévêque are more concerned with a public who speaks "proper" slang, a notion that completely subverted the efforts of regulatory institutions such as the French Academy, as well as the prescriptivist objectives of standard dictionaries that are typically "surrounded by myths of 'objectivity' and 'authority.'"[79] Unlike earlier dictionaries, Lermina and Lévêque's cataloguing of slang had less to do with the elimination of "bad" French and its speakers, and more to do with the bodily execution and performance of slang. The idea of performance is not entirely new to slang compilations: many of them contain theatrical dialogues between criminals or workers and argot songs that were meant to show the reader what these terms might look like in conversation. For example, in the 1849 dictionary entitled, *The New Complete Dictionary of Jargon and Slang, or the Language of Thieves Revealed* (*Le Nouveau Dictionnaire complet du jargon et de l'argot, ou Le Langage des voleurs dévoilé*), the cover page states that the back of the work contains "songs in French and in slang."[80] In 1887, Albert Barrère compiled a French slang-English dictionary for British audiences called, *Argot and Slang: A New French and English Dictionary of the Cant Words, Quaint Expressions, Slang Terms and Flash Phrases Used in the High and Low Life of Old and New Paris*, that included excerpts from medical texts, memoirs, novels, plays, poems, and songs. Nonetheless, Lermina and Lévêque explore new frontiers in linking the theatrical aspect of the language to the notion of proper speech. For them, to speak slang correctly one must manipulate their voice and gestures, and not just regurgitate what authors and lexicographers have written, which had the effect of establishing a new kind of prescriptivism[81]:

First of all, in order to speak slang, one needs slang's voice. Not the drawling and mischievous accent that one attributes to chic pimps and other slang academics, but something elusive and unique, that captures both the familiarity and the "Idontgiveadamn-ism" [. . .]. We will add all of the facial traits, the infinitesimal accentuations of the voice, the slightest gestures or simple shutters of the hand, of the hip, of the shoulder and of the foot which help with the interpretation of the word, of the interjection, and greatly increase its suggestiveness. A simple slap of the palm on the thigh accentuates a "Go to hell!" in the most energetic way.[82]

Lermina and Lévêque thus codify slang as an equally embodied language that requires attention to corporal stylization: a specific accent and intonation, facial expressions, and slight gestures of the hands, hip, shoulder, and foot are necessary components to the interpretation of the language itself. With slang, then, the body therefore becomes a function of language and language becomes a function of the body. Although French novelists in the early nineteenth century represented slang as simultaneously spoken and embodied via the criminal character, it would not be until the late nineteenth century that lexicographers overseeing the official enregisterment of this anti-language, validated this inherent characteristic of slang. From a sociolinguistic perspective indexicality, on a fundamental level, "arises from bodily engagement with the world,"[83] which Charles Sanders Peirce defined as "all natural signs and physical symptoms."[84] As Mary Bucholtz and Kira Hall note, "[e]mbodied motion has been theorized as the primordial source of indexicality, given Peirce's assertion that the most basic indexical form is the pointing gesture."[85] The "infinitesimal" manipulations of voice intonation and bodily gestures produce infinitesimal meanings of the same utterances, allowing for each individual to be read socially via their linguistic delivery through the body:

> Especially in slang, it is important to not imitate anybody. Everyone must mold their language to their own nature, in such a way that it is the perfect expression of individuality [. . .]. Speak to me in slang and I will tell you who you are. We are repeating it, everyone creates their slang based on the known elements.[86]

For Lermina and Lévêque, to perform slang implicates the entire body, not just the function of speaking; the body communicates key social information and constitutes an act of individuality, rather than a form of criminal imitation. The emphasis on voice, gestures, and facial expressions in the *Thematic French-Slang Dictionary* further reveals the corporal aspects of communication and social identity that constitute an embodied slang. Moreover, in addition to written text, the body becomes a new means of enregistering the language. The link between the body, language, and individuality thus distinguishes the *Thematic French-Slang Dictionary* from past slang dictionaries that sought to reveal criminal codes or rebrand slang as Parisian vernacular. By the end of the nineteenth century, dictionary writers such as Lermina and Lévêque placed a new value on individuality, as well as the ways in which both speech practices and bodily movements can create unique identities, rather than only serve as a strict identity marker of a criminal, the working class, or the bourgeoisie. This ideological differentiation reveals the formation of a new literary terrain in which writers increasingly valorize the experience of individuals from all class backgrounds, a practice that will come to fruition in the literature of the twentieth century.

NOUVEAU ENREGISTERMENT

An analysis of dictionaries and their enregisterment of slang reveals the slow paradigm shift away from this previously criminal language that culminated at the end of the nineteenth century. Starting with Pechon in the sixteenth century, the desire to eliminate slang, and ideally its speakers, from society transforms after 1850 into a desire to rebrand it as a distinctly Parisian form of speech undergoing a "bourgeoisification." By enregistering slang terms in dictionaries, writers expanded the social indexicalities related to slang. The definition of *argot* as the coded sociolect of criminals, which appears in earlier compilations such as Vidocq's *Thieves*, eventually gains social associations with the working classes, and finally, in the second half of the nineteenth century, with Parisians, in works published by Delvau, Larchey, and Rigaud. Because of this process of re-enregisterment, slang not only became indexical of a social type but also of a specific place—the city of Paris. In previous works, slang had been the product of the countryside, especially the Loire Valley, while in later works, it eventually came to be associated with Paris. As both fairs and the urban terrain possessed a steady free flow of goods, people, and language, these served as sites of linguistic encounter where interaction and language evolution could take place. The wide-sweeping urban changes instantiated under Haussmann's direction provoked new identity crises which broke down social barriers, thus allowing for the evolution of language practices as well as the emergence of new social orders in relation to these practices.

For dictionary writers, Larchey and Delvau, slang was no longer specific to the Parisian underworld, and in a subversive move, as well as an appropriation, they purveyed the slang of the criminal classes as fit for the fashionable urbanite. With this new marketing of slang as a Parisian vernacular, the lexicographer transforms into a figure who infiltrates society at all levels in order to harvest a lexicon composed of non-standard dialects, idiolects, and sociolects.

As did slang itself, the lexicographer also underwent a transformation, moving from reformed criminal who went slumming (Vidocq) to Parisian *flâneur*. This shift in roles allowed for the possibility of greater social awareness, change, and an acceptance of subcultures that demanded a discerning eye in order to fully appreciate slang's creative potential. In the prefaces to their dictionaries, these dictionary writers provide intricate geographical details of exact regions, cities, and neighborhoods, in order to create verbal maps of their wanderings that corresponded to linguistic markers.

By the end of the nineteenth century, lexicographers argue for slang's ability to create novel identities, if correctly performed via the body. The theatrical dialogues, metanarratives, and songs found in Pechon, Chereau, and Vidocq's compilations of slang provided the framework for future dictionary makers to include textual examples in order to show readers the embodied execution of the language. Following these writers, the publication of Lermina and Lévêque's *Thematic French-Slang Dictionary* validated the role of the body vis-à-vis slang language as well as the power of the individual to stylize language through the body (and vice versa), thus providing a radical interpretation of nonconventional speech practices. This emphasis on linguistic stylization in the late nineteenth century further affirms the corporal as slang's embodied form, and while slang still conveyed important social information in terms of the speaker's class background, profession, and perceived morality, it now did so with a different intention. While early nineteenth-century lexicographers set out to expose their middle-class audience in order to protect them from and eradicate evildoers, in contrast, late-nineteenth century lexicographers reveal linguistic innovation as a new means of enregistering the language, as well as the basis for individuality. As the following chapter reveals, this individuality, born of spoken and embodied slang, provided women with an opportunity to subvert gender norms through speech.

NOTES

1. *[À] la foire de la Chastaigneraye près Fontenay, où je fus accosté de tous les Pechons, Blesches & Coesmelotiers hurez pour sçavoir si j'entervois le gourd & toutime: me demandans le mot & les façons de la ceremonie, ce fut à moy à entrer en carriere & payer le soupper apres la foire passee: car ils cogneurent que je n'entervois que de beaux, c'est-à-dire que je n'entendois le langage ni les cérémonies.* (Pechon, 49)

2. Milroy and Milroy, *Authority in Language*, 27.

3. Benson, *Ethnocentrism*, 4.

4. Ibid., 28.

5. For more on the history of French language norms and standardization, see chapter 3, "Slang as Language Politics."

6. Lodge, *A Sociolinguistic History*, 6.

7. For Althusser, "ideological state apparatuses" refer to the institutions (religious, scholarly, familial, legal, political, informational, and cultural) that produce rules and regulations, and express certain perspectives that reinforce the dominant capitalist ideology. While non-violent, these institutions exercise a psychological hegemony over society in order to keep the dominated classes from achieving social mobility. See his essay "Idéologie et appareils idéologiques d'État (notes pour une recherche)" in *La Pensée* vol. 151, June 1970, pp. 3–38.

8. Benson, *Ethnocentrism*, 24.

9. Ibid., 8.

10. Agha, *Language and Social Relations*, 81.

11. Lodge, *A Sociolinguistic History*, 10.

12. Ibid.

13. Barbara Johnstone points out that "a linguistic act can enregister linguistic features with multiple contexts" (Johnstone, "Enregisterment," 635), while Lodge reveals that "a switch of register may entail a switch of dialect" (10).

14. Larchey published several versions from 1858 to 1889, but I will focus mainly on the sixth edition.

15. In addition, I exclude those more philological in nature, such as Francisque Michel's *Studies of Comparative Philology on Slang and on Analogous Idioms Spoken in Europe and Asia* (*Études de philologie comparée sur l'argot et sur les idiomes analogues parlés en Europe et en Asie*, 1856) and Georges Delesalle's *Dictionary of Slang-French and French-Slang* (*Dictionnaire argot-français et français-argot*, 1895), because of their repetition of terms already found in the previously mentioned works.

16. The term for the vernacular in French, *le vulgaire*, refers to the common language used by a nation of people, from the latin *vulgus* (the common people), while the French adjective *vulgaire* refers to that which is vulgar, crass, and obscene. While these definitions are conflated in the nineteenth century when referring to slang, Pechon immediately makes a distinction between jargon and the vernacular on the title page: *The Magnanimous Life of Dealers, Bandits, and Bohemians, Containing their Ways of Life, Subtleties and Jargon* (*La vie genereuse des Mercelots, Gueuz et Boesmiens, contenant leur façon de vivre, subtilitez et gergon*). The French word *jargon* (former spelling: *gergon*) is specifically the language used by the wandering beggars, merchants, and gypsies (equivalent to the definition of *argot* of the early nineteenth century). The vernacular, or the French of the people, was not jargon.

17. Nédélec, *Les Enfants de la Truche*, XIII.

18. In terms of jargon, those that appear in *The Magnanimous Life* overlap with the ones Bouchet includes. According to Denis Delaplace: "The similarities between the glossaries in *The Magnanimous Life* and the *Fifteenth Evening*, in spite of their differences, makes one think that either the latter text circulated before 1596, maybe in manuscript form, and was thus able to be known by Pechon de Ruby, or Guillaume Bouchet and Pechon de Ruby went to draw from a common tradition, or that a highly reworked version of the glossary in *The Magnanimous Life* was added *in extremis* by the editor at the end of the fifteenth evening which is not the last one of the book" (*[L]es ressemblances entre les glossaires de la* Vie genereuse *et de la quinzième*

serée, malgré leurs divergences, laissent à penser soit que le texte de la seconde circulait avant 1596, peut-être en manuscrit, et a donc pu être connu de Pechon de Ruby, soit que Guillaume Bouchet et Pechon de Ruby sont allés puiser à une tradition commune, soit qu'une version très remaniée du glossaire de la Vie genereuse a été ajoutée in extremis par l'éditeur à la fin de cette quinzième serée qui n'est pas la dernière du livre [Pechon, 164]).

19. Due to the heavy contextualization of slang as the coded language of criminals, Vidocq does not provide an official definition for the term *argot*, or its occasional synonym, *jargon*.

20. Gaitet, "From the Criminal's to the People's," 236.

21. According to Denis Delaplace, the terms that Vidocq borrows from Chereau's work come from the edition of *Jargon* that dates from the end of the seventeenth century. One asterisk indicates a term taken from Chereau's *Jargon* and two asterisks signal terms taken from Villon's ballads.

22. "*Peindre les voleurs tels qu'ils sont en réalité, avec leurs vices et leurs qualités*" (Vidocq, *Les voleurs*, 681–82).

23. Agha, *Language and Social Relations*, 165.

24. Vidocq claims that if this slang becomes more universal, criminals will eventually cease their use of this dangerous language (Vidocq, *Les voleurs*, 689).

25. "*J'ai cru que la connaissance de leur langage servirait à mieux les faire connaître, voilà pourquoi ce qui d'abord ne devait être qu'une étude de mœurs est devenu un Dictionnaire aussi complet que possible du langage argotique*" (Ibid., 682).

26. Johnstone, "Enregisterment," 640–41.

27. As Brett Bowles notes, the influence on dictionary writers was mutual. According to Bowles, Delvau borrowed etymologies from Larchey but that "[e]ven Larchey himself came to appreciate Delvau's method, for in 1872 he published a *Dictionnaire historique, étymologique et anecdotique de l'argot parisien*, which no longer classified slang as 'excentricités' and incorporated popular word etymologies into philological analysis" (217).

28. *Si j'ai qualifié mon dictionnaire de* parisien, *c'est qu'au point de vue du langage, comme à tout autre, Paris est le grand rendez-vous. Là, se fabriquent ou affluent tous les mots nouveaux: ceux du bagne comme ceux du sport, ceux du boudoir comme ceux de l'atelier, ceux de la caserne comme ceux des couloirs de l'Assemblée, ceux de la halle comme ceux du collège, comme ceux du journalisme [. . .]. À Paris seul appartient le privilège de les laisser mourir ou de leur donner la vie, car Paris fait la mode des mots, comme il fait la mode des chapeaux.* (Larchey, *Dictionnaire historique*, 2)

29. *Beaucoup s'imaginent que l'argot n'est que le langage des voleurs. La vérité est que son domaine est beaucoup plus grand. Son étymologie en fait foi. ARGOT dérive [du moins pour nous] du vieux mot argue, et ne signifie [comme argutie qui a la même origine] que: ruse, finesse, subtilité. Parler argot, c'est user d'une subtilité de langage. Pas autre chose [. . .] les précieuses en ont usé comme les voleurs. Chacun a son argot.* (Ibid.)

30. Johnstone, "Enregisterment," 641.

31. "*Sous une terminologie nouvelle, c'est le concept d'argot qui se dilue: excentricités du langage, langue verte, argot parisien, langue parisienne, jargon parisien constituent en quelque sorte des 'synonymes' recouvrant une notion assez confuse*" (Klein, 256).

32. Benson, *Ethnocentrism*, 33.

33. Larchey, *Dictionnaire historique*, 7.

34. "*Dans l'argot plus que dans tout autre langage, certains termes caractérisent un ordre d'idées, d'habitudes, d'instincts*" (Ibid., 10).

35. *En toute justice, cependant, on ne saurait traiter avec une sévérité absolue l'élément populaire qui sert de base aux observations précédentes. Comment le peuple se piquerait-il de délicatesse en son langage? [. . .] Si on veut donc bien ne pas se choquer de la rusticité de cette forme, l'étude de l'argot parisien fera découvrir, au degré le plus éminent, certaines qualités de couleur.* (Ibid., 11)

36. "Slang, trendy words and new ways of speaking, —all of that can be useful and not to be disdained. Our former authors agree on this point and we would not know to neglect their testimonies; they will be our aegis" (*Argot, mots à la mode et nouvelles façons de parler, — tout cela peut être utile et n'est pas à dédaigner. Nos anciens auteurs tombent d'accord sur ce point, et nous ne saurions négliger leurs témoignages; ils seront notre égide* [Ibid., 18]).

37. Bowles, "Alfred Delvau's Dictionaries," 214.

38. In fact, the dictionary's popularity inspired Delvau to write a second edition, which was published posthumously.

39. Bowles, "Alfred Delvau's Dictionaries," 217; Bowles also points out that Delvau went so far as to invent quotes by La Fontaine (217). Other lexicographers like Jules Lermina's and Henri Lévêque also subverted the French canon. Following this preface on slang and performance, the lexicographers include a translation of Racine's *Récit de Théramène* from Standard French into slang, a move that completely decenters the literary canon and its language (Lermina and Lévêque, *Dictionnaire thématique*, xi).

40. Delvau, *Dictionnaire érotique moderne*, 18.

41. "*Ce qui se parle doit s'écrire, et tout doit se parler*" (Ibid., 16).

42. According to Bowles, Delvau was aware of the potential dangers of his work and took precautionary measures to avoid punishment: "Scandalous words are either omitted altogether, toned down through euphemism, or defined using other slang terms in order to lose the potential censor in an endless labyrinth of cross-references, a practice that recalls the strategy Diderot used to protect *l'Encyclopédie* from censure" (215).

43. "*Le cant, c'est l'argot particulier; le slang, c'est l'argot général. Les voleurs parlent spécialement le premier; tout le monde à Paris parle le second*" (Delvau, *Dictionnaire de la langue verte*, i–ii). Julie Coleman explains that "*Canting* is from *cant* 'to speak in the whining tone of a beggar' (1567-1750), ultimately from the Latin *cantare* 'to sing'. It still usually implies some type of dishonesty and is now generally used with reference to the language of beggars, criminals, estate agents, politicians, and religious hypocrites" (119)

44. In his Preface, Rigaud cites the reference works of several of his predecessors as sources such as those by Charles Nisard, Francisque Michel, Lorédan Larchey, and Alfred Delvau (Rigaud, *Dictionnaire du jargon parisien*, xviii).

45. In his dictionary, Rigaud analyzes the slang of workers (*les ouvriers*), butchers (*les bouchers*), cobblers (*les cordonniers*), tailors (*les tailleurs*), roofers (*les couvreurs*), masons (*les maçons*), and acrobats (*les saltimbanques*) (Ibid., xiii–xiv).

46. This is not to say that *ancient argot* and *modern argot* are entirely different from a structural perspective. Rigaud acknowledged that there is a linguistic residue from earlier times, and that slang words that have survived from the fifteenth century have simply been reappropriated by a different social milieu, a transition which spurred the creation of new indexicalities (Ibid., xiv).

47. *Le jargon parisien est ce langage étrange, libre d'allures, tantôt sombre et bref, tantôt imagé et plaisant, tantôt masqué comme Arlequin, comme lui habillé de pièces et de morceaux, qui court les rues et se recrute dans la rue, dans les prisons, dans l'échoppe, à la boutique, au comptoir, à l'atelier, à la caserne, à l'école, au théâtre, chez les artistes et chez les gens de lettres, chez les banquiers et chez les banquistes. Chaque caste, chaque corps d'état possède son jargon en propre. Depuis le voleur jusqu'au diplomate, depuis* Lacenaire *jusqu'à* Talleyrand, *tout le monde parle plus ou moins argot.* (Ibid., v)

48. Ibid., vi–vii; Rigaud cites Chereau's *Jargon* as the work that exposed this language to the police and subsequently undid the work of these criminal scholars (Ibid., viii).

49. Ibid., x.

50. Ibid.

51. *François Villon a parlé cette langue et en a laissé de curieux spécimens, entre autres des ballades dont le sens n'est pas précisément facile à saisir. Plus tard, l'argot a compté des lexicographes nombreux qui ont essayé de le suivre dans ses évolutions. Il a eu ses écrivains attitrés; et, de nos jours, les romans de Balzac, d'Eugène Sue, de Victor Hugo n'ont pas peu contribué à en propager le goût parmi le public. Aujourd'hui quel est le fabricant de romans qui soit assuré du succès s'il ne va pas chercher ses héros dans le monde ténébreux où le langage argotique est monnaie courante [. . .].* (Ibid., vii)

52. "*rendre un grand service aux lettres françaises [. . .] car la plupart de nos auteurs retardent de cinquante ans sur l'argot tel qu'il se parle à présent*" (Ibid.).

53. *Tout cela forme un total considérable. Pris dans son ensemble, le jargon parisien est si multiple, il comprend un si grand nombre de mots et d'expressions, chaque jour son contingent s'accroît tellement que si on voulait le suivre pas à pas, il faudrait, chaque année, lui consacrer un lexique confié aux soins de quarante académiciens d'un nouveau genre, et quarante académiciens suffiraient à peine à ce travail, s'ils ne voulaient omettre aucune des locutions qui surgissent incessamment.* (Ibid., xv–xvi)

54. "*Tous les mauvais lieux de l'intérieur et des environs*" (Vidocq, *Mémoires*, 293).

55. Ibid., 284, 286.

56. "*[J]étais partout, je savais tout*" (Ibid., 294).

57. *Nous avons recueilli, avec soin, un peu partout, les éléments de ce livre: dans la rue, dans les ateliers, à la caserne, au théâtre, dans les endroits les plus gais et dans*

les lieux les plus sinistres; nous avons voulu entendre parler la haute et la basse pègre, nous avons fouillé un peu tous les mondes, tous les coins et recoins de la société, et de tous les mots absolument inédits que nous avons donnés, il n'en est pas un seul qui n'ait été l'objet d'un examen sévère. (Rigaud, *Dictionnaire du jargon parisien*, xvii–xviii)

58. "*la révolution littéraire*" (Ibid., xiii).

59. He only cites previous authors and works as his main sources. Like Larchey, neither Lermina nor Lévêque make any mention of time spent on the streets; however, their emphasis on gesture and performance signals their *Thematic French-Slang Dictionary* as a pioneer in the genre.

60. "*[S]on tort est de n'avoir pas ramassé ces orphelins-là dans la rue, mais dans les livres [. . .]*" (Delvau. *Dictionnaire de la langue verte*, ii).

61. "*En France, on parle peut-être français; mais à Paris on parle argot, et un argot qui varie d'un quartier à l'autre, d'une rue à l'autre, d'un étage à l'autre*" (Ibid.).

62. "*On pourrait s'étonner aussi, et tout aussi justement, de voir attribuer à la langue populaire une foule de mots sortis de la langue du bagne, de la prison et des mauvais lieux*" (Ibid., v).

63. *Une expression tombe des lèvres flétries d'un forçat, non pas au bagne, où il est défendu aux honnêtes gens d'aller, mais dans un cabaret, dans une rue de Paris, où il est interdit aux coquins de séjourner et où ils accourent tous comme des frelons sur un gâteau de miel: dix paires d'oreilles la ramassent et dix bouches la répètent—sans l'essuyer. Elle fait son chemin d'atelier en atelier, de faubourg en faubourg, jusqu'au jour où, tombant à son tour des lèvres d'un ivrogne, dans un café littéraire ou dans une brasserie artistique, elle est alors recueilli par quelque curieux aux écoutes, par quelque flâneur aux aguets, qui la trouve accentuée, originale, et la colporte çà et là,—tant et si bien que, finalement, elle entre dans un article, puis dans un livre, puis dans la circulation générale.* (Ibid., vi)

64. Harvey, *Paris*, 106.

65. This is not a new claim. Chereau makes a similar implication between the slang speakers (*Argotiers*) and the good poor (*les bons pauvres*), who are ostensibly connected by crime.

66. *[J']ai tant de fois déambulé par les compites et les quadrivies de l'urbs que l'on vocite Lutèce, j'ai cueilli sur leur tige et ramassé sur leur fumier natal tous les mots de mon Dictionnaire, tous les termes bizarres, toutes les expressions pittoresques qui s'y trouvent accumulées [. . .]* (Delvau, *Dictionnaire de la langue verte*, iii).

67. "That which, in my daily and nightly wanderings, I heard outrageous, racy, startling, ruthless words, which are like kicks from behind, or slaps in the face, to some poor devils of one sex or the other, afflicted, this one here of this infirmity, that one of mockery, that what I heard could fill one great big—unpublishable—book" (*Ce que, dans mes déambulations diurnes et nocturnes à travers Paris, j'ai entendu de phrases énormes, pimentées, saisissantes, cruelles, appliquées en plein dos comme des coups de pied, ou en plein visage comme des soufflets, à de pauvres diables de l'un ou de l'autre sexe, affligés, celui-ci de cette infirmité, celle-là de ridicule, ce que j'ai entendu composerait un gros livre—inimprimable* [Ibid., vi–vii]).

68. "There are a thousand ways a word can spread, and it's precisely that which universalizes slang. Firstly, the street where everyone passes by; the cabaret that is so diversely populated; the dubious hangout,—another street" (*Il y a mille moyens de contagion pour un mot, et c'est précisément ce qui universalise l'argot. La rue d'abord, où passe tout le monde; le cabaret, si diversement peuplé; le mauvais lieu,— une autre rue* [Ibid., vii]).

69. Harvey, *Paris*, 109.

70. [T]els que l'église, les guinguettes, les brasseries, les salons littéraires ou artistiques, les théâtres du boulevard du Temple, les halls d'exposition, les bals, les grands magasins, les gares [. . .] les révolutions, les fêtes publiques, les carnavals. (Nesci, 18–19)

71. Harvey, *Paris*, 109.

72. Agha, *Language and Social Relations*, 82.

73. Johnstone, "Enregisterment," 640.

74. In *Memoirs* there are many dialogues that recall scenes from a play: see pp. 389, 393, 488–91, 503, 517–20, 569–73, 592–602, 606–10.

75. "*Vidocq enfoncé*" (Vidocq, *Mémoires*, 394).

76. "There is no language more difficult to learn and speak than slang [. . .]. This fact can be explained easily: positive languages have a grammar, syntax, clear forms, an academy to maintain them and professors to defend them [. . .]. Slang, itself, is elusive, untamable, not able to be professed; without rules, without laws [. . .] it blows where it wants" (*Il n'est pas de langue plus difficile à apprendre et à parler que l'argot [. . .]. Le fait s'explique aisément: les langues positives ont une grammaire, une syntaxe, des formes nettes, une académie pour les garder et des professeurs pour les défendre [. . .]. L'argot, lui, est insaisissable, indomptable, improfessable; sans règles, sans lois [. . .] il souffle où il veut* [Lermina and Lévêque, Dictionnaire thématique, i]).

"Every minute of Parisian life witnesses a new word hatching or, at the very least, of manner of diction, a change of construction, a syllable elision, that targets a special, untranslatable meaning by any other means. So well that, really, no one can boast of, in good conscience, a knowledge of slang" (*Chaque minute de la vie parisienne voit éclore un mot nouveau ou, tout au moins, une manière de diction, un changement de construction, une élision de syllabe, qui vise un sens spécial intraduisible par tout autre moyen. Si bien que, réellement, nul ne peut se targuer, en toute sincérité de conscience, de savoir l'argot* [Ibid., ii]).

77. "But, from the most naïf kids to the most talented of artists, everyone has their slang [. . .]. Everyone speaks slang: listen to the private conversation of *high-life* gentlemen and you will hear language and expressions that would make Octave Feuillet's monkey blush" (*Mais, depuis le plus naïf des gamins jusqu'au plus génial des artistes, tout le monde fait de l'argot [. . .]. Tout le monde parle argot: écoutez la conversation intime des gentlemen les plus* high-life *et vous entendrez des propos et des expressions à faire rougir le singe d'Octave Feuillet* [Ibid., ii, xi]).

78. *Notre ambition est plus haute. Nous avons remarqué que les gens du monde tenaient grandement, sous prétexte d'air artiste, à parler argot. Sans discuter cette tendance – dont nous ne sommes pas juges – du moins avons-nous voulu fournir à ces*

ambitieux les moyens de parler purement et hardiment cette langue qu'ils balbutient à peine et qu'ils déparent par de cruelle erreurs [...]. Grâce à ce dictionnaire, chacun saura traduire ses impressions dans la langue des macs et des poniffes. (Ibid., x)

79. Benson, *Ethnocentrism*, 4.
80. The title page reads: "*Et terminé par Chansons en français et en argot.*"
81. "The simple imbecile, to be adaptable and numerous, believes that to speak slang, it suffices to learn by heart a few hundred words made popular by Eugène Sue, Balzac, Victor Hugo, Zola, Richepin or Bruant. Without going all the way back to Vadé, Saint-Amant or Villon, he is satisfied with flipping through the dictionaries by Delvau, Lorédan Larchey, or even Francisque Michel, and when his memory stored up some terms, he lets them go with confidences and believes to speak slang . . . A distressing error that it is suitable to dispel!" (*Le simple imbécile, être multiforme et nombreux, croit que, pour parler argot, il suffit d'apprendre par cœur quelques centaines de mots mis à la mode par Eugène Sue, Balzac, Victor Hugo, Zola, Richepin ou Bruant. Sans remonter jusqu'à Vadé, Saint-Amant ou Villon, il se contente de feuilleter les dictionnaires de Delvau, de Lorédan Larchey, voire de Francisque Michel, et quand sa mémoire a emmagasiné des vocables, il les lâche avec aplomb et croit parler argot . . . Douloureuse erreur qu'il convient de dissiper!* [Lermina and Lévêque, *Dictionnaire thématique*, ii]).
82. *Tout d'abord, pour parler argot, il faut la voix d'argot. Non point l'accent traînard, canaille, qu'on attribue de chic aux souteneurs et autres académiciens de bigorne, mais ce quelque chose d'insaisissable, de tout particulier, qui touche à la fois à la familiarité et au 'jemenfoutisme' [. . .]. Nous ajouterons que tous les traits du visage, les accentuations infinitésimales de la voix, les moindres gestes ou simples tressaillements de la main, de la hanche, de l'épaule, du pied, aident à l'interprétation du mot, de l'interjection, et décuplent sa suggestivité. Un simple renversement de la paume sur la cuisse accentue un 'Et ta sœur!' de la façon la plus énergique.* (Ibid., ii–iii, ix)
83. Bucholtz and Hall, "Embodied Sociolinguistics," 178.
84. Peirce, "On the Algebra of Logic," 181.
85. Bucholtz and Hall, "Embodied Sociolinguistics," 184.
86. *Surtout en argot, il importe de n'imiter personne. Chacun doit plier sa langue à sa propre nature, de telle sorte qu'elle soit la parfaite expression de l'individualité [. . .]. Parle-moi argot, je te dirai qui tu es. Nous le répétons, chacun se compose son argot d'après les éléments connus.* (Lermina and Lévêque, *Dictionnaire thématique*, ix)

Chapter 6

Slang as the Language of Whores

The babbling of whores is one-hundred times preferable to the slang of stockbrokers.

—Alfred Delvau, *Dictionnaire érotique moderne* (1864)

(*Le ramage des filles est cent fois préférable à l'argot des boursiers*)

In a caricature by Paul Gavarni that depicts an interaction at Carnival between a man and a masked woman who are both leaning against a wall, it takes on a new social meaning when the woman uses working-class slang.[1] From the caption, the audience learns that the woman dances the Cancan, drinks liquor, and speaks this vulgar anti-language. While perched against the wall facing the man, the woman, who is wearing pants, makes sexual advances. Her use of the informal "you" (*tu*) and the phonetic spelling of adverb "more" (*plus*, which is spelled "*pus*" in the caption) signifies both her lower class and profession as working-class prostitute.[2] Naturalist writers, such as Edmond and Jules de Goncourt, praised Gavarni for his use of slang as a linguistic shorthand for visual representations in popular culture of the marginal figures that made up the patchwork Parisian population.[3] Like Gavarni's caricature, literary representations of the woman slang speaker after 1850 established a strong indexical link between the visual, the aural, and the body.

In his analysis of women criminals in the city-mystery genre, Nicolas Gauthier establishes three categories of this character type: women who are seduced, women who seduce, and women exempt from seduction due to their resemblance to men.[4] Although Gauthier posits the hardened, masculine

Figure 6.1 "—J'ai cancanné que j'en ai pus de jambes, j'ai mal au cou d'avoir crié . . . et bu que le palais m'en ratisse . . . Tu n'es donc pas un homme?" Illus. Paul Gavarni. *Oeuvres choisies de Gavarni*, by Paul Gavarni. Paris: J. Hetzel, 1846–1848.

woman criminal as the only category free from the paradigm of male desire, in this chapter, I will demonstrate that "women who seduce" employ a slang indexical of working-class virility that, coupled with their sensual bodies, disrupts the sexual fantasies of male characters to such an extent that this category of women criminals can acquire subjectivity as well. Much like Gavarni's masked woman, the working-class slang used by prostitutes in naturalist French novels indexes a proto-feminist ideology that validates these women as agents, especially through the use of their bodies.

The nineteenth-century cultural discourse on women, their bodies, and their use of language demonstrated more radical shifts as representations of "bad women" in naturalist literature began to center on their sexuality. As discussed in earlier chapters, contemporary sociolinguists, Mary Bucholtz and Kira Hall, assert that language is "an embodied phenomenon."[5] Thus, corporal elements, such as gesture and gaze, can additionally serve as valuable communication tools:

[J]ust as bodies produce language, so the converse also holds: Language produces bodies. That is, language is a primary means by which the body enters the sociocultural realm as a site of semiosis, through cultural discourses about bodies as well as linguistic practices of bodily regulation and management.[6]

By the mid-to-late nineteenth century, slang's indexical shift from the language of criminals to the Parisian vernacular coincided with radical changes in the representations of speech for women characters in French literature, which now included a largely bodily component for women of a lower-class standing. Similar to the embodied language of the hardcore criminal, the slang-speaking prostitute possesses her own body language as expressed through gesture, mobility, and performance which operates in similar ways as her linguistic practices to index information about her social, professional, and moral status. In general, the use of the vernacular and slang in French novels was reserved for working-class women and prostitutes, while making only modest reference to their nonmarital relations with men. In the second half of the nineteenth century, however, representations of prostitutes evolved, as male writers now sought to portray these characters with a sense of realism; in other words, the speech and actions of prostitutes in French novels became explicitly vulgar, while indicating their sexual dealings, which fundamentally disrupted societal expectations on how women should behave in nineteenth-century France.[7]

In addition to an increased focus on women's bodies, a male-led quest for the causes of prostitution emerged as an object of study within a wide variety of social spheres. As Marjorie Rousseau-Minier points out, these "panoramic" investigations sought to study prostitutes from all angles, and pervaded several domains of discourse, not just religion but also French medicine, law, administration, and literature.[8] Although categories of prostitutes ranged from the working-class *grisette* to the high-class courtesan, within literature, male writers generally depicted these women as victims of a broken social system and the undeniable product of a tragic familial situation. In spite of predominately depressing representations of these women, naturalist French writers such as Émile Zola began to focus more on the role of entertainment venues, or sanctioned meeting places of "heterosocial interactions," such as cabarets and theaters that served as a narrative backdrop to the dealings of these working-class women.[9] French writers in the second half of the nineteenth century began to explore the linguistic and sexual complexity of the slang-speaking woman; her use of crass language in direct speech to socially mark herself as sexually available, and the writers' glimpse into the seedy underbelly of the entertainment world differentiates the naturalist prostitute from previous representations. However, in spite of this modernization of the prostitute in later works, these characters' acts of willfully defying the patriarchy nevertheless concluded in the same result as earlier texts: excluded from society, sexualized women characters were condemned to a narrative death.

In the work of nineteenth-century French male writers, such as Edmond and Jules de Goncourt and Zola, who depicted women characters as objects of sexual desire, the women never fully escape the male gaze. In her famous essay, "Visual Pleasure and Narrative Cinema," Laura Mulvey describes the portrayal of women in film as a "signifier for the male other, bound by a symbolic order in which man can live out his fantasies."[10] Although film serves as the ultimate medium for revealing male projection, pleasure, and desire, Mulvey's work has been widely applicable across many disciplines. As in early Silent film, late nineteenth-century literary representations of slang-speaking prostitutes portraying woman as erotic object becomes widespread practice.[11] For literary critic Charles Bernheimer, the ubiquity of the image of the prostitute in late-nineteenth-century art, film, and literature allowed her body to be an object for capitalist consumption as well as regulated. The appearance of the erotic woman in art and literature additionally became a means of "control [to] dispel her fantasmatic threat to male mastery."[12] While women characters in late-nineteenth-century literature, such as the Goncourt brothers' Germinie Lacerteux and Zola's Nana, are constructed as male fantasy, they nevertheless deploy a language indexical of working-class men that serves to disrupt and subvert this fantasy. Furthermore, the body functions as the alpha and the omega of agency, and language in particular is always anchored within a physical entity that "acts and is acted upon."[13] According to Kira Hall and Ayden Parish, "agency" is "the capacity for socially meaningful action" while "indexicality" is the principal sociolinguistic process through which agency can emerge, which renders the body as a basic element of indexicality.[14] In terms of embodiment, the body possesses "its own agency separate from the speaker."[15] As women whose identity is deeply intertwined with the abject actions of their bodies, an analysis of their language sheds insight into the ways in which nineteenth-century French prostitutes in naturalist works asserted themselves as agents, thus creating new avenues of meaning through their exploits.

Even though Germinie and Nana's bodies serve as sites of male pleasure and desire, the women's vulgar language and gestures that index them as low-class prostitutes grants them a form of female agency through their rejection of cultural expectations for women's speech. From a sociolinguistic standpoint, the overarching characteristic of cultural expectations for women's speech is politeness and "avoids the markers of camaraderie: backslapping, joke telling, nicknaming, slang, and so forth."[16] In nineteenth-century society, "women [were] the preservers of morality and civility," a cultural construction manifested in the speech practices expected of women.[17] This is an important point, and one that has been addressed in relation to the "sex goddess" in American cinema, a term that Jessica Hope Jordan uses to describe early twentieth-century hyperfeminine actresses such as Jean Harlow, Lana Turner, Jayne Mansfield, and Mae West. In her analysis of women's speech in *The Sex Goddess in American Film, 1930–1965*, Jordan looks at West's empowering use of "vulgar" language as a "turning back" of patriarchal language onto itself. West's use of double entendre and slang terms from the speakeasies and vaudeville scene gave the actress a masculine edge, but as Jordan so insightfully notes, West's talent resided in her ability "to deploy this language in a way that shifted its terms and meaning into a language that better described and empowered the feminine."[18] Similarly, in both the Goncourt brothers' *Germinie Lacerteux* (1865) and Zola's *Nana* (1880), language constructs the identity of the prostitute; however, the language the women use—slang—functions as a means of agency. Even in Zola's novel, which guarantees a grim outcome for Nana (as does the Goncourts' for Germinie), the women characters achieve empowerment through their speech that was not present in earlier literary representations of prostitutes, such as Fleur in Eugène Sue's *The Mysteries of Paris* and Esther in Honoré de Balzac's *Splendors and Miseries of Courtesans*.[19] While the characters of Germinie and Nana may fail to liberate themselves from a masculinist economy, I argue that they do, however, manage to displace the male gaze through their transgressive speech and bodily practices. They do so by resourcefully using their spoken language, as Judith Butler has written in terms of boundary-crossing bodies, to "inadvertently mobilize possibilities of 'subjects' that do not merely exceed the bounds of cultural intelligibility, but effectively expand the boundaries of what is, in fact, culturally intelligible."[20] However, as Rachel Mesch notes, despite the pejorative, depressing portrait of culturally deviant women characters in nineteenth-century French literature, such as prostitutes and hysterics (both the creations of male writers), these women characters functioned instead as pioneering emblems of female liberation that would come to fruition in the work of woman writers in the late-nineteenth and early twentieth centuries, such as Colette and Isabelle Eberhardt, and later, as Jordan argues in her book, through the early twentieth-century sex goddesses in American cinema and the actresses who played them, who were proto-feminists in their own right. Similarly, in the case of Germinie and Nana, an analysis of both their nonconforming speech practices and body language reveals their subversive gender practices that contributed to the advent of both an early twentieth-century feminism and queer identity.

After 1850, in addition to their transgressive speech practices, the corporal index in the form of a performance that was simultaneously theatrical and sexual further characterized women slang speakers and functions as the embodied equivalent of their speech. Unlike earlier representations of what was perceived as embodied criminal speech in the form of dance and song as discussed in chapter 2, this later embodied practice is one that pervaded a wider range of social domains due to the prostitute's inherent mobility. In the tradition of Judith Butler's gender performativity, the literary representation of Geminie and Nana's use of slang contributes to the stylization of their subversive gender performance and thus serves as an embodied language indexical of sexually indecent women. In the naturalist sense, the portrait of these women is both degrading and depressing because, while, ultimately, they do not escape their social circumstances, their use of masculine language, while nevertheless indexical of a certain social identity as prostitute, is a source of empowerment.[21] Even as the sexualized images of Germinie and Nana evokes a kind of eroticism for certain spectators, their speech practices and body language were undeniably considered unladylike for their time, a distinction that sets them apart from earlier images of women slang speakers as being either hyper-virginal or hypermasculine.

WOMEN SLANG SPEAKERS IN FRENCH LITERATURE BEFORE 1850

Like that of the criminal, the evolving image of the prostitute in French literature remained far from morally neutral. As Bernheimer notes, "[p]rostitutes, like criminals [. . .] reintroduce into the flat conformism of bourgeois society the elements of contestation, scandal, mobility, theatricality, extremism, and surprise."[22] As Jann Matlock asserts, the prostitute was the ultimate criminal because she "could be made an accessory to every crime against nature, against the family, and against the state [. . .]. No other social element could present so many dangers or prove so costly to the state."[23] Matlock points out that this moral scapegoating of the prostitute was necessary, as the dominant cultural discourse constructed her as an imminent threat to the bourgeois family; however, she was also essential to "the implementation of a policing network that would maximize collective and individual forces."[24] In other words, the prostitute was tolerated, in the sense of being a necessary, useful part of society, while simultaneously feared as potentially uncontrollable. Nevertheless, in the final analysis, overall, she remained emblematic of a fall from moral and social grace.

France's institutionalized measures to regulate prostitution in the nineteenth century became the standard for other European countries. As Rousseau-Minier acknowledges, for the French, "prostitution was no longer prohibited and it was no longer considered a criminal offense, but a socially necessary and inevitable evil that needed to be controlled."[25] The need for regulation, according to Alain Corbin, can be summarized into three main reasons: (1) to protect the public, especially vulnerable women, from moral corruption; (2) to defend and promote the commercial success of men; and (3) to guard the overall health of the public.[26] Prostitutes, as Corbin notes, became synonymous with putrefaction and death as well as emblematic of disease, especially syphilis.[27] French cities carefully decided where sanctioned brothels could be established, and even prohibited certain geographic areas from streetwalkers, and as Corbin points out, this became a power game of concealment and control. For these reasons, prostitutes had to register in their city municipalities, becoming either "number girls" (*les filles à numéro*), in which they lived at a brothel overseen by a Madame or "card girls" (*les filles en carte*), which gave them the ability to freely roam the streets as long as they had their identity card with them. In spite of regulation efforts, many women continued to pimp themselves out under the table, defying orders and risking arrest. French writers, such as the Goncourt brothers and Zola, often explored within their plotlines the prostitute's resistance to the formal measures imposed on her body by city authorities. However, in addition to the control over her biological sex, these writers simultaneously examined other bodily forms of the prostitute's resistance, such as her language.

The indexical relationship between gender and slang introduced a new twist on the ideological and moral struggle between good and bad. Sexuality, morality, and language pointed to a new kind of threat to traditional values through its implied nostalgia for a French society of the past, one in which there existed strong linguistic, moral, and national unity. The Revolution of 1789, however, had given license to the riotous woman within public discourse, while the Revolution of 1830 had further reinforced this image. Michèle Riot-Sarccy acknowledges the years both prior to and during the Revolution of 1789 as a time of women's political mobilization. According to Riot-Sarcey, it was during this time when gender construction came to the forefront of public debate as the notion of universal rights was now hotly debated.[28] The entrance of women into the political arena inspired a masculine cultural enterprise to clearly demarcate gender roles in order to control where women went and how they behaved.[29] A reliance on biology to control women's bodies further served as a political tool that acted as scientific proof (versus religious proof) for the enforcement of certain policies that limited the political mobilization of women, as well as to assert the biological superiority of men. The shift in focus from a two-sex model to a one-sex model following the French Revolution, Thomas Laqueur argues, occurred "through endless micro-confrontations over power in the public and private spheres."[30] The inequity in power relations between men and women served male dominance within bourgeois institutions but needed to be supported by biological evidence that women were indeed the weaker sex.[31] French policymakers thus used biology as a means of immobilizing the bodies of disorderly women through the construction of a so-called natural discourse of femininity.

However, in their work, male writers also included biological explanations for the behavior of disorderly women which was intertwined with the dominant cultural ideology of how a true woman was to behave and speak.

By 1848, the portrayal in the press of the riots at Saint-Lazare, an all-women's prison in Paris, shifted the image of lower-class women from that of victims of circumstance to uncontrollable criminals.[32] Even though the dawn of the Second Republic in 1848 saw the solidification of *Marianne* as emblematic of *Liberté, Égalité, Fraternité*, in reality, the inception of the new democracy in France was a time of "paradox" for women.[33] According to Riot-Sarcey, women mobilized on behalf of workers' and women's rights and actively contributed to feminist newspapers run by women that had previously been established to challenge the Napoleonic Code of 1804.[34] However, prominent men and women alike, such as writer, George Sand, were hesitant to back the women's movement, which resulted in an exclusion of women activists from the socialist struggle in France, as well as fines and imprisonment for those who were most vocal in the press. Consequently, unlike the explicit threat the criminal classes had already posed to French society, this new threat of the unorthodox woman was less tangible, as well as depicted in literature as more variable.

The intense scrutiny of women, their bodies, and sexuality in French society also fell under the realm of nineteenth-century medical and hygienic discourse, which concerned itself with the underlying threat of "bad" women and contributed to the male-led quest for causes and solutions to prostitution.[35] During this era, the French doctor Alexandre Parent-Duchâtelet's posthumously published study, entitled, *On Prostitution in the City of Paris* (*De la prostitution dans la ville de Paris*, 1836), catalogued the various causes, states, types, and characteristics of prostitution and the Parisian prostitute. Parent-Duchâtelet called for the regulation of such deviant bodies through the use of an official registration of all prostitutes, along with a dossier of their medical history.[36] In his study, Parent-Duchâtelet presents the question "Do prostitutes have a specific slang?" (*Les prostituées ont-elles un argot particulier?*), declaring that the slang used by prostitutes differs from that of criminals.[37] However, for Parent-Duchâtelet, prostitutes merely borrowed from criminal slang:

> [A]nd so the inspectors from the Office of the Vice Squad are known as *Johnny Law*, a police chief is a *cop*, a pretty prostitute is a *minx* or an *owl*, an ugly prostitute is a *floozy*; they call a man's mistress his *lady*, and the lover of a prostitute her *pimp*.[38]

In spite of his insistence that prostitutes do not have a special slang for their profession, Parent-Duchâtelet refers to their speech several times as a key identifier of the prostitute and the characteristics associated with this social type, such as sexual promiscuity and a lack of modesty and shame. Through his observation of both their speech practices and public behavior "one could believe that modesty, which makes the most beautiful woman's accessory, became a feeling that was completely foreign to them."[39] For Parent-Duchâtelet, language serves as a tool for identifying prostitutes and their moral shortcomings. In literature, too, writers such as Balzac and Sue commonly used slang as a sociolinguistic marker to allow their middle-class readers to be able to situate women characters both socially and morally. Nonetheless, such early nineteenth-century French writers did not present prostitute-speak as direct dialogue; this stylistic feature only appeared later in literary works in the latter half of the nineteenth century.

The lack of slang dialogue in early literary representations of prostitutes shifts in the late nineteenth-century with naturalist writers such as the Goncourt brothers and Zola who showcased the grim realities of the Parisian *demi-monde*. This change coincided with an overall rebranding of slang in fiction and nonfiction as a Parisian vernacular associated with the working classes, rather than the criminal classes. It is important to note that the representation of slang as a criminal code did not disappear; rather, with the publication of works such as Victor Hugo's *Les Misérables* (1862), a second indexical order in which slang indexed the poor, misery-stricken population emerged that coexisted with the first indexical order associated with criminality. While early nineteenth-century writers tended to masculinize slang speakers, whether they be men or women, through the use of slang itself, in the late nineteenth century sexuality becomes a major focus of the image of the woman slang speaker.

In terms of nineteenth-century French society, the expectation of women to stand as pillars of morality, and thus to speak in a way that reflected moral purity, surfaces in literary depictions as well as political and medical discourse. In her study of Japanese women's language, Miyako Inoue analyzes the evolution of women's speech practices in nineteenth-century Japan and how this led to the construction of a linguistic origin story, one dictated by upper-class Japanese men, in relation to modernity. Inoue defines "women's language" as

> a space of discourse—understood as a complex ensemble of practices, institutions, representations, and power—in which the Japanese woman is objectified, evaluated, studied, staged, and normalized through her imputed language use and is thus rendered a knowable and unified subject both to herself and to others.[40]

Thus, her way of speaking constitutes a historically bounded "Japaneseness" that contains "unbroken historical roots in an archetypical, imaginary

Japanese past."[41] Similarly, the historical divide between pre- and post-1789 France and the corresponding changes in representations of women in the public sphere reveal both a "traditional and archetypical imaginary" of French women and their speech.[42] Women's speech, in the sense of being polite and "ladylike," thus becomes symbolic of patriarchal control, power, and order that characterized the French monarchy before the collapse of the Ancien Régime.

Correspondingly, in Sue's *The Mysteries of Paris*, the slang-speaking lady of the night Fleur-de-Marie barely uses any slang, thus differing from representations of female slang speakers in later works, such as Zola's *Nana*. For instance, with his characterization of Fleur, Sue maintains a moral subtlety in his treatment of both her criminal character and scandalous profession. This subtleness not only speaks to Sue's propriety vis-à-vis his audience but also renders Fleur's noble birth as believable in the end. As Bernheimer notes, Sue's approach allows Rodolphe to act as Fleur's savior simply by "[recognizing] her inherent virtue."[43] At the beginning of the novel, the narrator states that the criminal classes communicate with one another in this "vile language" (*langue immonde*), a statement that implicates Fleur as a slang speaker.[44] When Fleur describes her housing with the Owl, she uses two slang expressions: a word for a "liquor joint" (*un rogomiste*) and the phrase "to be completely drunk" (*être dans les bringues-zingues*).[45] Apart from the above examples and a general statement made about criminals and their language, Fleur does not use any slang when speaking with other characters.

Like Fleur, in Balzac's *Splendors and Miseries of Courtesans*, the character Esther's use of slang is rarely employed. When Esther states that she wants to make the Baron de Nucingen happy, "like a rooster in plaster" (*comme un coq en plâtre*), an expression meaning to pamper someone, with a further play on the expression, "like a rooster in dough" (*comme un coq en pâte*), the narrator immediately follows with an informative detail on the phrase's connotation: "This word is becoming proverbial in the prostitute world."[46] Similarly, after using the verb, "*blaguer*," meaning "to joke around," Esther interrupts the indexical expectations of her interlocutor, Europe: "In hearing this word, Europe remained completely stupefied, as she could have been in hearing an angel blaspheme."[47] Despite Esther's inherent unworthiness, Balzac maintains this air of virtue, presenting to readers a politer version of a prostitute's language. When compared to their contemporary representations of slang-speaking criminal characters, the portrayals of prostitutes and their speech in *Mysteries* and *Splendors* presents a watered-down version of what later appears after 1850.

Aside from occasional details mentioning the profession and language of prostitutes, both Sue and Balzac notably shy away from any sexually explicit details and vulgar-laced tirades, preferring instead to emphasize the reformed aspects of their deviant female characters as inherently childlike and virginal;

however, nevertheless marked by indelible shame. This is because before 1850, these writers were still influenced by late eighteenth-century discourse on "virtue and vice" as well as Romanticism. Within their literary depictions of Fleur and Esther, Sue and Balzac thus fetishize the prostitutes as born-again virgins, returning them to a prepubescent state, rather than hypersexualized temptresses, also an influence of the cult of the little girl in the Victorian age.

In contrast, in the early nineteenth century, women characters that did employ slang in dialogue were made to possess hypermasculine qualities and constitute Gauthier's third category of women criminals: those exempt from seduction. Characters such as the Owl and She-Wolf in *Mysteries* and Asia in *Splendors* freely engaged in crime, and thus their speech habits resembled those of the cutthroat male criminals that also appeared in these works. Their bestial physical features further reflected their immoral nature, a characteristic that neutralized their physiological differences with male criminals, a trait that Cesare Lombroso later included in his extensive work on criminal physiognomies in the late nineteenth century, *Criminal Man* (1876). Illustrations from the 1843 edition of *The Mysteries of Paris* reveal the polarization between the ultrafeminine Fleur and her more masculine female counterparts such as the Owl, whose facial features resemble those of a man—strong square jawline, thin lips, hooked nose, and inwardly slanted eyebrows, coupled with a faint semblance of five-o-clock shadow, and a lack of pupil in her right eye (her "good" eye)—not only portray an unattractive woman by societal standards but also one whose facial features are definitively masculine.[48]

This portrayal of women criminals as testosterone-laden, with all of the physical characteristics that index a "manly" man, including her speech, incites questions on empowerment and these hypermasculine constructs. Unlike male criminals, such as Vautrin, same-sex relations never factored into these representations of virile women. Themes of lesbianism would appear in later novels that dealt with more nuanced versions of female criminality. In Balzac's prototypical naturalist novel *Cousin Bette* (*La cousine Bette*, 1846–1847), the text hints at same-sex relations between the spinster Bette and her gorgeous accomplice Valérie, and while Balzac describes Bette as having masculine qualities and being bestial in appearance (her name "Bette" is a homonym for the French word "bête" meaning "beast"), her criminality is limited to her personal vengeance on the Hulot family; Bette is not an ex-con, murderer, or thief. In later naturalist French works, like Zola's *Nana*, lesbianism would factor between the prostitutes Nana and Satin, but by the late nineteenth century, the extreme disfiguration and butch appearance of women criminals gave way to more sensual, complex versions of lady villains who spoke slang.

While the grotesque images of evil women in *Mysteries* and *Splendors* may have contributed to women's liberation movements, or even provided

Figure 6.2 "La Chouette." Illus. Charles Joseph Traviès. *Les Mystères de Paris* by Eugène Sue. Vol. 1. Paris: C. Gosselin, 1843–1844.

a Queer construct during the *fin-de-siècle*, early nineteenth-century writers such as Sue and Balzac, who were male, white, straight, cisgender, and dominant figures of canonical French literature, emphasized masculine features and qualities in their women criminal characters as a means of aligning them with their male counterparts. If women are going to engage in villainy, then they will resemble the degenerate men of society in appearance, deed, and speech. Homogenizing the physicality of men and women wrongdoers establishes a kind of race of criminals, and through these freakish depictions, these writers incited a racism in which middle-class readers could identify "criminals" based on a virile and borderline monstrous appearance, in addition to their language. The gender stylization of early nineteenth-century French writers, which included body language and speech, has less to do with gender identity and more to do with exhibiting a class and moral demarcation between virtuous women and dishonorable women through their appearance, one that also existed between non-slang and slang speakers. By fashioning criminal women more-or-less under the same physical portrait as predominately masculine, muscular, and large in build with deformed physiognomies and resemblances to wild animals, Balzac and Sue introduced concepts of criminal atavism that would only be officially in circulation by the end of the nineteenth century. However, this physical code created by French male authors in the early nineteenth century indexed speech practices as well.

In his follow-up to *Criminal Man*, Lombroso published a study entitled, *Criminal Woman, the Prostitute, and the Normal Woman* (1893) in which he examined the physiological differences between three types of women: (1) criminal, (2) prostitute, and (3) normal. He determined that "[t]he lower jaw of female criminals, and still more of prostitutes, is heavier than in moral women, and the cranio-mandibular index is nearly always as virile as it is heavy."[49] Although Lombroso's theories surface at the end of the nineteenth century (and greatly influenced naturalist writers such as Zola), these early illustrations of criminal women in Balzac and Sue's works exaggerate skull and jaw size, thus rendering characters such as the Owl and Asia more masculine in appearance, while communicating information about their behaviors, mannerisms, and gestures to readers. In this manner, early nineteenth-century writers established a clear-cut link between the physical and the moral, in addition to language, which granted readers tools for decoding the new social landscape following the French Revolution.

In contrast to the masculinity of early criminal women, the illustrations of Fleur, who ostensibly speaks slang and works as a prostitute, showcase her feminine features rather than masculine ones. Sue describes her as possessing blonde hair, a slim oval face, pale skin, heart-shaped lips, a button nose, and large eyes.[50] Fleur's gestures further posit her as simultaneously feminine and virginal, features that were atypical of slang-speaking women characters: her hands, facing upward and crossed at the chest, resemble the ubiquitous posturing of the Virgin Mary that appears in many artworks of the long Renaissance, including sculpture and altar works.[51] For example, the portraits of the Virgin in Medieval and Renaissance Italian works of the *Annunciation*, such as those by Lorenzo Veneziano (1371) and Fra Angelico (1451), contain similar wide-set eyes, dainty facial features, hand placement, and eye gaze.[52]

Figure 6.3 *"Fleur-de-Marie."* Illus. Crimolen and Nargeon. *Les Mystères de Paris* by Eugène Sue. Vol. 1. Paris: C. Gosselin, 1843–1844.

Similarly, images of Esther in the illustrated version of *Splendors* from 1851 to 1853 reveal a drastic contrast between her feminine figure and the ogre-like Asia who serves as her slang-speaking criminal counterpart. Sitting playfully on the lap of the Baron de Nucingen, Esther's long hair, styled in an updo, falls gently onto the nape of her neck, as her right hand extends to the Baron's shoulder, a gesture that simultaneously suggests flirtatious play and sexual resistance.[53] Her tiny waist and petite facial features (eyes and lips), as well as her "exotic" nose, contribute to her physical desirability and inherent femininity.[54]

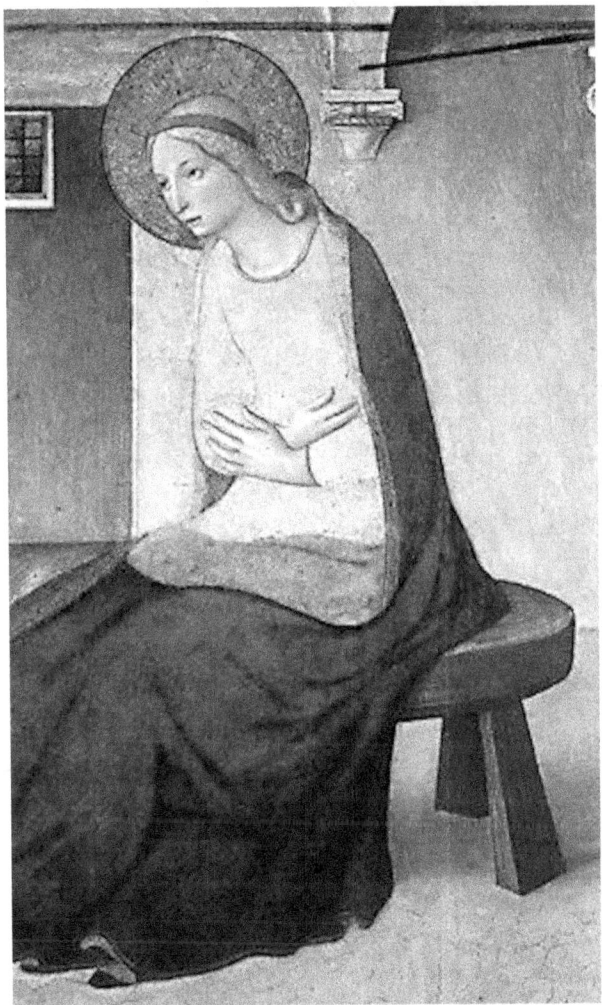

Figure 6.4 Detail from "The Annunciation" by Fra Angelico. Florence: Museum of San Marco, 1450.

In contrast, Asia's physical features are strikingly similar to those of the Owl's: her stout, round body, strong jawline, large nose and hands, as well as slanted eyebrows and long, thin mouth pursed into a frown, resemble masculine physical features instead of traditional feminine ones.[55] For nineteenth-century readers, this image of a criminal woman not only aligns with the indecent connotations of slang language but also provides a logical bodily context for this type of speech. Although Esther and Fleur are prostitutes, Balzac and Sue hardly vulgarize what would have been perceived by society at large as their sexual deviancy and crass way of speaking. In the opening scene of *Mysteries*, on the Rue aux Fèves in the seedy Parisian district, La Cité, Fleur appears under the light of the streetlamps on a dark, stormy night. Standing in a doorway along with fellow prostitutes, they are singing popular songs, waiting for clients to approach. Apart from this initial scene, Sue does not depict Fleur exercising her profession, and she renounces prostitution shortly after meeting Rodolphe.

However, the existential consequences of her immoral lifestyle remain, as Fleur grapples with chronic shame throughout the entire novel, a feeling that ultimately leads to her death.[56] Much like her slang, which barely appears throughout the one-thousand-page novel, Fleur's tale detailing how she ended up as a prostitute, as well as her shame-bounded inferiority complex, is the only indications of her promiscuity. There is no hypersexualized descriptions of Fleur or scenes in which she engages in sexual conduct, just as there

Figure 6.5 Esther and the baron de Nucingen. (Illustrator not specified.) *Splendeurs et misères des courtisanes* by Honoré de Balzac. Paris: 1851–1853.

exists barely any instances in which she directly uses slang expressions. In fact, certain passages insist on Fleur's "virginal" qualities. For example, in addition to her delicate physical features, the Slasher tells her: "you have the air of a virgin."[57]

In Part I, Chapter 14, Fleur adopts the name "Marie," recalling the devoted follower of Jesus, Mary Magdalene, in addition to the holy Virgin Mary.[58] Sue often portrays Fleur as more childlike than sensual, and while he does not sexualize Fleur, his objectifying lens shifts between that of virginal treasure and subhuman untouchable, which, again, speaks to the Victorian male fascination with the little girl, or prepubescent girl, a form of pedophilia in

Figure 6.6 Asie. Illus. Bertall. *Splendeurs et misères des courtisanes* by Honoré de Balzac. Paris: 1851–1853.

literature and culture. Fleur does not possess the same bodily and linguistic indexes that later portrayals of sexually deviant, slang-speaking women characters do and is thus unable to disrupt any form of male fetishization, even temporarily.

In fact, even when mention of prostitution occurs in other early nineteenth-century works, such as Balzac's *Splendors*, courtesans like Esther remain unable to shatter male expectations, either through their behavior or speech. In the opening scene of *Splendors*, the journalist Émile Blondet and aspiring writer Étienne Lousteau speak explicitly about the prostitute Esther, "the Torpedo" (*La Torpille*). Blondet says she is "the only prostitute with the makings of a beautiful courtesan,"[59] while Lousteau reveals that "[a]t eighteen years old, this whore has already known the highest opulence, the lowest misery, and men from all classes."[60] Although this blatant allusion to Esther's profession occurs in other scenes of *Splendors*, specific details concerning her sexual escapades are absent.[61] At the beginning of the novel Esther, in fact, no longer engages in prostitution, and "[h]er name, her deviant sexuality, her venality belong to the pre-novelistic past."[62] During a masked ball at the Opera, the men attempt to guess Esther's identity, an act that Bernheimer posits as "male power and control over female sexual deviance."[63] According to Bernheimer their gaze, in effect, "neutralizes the threat embodied in her prostitution," by de-eroticizing her body.[64] Unlike Nana and Germinie, however, Esther poses no real threat to these men because they determine her identity. She does not resist their objectifying gaze through violent outburst or slang-riddled tirades; instead, she allows herself to be controlled and molded to their liking.

For example, the male spectators are able to see "the ingenuousness of a virgin and the graces of childhood."[65] In Part I, Esther is seen exclusively in the company of Lucien de Rubempré, and while under the control of the master criminal Vautrin, Esther undergoes a total moral conversion. With the help of their male saviors, Rodolphe in *Mysteries* and Vautrin in *Splendors*, both Fleur and Esther become reformed visions of femininity, brimming with childlike innocence and newfound virginity. However, in the case of Esther, in Part II, the same character who polices her sexuality subsequently becomes her pimp. The respective situations of Fleur and Esther therefore reveal two women characters who engage in prostitution and speak slang, but they do so as the doll-like playthings of men; both women alter their subversive lifestyles at the hands of dominant male figures (Rodolphe and Vautrin), instead of supplanting the male gaze through shock and awe tactics via embodied and spoken slang in order to ultimately assert their agency.

In contrast, Balzac and Sue capitalize on the immoral and linguistic indecency of women characters completely void of feminine characteristics, such as Owl and Asia. As slang speakers, these exceedingly virile women criminals possess an agency akin to that of a man's and therefore evade the master and puppet dynamic that controls both Fleur and Esther. Nonetheless, promiscuous women, such as Fleur and Esther, function more fluidly on the spectrum of virtue and vice, tending not to exist on one extreme or the other for long, mainly because they do not ultimately possess control of their behaviors and language. These women are neither entirely bad nor entirely good, and, in some cases, are capable of degrees of moral reform. At the same time, Sue and Balzac frequently insinuate to their readers that she has sex for pay and speaks slang, traits which index her as criminal. Unfortunately, this also means that early representations of slang-speaking harlots almost never attempt to resist male dominance through the use of graphic body language or foul-mouthed speech. After 1850, in French naturalist novels, the prostitute's raunchy sexuality and uninhibited mobility serve as her embodied slang and, at the same time, the sleazy sexual conduct, physical movements, and vile language of these women, such as Germinie and Nana, grants them agency, even within the confines of male-driven narrative.

FEMININE BODIES, MASCULINE LANGUAGE

By the second half of the nineteenth century, the portrayal of the prostitute in literature created a paradoxical image of the woman slang speaker. On the one hand, she was a hyper sexualized being, who was rooted in her femininity and body. As Jessica Tanner argues, the prostitute was a figure that had the capability of both generating and withholding desire via her body, not unlike the writer of serial novels (*le feuilletoniste*) who withheld narrative closure from his readers by maintaining sinusoidal story arcs.[66] On the other hand, nineteenth-century French works on women's physiology define feminine beauty mainly in relation to their physical features but also her moral purity. In 1851, Auguste Debay claimed that beauty was culturally relative; however, for Europeans, the ideal woman possesses white skin, an oval face, and large, exaggerated eyes.[67] He asserted that perfection can only be obtained when physical beauty corresponds to a moral beauty as well: "But yet, man and woman who possess qualities of shape and expression, merit homage because physical beauty generally goes hand-in-hand with moral beauty; because these two kinds of beauty constitute perfection and perfection is an attribute of divinity."[68] Nearly ten years later, Ferdinand-Hippolyte Delaunay also claimed that there existed a link between female beauty and morality. In terms of objective beauty standards, Delaunay described the ideal female form:

The stature is small, the head cute and supported by a flexible neck of an admirable roundness; her neck is attached to soft, rounded shoulders [. . .]. In the front, the developed breast offers a true magnificence of charm in its form, of softness in its contours, and nicely breaks the monotony that a chest without depth would offer [. . .]. [T]he stomach is wide, the thigh very strong, the leg slim, the foot tiny. In this entire body, there exists no hardened or jagged trait. There is not anything that is neither angular nor sharp.[69]

Female voluptuousness and roundness, as opposed to masculine angularity and hardness, were desirable aspects of feminine beauty at the time. Both Debay's and Delaunay's respective assertions that there exists a positive correlation between physical beauty and morality appears in works such as Sue's *Mysteries* and Balzac's *Splendors*, wherein moral goodness ostensibly informs the "virginal" allure of Fleur and Esther. In contrast, compared to these literary ladies of the night, the descriptions of Germinie and Nana exploit their sexuality in order to reinforce not only their inherent immorality but also their sexual desirability for men. If the ideal feminine body—large breasts, hips, and thighs, petite face, and wide-set doe-eyes—characterizes these protagonists, their use of street slang in these novels does not correspond to the image of femininity, as it instead indexes the virility of the criminal and/or the working-class man.

In *Germinie Lacerteux*, the use of popular speech reminds readers of its working-class connotations, using italicization to distinguish the words as foreign to a bourgeois audience. In addition to making distinct their use of slang from Standard French via italics, in the works of Vidocq, Sue, and Balzac, the emphasis on class functions as a kind of distancing between the writer and the content. *Germinie Lacerteux* thus represents a literary crossroads in term of representations of the woman slang speaker. Based on the real life of Rose Malingre, the novel recounts the tragic life of a maid whose desire to love and to be loved ultimately leads to a string of addictions, loss, lovers, and fatal illness.[70] The figure of the maid, Corbin notes, is analogous to the prostitute in that she, too, belongs to a body of women who are "at the beck and call of the bourgeois body."[71] Although the Goncourt brothers' portrayal of Germinie evokes sympathy, there is nevertheless a bourgeois contemptibleness that frames the portrayal of her tragic life.

In terms of slang, Germinie and her peers speak in a way that indexes working-class men. In a scene in which Germinie tries absinthe for the first time, the conversation between her and her rival Adèle, the maid of a "kept women" (*une femme entretenue*),[72] is represented phonetically, while using several slang terms and expressions:

> One morning [. . .] Germinie found in the backroom two or three neighborhood maids who "were killing the worm" [. . .]

—Hey! said Adèle, while hitting her glass against the table, ther' you are (*te v'là*) already, mademoiselle de Varandeuil?
—What is this? said Germinie while taking Adèle's glass. I want some. . .
—You so thirsty at this hour in the morning? . . . eau-de-vie and absinth, nothing but that! . . . the *tap* of my *birdie*, you know? A military man . . . he only drank this . . . it's a little stiff, huh?[73]

These phonetic spellings contributed to the indexicalization of the woman slang speaker as working class, while further adding realism (*"te v'là"* instead of *"te voilà"*), rather than parody, as in earlier representations of unconventional speech habits in French literature (such as the Jewish hawker in Vidocq's *Memoirs* or the Baron de Nucingen in *Splendors*). This scene in which Germinie finds the "street" (*de la rue*) maids drinking absinthe in the morning, an act which is emphasized by the use of the popular idiom, "to drink on an empty stomach," translated as "to kill the worm" (*tuer le ver*), establishes an indexical link between language, class, and gender. The consumption of hard liquor and the use of slang are primarily indexes of working-class virility and the association of these two indexes with "working girls" in the naturalist novel adds another component to the same indexical field.[74] Like the hardened criminal men and women who possessed the same gruesome physical appearances in earlier works by Sue and Balzac, French writers post-1850 begin to conflate the behaviors between working-class men and women. And as Hall and Parish remind their readers, it is the transformation of actions into "meaningful signs" that serve as the basis of indexicality, which ultimately connects actions: "Agency in all its complexity refers both to the range of socioculturally mediated *acts* and also, interwoven, the possible *actors*."[75] When Adèle explains to Germinie that her "birdy" (*piou*, slang for "soldier")[76] only drinks absinthe, a sociolinguistic link surfaces between drinking absinthe and virility. Since the maids who are drinking and Adèle's lover share this common behavior, it further masculinizes the women characters.[77] The Goncourt brothers therefore play with the nature of absinthe-drinking in the morning by rendering it as indexical of lower-class women as well as military men, the ultimate figure of virility. The gestural and linguistic actions of the maids do not correspond to social notions of the day for a woman's behavior, and thus Adèle's act of violently hitting her glass on the table draws attention. Her use of language further contains aggressive undertones: the imperative (*Tiens!*) and exclamatory remarks (*Rien que ça!*) mark an assault on nineteenth-century linguistic norms regarding women's speech. The fact that Adèle can alter the indexicality of a highly masculinized language and gestures is therefore boundary-crossing, as she appropriates the speech habits of a masculine man.

Compared to Adèle, who expresses herself mainly through direct speech, Germinie's thoughts are mostly mediated through the narrator. Although

Germinie is the protagonist, the use of the third person omniscient narrator renders her much less vocal, contributing to a portrayal of her as being pathetic and weak. Nonetheless, Germinie's lack of direct speech throughout the text makes the times when she does speak up much more noticeable. The scene in which she speaks the longest takes place when her lover, the working-class painter Médéric Gautruche, suggests that she leave her spinster mistress, Mademoiselle de Varandeuil, and marry him. His proposal launches Germinie into an anger-driven rant, during which she reappropriates her power:

> Have you ever had pity on me when I was slaving away in the mud and in the snow, at the risk of kicking the bucket? Ah! Yes of course! And the things they said to me, they spit on my head, so that my blood boiled from one end of my body to the other. . . All that I've swallowed in insults waiting for you, and you are the one who couldn't care less![78]

Informal, vulgar expressions that are indexical of the working classes (*trimer*,[79] *crever*,[80] *cracher sur la tête*,[81] *manger*,[82] *et se ficher*[83]) characterize Germinie's speech. As with Adèle in the absinthe scene, an underlying violence simmers within Germinie's delivery. This embodied and linguistic violence thus serves to establish agency: the pejorative image of the immoral lower-class woman and her masculinized language is also capable of asserting herself as a subject. Germinie refuses the marriage proposal of a man, an act that in itself defies the normative expectations of women, as she chooses instead a life on her own in the household of Mademoiselle de Varandeuil, another unmarried woman character. By adopting masculine speech, in other words, both slang and the vernacular Germinie rebels against patriarchal gender conventions and norms in terms of what constitutes a proper woman and her speech, and therefore, in this instance, reasserts control of her own life.

In an 1866 critique for the newspaper *L'Événement*, Zola expressed the impact that the character *Germinie Lacerteux* had on him: "I must admit, from the beginning, that all of my being, my people and my intelligence brings me to admire the excessive and frenetic work that I am going to analyze."[84] Praising the Goncourt brothers for their raw, horrifying portrayal of the working-class maid, he further admonished the hypocrisy of critics who acclaimed bourgeois portrayals of fallen women, such as Gustave Flaubert's *Madame Bovary* (1856), while publicly condemning *Germinie Lacerteux*. More than twenty years after the appearance of *Germinie Lacerteux*, its influence became manifest in Zola's serialized publication of *Nana*, a novel that revealed the slang speech practices of lower-class women as far more obscene than those in earlier portrayals.

Similar to the embodied language of the criminal that served as a physical manifestation of his slang speech, the bodily and sexual deviance of the prostitute also emerged as the physical incarnation of her foul mouth. However, the slang speakers in earlier literary works indexed persons of the criminal and/or working classes who remained contained within specific physical locations, such as the urban metropolis, but more specifically, in taverns, sewers, brothels, soup houses, and prisons that were either on the periphery of the city or kept from plain sight. The prostitute, however, potentially represented a greater danger if she did not remain contained within the appropriate locations demarcated for her.[85] This lack of physical containment, most notable in the character Nana's, nonlinear social trajectory as a prostitute, and thus her capacity to frequent a wide-range of social milieus, in addition to her status as a public performer, highlight a breach in the physical and social boundaries previously imposed on those whose bodily and linguistic disorder threatened the social status quo. Nana, however, defies the typical representation of the ladylike courtesan, as she had her start as a common street prostitute. Despite her social ascent, her language consistently remains more indexical of the lower, rather than, upper classes. Throughout the novel, promiscuous women often characterize their speech with "muffled swear words" (*jurons étouffés*),[86] and Nana is no exception, as she "avenged herself of the problems that [her suitors] caused her, by mincing faint profanities against men. These curse words pained the chambermaid [. . .]."[87] She refers to the Count Muffat as her "little oaf" (*petit mufe*) and exclaims "dirty oaf!" (*sale mufe!*) to the men who pass by her on her nightly prowling for clients.[88] She also calls Muffat a "dirty nag" (*sale rosse*), while ordering him to imitate different animals.[89] Generally, Nana directs these expletives at men. When Steiner, the Marquis de Chouard, and Count Muffat arrive unexpectedly at her apartment on the boulevard Haussmann, she curses the undesired arrival of male suitors: "Ah! Yup, replied Nana crudely, they are bastards, they like that."[90] As with her body, Nana's words and ways of speaking are hers alone: "Holy! she murmured quietly to herself."[91] Although Nana's speech practices contribute to a pejorative portrait of the prostitute, emphasizing the fact that despite her newfound status as a courtesan, she will always be a working-class lowlife, they also highlight her refusal to capitulate to the patriarchal status quo. Nana swears both to herself and at the men who objectify her, thus disrupting their sexual fantasy. Her power resides in her ability to usurp the masculine position through her language and her body. In terms of performance, Mulvey notes that within the cinematic realm,

> A woman performs within the narrative, the gaze of the spectator and that of the male characters in the film are neatly combined without breaking narrative

verisimilitude. For a moment, the sexual impact of the performing woman takes the film into a no-man's-land outside its own time and space.⁹²

Nana, however, consistently shatters this moment devoid of time and space that Mulvey describes.⁹³ In a similar fashion, Mesch demonstrates that Nana possesses the ability to turn the male gaze back onto the male spectator. During the opening scene of Nana's performance in *La blonde Vénus*, the journalist Fauchery begins to chronicle the reactions of the male spectators because he "is driven to turn away from the female object of his analysis to record the effects of her behavior on men who come into contact with her."⁹⁴ According to Mesch, "Nana remains free from the imprints of the desire she evokes" when she participates in the spectacle of the male gaze through her act of laughing at the men, "thus eerily participating in the spectacle while remaining also outside of it, viewing the men as a spectacle as well."⁹⁵

Like other non-gender-conforming women before her, Nana's ability to break the male gaze and turn it back onto the spectators is a result of her refusal to capitulate fully to patriarchal standards regarding femininity. Her language thus accomplishes a similar feat as her laughter: by speaking in a

Figure 6.7 Actress Marlene Dietrich in *Blonde Venus* (1932). Directed by Josef von Sternberg.

manner that indexes the crude working-class man, a misalignment occurs between her body, viewed as the visual embodiment of female sexiness by men, and her speech, an aural marker, like laughter, that embodies virility. By not fully corresponding to male standards, a noticeable contrast occurs between the visual and the aural, which has a mirror effect on the spectator. The male interlocutor recognizes that Nana sounds more like a man than a woman, and in doing so, his sexualized fantasy of her thus partly collapses.

In fact, the badly behaved "ladies" of the *Théâtre des Variétés*, Bordenave's self-proclaimed "brothel" (*bordel*), freely spew vulgar expressions and swear words. When journalist Fauchery asks the streetwalker Satin, what she is doing, she responds, "I am bored shitless" (*Je m'emmerde*).[96] By 1830, the use of the expression "to be bored shitless" (*s'emmerder*), in addition to slight variations of the phrase, such as "that bores me shitless" (*ça m'emmerde*) or "to bore someone shitless" (*emmerder qqn*), was becoming more commonly used among colloquial French speakers, in spite of its vulgarity.[97] Satin's use of this expression signals the introduction of a new indexical relationship between the term and the image of the speaker that it conjures. *S'emmerder* is the crude expression of the convict, the working-class man, and now, the sexually promiscuous lower-class woman. This new indexicality associated with licentious women exists within the same indexical field as the previous social groups; however, elements of gender and sexual desirability have now begun to factor in.

Other vulgarities used by female slang speakers in *Nana* contain more nuanced meanings. When referring to the courtesan Lucy Stewart, Bordenave's star actress Rose Mignon lets the vulgar term "dirty crane!" (*sale grue!*) slip from her mouth.[98] The term *grue*, meaning "crane" (as in the animal), is slang for "prostitute" and inherently tied to the theater, as it also referred to an actress in the second half of the nineteenth century, while simultaneously signifying a person of minimal intelligence: "Thus to describe a girl with thin legs, with eyes bulging from the head, slow to understand—does one not fail to say: that's a *crane*. The crane is a type frighteningly common today [. . .]."[99] Lexicographer Alfred Delvau included the term *grue*, within both of his controversial slang dictionaries, emphasizing in each entry the sexual aspect of the term, as well as its relationship to stupidity. In his *Erotic Modern Dictionary* (1864), Delvau states that a *grue* is "[a] kept girl, because girls of this kind are often more stupid than beautiful—which means that one cannot explain the crazy things that dandies do for them."[100] In his *Dictionary of the Green Tongue* (1866), a *grue* constitutes

> A kept woman, that Nature blessed with as much stupidity as beauty that abuses of the former to in order to make the latter acceptable. It is a happy word that writers found as a response to the insolence of whores towards good women. *Stupid girls!* they cried. *Crane!* one replied. But this word, in its pejorative

sense, was not born of today. For a long time people use it to refer to a simpleton, an idiot and a vain person.[101]

Although there is no mention of the theater in the above definitions, Delvau's short exchange, included in the 1867 entry between an imagined group of insolent girls and literary people to demonstrate the usage of *grue* in a real-life context, incorporates both the literary and the theatrical into the definition. Whether in a novel or a play, this short dialogue gives a performative demonstration of its execution between women, and in a similar fashion to dialogues between criminal types that appeared in early nineteenth-century novels and dictionaries. The term "actress" further connoted sexual deviance, thus deepening the linguistic and professional interchangeability between the prostitute and the performer. According to Bernheimer's analysis of Parent-Duchâtelet, these "women of shows and of theaters" (*femmes de spectacles et de théâtres*) were to be feared the most due to "[their] ability to disguise [their] venality and control the signs of [their] sexual availability."[102] The term *grue* even further reinforces the pervasive notion of the criminal physique as being biologically similar to that of animals: *grue*, as crane, invokes a visual image of the prostitute-performer as physically resembling the long-legged bird, most notable for its deliberate march-like walk and long legs, considered to be an alluring female attribute and an embodiment of sensuality.[103]

As Jordan notes, throughout all the history of literature and film there has always been a strange admiring by male authors for a "woman who plays it like a man."[104] In later nineteenth-century French representations of the prostitute, an analysis of certain slang words uncovers a layered indexicality that links promiscuity to women actresses and dancers. Slowly over time, the layered meanings contained within these signs, that were once purely criminal, expands the domains of performance under which a woman slang speaker can be found. There is the sexual performance of the prostitute, who might also exercise a theatrical performance on the actual stage. Despite the public display of her body for the consumption of the male gaze, whether on the streets or in the theater, the prostitute's mobility and her appropriation of slang offers her the possibility of agency that would be strengthened over time with women writers increasingly portraying unconventional female protagonists.

EMBODIED LANGUAGE, SEXUALITY, AND PERFORMANCE

In addition to language, bodily disorders, such as hysteria and sexual deviancy, were also part of the discourse on the nineteenth-century prostitute, focusing on moral and pathological contamination but also other gestures, such as licentious dance, hysteric seizures, and the public display of her body in the brasserie, theater, or on the streets, all of which intersect to constitute a body that is simultaneously desired and marginalized.[105] Her adoption of slang and popular speech, coupled with her frenzied body language and sexual debauchery, resulted in a physical index that is deeply embodied, implying a mobility within the urban environment, hence the social mobility of the language, a mobility that had previously been the sole right of men. However, this mobility challenged not so much man's terrain because, as Janet Wolff exposes, nineteenth-century women had always been a part of the public sphere, but "the invisibility of women in the literature of modernity has nothing much to do with women's actual lives in the period. Rather it is a product of the discourse of modernity itself."[106] Therefore, the prostitute within the public discourse did not so much threaten the physical terrain of men, but rather his appropriation of the right to inhabit any place he chose. The prostitute's vulgar language, sexual promiscuity, and mobility rendered her the greatest threat to the preservation of social order as well as behavioral, gender, and linguistic norms. As Elizabeth Wilson acknowledges,

> The prostitute was a "public woman", but the problem in nineteenth-century urban life was whether every woman in the new, disordered world of the city— the public sphere of pavements, cafés and theatres—was not a public woman and thus a prostitute. The very presence of unattended—unowned—women constituted a threat both to male power and to male frailty. Yet although the male ruling class did all it could to restrict the movement of women in cities, it proved impossible to banish them from public spaces. Women continued to crowd into the city centres and the factory divides.[107]

The urban changes taking place in Paris after 1850 included the creation of public spaces for women, such as department stores. As Wilson notes, the shift in the physical and social landscapes rendered it difficult to distinguish between good and bad women. The mobility that prostitution offered to women threatened male control over public space, as she was a woman that could not be subjected to patriarchal restriction; she roamed freely and uncontrolled, while spreading disease and moral chaos. Her body became the physical equivalent of her unrefined speech.

The prostitute's wandering, albeit solitary, is, of course, motivated by money (whether hers alone, or that of her pimp) since her public exposure is an embodied transaction. At the same time, she does not typically possess the existential introspection of the *flâneur*, which was usually due to a lack of evolution in terms of her consciousness that placed her on the same intellectual playing field as an animal, or as one acting solely from instinct and desire. Perhaps she is aware of her desires; however, she lacks the ability to contextualize her existence within the developing urban metropolis. Nonetheless, the portrayal of her uninhibited mobility marked her as a post-Revolutionary woman in the urban terrain that not only challenged the rights of men alone to dominate this terrain but which was also the primary means through which the prostitute could simultaneously acquire both linguistic and literary liberation.

Germinie's street slang, as well as that of other prostitutes in the novel, indexes them as both working class and masculine. Unlike Nana, Germinie's social trajectory, however, is not as varied. At the beginning of the novel, the reader meets her as a working-class maid, while her downward spiral into alcoholism by the novel's end transforms her into a lowly streetwalker, a social descent that influenced later cinematic portrayals of the vamp, such as Greta Garbo as the man-eating seductress Elena, in the silent film, *The Temptress* (1926).[108]

Additionally, unlike Sue's *Mysteries* and Balzac's *Splendors*, there are no interactions between characters from a wide variety of social strata; instead, the main interactions tend to take place between characters who are socially separated by only a few degrees. Nonetheless, even though Germinie does not frequent high-society (like the slang-speaking Nana), her jaunts about Paris still mark a high level of mobility for an unaccompanied woman. For

Figure 6.8   Actress Greta Garbo in *The Temptress* (1926). Directed by Fred Niblo.

instance, the most vivid descriptions of her wanderings occur when she secretly follows Jupillon, the son of the dairywoman Madame Jupillon and the object of Germinie's affection, throughout the city, and when she falls into prostitution following her breakup with Gautruche. One morning, she sees Jupillon on the sidewalk and follows him to *la place Bréda* to find that a young woman (Jupillon's cousin) joins him.[109] This encounter includes a precise detailing of her urban trajectory:

> They headed towards rue de Navarin [. . .]. They were walking slowly [. . .]. They climbed up rue des Martyrs, crossed rue de la Tour-d'Auvergne, and went down rue Montholon [. . .]. Arrived at rue Lamartine in front of the passage des Deux-Sœurs they turned around; Germinie only had enough time to fling herself into an alley door. They passed by without seeing her.[110]

Eventually, the two lovers slip away into a hotel, while Germinie looks on in an act of voyeuristic flânerie. Interestingly, her urban mobility in the novel appears to be almost entirely motivated by an obsession with the male subject.[111] Germinie thus descends into the most sinister quarters of Paris and walks "for hours" (*souvent des heures*).[112] When she is working the streets, however, Germinie both watches and is watched:

> The passersby who pass there, the male worker who climbs up Paris while whistling, the female worker who comes back, her day completed, hands under her armpits to keep warm, the prostitute in a black bonnet who roams, crossed paths with [Germinie] and looked at her. Strangers seemed to recognize her; the light made her ashamed.[113]

The Goncourt brothers describe Germinie's time on the streets as a sort of reverse theatricality. The play between darkness and light resembles the lighting of a stage; however, instead of desiring the spotlight, Germinie actively flees it.[114] Like Fleur, Germinie incarnates the stigma attached to street prostitution, and thus cannot rid herself of the shame. At the same time, she becomes the eyes and ears of the streets as she maneuvers her body in and out of the shadows. Eventually, following her split from Gautruche, it is as if Germinie's prostitution renders her "thrown outside of her sex" (*jetée hors de son sexe*):

> From this breakup, Germinie fell where she had to have fallen, beneath shame, beneath nature even. From fall to fall, the miserable and passionate creature wandered the street. She collected loves that wear themselves out in one night, those which pass, those which one meets, those which the luck of the cobblestones makes one find the woman who roams.[115]

Germinie eventually reaches the point of degradation wherein she surpasses any kind of emotional state, functioning purely on a mechanical level.[116] Men are no longer individuals, but rather, cookie-cutter representations of one another.[117] This is not to say that subjectivity is exchanged in this situation, quite the contrary, as Germinie is objectified to the point of transforming herself into a machine (much like the mechanical metaphors that Zola so liberally uses to describe Nana). Her mobility, coupled with her discretion, gives her the phantom-like ability to freely roam the city streets. Although her mobility alone does not imply corporal performance, it does endow Germinie with a kind of body language, a physical equivalent of slang, that indexes a masculine independence in the eyes of a nineteenth-century audience; in this manner, she occasionally asserts her subjectivity and repels the objectifying male gaze. As Wilson notes, "Bourgeois men, by contrast, were free to explore urban zones of pleasure such as—in Paris especially—the Folies-Bergère, the restaurant, the theatre, the café and the brothel, where they met working-class women."[118] Spatial restrictions on women began to loosen following the rise of women's spaces such as the department store, which made differentiating between moral and immoral women even more difficult. Such mobility granted the possibility of greater social access in ways similar to the disguise-wearing characters of the male criminal popularized in early nineteenth-century works, such as Vidocq, Vautrin, and Jean Valjean.

Although linguistic vulgarities abound in *Nana* and *Germinie Lacerteux*, Zola's text differs in that it relies less on the medical discourse influenced by the prominent French neurologist Jean-Martin Charcot to explain the existence of the prostitute.[119] Unlike Germinie, who is a transitional figure, as she, too, is plagued by the same shame that defines earlier slang-speaking women, such as Esther and Fleur, Nana evokes contempt through her ostensible unawareness of others and their negative perception of her, as well as an unawareness of herself. The character of Nana thus embodies the late nineteenth-century, early twentieth century construct of the Vamp: her narcissism serves to eliminate the shame that once characterized earlier portrayals of prostitutes in literature, which renders Nana even more dangerous because she freely indulges her selfish desires, while being devoid of any empathy toward those she ruins.

Nana's danger further lies in her social mobility. She takes up with a variety of upper- and lower-class lovers, men and women alike: the Count Muffat, the journalist Fauchery, Madame Hugon's youngest son Georges Hugon, the actor Fontan, and fellow streetwalker-turned-lover Satin, and thus frequents a wide-range of social milieus. With her unsanctioned access, she threatens to destabilize the illusion of social control for the upper classes not only physically but morally and linguistically as well. Simultaneously, there is a permeation occurring between interior and exterior spaces, one that brings the otherwise contained physical and linguistic transgressions of the theater to the boulevard. For example, from the outset of the novel, Nana's mobility becomes a topic of discussion among the supporting characters. Both the Count Xavier de Vandeuvres and Fauchery claim to have already seen Nana on la Rue de Provence.[120] The banker, Steiner, also claims to have seen her before.[121]

Nana eventually falls into street prostitution in order to support Fontan; she

> had resigned herself in order to keep the peace in her household [. . .]. Nana fell back into the same shit from the past. She walked around, hitting the streets of her former clients from her streetwalker days, in search of a coin for one-hundred sous.[122]

While the boulevards that Nana and Satin frequent stage the scene, Zola uses similar vocabulary to describe the Parisian streets as he does Bordenave's theater, a sanctioned place of vice:

> [I]n this vice from below which roamed the length of muddy alleyways, under the obscured clarity of gas [. . .]. Both of them ran, frequented balls and neighborhood cafés, climbing staircases humid from spit and spilled beer; or else they walked leisurely and went up streets, standing upright against the large passageways.[123]

The description of the streets evokes a similar one that takes place earlier at the *Théâtre des Variétés* when Fauchery brings Muffat to the actresses' dressing rooms. Both passages conjure up images that denote filth, heat, humidity, and machinery. While climbing the stairs, Muffat is also figuratively descending into the vice of the Parisian demi-monde, thus falling further from his aristocratic morals into the sexual debauchery:

> Within the lanterns fixed to the walls, gas flames burned, crudely lighting this misery, releasing a heat that climbed and amassed underneath the narrow spiral of the floors [. . .]. Humidity was seeping from the walls. The steps sounded on the tiled floor, as if in an underground tunnel.[124]

Muffat is inundated by the "womanly scent" (*odeur de femme*) that permeates the floors, which further permeates the districts that the street prostitutes work as well. This similarity in descriptions between spaces obliterates the boundary between interior and exterior, between the theatrical and the real, and between the high and the low. In this regard, the streets are as much a place of embodied language as Bordenave's theater, which is as much a place of sexual deviancy as are the sleazy haunts of prostitutes.[125] In ways similar to the disguise-swapping criminal, the figure of the prostitute in the naturalist novel possessed her own embodied language that became the physical manifestation of her slang speech. Fornication, prostitution, dance, and other corporal transgressions (alcohol and drug use), of course, constituted the basis of this dangerous body language that, like its linguistic counterpart, could easily permeate all echelons of society in both public and private spaces. Thus, the slang-speaking woman who belongs to Gauthier's second category of women criminals, that is, "women who seduce," may also occasionally profit from a subjectivity that "women exempt from seduction" typically possess due to their physical resemblance to men. These sensual figures of slang prove that their virile speech and embodied language can temporarily remove them from projections of masculine desire and extend to them an agency akin to that of a man's.

Characters such as Nana and Germinie utilize their transgressive bodies and speech to temporarily supplant the confines of male objectification, while expanding categorical possibilities for women. While the character of Germinie is mainly designed as a social untouchable, there nevertheless exist subtle details throughout the narrative that showcase her sexual potency. For instance, when describing her physical features, the authors emphasize her undisputable homeliness: "Germinie was ugly."[126] Simultaneously, however, there exists a certain *je ne sais quoi* that erupts out of Germine's unattractiveness:

> Out of this ugly woman escaped a violent and mysterious seduction [. . .]. Everything about her, her mouth, her eyes, even her ugliness, contained a provocation and an appeal. An aphrodisiac charm sprang from her, which attacked and attached itself to the opposite sex.[127]

Germinie's "violent seduction" further recalls other instances of female aggressiveness in the text such as Adèle's slamming down her absinthe glass and Germinie's anger-laden refusal of Gautruche's marriage proposal. Albeit ugly, masculine, and violent, these women slang speakers nevertheless remain both desirable and mysterious to the opposite sex.[128] The virility expressed through their gestures and speech habits disrupts the phantasmatic nature of the male gaze, while simultaneously captivating it, thus encompassing Jacques Lacan's notion of desire as an ongoing fascination that is never obtained or fulfilled.

Despite her masculinized spoken and embodied language, through her descent into street prostitution, Germinie often demonstrates a lack of subjectivity that differentiates her from Nana, who regularly takes the stage at

Figure 6.9 "Germinie Lacerteux se montrant dans sa robe de demoiselle d'honneur à Mademoiselle de Varandeuil." Illus. Jeanniot and L. Muller. *Germinie Lacerteux* by Edmond and Jules de Goncourt. Paris: 1886.

Bordenave's *Théâtre des Variétés*, as well as transforms the street into her own stage. In fact, Germinie's ventures into the streets of Paris, transform her into the author of her own narrative, thus providing the foundation for her personal agency through her wild bodily gestures and working-class speech that resist male dominance. Through her urban wanderings, Germinie becomes a veritable storyteller (*conteuse*), an ability that shines forth in her fondness for telling Mademoiselle de Varandeuil stories of the various social types in their neighborhood:

Figure 6.10 "Germinie Lacerteux chez Gautruche." Illus. Jeanniot and L. Muller. *Germinie Lacerteux* by Edmond and Jules de Goncourt. Paris: 1886.

[Germinie] as well had set herself out, had educated herself and had been open to the education of Paris. Mlle de Varandeuil, unoccupied and curious in the way a spinster is about the neighborhood stories, had always told [Germinie] what news she had gathered, what she knew about the renters, all the gossip from the house and the street; and this tradition of storytelling, to chat like a lady-in-waiting with her mistress, to paint people, to draw their silhouettes, had developed within [Germinie] a long-term aptitude for lively expressions, happy and elusive traits, a zesty and sometimes biting observation particular to a servant's mouth.[129]

Germinie thus transforms the neighborhood happenings, both on and off the streets of Paris, into a serialized story (*chronique*). However, Germinie's stories are not written down, but rather transmitted both orally and through her lively facial expressions; in other words, through her body language. Nonetheless, in spite of Germinie's ability to read and write, she prefers to keep her stories to herself, but then begins to imagine scenarios that allow her to function as the subject of her own narrative, thus providing the foundation for actual demonstrations of agency.[130] For instance, after witnessing Jupillon's romantic affair with his cousin, Germinie creates an elaborate revenge fantasy—one that she never fulfills in reality, but that only exists within her mind.[131] In a similar fashion, Germinie fantasizes about Gautruche beating her, so she can reveal everything to the chief of police.[132]

Germinie possesses a strong urge to tell these stories; however, she is never able to satisfy this need; instead, her thoughts forever remain in the realm of fantasy. Notably, she constructs her fantasies around the same plotline: escaping masculinist projections that forbid her from asserting her own subjectivity. This subconscious desire of Germinie to speak as subject surfaces in another scene in which Mademoiselle de Varandeuil catches Germinie sleep talking:

> Mademoiselle leaned forward horrified by this abandoned body, no longer belonging to itself, in which the past came back like a spirit in an abandoned house [. . .]. [S]he felt like she was next to a cadaver possessed by a dream [. . .]. [H]er speech also became unrecognizable [. . .]. It was like the language of a people purified and transfigured by passion [. .]. Mademoiselle remained confused, stupefied, listening as if in a theater.[133]

In what appears to be an episode of a Biblical form of possession, when sleep-talking Germinie passionately speaks in tongues, and like Balzac's Esther and Asia who speak in onomatopoeias, Germinie's language is "unrecognizable" to Mademoiselle de Varandeuil. Instead of animal-like noises, however, Germinie's language is a "purified" form of the vernacular. In *Ventriloquized Bodies* (1994), Janet Beizer examines the "narrative power" of the hysteric's body in the nineteenth century and its semiotic use in literature. Beizer notes that one of the common characteristics of hysterics was the adoption of a "socially unacceptable speech": "Hysterics laugh or cry indiscriminately, sing or speak nonsense words, make animal noises, and give free rein to unseemly body sounds: hiccups and borborygmi (stomach rumblings) are most frequently cited."[134] This speech characteristic of the hysteric is as developed (or even less so) as that of an animal. Devoid of any kind of intelligible means of communication, the hysteric resorts to melodramatic gestures and bestial babble. Like the hysteric, the lower-class woman also does not possess the same capacity to speak intelligibly.[135] Germinie's episode of sleep talking captivates the old spinster as well as introduces a corporal element to the characterization of the woman slang speaker. While Germinie's body is disorderly, in the sense that she engages in sexual promiscuity and freely roams the urban streets unaccompanied, she further possesses a chaotic body that becomes slang incarnate. The confusion and stupefaction that Mademoiselle de Varandeuil experiences as if "listening like at the theater" emphasize the transformation of Germinie's body and language when sleep talking into a performance.[136] Her working-class speech, while indexically masculine, grants her the capacity to assert herself as a subject against a traditionally masculine oppression. Germinie's street speak, coupled with her embodied language, in the form of her mobility, sexuality, and demonstrations of anger and hysteria, presents this new woman slang speaker as an agent capable of evading categorical notions of gender, femininity, and even sexual desirability (as demonstrated by Germinie's objective ugliness).

Germinie's initial attempts at breaking free from the hold the male gaze manifests through more violent bodily and linguistic outbursts. Throughout the novel, Germinie possesses at times "the ghost of a woman from the Salpêtrière hospital,"[137] as she is susceptible to hysterical attacks. After learning of her daughter's death, Germinie enters Madmoiselle de Varandeuil's bedroom and undergoes a frenzied physical reaction:

> [W]hen Germinie entered into her bedroom [. . .] after two or three long, profound, wrested and painful sighs, Mademoiselle saw her, bending backwards and twisting, rolling at the foot of the chair and falling to the ground. She wanted to pick her up; but Germinie was agitated by convulsive movements that were so violent that the old lady was forced to let this raging body, whose members contracted and picked themselves up for a moment and lanced themselves randomly to the right and to the left, fall again onto the wood floor.[138]

The contortions of Germinie's body predate the infamous images found in the *Photographic Iconography of the Salpêtrière* (*Iconographie photographique de la Salpêtrière*, 1876) which captured images of the hysterical fits of young women, who twist and arch their bodies in chaotic, sexually suggestive ways.[139] These wild, animal-like movements defy the bodily constraints imposed on women in the nineteenth century: their tightly pulled corsets, their imprisonment in the home, and their mandate to remain silent and physically small.[140] Like Hugo's prisoner who appears to be half snake and half woman, Germinie's hysterical body acts as the physical embodiment of her working-class speech. In the same way as slang, this kind of bodily spectacle is made unpredictable and untamable by spectators. Although Mademoiselle

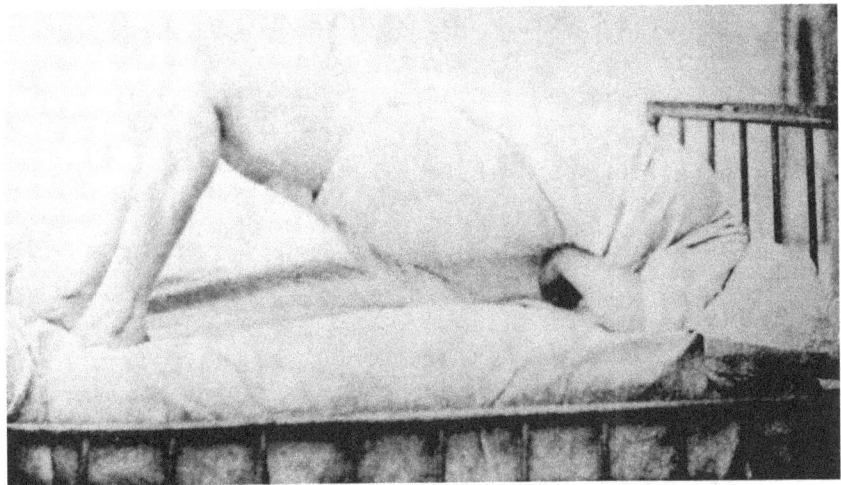

Figure 6.11 "Attaque hystéro-épileptique: arc de cercle." *Iconographie photographique de la Salpêtrière* by Bourneville and Régnard. Aux Bureaux du Progrès médical/Delahaye & Lecroisnier, Paris: 1878.

de Varandeuil wishes to pick Germinie up, she cannot handle her intense, full-bodied spasms. As attempts at containment can never be fully realized, Germinie enters a realm where she refuses, albeit momentarily, the societal restraints imposed onto women by men.[141]

In her book *The Hysteric's Revenge: French Women Writers at the Fin de Siècle*, Mesch asserts that the nineteenth-century explosion in interest concerning the female body, sexuality, and hysteria

> at the same time as it perpetuated female subjugation, made possible the critique of the body that would eventually empower modern feminism. The discursive production of sexuality exposed the mechanisms of patriarchal power over the female body, opening them up to challenge and subversion as women writers began to speak on their own behalf.[142]

The dynamic between women's bodies, language, and "patriarchal power" that surfaces in *Germinie Lacerteux*, with its representations of lower-class women who defy patriarchal norms (and are thus prone to promiscuous behavior, vile language, and violent outbursts), however, makes for a depressing image of female empowerment. Like her body, the representation of deviant women and their language in literature subvert cultural expectations of women's speech, presenting instead the slang-speaking woman as both virile and vulgar. Nonetheless, as Mesch

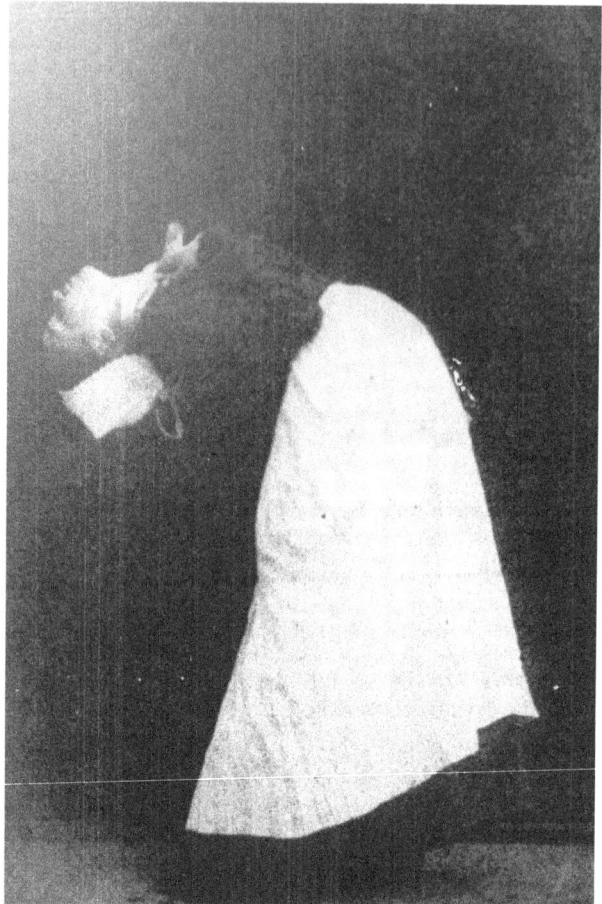

Figure 6.12 Photographie d'Augustine *Iconographie photographique de la Salpêtrière* **by Bourneville and Régnard.** Aux Bureaux du Progrès médical/Delahaye & Lecroisnier, Paris : 1878.

notes with regards to women's bodies and sexuality, that this is the same dynamic that propelled women in the late-nineteenth and early twentieth centuries to regain control over the patriarchal discourse concerning proper women's speech.

Like Germinie, the vulgarity of the woman slang speaker in *Nana* constitutes a bodily disorder in the form of an embodied language that is also mobile and refuses categorical gender norms.[143] The notion of public exposure, in addition to that of physical establishment (in the form of standing or otherwise) is inherent to the concept of the prostitute, which relies on the movement of the body. As Stephanie Wooler notes, Nana's mobility also offers her the possibility of performing "femininity" offstage. For instance, it is only when Nana exits the gender-confining atmosphere of the theater that she can truly play the role of the *grande dame*.¹⁴⁴ By the second half of the nineteenth century, gesture (*le geste*) possessed an inherently performative function. For Debay, "the art of gesture" (*l'art du geste*) included song, public speaking, and theatrical performance, including dance and pantomime.¹⁴⁵ In turn, these gestures made up what Debay calls "attitudes," which can be either natural or acquired:

> The diverse positions that the body is obligated to take, according to moral or physical circumstances under which one finds oneself, are attitudes. The elegant, the vain, the courtesan, the prideful, the coquette, the fop, the prude, the modest woman, etc., offer attitudes that are suitable for them, and with which it is easy to recognize them.¹⁴⁶

While less interested in gender and its subversion, Debay is more interested in the construction of social types in terms of these "attitudes." The centrality he gives to gesture vis-à-vis the creation of these types, thus reveals gesture as a key source of embodied language and indexicality, which was included among many other social indexes, such as spoken language.¹⁴⁷ For the woman slang speaker of the late nineteenth century, the combination of her theatrical and sexual performance, along with language, not only revealed an embodied language that disrupted and subverted male expectations and thus, momentarily asserting female agency, but it also created a nuanced combination of masculine and feminine qualities that paved the way for more gender-fluid representations of women in literature whose agency endured.

The relationships between slang, body language, and sexuality, as means of creating a new social vision of women, are best embodied in Nana's entrance, both into the narrative and Bordenave's play as "The Blond Venus" (*La blonde Vénus*). Before speaking, the audience is immediately captivated by the movements of her body:

> Nana was so white and so fleshy, so natural in this character armed with large hips and a mug that right away she won over the entire room [. . .]. [H]er round shoulders, her Amazonian throat [. . .], her large hips that turned in a voluptuous sway, her thighs of blonde flesh, all of her body was made out, was seen under a light fabric, of a white foam [. . .]. And when Nana lifted her arms, one saw, in the footlights, the golden hairs of her armpits.¹⁴⁸

Nana not only incarnates her role as Venus via her physical resemblance to Botticelli's Venus, but she is also an inversion of this classical image.¹⁴⁹ Nana is the anti-Venus: *Blonde*, not just in the physical sense, but in the figurative

NANA, EN VÉNUS, CHANTANT.
« Elle commença le second couplet. » — (Page 34.)

Figure 6.13 "Nana, en Vénus, chantant." Illus. André Gill, Bertall, et al. *Nana* by Émile Zola. Paris: 1882.

sense as well, as two common definitions for *Blonde* at this time were also "lover" and "mistress."[150] Similarly, she is not Venus as a goddess, but rather as "a streetwalker, who only asks for two francs for a voyage to Cythera."[151] This inverted image of the Goddess of Love eventually transforms itself into word incarnate, as in the twentieth century, "nana" becomes a slang term, standing in for both a "young woman of little virtue, a young prostitute" (*[j]eune femme de petit vertu, jeune prostituée*) as well as "a girl, woman, as opposed to a guy or man" (*[f]ille, femme, opposée à mec, homme*).[152] In the twentieth century, the French word, "nana," now embodies a new linguistic meaning of "woman," while also carrying the derogatory connotation of prostitute. Despite her deeply negative representation and gruesome death by the novel's end, Zola's Nana literally redefines "woman" by the twentieth century. Woman thus becomes word embodied, as she possesses the ability to transform not only the social terrain but the linguistic terrain as well.

THE AGENCY OF WOMEN SLANG SPEAKERS

The perversion of Standard French to create criminal meanings in slang corresponds to the perversion of social image. In the second half of the nineteenth century, a sociolinguistic evolution takes place with regards to the literary representation of the woman slang speaker, an evolution that corresponds to both a corporal and moral evolution as well. Earlier in the century, the figure of the woman slang speaker typically fell under two categories: (1) the ultrafeminine, even virginal, prostitute (Gauthier's "women who are seduced") and (2) the hypermasculine criminal woman (Gauthier's "women exempt from seduction"). However, the overwhelming portrayal of the sexually deviant woman as a slang speaker (Gauthier's "women who seduce") in literary works throughout the nineteenth century corresponded to a seemingly endless discourse generated during this time surrounding her problematic body, one that also constituted an embodied slang. A site of perceived physical and moral filth, the prostitute's physical permeation of the upper classes occurred through the exchange of her bodily fluids with clients as well as through her unaccompanied sojourns through the streets of Paris, granted her the same unsanctioned social access to various class milieus as bourgeois men. Her power to spread venereal disease through the act of sex was just as socially dismantling as her power to morally infect the upper classes through her invasion into their artistic, physical, and intellectual terrain. In addition to the threat of moral and pathological contamination the prostitute embodied, she often engaged in other dramatic gestures relative to a kind of bodily performance: raunchy forms of dance, such as the Cancan (*le chahut* or *le cancan*), hysterical fits of violence, and sensual unveilings of her body for a public audience, all of which contributed to the long list of physical transgressions that constituted the prostitute in the collective imaginary as well as to a body language analogous to her linguistic practices that granted her the temporary power of her own agency.

Other embodied functions, such as spoken language, also served as key components of the prostitute's social threat and subversive power. Combined with the fluid use of her body (paradoxically marginalized and feared while still desired), representations of the prostitute as a slang speaker in literature served as a crucial marker in order to index the abstract qualities this social figure possessed: sexual promiscuity, as well as a lack of modesty and morals. While earlier literary characters, such as Fleur and Esther, were more innocent than criminal in terms of their speech practices, later nineteenth-century portrayals of women slang speakers attempted to realistically showcase their dialogue—vulgarities, and all. The phonetic spelling of words and the use of idiomatic and slang expressions contributed to the realism of works such as *Germinie Lacerteux* and *Nana*, rather than the blatant parody of them as found in earlier works, such as *Splendors*. While Germinie represents a transitional figure of the woman slang speaker, in the middle of the continuum between the shame-filled Fleur and the narcissistic-driven Nana, Geminie's working-class speech did not align with her sexual desirability, a trait that further misaligned with her physical unattractiveness. In contrast, for Nana, her voluptuous movements within the public domain, her identity as a desired sex object, and her masculine street speak also implicated language and the body (one the function of the other) as part of her radical gender stylization which contained the power to shatter the erotic fantasies of male characters within the novel. While both representations are highly pejorative, this image of the new woman slang speaker as possessing a hypersexual body language combined with a spoken language predominately indexical of working-class men, granted her a kind proto-feminist agency that does not appear in earlier portrayals of women slang speakers such as Esther and Fleur, the Owl, Asia, and She-Wolf. Finally, the radical nature of Germinie and Nana further introduced the possibility of new literary visions of women characters that actively challenged social perceptions of gender norms through their more empowered deployment of language and the body.

Coinciding with this linguistic transition was a bodily transition in which characters such as Germinie and Nana constitute the making of a corporal index via a performance that was both theatrical and sexual as well as no longer physically and/or socially containable. Unlike the licentious dancers and singers of the slang speakers in past literary works, this new version of the woman slang speaker did not keep her sensual physical movements confined to underground taverns or brothels, but instead brought her indecent body to the public stage of the streets. Germinie and Nana thus possess a language that distinguishes them from earlier nineteenth-century representations of prostitutes, while simultaneously creating a new category of woman slang speaker at the end of the century that enters the collective imaginary. Their masculinized language and vulgar gestures notably do not align with their sensual bodies (both the results of, as well as testimonies to, their femininity). The mélange of masculine and feminine characteristics contained within these characters speak to a power of subversion; however, more importantly it established new possibilities for women's behavior, speech, sexuality, and body language that ultimately registered an agency that has endured.

While, again, mostly pejorative, these new images of the woman slang speaker at the end of the nineteenth century paved the way for women authors to write more gender-ambiguous figures (in terms of dress, profession, language, physical mobility, and sexuality) into their works. As Mesch notes, the inability of women to write outside of the limits of "patriarchal discursive categories" in the late-nineteenth century resulted in characters such as Nana written by men who wished to portray "deviant female sexual behavior as a threat to male authority."[153] Ironically, this admittedly depressing image of bad women ultimately introduced new versions of women characters that could be simultaneously sexy and virile. By subverting "women's speech" through their appropriation of a man's working-class slang, the characters, Germinie and Nana, effectively catalyzed a reappropriation of women's agency.

Following these boundary-crossing women characters, late nineteenth-century and early twentieth-century figures such as Rachilde's gender-bending enchantress Raoule de Vénérande in *Monsieur Vénus* (1885); Isabelle Eberhardt's autobiographical memoirs as an androgynous nomad in *Amours Nomades* (1904); and Colette's divorcée-turned-dancer Renée Néré in *La Vagabonde* (1910) represented a form of French gynocriticism, as a new wave of radically unconventional women, written *by women*, whose bodies were stylized as much by their language as their language was by their bodies.

NOTES

1. The slang words and their meanings that appear in the caption are *"cancanner"* (to dance the Cancan), *"le palais"* (a coin of five francs), and *"ratisser"* (to clean someone out).
2. See figure 6.1.
3. Goncourt, *Gavarni, L'homme et l'œuvre*, 272–73.
4. Gauthier, *Lire la ville*, 164.
5. Bucholtz and Hall, "Embodied Sociolinguistics," 173.
6. Ibid.
7. Realistic depictions of working-class women and prostitutes also appeared in visual media as seen in the Gavarni caricature. In eighteenth- and nineteenth-century French literature, prostitution officially referred to women or the "prostituée." Male characters analogous to the prostituée in literature were often aristocratic and would engage with women of the nobility in acts of libertinage. The prostitution of men following the Revolution was not addressed in the laws at the time, although in the nineteenth century, authorities associated men engaging in prostitution with male-male sex and sodomy. It was not until the twentieth century that the concept of the heterosexual "prostitué" would begin to appear.

8. Rousseau-Minier, *Des filles sans joie*, 70.

9. Peiss, "Charity Girls," 77; in her study on working girls living in New York City during the Progressive Era, Kathy Peiss explores the morally ambiguous lifestyles of a subculture of women known as "charity girls." This American slang term referred to women who received attention, material presents, and sexual pleasure, an act known as "treating," from men in exchange for "sexual favors of varying degrees" (Ibid., 78). Although not technically prostitution in the formal sense, these girls engaged in this behavior as a means of supporting themselves economically (in ways akin to the contemporary concept of the "sugar baby"), and "the growth of large public dance halls, cabarets, and metropolitan amusement resorts provided an anonymous space in which the subculture of treating could flourish" (Ibid., 83). As Peiss notes, these women spoke in vulgar slang in order to cut to the sexual chase, so-to-speak, as well as to avoid any obscurity in their intentions (Ibid., 79).

10. Mulvey, "Visual Pleasure," 58.

11. In the late nineteenth-century and early twentieth century, in early Silent cinema, women were also portrayed as prostitutes.

12. Bernheimer, *Figures of Ill Repute*, 2.

13. Hall and Parish, "Agency," 4.

14. Ibid., 1.

15. Bucholtz and Hall, "Embodied Sociolinguistics," 184.

16. Lakoff, *Language and Women's Place*, 99.

17. Ibid., 77.

18. Jordan, *The Sex Goddess*, 93.

19. As David Bellos notes, Victor Hugo's description of Fantine's descent into prostitution "is dealt with in just seven words" (20). For this reason, this book does not treat the representation of prostitution in *Les Misérables*.

20. Butler, *Gender Trouble*, 39.

21. It is important to acknowledge that some pro-sex feminists would argue that prostitution itself can be a source of empowerment if it is a chosen profession, rather than an economic imperative.

22. Bernheimer, "Prostitution and Narrative," 24.

23. Matlock, *Scenes of Seduction*, 33.

24. Ibid.

25. "*La prostitution n'est plus interdite, elle n'est plus considérée comme un délit, mais comme un mal social nécessaire et inévitable qu'il faut pouvoir contrôler*" (Rousseau-Minier, 86).

26. Corbin, "Commercial Sexuality," 209.

27. Ibid., 211.

28. Riot-Sarcey, *Histoire du féminisme*, 19.

29. Ibid., 20.

30. Laqueur, *Making Sex*, 193.

31. Ibid., 194.

32. Matlock, *Scenes of Seduction*, 97.

33. Matlock states that "Although the revolutions of 1789 and 1830 contributed to the invention of this woman of the people as allegory of the Republic, the

revolutionaries of 1848 were the ones to define her, draw her, popularize her, and baptize her Marianne" (Ibid., 87–88).

34. Examples of feminist newspapers include: *La Femme libre, Le Journal des femmes, Le Conseiller des femmes, Le Citateur féminin, La Mosaïque lyonnaise,* and *La Voix des femmes* (Riot-Sarcey, 33, 39).

35. Historian Alain Corbin points out that, interestingly, women's pleasure never surfaces in these discourses as potential cause (213).

36. The implementation of the Napoleonic Code (1804) mandated that prostitutes register and undergo regular health examinations. The Code also established licensed brothels known as *maisons de tolérance* or *maisons closes*.

37. Parent-Duchâtelet, *De la prostitution*, 137.

38. *[A]insi les inspecteurs du Bureau de Mœurs sont des* rails, *un commissaire de police un* flique, *une fille publique jolie est une* gironde *ou une* chouette, *une fille publique laide est un* roubiou; *elles appellent la maîtresse d'un homme sa* largue, *et l'amant d'une fille publique son* paillasson. (Ibid.)

39. "*On pourrait croire que la pudeur, qui fait la plus bel ornement de la femme, leur est devenue un sentiment tout-à-fait étranger*" (Ibid., 113).

40. Inoue, *Vicarious Language*, 1.

41. Ibid., 2.

42. Ibid.

43. Bernheimer, *Figures of Ill Repute*, 47.

44. Sue, *Mystères*, 35; this quote does not appear in Betensky and Loesberg's English translation.

45. Ibid., 56, 57.

46. "*Ce mot devient proverbial dans le monde-Fille*" (Balzac, *Splendeurs*, 289).

47. "*En entendant ce mot, Europe resta tout hébétée, comme elle eût pu l'être en entendant blasphémer un ange*" (Ibid., 255).

48. See figure 6.2.

49. Lombroso, *Criminal Woman*, 113.

50. Sue, *Mystères*, 45.

51. See figure 6.3.

52. See figure 6.4.

53. See figure 6.5.

54. When the narrator describes Esther's physical features, there is an emphasis on her "Arab-ness." For example, when referring to her nose as reminiscent of "an Arab one" (*celui des Arabes* [Balzac, *Splendeurs*, 79]). Her physical appearance also changes midway through the text when Balzac describes her as blonde.

55. See figure 6.6.

56. Despite discovering that she is Rodolphe's daughter and of noble birth, Fleur cannot escape her deviant past and remains aware of the fact that she is forever tarnished (Sue, *Mystères*, 1186, 1189; English translation, 1328, 1331).

57. "*Tu as l'air d'une vierge*" (Sue, *Mystères*, 62, my translation). The English translation by Betenksy and Loesberg interprets this quote as "you have a maidenly air" (28).

58. In the Western tradition, Mary Magdalene is often conflated with the sinful woman in Luke 7:36–50 and Mary of Bethany described in the New Testament. The figure of Mary Magdalene is generally represented as a prostitute who renounces her life of sin to become a disciple of Jesus.

59. "*La seule fille de joie en qui s'est rencontrée l'étoffe d'une belle courtisane*" (Balzac, *Splendeurs*, 50).

60. "*[à] dix-huit ans, cette fille a déjà connu la plus haute opulence, la plus basse misère, les hommes à tous les étages*" (Ibid., 51).

61. In *Splendors*, supporting characters explicitly discuss Esther's status as a courtesan. For example, Vautrin, disguised as the Spanish priest Carlos Herrera, tells Esther that despite her conversion to Christianity, she will forever remain a prostitute (Ibid., 72). Additionally, he tells Lucien, in reference to his love for Esther, that loving a lowlife prostitute, whose status cannot be elevated, is an error (Ibid., 92). Like Fleur, Esther cannot heal the existential consequences of her immoral lifestyle, and eventually commits suicide after sleeping with the Baron de Nucingen.

62. Bernheimer, "Prostitution and Narrative," 26.

63. Ibid., *Figures of Ill Repute*, 40.

64. Ibid., 41.

65. "*L'ingénuité d'une vierge, les grâces de l'enfance*" (Balzac, *Splendeurs*, 54).

66. Tanner, "Turning Tricks," 256.

67. Debay, *Hygiène générale de la beauté humaine*, 29.

68. *Or, l'homme et la femme, qui possèdent les qualités de formes et d'expression, méritent des hommages parce que la beauté physique marche généralement avec la beauté morale; parce que ces deux beautés constituent la perfection et que la perfection est l'attribut de la divinité.* (Ibid., 66)

69. *La stature est petite, la tête mignonne et supportée par un col flexible, d'une admirable rondeur; ce col s'attache à des épaules mollement arrondies [. . .]. En avant, le sein développé offre une vraie magnificence de grâce dans la forme, de mollesse dans les contours, et rompt agréablement la monotonie qu'offrirait la surface de la poitrine sans reliefs [. . .]. [L]'abdomen est vaste, la cuisse très-forte, la jambe fine, le pied petit. Dans tout ce corps il n'y a pas un trait dur ou heurté, rien n'y est anguleux ni brusque.* (Delaunay, 14)

70. In the Preface, the Goncourt brothers defend the veracity of their novel (*Germinie Lacerteux*, 55). The "street" as the source of their work recalls the claims made by various nineteenth-century lexicographers of slang and their respective claims for linguistic authenticity.

71. Corbin, "Commercial Sexuality," 213.

72. Goncourt, *Germinie Lacerteux*, 107.

73. "*Un matin [. . .] Germinie trouva dans l'arrière-boutique deux ou trois bonnes de la rue qui 'tuaient le ver' [. . .] —Tiens! dit Adèle, en frappant de son verre contre la table, te v'là déjà, mademoiselle de Varandeuil?*

Qu'est-ce que c'est que ça? fit Germinie en prenant le verre d'Adèle. J'en veux . . .

T'as si soif que ça à ce matin? . . . De l'eau-de-vie et de l'absinthe, rien que ça! . . . le mélo *de mon* piou, *tu sais bien? le militaire . . . il ne buvait que ça . . . C'est raide, hein?*" (Ibid., 150–51).

74. "Worm (to kill the): To drink eau-de-vie or white wine: a morning libation, designated by the saying to kill the worm" (*Ver [tuer le]: Boire de l'eau-de-vie ou du vin blanc: libation matinale, désignée par le dicton tuer le ver.* [Larchey, *Les excentricités du langage*, 1865]).

75. Hall and Parish, "Agency," 2–3.

76. "Birdy. Soldier. One says birdie, rather" (*Piou s.m. Soldat. On dit plutôt Pioupiou* [Delvau, *Dictionnaire de la langue verte*, 1867]).

77. The act of drinking hard liquor in the morning implies a high alcohol tolerance. A reader may assume that absinthe drinking is a regular part of their morning routine.

78. *As-tu eu seulement pitié de moi, quand je trimais dans la boue, dans la neige, au risque de crever? Ah! bien oui! Et ce qu'on me disait, ce qu'on me crachait sur la tête, que mon sang ne faisait qu'un bouillon d'un bout à l'autre... Tout ce que j'ai mangé d'affronts à t'attendre, c'est toi qui t'en fichais pas mal!* (Goncourt, *Germinie Lacerteux*, 224)

79. "To slave away: to walk" (*Trimer: marcher* [D'Angers, *Le Nouveau dictionnaire complet*, 1849]).

80. "To kick the bucket: to fight, to kill, often" (*Crever: v. a. Battre, — à tuer, souvent* [Delvau, *Dictionnaire de la langue verte*, 1867]).

81. "To spit on something: to be contemptible of it, — in commoner slang, which ordinarily uses this expression in the negative: He doesn't spit on the harvest, meaning he likes wine" (*Cracher sur quelque chose: v. n. En faire mépris, — dans l'argot du peuple, qui emploie plus ordinairement cette expression avec la négative: Il ne crache pas sur la vendange, c'est-à-dire il aime le vin* [Ibid.]).

82. "To swallow: undergo, to have, to do, — in commoner slang. To swallow up misery. To be difficult, miserable" (*Manger: v. a. Subir, avoir, faire, — dans l'argot du peuple. Manger de la misère. Être besogneux, misérable* [Ibid.]).

83. "To not care about: to laugh at. To not give a damn about anyone. To not have any self-control or modesty. I don't give a damn about you! Said as if to defy someone of this or that thing" (*Ficher (se): v. réfl. Se moquer. Se ficher du monde. N'avoir aucune retenue, aucune pudeur. Je t'en fiche! Se dit comme pour défier quelqu'un de faire telle ou telle chose* [Ibid.]).

84. "*Je dois déclarer, dès le début, que tout mon être, mes gens et mon intelligence me portent à admirer l'œuvre excessive et fiévreuse que je vais analyser*" (Zola, *Mes haines, causeries littéraires et artistiques*, 67).

85. In her *Promenades in London* (*Promenades dans Londres*, 1840), French socialist and writer Flora Tristan explains how London prostitutes would pick up clients at "finishes," or "gorgeous lounges, where up to two-hundred stylishly dressed prostitutes gathered. These places were visited by the fashionable and rich youths who choose women there" (*De splendides salons où s'assemblent jusqu'à deux cents prostituées richement vêtues. Ces lieux sont visités par des fashionables et riches jeunes gens qui choisissent là des femmes* [Tristan, 75]). Although located in taverns, English "finishes" were located along the River Thames in the West End and around Temple Bar. They also catered to a much wealthier clientele, marking a drastic social shift from the seedy taverns of thieves found in Vidocq's *Memoirs* and Sue's *Mysteries*. According to Judith Walkowitz, by the end of the nineteenth century, "the

West End no longer signified the home and fixed reference of the privileged urban *flâneur*; it became known as a 'pleasure capital' and second business district used by men and women of different classes" (3). Although published in 1840 about London, Tristan's account of prostitution signals a similar underlying fear of the infiltration of the lower classes into the establishments designated for the higher class that could be found within French literary, medical, and political discourse.

86. "The concierge of the theater, Mme Bron, passed in front of the door with an enormous bouquet under her arms [. . .]. This Nana! They showered her with flowers. Then, since Mme. Bron came back, she returned a letter to Clarisse, who swore under her breath" (*[L]a concierge du théâtre, Mme Bron, passait devant la porte, avec un énorme bouquet entre les bras [. . .]. Cette Nana! on la couvrait de fleurs. Puis, comme Mme Bron revenait, elle remit une lettre à Clarisse, qui laissa échapper un juron étouffé* [Zola, *Nana*, 147]); "As the prince walked down the small wooden staircase, a strange noise, muffled swear words, and the stampings of struggle, erupted from the other side of the theater" (*Comme le prince descendait le petit escalier de bois, un bruit étrange, des jurons étouffés, des piétinements de lutte, éclataient de l'autre côté du théâtre* [Ibid., 164]).

87. "*Nana se vengea des ennuis qu'on lui causait, en mâchant de sourds jurons contre les hommes. Ces gros mots chagrinaient la femme de chambre [. . .]*" (Ibid., 70).

88. Ibid., 278, 429, 439, 449. The term *mufe* is perhaps a deformation of the word *mufle*, which Emile Littré defines as an "ugly and unpleasant person" (*Personne laide et désagréable* [Littré, *Dictionnaire de la langue française*, 1873–1874]).

89. Zola, *Nana*, 452; Rosse can refer to an older horse, but in slang it can also mean "An ugly, cowardly man" (*homme mou, lâche* [Larchey, *Les Excentricités du langage*, 1865]).

90. "*Ah! ouiche, répondit Nana crûment, ce sont des salauds, ils aiment ça*" (Zola, *Nana*, 70).

91. "*Cré nom!' murmura-t-elle très bas, pour elle-même*" (Ibid., 211).

92. Mulvey, "Visual Pleasure," 62.

93. In her article on women who "break the fourth wall" in literature and cinema, Jessica Hope Jordan analyzes the refusal of Queen Thryth to accept the male gaze in *Beowulf*, a withholding that prompts a digression from the narrator on the duty of women to serve as the object of the gaze. Jordan notes that Thryth's resentment at being appropriated by the male gaze prompts in her both a "refusal" and a "challenge of the gaze", for which the narrator's subsequent interruption of the narrative not only reveals the "patriarchal attitudes" but also grants Thryth the opportunity to take control over the gaze, to turn "the gaze back onto the subjects themselves, thereby breaking the male gaze or the 'fourth wall of cinema,' as she kills off her own spectators" (Jordan, "Women Refusing the Gaze").

94. Mesch, *The Hysteric's Revenge*, 31.

95. Ibid.; the description of Nana's entrance in *La blonde Vénus* appears as the sensual cabaret performance of actress Marlene Dietrich in the 1932 film, *Blonde Venus*, directed by Josef von Sternberg. It is obvious that the inspiration came in part from Zola's infamous femme fatale, Nana, and her lewd portrayal of the

goddess Venus for an eager male audience. In any case, Dietrich's cabaret scene fits Zola's representation of Nana in her theatrical debut. In a scene that resembles a strip-tease, Dietrich's character Helen Faraday sensually undresses from a gorilla costume, an outfit choice that mocks notions of male desire, while a room of crowded men look on. The camera alternates between the looks of the male spectators, especially that of wealthy politician Nick Townsend, played by actor, Cary Grant. See figure 6.7.

96. Zola, *Nana*, 46.
97. Cellard and Rey, *Dictionnaire du français non-conventionnel*.
98. Zola, *Nana*, 137.
99. "*Aussi pour qualifier une fille aux jambes maigres, aux gros yeux à fleur de tête, à l'intelligence épaisse—ne manque-t-on pas de dire: c'est une grue. La grue est un type effrayamment répandu aujourd'hui [. . .]*" appeared in the French newspaper, *Le Figaro* (1858), (qtd. in Klein, 91).
100. "*Grue. Fille entretenue, parce que les filles de cette espèce sont souvent plus bêtes que belles—Ce qui fait qu'on ne s'explique pas les folies que les gandins font pour elles*" (Delvau, *Dictionnaire érotique moderne*, 1864).
101. *Grue s.f. Femme entretenue, que la Nature a douée d'autant de bêtise que de beauté, et qui abuse de celle-ci pour faire accepter celle-là. C'est un mot heureux que les gens de lettres ont trouvé là pour répondre à l'insolence des filles envers les honnêtes femmes.* Bécasses! *disaient-elles.* Grue! *leur répond-on. Mais ce mot, dans ce sens péjoratif, n'est pas né d'hier, il y a longtemps que le peuple l'emploie pour désigner un niais, un sot, un prétentieux.* (Ibid., *Dictionnaire de la langue verte*, 1866)
102. Bernheimer, *Figures of Ill Repute*, 34.
103. In addition to *grue*, animal comparisons in *Nana* abound that range from sexy to the grotesque. While turning her body at various angles in order to get warm in front of the fireplace, Nana refers to herself as "oie à la broche" (Zola, *Nana*, 233), and in his article "La Mouche d'Or," Fauchery compares Nana to a golden fly (Ibid., 224). Similarly, the spectators at the Grand Prix horse race conflate real-life Nana with the mare, Nana, who also possesses "the fairness of a redheaded girl" (*une blondeur de fille rousse* [Ibid., 380]).
104. Jordan, "Women Refusing the Gaze."
105. The prostitute's body thus functioned as a synecdoche "for the social system" and was the epitome of what Butler describes as "unregulated permeability" that "constitutes a site of pollution and endangerment" (*Gender Trouble*, 168). Therefore, the prostitute entered nineteenth-century discourse primarily as a "polluted" social and physical site as well as a semiotic one.
106. Wolff, "Gender and the Haunting of Cities," 22.
107. Wilson, "The Invisible Flâneur," 9.
108. See figure 6.8.
109. Goncourt, *Germinie Lacerteux*, 168–69.
110. *[I]ls se dirigèrent vers la rue de Navarin [. . .]. Ils marchaient lentement [. . .]. Ils montèrent la rue des Martyrs, traversèrent la rue de la Tour-d'Auvergne, descendirent la rue Montholon [. . .]. Arrivés à la rue Lamartine devant le passage*

des Deux-Sœurs, ils tournèrent sur eux-mêmes; Germinie n'eut que le temps de se jeter dans une porte d'allée. Ils passèrent sans la voir. (Ibid., 169)

111. For example, when walking in hopes of finding Gautruche, Germinie is completely motivated by her desire (Ibid., 216).

112. Ibid., 215.

113. *Les passants qui passent là, l'ouvrier qui remonte de Paris en sifflant, l'ouvrière qui revient, sa journée finie, les mains sous les aisselles pour se tenir chaud, la prostituée en bonnet noir qui erre, la croisaient et la regardaient. Les inconnus avaient l'air de la reconnaître; la lumière lui faisait honte.* (Ibid., 215–16)

114. Ibid., 226–27.

115. *De cette rupture, Germinie tomba où elle devait tomber, au-dessous de la honte, au-dessous de la nature même. De chute en chute, la misérable et brûlante créature roula à la rue. Elle ramassa les amours qui s'usent en une nuit, ce qui passe, ce qu'on rencontre, ce que le hasard des pavés fait trouver à la femme qui vague.* (Ibid., 226)

116. Ibid.

117. Ibid.

118. Wilson, "The Invisible Flâneur," 93.

119. In particular, Charcot's work on hysteria in the late nineteenth century greatly influenced popular opinions on perceived links between women's brains, emotions, and sexual desires.

120. Zola, *Nana*, 43.

121. Ibid., 37.

122. *Nana s'était résignée, pour avoir la paix dans son ménage [. . .]. Nana retomba dans la crotte du début. Elle roula, elle battit le pavé de ses anciennes savates de petit torchon, en quête d'une pièce de cent sous.* (Ibid., 276)

123. *[D]ans ce vice d'en bas qui rôde le long des ruelles boueuses, sous la clarté trouble du gaz [. . .]. Toutes deux couraient, faisaient les bals et les cafés d'un quartier, grimpant des escaliers humides de crachats et de bière renversée; ou bien elles marchaient doucement, elles remontaient les rues, se plantaient debout, contre les portes cochères.* (Ibid., 277)

124. *Dans des lanternes scellées aux murs, des flammes de gaz brûlaient, éclairant crûment cette misère, dégageant une chaleur qui montait et s'amassait sous la spirale étroite des étages [. . .]. Une humidité suintait des murailles. Les pas sonnaient sur le sol dallé, comme dans un souterrain.* (Ibid., 171, 177)

125. In her real-life account of London prostitutes, Tristan makes a similar discovery when, after touring Waterloo Road and the adjacent streets, she and a couple of friends sit down on the Waterloo bridge "to observe another spectacle" (*pour observer un autre spectacle* [Tristan 74]). Between eight and nine at night, Flora and her friends witness groups of prostitutes run to the West End of London where wealthy businessmen are leaving the theater. Here, again, the street becomes spectacle as swarms of prostitutes gather around the theater exits. As the wealthy crowd leaves the theater, they intermingle with the disgraced bodies of deviant ladies who follow them to the *finishes* in the hopes of landing a client for the night. In the anonymously written *Mémoires d'une dame du monde* (1861), the writer confirms a

similar occurrence in France: "The demi-monde took precedence over the real world. The kept woman, the lower-class mistress, the courtesan, call her whatever you would like [. . .]. These *ladies* flaunted themselves in the woods or the horse races, at the theater or the beach, appearing to mock us with their diamonds and their outfits that our sons and our husbands paid" (*Le demi-monde a pris le pas sur le monde véritable. La lorette, la biche, la courtisane, appelez-la comme vous voudrez [. . .]. Ces dames s'étalent au bois ou aux courses, au théâtre ou aux eaux, semblant nous narguer avec leurs diamants et leurs toilettes que nos fils ou nos mariés ont payés* [6]).

126. "*Germinie était laide*" (Goncourt, *Germinie Lacereux*, 95).

127. "*De cette femme laide, s'échappait une âpre et mystérieuse séduction [. . .]. Tout en elle, sa bouche, ses yeux, sa laideur même, avait une provocation et une sollicitation. Un charme aphrodisiaque sortait d'elle, qui s'attaquait et s'attachait à l'autre sexe*" (Ibid., 97).

128. See figures 6.9 and 6.10.

129. *[Germinie] aussi s'était dégrossie, s'était formée, s'était ouverte à l'éducation de Paris, Mlle de Varandeuil, inoccupée, curieuse à la façon d'une vieille fille des histoires du quartier, lui avait longtemps fait raconter ce qu'elle glanait de nouvelles, ce qu'elle savait des locataires, toute la chronique de la maison et de la rue; et cette habitude de conter, de causer comme une sorte de demoiselle de compagnie avec sa maîtresse, de peindre les gens, d'esquisser les silhouettes, avait développé à la longue en elle une facilité d'expressions vives, de traits heureux et échappés, un piquant et parfois un mordant d'observation singuliers dans une bouche de servante.* (Goncourt, *Germinie Lacerteux*, 210)

130. In one scene, Adèle requests that Germinie write a letter on her behalf (Ibid., 120–21). Germinie also indulges in the kind of dangerous reading of serialized literature that women were advised against in the nineteenth century (Ibid., 210).

131. Ibid., 170.

132. Ibid., 228.

133. *Mademoiselle était penchée avec une sorte d'épouvante sur ce corps abandonné et ne s'appartenant plus, dans lequel le passé revenait comme un revenant dans une maison abandonnée [. . .]. [E]lle avait l'impression d'être à côté d'un cadavre possédé par un rêve [. . .]. [S]on langage devenait aussi méconnaissable [. . .]. C'était comme une langue du peuple purifiée et transfigurée dans la passion [. . .]. Mademoiselle restait confondue, stupéfaite, écoutant comme au théâtre.* (Ibid., 190–91)

134. Beizer, *Ventriloquized Bodies*, 43.

135. For medical doctors, such as Debay, this lack of articulated speech signaled a biological devolution (Debay, *Hygiène de la voix*, 33–34).

136. The influence of Jean Louis Brachet's *Treaty on Hysteria* (*Traité de l'hystérie*, 1847) and the work of Hippolyte Taine on the Goncourt brothers' construction of Germinie, introduce a narrative that hinges on the clinical gaze as well as the performance of the hysteric. In the preface to the first edition of *Germinie Lacerteux*, the Goncourt brothers describe their book as a sort of Charcot-esque study (Goncourt, *Germinie Lacerteux*, 55).

137. "*l'ombre d'une femme de la Salpêtrière*" (Goncourt, *Germinie Lacerteux*, 164).

248   *Chapter 6*

138. *[Q]uand Germinie entra dans sa chambre [. . .] après deux ou trois soupirs, longs, profonds, arrachés et douloureux, mademoiselle la vit, se renversant et se tordant, rouler à bas de la chaise et tomber à terre. Elle voulut la relever; mais Germinie était agitée de mouvements convulsifs si violents que la vieille femme fut obligée de laisser retomber sur le parquet ce corps furieux dont tous les membres contractés et ramassés un moment sur eux-mêmes se lançaient à droite, à gauche, au hasard.* (Ibid., 146)

139. See figures 6.11 and 6.12.

140. In *Scenes of Seduction* (1994), Matlock notes that the nineteenth-century discourse on hysteria was a means of containment; however, it was generally focused on middle-class women and their sexual desires. In parallel with, as well as intersecting the discourse of the hysteric, the nineteenth-century discourse on the prostitute functioned as opposing representations of female hysterics: Middle-class women were plagued by a repression of sexual desire, while the prostitute's body was a physical site where this desire could be expressed. For Matlock, "the prostitute summoned fantasies of seduction and in turn produced plots of containment. Her body became a matrix for struggle aimed at reading women. It was also at the center of a contest through which women could be made readable" (*Scenes of Seduction*, 9).

141. Instead of taking place in the seedy taverns or on the peripheral boundaries of the city, Germinie's violent bodily movements invade the aristocratic household of Mademoiselle de Varandeuil. Like Bordenave's actresses whom he sells and the street prostitutes who sell themselves, the spectacle of the hysteric is not far from the spectacle of the licentious actress or dancer (Zola, *Nana*, 25). Minus the choreographed movements and stage directions, Germinie shapes and twists her body in order to convey an emotional state to her audience. Although limited by the medical discourse framing the Goncourts' representation of the prostitute, Germinie's status as a slang-speaking woman not only implies sexually promiscuity but also a public display of bodily violence that is no longer contained within socially designated locations.

142. Mesch, *The Hysteric's Revenge*, 8.

143. Etymologically, the verb *prostitute* comes from the "Latin *prostitutus*, past participle of *prostituere* 'to expose to prostitution, to expose publicly,' from *pro-* 'before' and *statuere* 'cause to stand, establish.'" See the definition for "Prostitute" in the *Online Etymology Dictionary*.

144. Wooler, *Performance Anxiety*, 46–47.

145. Debay, *Hygiène de la voix*, 151.

146. *Les diverses positions que le corps est obligé de prendre, selon les circonstances morales ou physiques dans lesquelles on se trouve, sont des attitudes. L'élégant, le fat, le courtisan, l'orgueilleux, la coquette, la précieuse, la prude, la femme modeste, etc., offrent des attitudes qui leur sont propres, et auxquelles il est facile de les reconnaître.* (Ibid., 149–50)

147. The link between embodiment and indexicality dates back to semiotician Charles Peirce who asserted that the act of pointing served as a rudimentary indexical gesture.

148. *Nana était si blanche et si grasse, si nature dans ce personnage fort des hanches et de la gueule, que tout de suite elle gagna la salle entière [. . .]. [S]es épaules rondes, sa gorge d'amazone [. . .], ses larges hanches qui roulaient dans un balancement voluptueux, ses cuisses de blonde grasse, tout son corps se devinait, se voyait sous le tissu léger, d'une blancheur d'écume [. . .]. Et lorsque Nana levait les bras, on apercevait, aux feux de la rampe, les poils d'or de ses aisselles.* (Ibid., 41, 47)

149. See figure 6.13.

150. "Blonde: Female lover" (*Blonde: Amante* [Larchey, *Les Excentricités du langage*, 1865]). "Blonde: Mistress, in working-class slang" (*Blonde s.f Maîtresse, dans l'argot des ouvriers* [Delvau, *Dictionnaire de la langue verte*, 1867]).

151. "*La fille du trottoir, qui ne demande que deux francs pour un voyage à Cythère,*" "Vénus populaire [la]" (Ibid., *Dictionnaire érotique moderne*, 1864).

152. Cellard and Rey, *Dictionnaire du français non-conventionnel*.

153. Mesch, *The Hysteric's Revenge*, 38.

Epilogue
Literary Slumming across Cultures

This book has outlined the concept of literary slumming, a sociolinguistic phenomenon in the nineteenth century based on the use of the language of slang as criminal code, which French writers employed for both economic and artistic purpose. In nineteenth-century France, literary slumming was a twofold phenomenon: first, literary slumming referred to the degradation of literary content, primarily in the form of representing lower-class degeneracy and vice. From criminals to prostitutes (and everything in between), French writers sought to seduce their public with realistic depictions of society's deviants in all their criminal glory. Second, literary slumming referred to the degradation of the literary standards that were formally mandated in the seventeenth century. This literary degeneration included the publication of serial novels, the inclusion of nonstandard dialects and sociolects, especially slang, the cheapening of book binding, and the mass production of stories filled with violence and sexual intrigue.

As this book has demonstrated, literary slumming occurred in wide variety of printed media: memoirs, serials, bound novels, dictionaries, in addition to plays and song lyrics. Assisted by technological innovations in the printing press that allowed for mass distribution of serial novels and other publications, such as bound novels and dictionaries, these writers' use of slang furthered the development of the late-nineteenth and early twentieth centuries' stylistic literary movements of Realism and Naturalism. This is not to say, however, that literary slumming had not occurred in earlier periods of French history. Throughout the long Renaissance, instances in which poets, playwrights, and writers of the Arthurian adventures, romances, and farces, incorporated elements of literary slumming and criminal culture, such as slang and other aspects of their villainous lifestyles, can be found. Even though the premodern texts analyzed in this book were destined for a minority audience of elite readers, and authorities had not yet implemented any formal institutionalized conventions concerning literature and the French language, they nonetheless figure as subversive detours into criminal culture as depicted by writers from a higher social class. Similar class dynamics are at work in which members of the dominant culture both appropriate and translate elements of the dominated culture which were intended for a noble readership. Conversely, a reverse cultural appropriation also takes place as these prototypical criminal characters and their slang invade upper-class domains, both on the page and off. In fact, what occurs from the fifteenth century to the nineteenth is simply an evolution of this sociolinguistic phenomenon. After 1789, the modernizations of the printing and papermaking realms coincided with major upheavals in the French political climate, which generated the ideal social conditions and an artistic realism that effectively worked to dismantle previous oppressive literary and linguistic protocols.

While early modern works, such as François Villon's slang ballads, Pechon de Ruby's *The Magnanimous Life*, and Guillaume Bouchet's *Fifteenth Evening* (to name a small few), also engaged in earlier forms of literary slumming, as they sought to reveal the inner workings of criminal culture and language, in the nineteenth century, in contrast, the act of literary slumming involved actual forays into criminal realms as well as much more realistic depictions of criminal types, while leading to a perceived cheapening of the novel via its publication in serial format in newspapers. This lowbrow content, coupled with the perceived deteriorating literary formats and style, reached readers *en masse*, even those who could not afford newspaper subscriptions. Bourgeois writers and readers could therefore access an antisociety previously inaccessible to them, while also vicariously experience new social identities from the safety of their home. Literary slumming thus constituted a mutual cultural appropriation: as the upper classes effectively collected and rebranded elements of criminal and working-class culture, in turn, marginalized social types began to invade bourgeois spaces within both the narrative and real worlds.

As this book argues, the role of the language of slang in literary slumming was pivotal for creating realistic images of the criminal and working-class types. Beginning with Vidocq's *Memoirs* and ending with Zola's novel *Nana* that indexical evolution of slang is revealed in this book. In the first half of the nineteenth century, slang had functioned as a criminal anti-language, reflecting the alternative perspectives and values of the criminal underworld that stood in contrast to the bourgeois overworld. Hardcore criminal characters, such as Vidocq and Balzac's Vautrin, and the variety of slang-speaking villains in Sue's *The Mysteries of Paris*, spoke slang as an index of their immorality. For bourgeois writers and readers, slang thus became the basis of criminal identity, serving as a key means for the upper classes with which both to read and identify lower class and criminal types. As readers became exposed to slang and other codes of criminality, slang's first indexical order began to take shape as referential of criminals.

Moreover, the stylization of the criminal body in the form of additional nonreferential indexes that constituted an embodied slang, such as appearance and physique, accent and voice manipulation, as well as choice of language, dialect, or sociolect, further rendered slang iconic of the criminal classes. These additional indexes revealed the criminal as a performer of multiple identities and public spectacles. Capturing these bodily aspects of criminals not only appeared in novels but also in slang dictionaries, which sought to give readers instructions on slang and its linguistic performance with the use of interlocutors who demonstrated the gestures, accents, and deliveries associated with slang, serving as an embodied form of criminal linguistic practices.

By the mid-nineteenth century, a demonstrative shift in the use of slang had occurred with the publication of slang dictionaries destined for a bourgeois public, as well as, most notably, the publication of Victor Hugo's *Les Misérables*, in which the slang speaker becomes indexical of the lower classes who are afflicted by misery and poverty, and who are in need of upper-class aid, rather than disdain. In Hugo's novel, a second indexical order appears that builds on the first, while further introducing new social connotations of slang. In *Les Misérables*, bourgeois contempt for the slang speaker is transformed into pity, as the slang speaker is no longer coded as purely indexical of the criminal type, but who has now become a more nuanced social figure that straddles the line between the criminal and the working classes. Although, in his work, Hugo posits slang as the language of the grotesque, he simultaneously lauds it as capable of the sublime. As Karen Masters-Wicks has examined, Hugo's slang is a language of contrasts in which "the author brings the spectacles of the grotesque and the sublime to the same dramatic arena, showing their metamorphoses on both visual and linguistic levels."[1] For Hugo, therefore, it is through this criminal anti-language that new poetic heights may be obtained.

Throughout this quest to dominate and exploit criminal and working-class culture, nineteenth-century writers did not shy away from acknowledging the inherent literariness of slang, especially in their use of metaphor. The puzzling incompatibility between style and content apparent in slang terms and expressions thus results in a linguistic paradox: despite the vulgar images these terms may evoke, the expressions themselves stylistically resemble a kind of poetry. As evidenced in Balzac's *Splendors*, the metaphoric nature of slang oftentimes comes from a lexical perversion of Standard French terms that have been appropriated by thugs and thieves to connote criminal meanings, a concept that is fully developed within Hugo's *Les Misérables*. Moreover, there exists both a literary and social evolution in terms of the emphasis on slang's poetic value within these works. The development of slang-speaking characters from *Memoirs* to *Splendors* thus reveals the transformation of the criminal's anti-language from a crude code to an aesthetically inventive language, which, again, reaches its pinnacle within Hugo's epic novel. This shift in attitude toward slang as well as its role in fictional works therefore points to an acknowledgment of the literary richness of the anti-language of slang.

Adding to this second indexical order, slang dictionaries published after 1850 contain terms that reflect the social complexities found in Hugo's novel. Initially, compilations of slang words, such as in Vidocq's *Thieves*, reflected the coded uses of this criminal anti-language inherent in the first indexical order. Over time, however, definitions of slang words contained increasing connotations of the working classes, including prostitutes, as well as Parisian vernacular. Like the novelist, the lexicographer also engaged in his own particular brand of slumming, both literary and literal, in which he boasted of his firsthand experience within the various districts of Paris, while observing and taking notes on the slang used by everyday city dwellers. Not only was the lexicographer a key figure in the codification and standardization of slang words, thus rendering the language more mainstream for a bourgeois public, he also stood as a kind of linguistic *flâneur*, whose empirical study of urban speech practices came directly from his city jaunts. Similar to Charles Baudelaire's avant-garde *flâneur*, the linguistic *flâneurie* of lexicographers after 1850 sought to embrace the modern changes occurring in Paris, as well as to present a panoramic vision of the French language and all its varieties in their slang dictionaries.

Concerning the realm of gender, the appearance of slang-speaking prostitutes in naturalist novels in the second half of the nineteenth century marked the use of a lexicon by women that had traditionally indexed working-class virility. Protagonists, such as Émile Zola's Nana and Edmond and Jules de Goncourt's Germinie Lacerteux, provide new representations of the woman slang speaker that differs from earlier depictions, such as Sue's Fleur or Balzac's Esther, or even the more masculinized women criminal characters, such as the Owl, She-Wolf, Asia, or Europe. However, a difference in these representations exists in terms of the degree of vulgarity and the use of free indirect speech used to portray the language and psychology of these deviant women. In both *Germinie Lacerteux* (1865) and *Nana* (1880), the women protagonists speak a working-class slang filled with obscenities, while their speech provides a stark contrast to their hyper-sexualized bodies. In fact, Germinie and Nana temporarily disrupt the male fantasy through their foul language, by presenting a highly nuanced vision of women slang speakers as simultaneously sexy, yet virile, through the characteristics of their bodies and speech. This combination laid the groundwork for the advent of women characters who demonstrate true agency, and that influenced later women writers, such as Rachilde and Colette, who created subversive women characters.

Within these nineteenth-century memoirs, novels, dictionaries, and debates, a tension between dominant and dominated (sub)cultures is in perpetual motion. Although the literary slumming of white, male, and upper-class writers paints a depressing picture for the marginalized social classes and minorities who did not have the ability to self-represent, minority writers nevertheless began to emerge at this time in spite of the mechanisms in place that maintained bourgeois hegemony. Within the nineteenth century and into the twentieth century, these dominated cultures begin to realize their own empowerment by creating their own cultural and literary spaces; for example, autobiographies and memoirs by workers and infamous ladies-of-night, such as famed courtesan Cora Pearl's *Memoirs of Cora Pearl* (*Mémoires de Cora Pearl*, 1886) or Norbert Truquin's *Memoirs and Adventures of a Proletarian throughout the Revolution, Algeria, the Argentinian Republic, and Paraguay* (*Mémoires et aventures d'un prolétaire à travers la Révolution, l'Algérie, la République argentine et le Paraguay*, 1888),[2] speak to the emergence of literary working classes. In the 1830s and 1840s, women writers, such as Flora Tristan and George Sand, sought social justice for women and workers through both their writings and political presence. The foundation of working-class newspapers, such as *Atelier* (*L'Atelier*) and *The Workers' Hive* (*La Ruche Populaire*), as well as the emergence of worker-poets in nineteenth-century France, such as Agricole Perdiguier, Charles Poncy, Jules Vinçard, Reine Garde, and Savinien Lapointe, signals the reappropriation of a literary space by minorities that was, in part, due to the democratizing effects of the press as well as the widespread emphasis on marginalized social types in popular literature.

In the late nineteenth and early twentieth centuries, women writers, such as Rachilde and Colette, further created representations of women and men who were both gender fluid and sexually liberated, while also including realistic depictions of lower-class speech practices. In *La Vagabonde* (1910), Colette employs the colloquial speech of the Parisian music hall during the Belle Époque through her unconventional protagonist Renée Néré, a divorced performer and woman writer. In Marcel Proust's masterpiece, *In Search of Lost Time*, taboo references to same-sex relations abound, and working-class characters, such as Marcel's maid Françoise, become marked by their nonstandard ways of speaking. The twentieth-century texts treated by Pascale Gaitet, such as Louis-Ferdinand Céline's *Journey to the End of the Night* (*Voyage au bout de la nuit*, 1932) and Raymond Queneau's *Zazie in the Metro* (*Zazie dans le métro*, 1959), are composed using working-class and military slang and word play that had become much more commonplace in literary works by 1950. In addition to novels, autobiographies written by peasants, such as Émile Guillaumin, Antoine Sylvère, and Pierre-Jakez Hélias, also emerged in the early twentieth century.

The weakening of literary norms throughout the nineteenth century, while highly condemned by some, ultimately meant greater creative possibilities for language as well as the social, gender, and racial reappropriation by minority writers of their own culture that comes to fruition in the twentieth century. Although slang in the nineteenth century had functioned as a linguistic scapegoat onto which writers conflated other nonstandard dialects and foreign languages, in the first half of the twentieth century, writers began to employ alternative speech practices within their works as a means of encompassing a fuller culture of slang, for both working-class and urban characters.

Of course, the practice of literary slumming is not particular to French culture, or even to the nineteenth century. Depictions of criminal characters were also occurring outside the realm of French literature, from which other great writers derived their influence. The mass reception and popularity of Sue's *Mysteries* crossed continents as American, British, and European writers generated their own versions, launching the new city-mysteries genre. As Marjorie Rousseau-Minier notes, the publication of Zola's *Nana* altered the literary landscape for naturalist writers not only in France but also across Europe and in the United States.[3] In Spain, translations of French naturalist novels began to appear, as Spanish writers, such as Benito Pérez Galdós and Eduardo López Bago, began to write their own depictions of the prostitute who used working-class vernacular.[4] Other writers, such as Clarín, Alejandro Sawa, and José Zahonero, gained tremendous influence from Zola in their naturalist works.[5] Carlo Righetti's *Nanà a Milano* (1880) is an Italian spinoff that depicts Nana's new escapades, and in Greece, Zola's work had also become well-known following the publication of *Nana* and references to the French author in newspapers, reviews, and almanacs, as well as photographic prints of Zola entered into circulation.[6]

In British literature, the use of language to index social class and profession can be found as far back as the Arthurian cycles, Chaucer, and Shakespeare. Shakespeare's lower-class characters used language that coded their class and work, such as Iago, who spoke a kind of slang that revealed his criminal character, and the Rude Mechanicals' language in *A Midsummer's Night Dream*, which was further coded by their professions. Of course, dialect, as a literary technique, has a long history in literature, as one can consider *The Adventures of Huckleberry Finn* (1885), for instance, or the Puritan colonists' and early American settlers' use of regional and immigrant dialects, as well as their appropriation of Native American languages. Charles Dickens' portrayal of crime and slang in *Oliver Twist* (1837–1839), and his depiction of the slums of London in *Bleak House* (1852–1853), center on the lower-class misery that is a product of poverty in ways akin to Hugo's *Les Misérables*.

Foreign writers also played with the fluid social identities of protagonists, such as Edward Bulwer-Lytton's Paul Clifford, who passes between high society and the criminal anti-society of thieving highwaymen. Other novels and discourses that were more socialist in nature similar to Sue's *Mysteries*, such as Benjamin Disraeli's *Sybil* (1845) and Friedrich Engels' *The Condition of the Working Class in English* (1845), reveal a heightened interest in the sordid work environment of the lower classes by the upper classes. Literary slumming as the exploration and appropriation of criminal and working-class culture by bourgeois writers, in France and elsewhere in the world, whether for aesthetic, comedic, economic, or socialist objectives, included representations of speech practices (accent, delivery, and lexicon) and body language through gesture and movement, dress, physique and physiognomy, that resulted in a collective upper-class vision of the criminal and working classes.

A tiny glimpse at the European and transatlantic influence that these French texts had decades later denotes literary slumming as a gateway sensation: the sparse instances of criminal depictions and the incorporation of slang in literary works throughout the long Renaissance and even in the eighteenth century exploded in the nineteenth century and, as this book shows, slowly began to integrate plot and character details that were increasingly taboo in nature. By the twentieth century, the complexity of these portraits went beyond slang, theft, murder, and prostitution. The formulaic characterizations of criminal and working-class culture in early nineteenth-century French culture that constituted the bulk of literary slumming evolved into attempts at representing gay men and lesbians, or "disgraced" women who were newly empowered, and even gender stylization, not as a professional means of the thieving con-artist, but as an actual stance on gender identity. Slang, while originally the basis of criminal characterizations, permitted writers to represent additional nonstandard languages and minority cultures, ultimately to open the literary Pandora's box of possibility for writers of all class ranks.

Overall, nineteenth-century French writers infused criminal characters with a kind of social realism, and even naturalism, that was particular to the French milieu, as well as highly influential on literary development as well as social progress. From a sociolinguistic perspective, a study of the literary slumming at this particular juncture in French history is significant because of the extent to which elements of lower-class culture now appeared in written form and impacted writers and readers across countries and continents; in years past, the language and lifestyles of dominated cultures were primarily transmitted orally by their guardians within a closed community. And although analogous sociolinguistic happenings in which artists appropriate, rebrand, and market minority culture on a mass scale can transpire in song (take for instance the prevalence of Ebonics used by white hip-hop artists, such as Eminem and Iggy Azalea, or pop stars such as Justin Bieber) or in cinematic form (for example, the controversial castings of white, straight, cisgender actors as ethnic, racial, or queer minorities, or even the emergence of social media iterations of "blackface," such as "blackfishing"), literary slumming is especially significant because it involves the codification of these cultural and linguistic representations in written form (unlike song, which is an oral medium) and predates cinema as a form of popular culture intended for entertainment or educational purposes.

If language constitutes, as Bucholtz and Hall state, "the most flexible and pervasive" resource for "the cultural production of identity,"[7] then the preservation of anti-languages, dialects, and sociolects constitutes a societal acknowledgment of that identity (as found in French literature) which can be positive or negative. Literary slumming thus catalyzes the standardization of nonstandard language precisely because it is committed to paper, a prerequisite for linguistic codification of any kind as well as an official means of recognizing communities and cultures. While codification and standardization can occur in reference works, such as grammars and dictionaries, the role of literature was especially pivotal in its ability to reach audiences well before the explosion of the film industry. Before visual cinematic representations of lower-class lifestyles and speech practices became the preferred medium by audiences, readers consumed tantalizing serials, novels, and memoirs that exposed them to foreign ways-of-life and thus codified these practices as interpreted by bourgeois, male writers, making for a grim and depressing image of reality as controlled by dominant members of society; however, perhaps unintentionally, nevertheless elevating the role of lower-class characters in fictional works.

It is important to note here that the appropriation of minority culture by the upper classes happened (and continues to happen) as a result of class, ethnic, racial, and sexual inequality. Although literary slumming highlights the tragedy of discrimination, what one witnesses over time is the eventual waning of formerly "taboo" elements: as these pejorative representations, while wholly unjust, become more mainstream, they also tend to neutralize as audiences become habituated to them (one could argue that this is because these representations are tailored to their readers' sensibilities in the moment), and then undergo yet another cycle of reappropriation by those minorities who stand as the rightful owners of these linguistic and cultural elements.

The topic of this book is more expansive than what could be treated here, and thus calls for further scholarship on literary slumming across various cultures and time periods wherever slang has served as a basis of criminal and/or lower-class representation. Further research in this area will continue to allow the socially marginalized within literature to reassert their voices, as former criminals and working-class men and women have often used the growing visibility of lower-class and criminal characters in literature and culture as an impetus for their own self-representation. Additionally, the existence of comparable sociolinguistic phenomena in other forms of popular culture, such as song and film, are in need of interdisciplinary analysis by cultural historians, literary scholars, and sociologists. Extensive studies on specific cultures and time periods, the mechanisms at play in these representations of criminal and other minority cultures, the motives behind the production of these depictions, and the sociolinguistic stylization, both linguistic and embodied, that occurs within these media, could be examined as isolated occurrences or as ones that interacted with or developed out of literary slumming. Regardless of the chosen artistic medium, the end of this book nevertheless calls for the next step of focusing on the further revealing of the dominated classes reappropriation of their own uniquely stylized languages and literatures as acts of resistance against the dominant culture.

NOTES

1. Masters-Wicks, *Victor Hugo's Les Misérables*, 148–49.
2. See also the anonymously written *Memoirs by a Lady of the Night* (*Mémoires d'une dame du monde*, 1861), Martin Nadaud's *Leonard's Memoirs: Former Boy Bricklayer* (*Mémoires de Léonard, ancien garçon maçon*, 1895), and Victorine Brocher's *Memories of a Living Dead Woman* (*Souvenirs d'une morte vivante*, 1909).
3. Rousseau-Minier, *Des filles sans joie*, 168–69.
4. See Pérez Galdós' *La desheredada* (1881) and López Bago's trilogy *La prostituta* (1884).
5. See Sawa's *La mujer de todo el mundo* (1885) and Zahonero's *La carnaza* (1885).
6. Rousseau-Minier, *Des filles sans joie*, 169.
7. Bucholtz and Hall, "Language and Identity," 369.

Bibliography

Agha, Asif. *Language and Social Relations*. Cambridge, Cambridge UP, 2007.
———. "The Social Life of Cultural Value." *Language & Communication*, vol. 23, no. 3–4, 2003, pp. 231–73.
Allen, James Smith. *In the Public Eye: A History of Reading in Modern France, 1800–1940*. Princeton, Princeton UP, 1991.
Althusser, Louis. "Idéologie et appareils idéologiques d'État (notes pour une recherche)." *La Pensée*, vol. 151, 1970, pp. 3–38.
Angenot, Marc. *1889. Un état du discours social*. Montréal: Éditions du Préambule, 1989, http://www.medias19.org/index.php?id=11003. Accessed 2 Jan. 2020.
"Argot." *Le Dictionnaire de l'Académie française*, 6th ed., vol. 1. Firmin Didot Frères, 1835, p. 101.
Balibar, Renée et Dominique LaPorte. *Le français national. Politique et pratiques de la langue nationale sous la Révolution française*. Paris, Hachette, 1974.
Balzac, Honoré de. "De l'État actuel de la librairie." *Œuvres diverses*. Gallimard, 1996, pp. 662–70.
———. *Splendeurs et misères des courtisanes*. 1838–47, edited by Pierre Barbéris. Gallimard, 1973.
Baudelaire, Charles. "Crowds." *Paris Spleen*. Translated by Martin Sorrell. OneWorld Classics, 2010.
Beizer, Janet. *Ventriloquized Bodies: Narratives of Hysteria in Nineteenth-Century France*. Ithaca, Cornell UP, 1994.
Bellos, David. *The Novel of the Century: The Extraordinary Adventure of Les Misérables*. New York, Farrar, Straus and Giroux, 2017.
Benjamin, Walter. *Charles Baudelaire: Un poète lyrique à l'apogée du capitalisme*. Translated by Jean Lacoste. Payot, 2002.
Benson, Phil. *Ethnocentrism and the English Dictionary*. London, Routledge, 2001.
Berlanstein, Lenard R. "Breeches and Breaches: Cross-Dress Theater and the Culture of Gender Ambiguity in Modern France." *Comparative Studies in Society and History*, vol. 38, no. 2, 1996, pp. 338–69.

Bernheimer, Charles. *Figures of Ill Repute: Representing Prostitution in Nineteenth-Century France.* Cambridge, Harvard UP, 1989.

———. "Prostitution and Narrative: Balzac's 'Splendeurs et misères des courtisanes'." *L'Esprit Créateur*, vol. 25, no. 2, 1985, pp. 21–31.

Berrong, Richard. "Vautrin and Same-sex Desire in 'Le Père Goriot.'" *Nineteenth-Century French Studies*, vol. 31, no. 1–2, 2002–2003, pp. 53–65.

"Blonde." *Dictionnaire érotique moderne*, Bale, 1864, p. 61.

———. *Dictionnaire de la langue verte: argots parisiens comparés.* E. Dentu, 1866, p. 36.

———. *Les excentricités du langage.* E. Dentu, 1865, p. 34.

Bouchet, Guillaume. *Les Serées (1548–1597–1598) du libraire-imprimeur Guillaume Bouchet (1514–1594)*, edited by André Janier. Honoré Champion, 2006.

Bourdieu, Pierre. *Language and Symbolic Power.* Cambridge, Harvard UP, 1991.

———. "L'économie des échanges linguistiques." *Langue française*, vol. 34, 1977, pp. 17–34.

———. "Reproduction culturelle et reproduction sociale." *Sociologie de l'éducation*, 1969, pp. 45–79. Web. http://ssi.sagepub.com/content/10/2/45.full.pdf.

Bowles, Brett. "Alfred Delvau's Dictionaries: Vehicles of Lexical and Sociocultural Change in Second-Empire Paris." *The French Review*, vol. 71, no. 2, 1997, pp. 213–24.

Brunot, Ferdinand. *Histoire de la langue française des origines à 1900. Tome I, De l'époque latine à la Renaissance*, 4th ed. Paris, A. Collin, 1933.

Bucholtz, Mary. "Word Up: Social Meanings of Slang in California Youth Culture." *A Cultural Approach to Interpersonal Communication*, 2nd ed., edited by Leila Monaghan et al. Oxford, Wiley-Blackwell, 2012.

Bucholtz, Mary and Kira Hall. "Embodied Sociolinguistics." *Sociolinguistics: Theoretical Debates*, edited by Nikolas Coupland. Cambridge UP, 2016, pp. 173–97.

———. "Language and Identity." *A Companion to Linguistic Anthropology*, edited by Alessandro Duranti. Blackwell publishing, 2004, pp. 369–94.

Busby, Keith. "'*Plus acesmez qu'une popine*': Male Cross-Dressing in Medieval French Narrative." *Gender Transgressions: Crossing the Narrative Barrier in Old French Literature*, edited by Karen J. Taylor. Garland Publishing Inc., 1998, pp. 45–59.

Butler, Judith. *Gender Trouble: Feminism and the Subversion of Identity.* New York, Routledge, 1990.

———. "Performative Acts and Gender Constitution: An Essay in Phenomenology and Feminist Theory." *Theatre Journal*, vol. 40, no. 4, 1988, pp. 519–31.

Cameron, Deborah. *Verbal Hygiene.* London, Routledge, 1995.

"Cancaner." *Dictionnaire de la langue verte: argots parisiens comparés*, E. Dentu, 1866, p. 58.

Castille, Hippolyte. *Les Hommes et les mœurs sous le regne de Louis-Philippe.* Paris, P. Henneton, 1853.

Cellard, Jacques. *Anthologie de la littérature argotique.* Paris, Mazarine, 1985.

Cellard, Jacques, and Alain Rey. *Dictionnaire du français non-conventionnel*. Paris, Hachette, 1991.
Cérésa, François. *Les Princes de l'argot*. Éditions Écriture, 2014.
Chapuys-Montlaville. "Discours à la Chambre des députés, 13 juin 1843." *Le Moniteur universel*. 14 juin 1843. Dumasy-Queffélec, pp. 80–86.
———. "Discours à la Chambre des députés, 14 mars 1845." *Le Moniteur universel*. 15 mars 1845. Dumasy-Queffélec, pp. 95–103.
———. "Discours à la Chambre des députés, 6 avril 1847." *Le Moniteur universel*. 7 avril 1847. Dumasy-Queffélec, pp. 104–16.
Chereau, Ollivier. *Le Jargon, ou langage de l'argot réformé, comme il est au présent en usage parmi les bons pauvres* (1630, 1632, 1634), edited by Denis Delaplace. Champion, 2008.
Chevalier, Louis. *Laboring Classes and Dangerous Classes: In Paris During the First Half of the Nineteenth Century*. Translated by Frank Jellinek, Howard Fertig, 1973.
Coleman, Julie. *The Life of Slang*. Oxford, Oxford University Press, 2012.
Corbin, Alain. "Commercial Sexuality in Nineteenth-Century France: A System of Images and Regulations." *Representations*, vol. 14, 1986, pp. 209–19.
Daumard, Adeline. *La Bourgeoisie parisienne de 1815 à 1848*. Paris, Éditions Albin Michel, 1963.
Debay, Auguste. *Hygiène de la voix et gymnastique des organes vocaux*. Paris, E. Dentu, 1861.
———. *Hygiène générale de la beauté humaine, spécialement chez la femme*. Paris, Moquet, 1851.
De Certeau, Michel, Dominique Julia, and Jacques Revel. *Une politique de la langue. La Révolution française et les patois: l'enquête de Grégoire*. Paris, Gallimard, 2002.
Delaunay de Fontenay, Ferdinand-Hippolyte. *Tempérament physique et moral de la femme*. Paris, Librairie moderne, 1862.
Delesalle, Georges. *Dictionnaire argot-français et français-argot*. Paris, 1895.
Delvau, Alfred. *Dictionnaire érotique moderne (1864)*. Paris, Les Éditions, 1900.
———. *Dictionnaire de la langue verte: argots parisiens comparés*. Paris, E. Dentu, 1866.
Dentith, Simon. *Parody*. London, Routledge, 2000.
Desnoyers, Louis. "Un Peu d'histoire à propos de roman." *Le Siècle*. 5 septembre 1847. Dumasy-Queffélec, pp. 121–33.
———. "Un Peu d'histoire à propos de roman." *Le Siècle*. 28 septembre 1847. Dumasy-Queffélec, pp. 134–41.
———. "Un Peu d'histoire à propos de roman." *Le Siècle*. 29 septembre 1847. Dumasy-Queffélec, pp. 142–54.
Desrat G. *Dictionnaire de la Danse historique, théorique, pratique et bibliographique, depuis l'origine de la danse jusqu'à nos jours*. Paris, Librairies-Imprimeries Réunies, 1895.
Dufour, Philippe. *La Pensée romanesque du langage*. Paris, Editions du Seuil, 2004.

Dumasy-Queffélec, Lise. *La Querelle du roman-feuilleton: littérature, presse et politique un débat précurseur (1836-1848)*. Grenoble, ELLUG, 1999.
Eckhert, Penelope. "Variation and the Indexical Field." *Journal of Sociolinguistics*, vol. 12, no. 4, 2008, pp. 453–76.
Eco, Umberto. "Rhetoric and Ideology in Sue's *Les Mystères de Paris*." *International Social Sciences Journal*, vol. 19, no. 4, 1967, pp. 551–69.
Emsley, Clive. "A Typology of Nineteenth-Century Police." *Crime, History & Societies*, vol. 3, no. 1, 1999, pp. 29–44.
Erickson, Paul. *Welcome to Sodom: The Cultural Works of City-Mysteries Fiction in Antebellum America*. 2005. University of Texas at Austin, PhD dissertation.
Flaubert, Gustave. *Correspondance*. Paris, Gallimard, 1973. 6 vols.
Foucault, Michel. *Histoire de la sexualité*. Vol I. Editions Gallimard, 1976.
Gaitet, Pascale. "From the Criminal's to the People's: The Evolution of Argot and Popular Language in the Nineteenth Century." *Nineteenth-Century French Studies*, vol. 19, no. 2, 1991, pp. 231–46.
———. *Political Stylistics: Popular Language as Literary Artifact*. London, Routledge, 1992.
Gal, Susan and Judith Irvine. "Language Ideology and Linguistic Differentiation." *Regimes of Language: Ideologies, Polities and Identities*, edited by P. Kroskrity, School of American Research, 2000, pp. 35–83.
Gaschon de Molènes. "Revue littéraire." *Revue des deux mondes*. 15 décembre 1841. Dumasy-Queffélec, 157–83.
Gauthier, Nicolas. *Lire la ville, dire le crime: mise en scène de la criminalité dans les mystères urbains*. Limoges, Presses Universitaires de Limoges, 2017.
Gillis, A. R. "Institutional Dynamics and Dangerous Classes: Reading, Writing, and Arrest in Nineteenth-Century France." *Social Forces*, vol. 82, no. 4, 2004, pp. 1303–32.
Glinoer, Anthony. "Classes de textes et littérature industrielle dans la première moitié du XIXe siècle." *Contexte. Revue de sociologie de la littérature*, 2009. http://contextes.revues.org/4325?lang=en#authors. Accessed 2 Jan. 2020.
———. "Des Éditeurs de romans pour cabinets de lecture." *Le Rocambole: bulletin des amis du roman-populaire*, vol. 50, 2010, pp. 15–17. https://www.academia.edu/7336693/Des_%C3%A9diteurs_de_romans_pour_cabinets_de_lecture. Accessed 2 Jan. 2020.
Gobineau, Arthur. "Essais de critique. *Esther, Splendeurs et misères des courtisanes*, Par M. de Balzac." *Le Commerce*. 29 octobre 1844. Dumasy-Queffélec, 87–103.
Goncourt, Edmond and Jules de. *Gavarni. L'homme et l'oeuvre*. 1873. Paris, Bibliothèque Charpentier, 1912.
———. *Germinie Lacerteux*. 1865. Paris, Flammarion, 1990.
Goulet, Andrea. "Apache Dancers and Savage Boxers: Criminal Choreographies from *Les Mystères de Paris* to *The Wire*." *Les Mystères urbains au XIXe siècle: circulations, transferts, appropriations*, edited by Dominique Kalifa and Marie-Ève Thérenty, 2015, *Médias 19*, www.medias19.org/docannexe/file/21375/andrea_goulet.pdf.

———. *The Legacies of the Rue Morgue: Science, Space, and Crime Fiction in France*. U of Pennsylvania P, 2016.

Gourden, Jean-Michel. *Le Peuple des ateliers: les artisans du XIXe siècle*. Paris, Créaphis, 1992.

"Grue." *Dictionnaire érotique moderne*, Bale, 1864, p. 217.

———. *Dictionnaire de la langue verte: argots parisiens comparés*, E. Dentu, 1866, p. 143.

Hall, Kira and Ayden Parish (in press). "Agency." *The International Encyclopedia of Linguistic Anthropology*, edited by James M. Stanlaw, John Wiley & Sons, 2021, pp. 1–6.

Halliday, M. A. K. "Anti-Languages." *American Anthropologist*, vol. 78, no. 3, 1976, pp. 570–83.

Harvey, David. *Paris: The Capital of Modernity*. New York, Routledge, 2003.

Haynes, Christine. *Lost Illusions: The Politics of Publishing in Nineteenth-Century France*. Cambridge, Harvard University Press, 2010.

Heller-Roazen, Daniel. *Dark Tongues: The Art of Rogues and Riddlers*. New York, Zone Books, 2013.

Hugo, Victor. *Le Dernier Jour d'un condamné*. Charles Gosselin, 1829.

———. *Les Misérables*. Paris, Librairie Générale française, 1998. 2 vols.

———. *Les Misérables*. Translated by Julie Rose, Modern Library, 2008.

———. *Notre-Dame de Paris*. Gallimard, 2009.

Hugo Victor and Paul Meurice. *Correspondance entre Victor Hugo et Paul Meurice*, edited by Jules Claretie. Paris, E. Fasquelle, 1909.

Hutcheon, Linda. *The Politics of Postmodernism*. London, Routledge, 2002.

Inoue, Miyako. *Vicarious Language: Gender and Linguistic Modernity in Japan*. Berkeley, University of California Press, 2006.

"Jargon." *Dictionnaire français (1680)*, vol. I, Slatkine, 1970, p. 413.

Johnstone, Barbara. "Enregisterment: How Linguistic Items Become Linked with Ways of Speaking." *Language and Linguistics Compass*, vol. 10, no. 11, 2016, pp. 632–43.

———. "Locating Language in Identity." *Language and Identities*, edited by Dominic Watt and Carmen Llamas. Edinburgh University Press, 2010, pp. 29–36.

Jordan, Jessica Hope. *The Sex Goddess in American Film, 1930-1965*. Amherst, Cambria Press, 2009.

———. "Women Refusing the Gaze: Theorizing Thryth's 'Unqueenly Custom' in *Beowulf* and The Bride's Revenge in Quentin Tarantino's *Kill Bill, Volume I*." *The Heroic Age*, vol. 9, 2006, http://www.heroicage.org/issues/9/forum2.html. Accessed 17 June 2020.

Jullien, Dominique. *Les Amoureux de Schéhérazade. Variations modernes sur les Mille et Une Nuits*. Genevia, Librairie Droz, 2009.

———. "Vautrin génie balzacien." *Francofonia*, no. 69, 2015, pp. 83–104.

Kalifa, Dominique. *Crime et culture au XIXe siècle*. Paris, Perrin, 2005.

———. *La Culture de masse en France 1860-1930*. Paris, La Découverte, 2001.

———. *Les bas-fonds: histoire d'un imaginaire*. Paris, Éditions du Seuil, 2013.

Klein, Jean René. *Le vocabulaire des mœurs de la 'vie parisienne' sous le Second Empire. Introduction à l'étude du langage boulevardier*. Louvain, Éditions Nauwelaerts, 1976.

Knight, Stephen. *The Mysteries of the Cities: Urban Crime Fiction in the Nineteenth Century*. London, McFarland & Company, 2012.

Koven, Seth. *Slumming: Sexual and Social Politics in Victorian London*. Princeton, Princeton UP, 2004.

Lakoff, Robin. *Language and Women's Place: Text and Commentaires*, edited by Mary Bucholtz, Oxford, Oxford University Press, 2004.

Laqueur, Thomas. *Making Sex: Body and Gender from the Greeks to Freud*. Cambridge, Harvard University Press, 1992.

Larchey, Lorédan. *Les excentricités du langage*. Paris, E. Dentu, 1865.

———. *Dictionnaire historique, étymologique et anecdotique de l'argot parisien*. 6th ed. Paris, F. Polo Libraire, 1872.

Lermina, Jules, and Henri Lévêque. *Dictionnaire thématique français-argot*. Paris, Bibliothèque Chacornac, 1897.

Lerner, Bettina. *Inventing the Popular: Printing, Politics, and Poetics*. New York: Routledge, 2018.

Littré, Émile. *Dictionnaire de la langue française*, vol. III. Paris, L. Hachette, 1873–74.

Lodge, Anthony. *A Sociolinguistic History of Parisian French*. Cambridge, Cambridge University Press, 2004.

Lombroso, Cesare. *Criminal Man*. 1876. Translated by Mary Gibson and Nicole Hahn Rafter, Duke UP, 2006.

———. *Criminal Woman, the Prostitute, and the Normal Woman*. 1893. Translated by Nicole Hahn Rafter and Mary Gibson, Durham, Duke UP, 2004.

Lyon-Caen, Judith. "Lecteurs et lectures: les usages de la presse au XIXe siècle." *La Civilisation du Journal. Histoire culturelle et littéraire de la presse française au XIXe siècle*, edited by Dominique Kalifa, Philippe Régnier, Marie-Ève Thérenty et Alain Vaillant, Nouveau Monde Éditions, 2011, pp. 23–60.

Lyons, Martyn. *Reading Culture and Writing Practices in Nineteenth-Century France*. Toronto, University of Toronto Press, 2008.

———. *Readers and Society in Nineteenth-Century France: Workers, Women and Peasants*. New York, Palgrave, 2001.

Martens, David, editor. *Lettres de noblesse I. Le versant aristocratique de la modernité littéraire en France (XIXe siècle)*. Lettres Modernes Minard, 2016.

Masters-Wicks, Karen. *Victor Hugo's Les Misérables and the Novels of the Grotesque*. New York, Peter Lang Publishing Inc., 1994.

Matlock, Jann. "Masquerading Women, Pathological Men: Cross-Dressing, Fetishism, and the Theory of Perversion, 1882–1935." *Fetishism as Cultural Discourse*, edited by Emily Apter and William Pietz, Cornell University Press, 1993, pp. 31–61.

———. *Scenes of Seduction: Prostitution, Hysteria, and Reading Difference in Nineteenth-Century France*. New York, Columbia University Press, 1994.

Mémoires d'une dame du monde. Paris, L. Marpon, 1861.

Merle, Pierre. *L'Argot: cette langue que l'on dit verte*. Paris, Hachette, 1996.
Mesch, Rachel. *The Hysteric's Revenge: French Women Writers at the Fin de Siècle*. Nashville, Vanderbilt University Press, 2006.
Michel, Francisque. *Études de philologie comparée sur l'argot et sur les idiomes analogues parlés en Europe et en Asie*. Paris, Librairie de Firmin Didot Frères, 1856.
Michelet, Jules. *Le Peuple*. 1846. Paris, Flammarion, 1974.
Milroy, Lesley, and James Milroy. *Authority in Language: Investigating Language Prescription and Standardisation*. London, Routledge, 1985.
"Misère." *Le Dictionnaire de l'Académie française*, 6th ed., vol. 2, Firmin Didot Frères, 1835, p. 212.
Mulvey, Laura. "Visual Pleasure and Narrative Cinema." *Feminism and Film*, edited by Constance Penley, Routledge, 1988, pp. 57–68.
"Narquois." *Dictionnaire français (1680)*, vol. II, Slatkine, 1970, p. 62.
Nédélec, Claudine. *Les Enfants de la Truche: la vie et le langage des argotiers, quatre textes argotiques (1596–1630)*. Paris, Klincksieck, 1998.
Nesci, Catherine. *Le flâneur et les flâneuses: les femmes et la ville à l'époque romantique*. Grenoble, ELLUG, 2007.
Nettement, Alfred. *Études critiques sur le roman-feuilleton*. Paris, Lagny Frères, 1847.
Normington, Katie. *Gender and Medieval Drama*. Rochester, D.S. Brewer, 2004.
Ochs, Elinor. "Indexicality and Socialization." *Cultural Psychology: Essays on Comparative Human Development*, edited by Gilbert Herdt, Richard A. Shweder and James W. Stigler, Cambridge UP, 1990, pp. 287–308.
"Palais." *Dictionnaire d'argot fin-de-siècle*, A. Charles Libraire, 1894, p. 204.
Parent-Duchâtelet, Alexandre. *De la prostitution dans Paris*. Vol. I. Paris, J.B. Baillière, 1837.
Parent-Lardeur, Françoise. *Les Cabinets de lecture: La lecture publique à Paris sous la Restauration*. Paris, Payot, 1982.
Partner, Nancy F. "No Sex, No Gender." *Studying Medieval Women: Sex, Gender, Feminism*, edited by Nancy F. Partner. Medieval Academy of America, 1993, pp. 117–41.
Pechon de Ruby. *La Vie généreuse des mercelots, gueuz et boesmiens, contenans leur façon de vivre, subtilitez & gergon mis en lumière*. 1596, edited by Denis Delaplace. Champion, 2007.
Peirce, Charles Sanders. "On the Algebra of Logic: A Contribution to the Philosophy of Notation." *American Journal of Mathematics*, vol. 7, no. 2, 1885, pp. 180–96.
Peiss, Kathy. "Charity Girls and City Pleasures: Historical Notes on Working Class Sexuality, 1880–1920." *Powers of Desire: The Politics of Sexuality*, edited by Ann Snitow et al. Monthly Review Press, 1983, pp. 74–87.
Pike, David. *Metropolis on the Styx: The Underworlds of Modern Urban Culture, 1800–2001*. Ithaca, Cornell UP, 2007.
"Piou." *Dictionnaire de la langue verte: argots parisiens comparés*, E. Dentu, 1866, p. 302.

Prendergast, Christopher. *For the People by the People?: Eugène Sue's Les Mystères de Paris: a Hypothesis in the Sociology of Literature.* Oxford, Legenda, 2003.

"Prostitute." *Online Etymology Dictionary.* http://www.etymonline.com/index.php?term=prostitute&allowed_in_frame=0.

"Ratisser." *Dictionnaire de la langue verte: argots parisiens comparés,* E. Dentu, 1866, p. 331.

Richelet, Pierre. *Dictionnaire français (1680).* 2 Vols. Genève: Slatkine, 1970.

Rigaud, Lucien. *Dictionnaire du jargon parisien. L'Argot ancien et l'argot moderne.* Paris, Paul Ollendorff, 1878.

Riot-Sarcey, Michèle. *Histoire du féminisme.* Paris, La Découverte, 2002.

Roberts, Anna Klosowska. *Queer Love in the Middle Ages.* New York, Palgrave Macmillan, 2005.

Rosa, Guy. "Essais sur l'argot: Balzac (*Splendeurs et misères des courtisanes*) et Hugo (*Les Misérables,* IV, 7)." *Hugo, les Misérables,* edited by Pierre Brunel. Éditions Interuniversitaires, 1994, pp. 149–64.

Rousseau-Minier, Marjorie. *Des filles sans joie: le roman de la prostituée dans la seconde moitié du XIXe siècle.* Geneva, Droz, 2018.

Sainéan, Lazare. *L'Argot ancien (1455-1850).* Paris, 1907.

Sainte-Beuve. "De la littérature industrielle." *Revue des deux mondes.* 1er septembre 1839. Dumasy-Queffélec, 25–43.

"S'encanailler." *Dictionnaire de l'Académie française* (1694), https://artflsrv03.uchicago.edu/philologic4/publicdicos/query?report=bibliography&head=s%27encanailler. Accessed October 13, 2019.

Silverstein, Michael. "Indexical Order and the Dialectics of Sociolinguistic Life." *Language & Communication,* vol. 23, 2003, pp. 193–229.

"Slum." *OED Online,* Oxford University Press. https://www-oed-com.sandiego.idm.oclc.org/view/Entry/182267?rskey=EYhjvo&result=1. Accessed 24 Nov. 2019.

Smith, Eliza Jane. "Dissonant Voices: Noise and the Criminal Leitmotiv in Vidocq and Victor Hugo." *Nineteenth-Century French Studies,* vol. 48, nos. 1 & 2, 2019–2020, pp. 32–48.

Stiénon, Valérie. *La Littérature des Physiologies: sociopoétique d'un genre panoramique, 1830–1845.* Paris, Classiques Garniers, 2012.

Sue, Eugène. *Les Mystères de Paris.* 1842-43, edited by Judith Lyon-Caen. Éditions France Loisirs, 2009.

———. *The Mysteries of Paris.* Translated by Carolyn Betensky and Jonathan Loesberg. Penguin Classics, 2015.

Tannenbaum, Edward R. "The Beginnings of Bleeding-Heart Liberalism: Eugène Sue's *Les Mystères de Paris.*" *Comparative Studies in Society and History,* vol. 23, no. 3, 1981, pp. 491–507.

Tanner, Jessica. "Turning Tricks, Turning the Tables: Plotting the Brasserie à femmes in Tabarant's *Virus d'Amour.*" *Nineteenth-Century French Studies,* vol. 41, nos. 3 & 4, 2013, pp. 255–71.

Thérenty, Marie-Eve. *Mosaïques: être écrivain entre presse et roman, 1829-1836.* Paris, H. Champion, 2003.

Thérenty, Marie-Eve and Alain Vaillant. *1836. L'an 1 de l'ère médiatique: étude littéraire et historique du journal La Presse, d'Emile de Girardin*. Paris, Nouveau Monde Editions, 2001.

Thérenty, Marie-Eve and Élisabeth Pillet, editors. *Presse, chanson et culture orale au XIXe siècle. La parole vive au défi de l'ère médiatique*. Nouveau Monde Éditions, 2012.

"Trimer." *Le Nouveau Dictionnaire complet du jargon et de l'argot, ou Le Langage des voleurs dévoilé*, Le Bailly, 1849, p. 23.

Tristan, Flora. *Promenades dans Londres. L'aristocratie et les prolétaires anglais*. 1842. Paris, Indigo, 2001.

Vaillant, Alain. "Invention littéraire et culture médiatique au XIXe siècle." *Culture de masse et culture médiatique en Europe et dans les Amériques 1860–1940*, edited by Jean-Yves Mollier, Jean-François Sirinelli and François Vallotton. PUF, 2006, pp. 11–22.

"Vénus populaire [la]." *Dictionnaire érotique moderne*, Bale, 1864, p. 367.

"Ver [tuer le]." *Les excentricités du langage*, E. Dentu, 1865, p. 325.

Vidocq, Eugène François. *Les voleurs: physiologie de leurs mœurs et de leur langage*. Paris, Robert Laffont, 1998.

———. *Mémoires de Vidocq: chef de la police de sureté jusqu'en 1827*. 1828. Paris, Bouquins Laffont, 1998.

Walkowitz, Judith R. "Going Public: Shopping, Street Harassment, and Streetwalking in Late Victorian London." *Representations*, vol. 62, 1998, pp. 1–30.

Wilson, Elizabeth. "The Invisible Flâneur." *New Left Review*, vol. 191, 1992, pp. 90–110.

Wolff, Janet. "Gender and the Haunting of Cities (Or, the Retirement of the Flâneur)." *The Invisible Flâneuse? Gender, Public Space, and Visual Culture in Nineteenth-century Paris*, edited by Aruna D'Souza and Tom McDonough, Manchester University Press, 2006, pp. 18–31.

Woolard, Kathryne. "Why *dat* Now?: Linguistic-Anthropological Contributions to the Explanation of Sociolinguistic Icons and Change." *Journal of Sociolinguistics*, vol. 12, no. 4, 2008, pp. 432–52.

Wooler, Stephanie Grace. *Performance Anxiety: Hysteria and the Actress in French Literature 1880–1910*. 2012. Harvard University, PhD dissertation.

Wulf, Judith. *Étude sur la langue romanesque de Victor Hugo: Le partage et la composition*. Paris, Classiques Garnier, 2014.

Zola, Emile. "Germinie Lacerteux." *Mes haines, causeries littéraires et artistiques*, edited by G. Charpentier and E. Fasquelle, Paris, 1893, pp. 67–84.

———. *Nana*. 1880. Paris, Pocket Classiques, 1991.

Index

Note: *Italic* page numbers refer to figures and page numbers followed by "n" denote endnotes.

AABB rhyme scheme, 148
agency, 200; of women slang speakers, 237–39
Agha, Asif, 5, 19, 25n13, 99–100, 170, 183
Althusser, Louis, 167, 189n7
Ancien Régime, 96–98, 206
ancient argot, 176
Angenot, Marc, 100, 103
Annunciation, 209, *211*
anti-language, 13, 19, 26n43, 34, 37, 38, 59, 121–22, 133, 136, 150, 197, 254
anti-society, 12–13, 36–38, 40, 41, 43, 44, 46, 136
argot. *See* slang (*argot*)
Argot and Slang: A New French and English Dictionary of the Cant Words, Quaint Expressions, Slang Terms and Flash Phrases Used in the High and Low Life of Old and New Paris (Barrère), 185
Argot Order, 132, 165, 184
auto-da-fé, 118

Bago, Eduardo López, 256
Balibar, Renée, 97, 98

Ballades en jargon (Villon) xiii
Balzac, Honoré de, 4, 7, 15, 18, 29–33, 44, 51, 55n41, 72, 95, 106, 109, 114, 131, 133, 136, 150, 205; *Le Père Goriot*, 69, 86n38; *Splendors and Miseries of Courtesans*, 16, 17, 21, 23, 29, 36–37, 60, 152, 201, 206, 210–15, *212*, *214*, 253
Barrère, Albert: *Argot and Slang: A New French and English Dictionary of the Cant Words, Quaint Expressions, Slang Terms and Flash Phrases Used in the High and Low Life of Old and New Paris*, 185
bas-fonds, 2
Baudelaire, Charles, 59, 254
"beautiful French language," 110, 111
Beizer, Janet: *Ventriloquized Bodies*, 231
Belles heures de Jean de France (Jean de Berry), 89n64
Benjamin, Walter, 128n53
Benson, Phil, 166, 167
Bernheimer, Charles, 200, 202, 214, 222
Berrong, Richard, 86n38
Bertin, Louis-François, 102

Bertin, Pierre Louis, 102
blesquin, 13–14
Blonde Venus (Sternberg), *220*, 244
body language, 199, 201, 209, 215, 223, 226, 228, 231, 235, 237, 238
Book of Revelation, 155, 162n121
Bouchet, Guillaume, 12, 132, 170, 189n18; *Fifteenth Evening*, xiv, 169, 252
Bourbon Restoration, 118
Bourdieu, Pierre, 117, 122
bourgeoisie, 114, 118, 119
"bourgeoisification," 171, 181, 187
bourgeois literature, 119, 178
Bowles, Brett, 190n27, 191n39, 193n59
Brachet, Jean Louis: *Treaty on Hysteria*, 247n136
British literature, 256
Brunot, Ferdinand, xiii
Bucholtz, Mary, 8, 59–61, 71, 74, 85n29, 186, 198, 258
Bulwer-Lytton, Edward, 257
Busby, Keith, 72, 88nn58, 62
Butler, Judith, 88n51, 201, 202

Callot, Jacques, 144
Cameron, Deborah, 110
Cartouche, Louis-Dominique, xiv, xvn8
Castille, Hippolyte, 126n44
Catholic Church, 14, 97, 101, 116, 118
Céline, Louis-Ferdinand: *Journey to the End of the Night*, 4, 255
Cellard, Jacques, 14
chahut, 78–79; Can-can, 78
Changer (*le Changeur*), 141
Chapuys-Montlaville, Baron Benoît-Marie, 110–12
characterological figures, 5, 170
Charcot, Jean-Martin, 226
charity, 8–10
Chereau, Olivier: *Jargon or the Language of Reformed Slang*, xiv, 135–36, 170, 177, 184
Chevalier, Louis, 114, 135
"child readers," 108

Christian morality, 149, 150
cinema/film, 60, 141, 201
class distinctions, use of, 112–13
class dynamics, 252
Classical Antiquity, 139, 155
class nuance, 141
coded criminal language, xiii
codification, of criminal anti-language, 181
Coleman, Julie, 88n53
Colette: *La Vagabonde*, 255
Collin, Jacqueline, 15
common people (*le peuple*), 114, 117, 134; vision of, 120
"communicative isolation," 168
The Condition of the Working Class in English (Engels), 257
conservatism, 77
Cooper, James Fenimore: *The Last of the Mohicans*, 150–51
Coquillars (*les Coquillards*) xiii, xvn5, 13
Corbin, Alain, 202, 203, 241n35
criminal: coded anti-language of, 47; embodied language of, 199, 219; embodied slang and, 61–71; in French literature, 94; iconization of, 83–84; indexical of, 30; language of, 117; public interest in, 99; representations of, 4, 5; social discourse on, 100; social types of, 98; stereotypes of, 131; and working classes, 137
criminal anti-society, 32, 34
criminal atavism, 62, 83, 84n7
criminal body, stylization of, 253
criminal characters, inherent theatricality of, 88n51
criminal culture, 5, 94; in French novels, 2
criminal descents, 32–37
criminal disguise, 70–71, 141
criminal identity, 17, 18, 77, 171
criminality, xiv; non-referential index of, 59; and physique, 61; realistic version of, 29–30; realm of, 17

criminal language, xiv; use of, 109–10
Criminal Man (Lombroso), 62, 207, 209
criminal metaphor, 151
criminal type: function, 134; twist on, 137–42
criminal underworld, 41
criminal women, masculinity of, 209
cross-dressing, 18, 72–74, 77, 84
cultural capital, 10, 12, 34, 40, 41, 53, 122

dance, 18, 60, 61, 77–84, 183, 201, 237
dangerous classes, 113, 118, 121; bourgeois fears of, 107–12; collective societal fear of, 115
dangerous language, 15, 19, 20, 113, 121, 134, 135, 136, 148, 152
Daumard, Adeline, 114
Debay, Auguste, 215–16, 235
de Certeau, Michel, 97
Delaplace, Denis, 189n18, 190n21
Delaunay, Ferdinand-Hippolyte, 215–16
Delvau, Alfred, 4, 171, 172, 221; *Dictionary of Green Tongue: Comparative Parisian Slang*, 21, 22, 168, 175–76, 180–83, 221–22; *Erotic Modern Dictionary*, 174–75, 221
demi-monde, 205, 227, 247
democratization, 169; of *argot*, 176; of education, 109; of literature, 102–4; social and geographical spaces, 179–80; of urban space, 183; of writer, 107
Dentith, Simon, 44, 89n64
Desnoyers, Louis, 103, 110–12
Desrat, Gustave: *Dictionnaire de la danse*, 78
Dickens, Charles: *Oliver Twist*, 256–57
dictionary, 167; analysis of, 167–68; authenticity for, 182
Dictionary of Green Tongue: Comparative Parisian Slang (Delvau), 21, 22, 168, 175–76, 180–83, 221–22

Dictionary of Parisian Jargon: Ancient and Modern Slang (Rigaud), 21, 168, 176–79
Dictionnaire de la danse (Desrat), 78
Dietrich, Marlene, 220, 244–45
disguise, 13, 18, 45, 51; criminal, 70–71, 141
Disraeli, Benjamin: *Sybil*, 257
The Drinking Den (Zola), 4
Dufour, Philippe, 131, 134, 144

The Eccentricities of the French Language (Larchey), 21, 168, 171–74
Eckhert, Penelope, 6
Eco, Umberto, 104
embodied criminal performance, 77–83
embodied language, 222–37
embodied slang: and criminal, 61–71; gender-bending as, 72–77, 75, 76
Engels, Friedrich: *The Condition of the Working Class in English*, 257
enregisterment, 10–12, 21, 22, 30, 168, 171, 183, 186
Erickson, Paul, 39
Erotic Modern Dictionary (Delvau), 174–75, 221

fabliaux, 72, 73
fascination, 3; public, 19
feminine bodies, 215–22
femininity, natural discourse of, 203
Fifteenth Evening (Bouchet), xiv, 169, 252
first indexical order, 131, 138, 254
flânerie, 179, 183
flâneur, 167, 174, 180, 187, 223, 254
Flaubert, Gustave: *Madame Bovary*, 218
Foucault, Michel, 89n65
Fra Angelico, 209
French Academy, xiv, 14, 101, 116, 166, 185
French convention, 106
French culture, 110
French language, 97

French literature, 2; degradation of, 95; democratization of, 102–4; evolution of, 112; press and, 100; representations in, 131; role of slang in, 30; slang speaker and, 115–21; slang-speaking characters in, 5; types of, 106; unconventional speech habits in, 217; women slang speakers in, 202–15
French Penal Code, 99
French prison system, 41
French Revolution, 23–24, 98, 99, 115, 203, 209
French society, 3, 11, 44, 203; sexuality in, 204
functional literacy, 115, 128n65

Gaitet, Pascale, 24n10, 30, 149, 170, 255; *Political Stylistics*, 4
Galdós, Benito Pérez, 256
Garbo, Greta, 224, *224*
Garde, Reine, 255
Garnier-Pagès, Louis-Antoine, 114
Gauthier, Nicolas, 2, 8, 33, 197–98
Gautruche, Médéric, 218
Gavarni, Paul, 197
gender: indexical relationship between slang and, 203; realm of, 254
gender-bending, as embodied slang, 72–77, *75*, *76*
gender identity, 69, 209
gender performativity, 88n51, 202
gender stylization, 209, 238
Germinie Lacerteux (Goncourt and Goncourt), 22, 201, 254; agency of women slang speakers, 237–39; embodied language, sexuality and performance, 224–35, *229*, *230*; feminine bodies, masculine language, 215–18
Gillis, A. R., 115–17, 128n64
Girardin, Émile, 103
Glinoer, Anthony, 105, 106, 117
Gobineau, Arthur de, 108–9, 126n44
Goncourt, Edmond de, 197, 200, 254

Goncourt, Jules de, 197, 200, 254
Goulet, Andrea, 8, 25n10, 78, 80
Gourden, Jean-Michel, 113
Greek mythology, 155, 156
Grégoire, Abbé, 97, 166
Gringoire, Pierre, 132
grue, 221, 222, 245n103
Guillaumin, Émile, 256

Hall, Kira, 60, 61, 71, 74, 85n29, 123n3, 138, 186, 198, 200, 258
Halliday, M. A. K., 12–13, 15, 26n43, 43, 44, 150
Harvey, David, 7, 43, 80, 182
Haussmann, Georges-Eugène, 182, 183
Haynes, Christine, 119
Heldris de Cornuälle: *Roman de Silence*, 89n64
Hélias, Pierre-Jakez, 256
Heller-Roazen, Daniel, 13, 32
Historical, Etymological, and Anecdotal Dictionary of Parisian Slang (Larchey), 172–74
honorable literature, 105–7
Hugo, Victor, 4, 17, 133; *The Hunchback of Notre Dame*, 132; *The Last Day of a Condemned Man*, 132; *Les Misérables*, 7, 16, 20–21, 80, 113, 132–35, 166, 205, 253–54, 257; *Lirlonfa*, 82
The Hunchback of Notre Dame (Hugo), 132
Hutcheon, Linda, 44
hypermasculine criminal woman, 207, 237
hysteria, 81, 222, 232, 233
The Hysteric's Revenge: French Women Writers at the Fin de Siècle (Mesch), 233–34

iconization, 30, 69; of criminal, 83–84
identity, expansion of, 121–23
"ideological state apparatuses," 167, 189n7
indexical field, 7

indexicality, 6, 200
indexical orders, 30, 53n1
indexical relationship: between gender and slang, 203; between slang and criminal identity, 171
industrial literature, 96, 104, 105; readership of, 117
Industrial Revolution, in France, 113
industrial writer, 106
Inoue, Miyako, 205
In Search of Lost Time (Proust), 255
in-text codification, 32, 51

jargon, xiii, xiv, 14, 16; of beggars and thieves, 13–14
Jargon or the Language of Reformed Slang (Chereau), xiv, 135–36, 170, 177, 184
Jean de Berry: *Belles heures de Jean de France*, 89n64
Johnstone, Barbara, 6, 30, 95, 171, 173, 183, 189n13
Jordan, Jessica Hope, 201, 222, 244n93
Journal des débats, 102
Journey to the End of the Night (Céline), 4, 255
Jullien, Dominique, 9

kaleidoscopic identity, 7, 25n20
Kalifa, Dominique, 2, 3, 15, 34, 99, 104, 105, 113, 122, 150
Klein, Jean-René, 16, 173
Knight, Stephen, 8, 9
Koven, Seth, 10; *Slumming: Sexual and Social Politics in Victorian London*, 8

Lacan, Jacques, 228
language: association between identity and, 171; deviations in, 181; "an embodied phenomenon," 198; of slang, 251, 252; of working-class Parisians, 166
language policy, 96–98
Lapointe, Savinien, 121, 255

LaPorte, Dominique, 97, 98
La Poste, 103
La Presse, 103
Laqueur, Thomas, 203
Larchey, Lorédan, 193n59; *The Eccentricities of the French Language*, 21, 168, 171–74; *Historical, Etymological, and Anecdotal Dictionary of Parisian Slang*, 172–74
La Ruche populaire, 120
The Last Day of a Condemned Man (Hugo), 132
The Last of the Mohicans (Cooper), 150–51
L'Atelier, 120
La Vagabonde (Colette), 255
Le Père Goriot (Balzac), 69, 86n38
Lermina, Jules, 191n39; *Thematic French-Slang Dictionary*, 21, 168, 184–88
Les Archisuppôts, 177
Le Siècle, 103, 111, 112
Les Misérables (Hugo), 7, 16, 20–21, 80, 113, 132–35, 166, 205, 253–54, 257; aesthetics of slang, 155–57; criminal type, twist on, 137–42; remaking misery in, 148–50; slang as metaphor, 150–55; slang speaker as poet, 142–48; slang's second indexical order, 135–37
L'Événement, 218
Lévêque, Henri, 191n39, 193n59; *Thematic French-Slang Dictionary*, 21, 168, 184–88
le vulgaire, 189n16
lexicographer, 187; argue for slang, 188; evolution of, 174–75
L'Héritier, Louis-François, 33
linguistic *flâneurie*, 254
linguistic normativity, 110
linguistic realism, 145
linguistic scapegoating, 18
Lirlonfa (Hugo), 82
literacy gap, 117

literacy rates, 99, 115, 116, 118, 120, 129n79
literal slumming, 7–12, 31, 169
literary realism, 29
literary slumming, 7–12, 17, 22, 31, 37, 94, 134, 156, 168, 169, 251, 255, 257–59; mutual cultural appropriation, 252; practice of, 256
Lodge, Anthony, 97, 100, 167, 168
Lombroso, Cesare, 67, 84n7; on criminal atavism, 83; *Criminal Man*, 62, 207, 209; *Criminal Woman, the Prostitute, and the Normal Woman*, 209
Lorenzo Veneziano, 209
Louis XIV, 11
Louis XVIII, 102
Lousteau, Étienne, 214
lower-class culture, 257; construction and consumption of, 96
Lyon-Caen, Judith, 117
Lyons, Martyn, xvn7, 115, 116, 124n26, 129n75

Madame Bovary (Flaubert), 218
mademoiselle (*mamselle*), 145
Maggiolo, Louis, 115–16
The Magnanimous Life of Dealers, Bandits, and Bohemians (Pechon), xiii–xiv, 33, 38, 148, 150, 169, 252
Martens, David, 114
Marx, Karl, 70, 142
masculine language, 215–22
mass culture, 124n26
Masters-Wicks, Karen, 144, 160n64, 253
Matlock, Jann, 202; *Scenes of Seduction*, 248n140
media regime (*régime médiatique*), 19
Memoirs (Vidocq), xiv, 15, 17, 21, 29, 33–35, 54n18, 57n72, 58n85, 93, 152, 252; criminal disguise in, 70; criminal figures in, 60; embodied criminal performance, 77–79; first indexical order, 51–53;

gender-bending, 72–74; linguistic scapegoating in, 47–49; slang and dangerous classes, 37–39
Memoirs and Adventures of a Proletarian throughout the Revolution, Algeria, the Argentinian Republic, and Paraguay (Truquin), 255
Memoirs of Cora Pearl (Pearl), 255
Mesch, Rachel, 201, 220, 233–34, 239; *The Hysteric's Revenge: French Women Writers at the Fin de Siècle*, 233–34
Michelet, Jules: *The People*, 120
A Midsummer's Night Dream (Shakespeare), 256
minority: readerships, 118; social effects on, 116; of working-class intellectuals, 118–19
misery, defined as, 136
modern argot, 176
modernizations, of printing and papermaking realms, 252
Molière, 144
morality, 137, 149, 150
Morice, Émile, 33
Mulvey, Laura, 219–20; "Visual Pleasure and Narrative Cinema," 200
The Mysteries of London (Reynolds), 8
The Mysteries of Paris (Sue), 1, 2, 8, 15, 17, 21, 23, 29, 36, 44, 83, 104, 107, 150–52, 168, 201, 206, *208*, *210*, 252; criminal disguise in, 70–71; criminal figures in, 60; embodied criminal performance, 79–80, 82; embodied slang, 63–67, *64–66*; first indexical order, 51–53; gender-bending, 74, *76*, 76–77; linguistic scapegoating in, 50–51; slang and dangerous classes, 39–41

Nana (Zola), 22, 80, 201, 252, 254; agency of women slang speakers, 237–39; embodied language, sexuality and performance, 226,

227, 234–37, *236*; feminine bodies, masculine language, 218–21
Nanà a Milano (Righetti), 256
Napoléon, 99, 103
Napoléon III, 174, 175, 181
Napoleonic Code (1804), 204, 241n36; French Penal code, 99
Naturalism, 101, 142, 251
Nédélec, Claudine, 14, 27n53, 30, 150, 170
Nesci, Catherine, 183
Nettement, Alfred, 107–9
newspaper, 94; circulations in France, 120–21; drop in subscription prices, 103; format of, 102; innovations in production and distribution, 96; role of, 95; working-class, 120
Nicolas Ragot de Granval, xiv
non-gender-conforming women, 220
non-referential indexes, 6, 7, 18, 59, 60, 253
non-Standard French, 94, 96
Normington, Katie, 72

Oliver Twist (Dickens), 256–57
Ordinance of Villers-Cotterêts (1539), 97
ouvrier, 30

panoramic literature, 128n53
paper-passing, 120
Parent-Duchâtelet, Alexandre: *Prostitution in the City of Paris*, 204–6
Parent-Lardeur, Françoise, 120
Parish, Ayden, 123n3, 138, 200
Parisian demi-monde, 205, 227
Parisian newspapers, 103
Parisian society, 34, 43
Parisian vernacular, 166, 168
parody, 44
Paul Gaschon de Molènes, 107
Pearl, Cora: *Memoirs of Cora Pearl*, 255
Pechon de Ruby, 12, 132, 155, 165, 166, 187, 189n18; *The Magnanimous Life*, 33, 38, 169, 252; *The Magnanimous Life of Dealers, Bandits, and Bohemians*, xiii–xiv, 27n50, 148, 150
Peirce, Charles Sanders, 186
Peiss, Kathy, 240n9
The People (Michelet), 120
Perdiguier, Agricole, 255
performance: embodied language, sexuality and, 222–37; and slang, 183–87
peuple, 137, 149
philological novel, 131
physiognomy, 62, 63
Pike, David L., 8
Political Stylistics (Gaitet), 4
Poncy, Charles, 121, 255
porosity, 34
post-Revolutionary woman, 224
Prendergast, Christopher, 120
pre-Revolutionary French literature, 112
prescriptivism, 167, 175, 185
press, 98–102; innovations in, 102–4; and literature, 100
primitive argot, 176–77
printed media, 251
"processes of socialization," 10
Promenades in London (Tristan), 243n85
prostitute, 203; in late-nineteenth-century, 200; literary representations of, 210; portrayal in literature, 215; realistic depictions of, 239n7; representations of, 199
prostitution: characteristics of, 204; institutionalized measures to regulate, 202
Prostitution in the City of Paris (Parent-Duchâtelet), 204–6
Proust, Marcel: *In Search of Lost Time*, 255
psychological complexity, 138

Queneau, Raymond: *Zazie in the Metro*, 4, 255

querelle du roman-feuilleton, 104–7, 120–21

Rachilde, 255
racism, 209
Realism, 3, 101, 251
referential indexes, 6, 22
Reynolds, George W. M.: *The Mysteries of London*, 8
rez-de-chaussée, 102
Richelet, Pierre, 14
Rigaud, Lucien, 170, 172; *Dictionary of Parisian Jargon: Ancient and Modern Slang*, 21, 168, 176–79
Righetti, Carlo: *Nanà a Milano*, 256
Riot-Sarcey, Michèle, 203, 204
Roge, Edma, 133
Rosa, Guy, 133
Rousseau-Minier, Marjorie, 199, 202, 256

Sainéan, Lazare, 159n37
Sainte-Beuve, Charles Augustin, 96, 104–6, 109
Sand, George, 255
Scenes of Seduction (Matlock), 248n140
second indexical order, 134–37, 156, 254; emergence of, 138
"semiotic encounter," 19, 27n66
"semiotics of style," 85n29
serialized literature, 94, 95, 107–9, 111, 112, 117, 120
serialized novel/serial novels (le roman feuilleton), 11, 19, 95, 96, 99, 102, 104, 105, 108, 109, 118, 121–23
sexual debauchery, 223, 227
sexuality: in French society, 204; performance and embodied language, 222–37; social repression of, 89n65
sexual promiscuity, 205
Shakespeare, William: *A Midsummer's Night Dream*, 256
Silverstein, Michael, 6, 30
slang (*argot*), 169, 171; aesthetics of, 155–57; and bourgeois fears of dangerous classes, 107–12; conception of, 172; as criminal code, 12–15; and dangerous classes, 37–46; demonstrative shift in use of, 253; as embodied criminal performance, 77–83; embodiment of, 70–71; enregisterment of, 187–88; and expansion of identity, 121–23; first indexical order, 51–53; in French literature, 1; geographical makeup of, 179; indexical relationship between gender and, 203; as language of Parisians, 176; as linguistic scapegoat, 47–51; mass distribution in French literature, 4; meaning of, 169–78; as metaphor, 150–55; nineteenth-century sociolinguistic evolution of, 15–24; performance and, 183–87; pervasiveness of, 10; portrayal of, xiv; as premodern anti-language, xiii–xv; and press, 98–102; re-enregisterment of, 176; second indexical order, 135–37; sociolinguistic evolution of, 24; an urban language, 2
slang dialogue, lack of, 205
slang dictionaries, 167, 169, 171, 173, 177–78
slang function, 132, 135
slang speaker (*argotier*), 140; and literacy, 115–21; as poet, 142–48; social types and, 112–15
slum, defined as, 31
slumming, defined as, 10
Slumming: Sexual and Social Politics in Victorian London (Koven), 8
Social Darwinism, 83, 84n7
social discourse (*le discours social*), 100–101
social generalization, 127n53
"socially unacceptable speech," 231
social reform, 9
social status, 134, 137
social types, 112–15, 127n53

sociolinguistic analysis, 5–7
sociolinguistic phenomenon, 11, 31, 53, 251, 252
song, 18, 61, 81–84, 147, 148, 257
speech chain network, 99–100
Splendors and Miseries of Courtesans (Balzac), 16, 17, 21, 23, 29, 36–37, 152, 201, 206, 210–15, *212*, *214*, 253; criminal disguise in, 71; criminal figures in, 60; embodied slang, 67–69; first indexical order, 51–53; gender-bending, 74–77, *75*; linguistic scapegoating in, 49–50; slang and dangerous classes, 41–46
spoken language, 201, 235, 237, 238
Standard French, 6, 13, 15, 22, 32, 34, 39, 45, 47–49, 51–53, 91n102, 97, 136, 139, 167, 178, 180, 237, 253
Sternberg, Josef von: *Blonde Venus*, 220, 244
Stiénon, Valérie, 127n53
Sue, Eugène, 4, 7, 9, 18, 29–33, 44, 51, 55n41, 84n15, 85n34, 91n102, 95, 105, 131, 136, 205; *Mysteries*, 60, 104, 107, 150–52; *The Mysteries of Paris*, 1, 2, 8, 15, 17, 21, 23, 29, 36, 44, 83, 168, 201, 206, *208*, *210*, 252
Sybil (Disraeli), 257
Sylvère, Antoine, 256

taboo sexuality, 74, 77, 255, 258
Tannenbaum, Edward, 8, 9
Tanner, Jessica, 215
The Temptress (Niblo), 224, *224*
theater, 49, 82, 199, 221–23, 227, 228, 235
Thematic French-Slang Dictionary (Lermina and Lévêque), 21, 168, 184–88
Thérenty, Marie-Ève, 127n53
Thieves: The Physiology of Their Ways and of Their Language (Vidocq), 15, 21, 168, 170–71
transvestism, 77, 89n65

Treaty on Hysteria (Brachet), 247n136
Tristan, Flora, 246n125, 255; *Promenades in London*, 243n85
Truquin, Norbert: *Memoirs and Adventures of a Proletarian throughout the Revolution, Algeria, the Argentinian Republic, and Paraguay*, 255

ultrafeminine, 207, 237
underworld (*les bas-fonds*), 2, 94
urban innovations, 181

Vaillant, Alain, 100, 101, 103
veillée, xvn7; *veillée d'hiver*, 116
Ventriloquized Bodies (Beizer), 231
vernacular, 16, 30, 169, 189n16, 199, 218, 231
Vidocq, Eugène François, 3, 4, 7, 9, 18, 29–33, 44, 51, 95, 122, 131, 136, 148–49, 171, 179; *Memoirs*, xiv, 15, 17, 21, 29, 33–35, 54n18, 57n72, 58n85, 60, 93, 152, 252; role as linguistic authority, 35; *Thieves: The Physiology of Their Ways and of Their Language*, 15, 21, 168, 170–71
Villon, François, xvn5, 14, 132, 177, 252; *Ballades en jargon*, xiii
Vinçard, Jules, 121, 255
violent seduction, 228
Virmaître, Charles, 172
"Visual Pleasure and Narrative Cinema" (Mulvey), 200

Walkowitz, Judith, 243n85
Wilson, Elizabeth, 223, 226
winter vigil (*veillée d'hiver*), 116; *veillée*, xvn7
Wolff, Janet, 223
women: expectation of, 205; intense scrutiny of, 204; types of, 209
women criminals, 67, 69; portrayal of, 207; second category of, 228
women slang speakers: agency of, 237–39; in French literature, 202–15

"women's language," 205
Wooler, Stephanie, 234
working-class culture, 5
working classes (*classes ouvrières*), 113, 116–18; indexical of, 218
working-class intellectuals, 118–20, 129n75
working-class language, 181
working-class newspapers, 120, 255
working-class Parisians, language of, 166
working-class slang, 197, 198
working-class women, 199; realistic depictions of, 239n7
Wulf, Judith, 133, 142

Zazie in the Metro (Queneau), 4, 255
Zola, Émile, 199, 200, 203, 254; *The Drinking Den*, 4; *Nana*, 22, 80, 201, 206, 252

About the Author

Eliza Jane Smith is an assistant professor of French and Francophone Studies at the University of San Diego. She has published articles on representations of French slang in the city-mystery genre, criminal noise in the works of Victor Hugo and Vidocq, and on teaching Francophone culture through project-based learning. Her primary research interests include nineteenth-century French literature, sociolinguistics, and second-language acquisition.

www.ingramcontent.com/pod-product-compliance
Lightning Source LLC
Chambersburg PA
CBHW061707300426
44115CB00014B/2589